AMERICAN EDUCATION SERIES

GEORGE DRAYTON STRAYER, GENERAL EDITOR

AN INTRODUCTION TO THE
PHILOSOPHY OF EDUCATION

MICHAEL DEMIASHKEVICH, Ph.D.

GRADUATE OF THE IMPERIAL HISTORICO–PHILOLOGICAL
INSTITUTE (PETROGRAD)

Officier d'Académie

PROFESSOR OF EDUCATION AT GEORGE PEABODY
COLLEGE FOR TEACHERS

AMERICAN BOOK COMPANY
NEW YORK   CINCINNATI   CHICAGO   BOSTON   ATLANTA

PHILOSOPHY IS NOT A POTENTATE'S THRONE, BUT
A BATTLEFIELD OF IDEAS.

"PROVE ALL THINGS; HOLD FAST THAT WHICH IS
GOOD." (*1 Thess. 5:21.*)

EDITOR'S INTRODUCTION

Many of the treatises dealing with the philosophy of education consist of an exposition of the particular philosophy of the individual making the contribution. While this sort of treatment may have the merit of giving to the student the arguments in favor of an individualized point of view, its limitations are obvious.

A different type of treatment requires that the student become familiar with many points of view, with many philosophies of education, that he assume a critical attitude toward each of them, and that he reach certain conclusions with respect to the validity of each of the many theories brought to his attention.

Contemporary educational philosophies get their meaning when viewed in the perspective of the history of philosophy. One may question whether the student has any right to claim that he has developed a philosophy of education except as he has reached his conclusions out of a rich experience in the study of current philosophies of education and of the history of philosophy.

A philosophy of education is not something which stands apart in the experience of the individual. If it is significant at all, it must give meaning to methods of teaching and of learning; it must make its contribution to the understanding and development of character; it must furnish criteria for the judgment of social progress; and it must throw light upon the current scene, whether national or international. The author of this text has met these requirements out of his unusual scholarship in the fields of philosophy, sociology, and government. He has written most interestingly and yet critically of the philosophies which men have held, and has without dogmatism sought to guide the student in his thinking in such fashion as to lead him to the intelligent formulation of his own philosophy. In no case is he more helpful than in the consideration of education for leadership in a democracy.

College and university students preparing to teach will find the book a mine of information and a source of inspiration. The more mature and more experienced teachers and administrators who read the book will be stimulated to analyze critically beliefs which they may have held without fully understanding their source or their implications.

GEORGE D. STRAYER

CONTENTS

PART ONE

THE SOURCES OF THE PHILOSOPHY OF EDUCATION

PART TWO

THE FUNCTIONING OF THE PHILOSOPHY OF EDUCA-
TION IN THE SCHOOL'S RESIDUAL SERVICE
TO THE INDIVIDUAL

PART THREE

THE FUNCTIONING OF THE PHILOSOPHY OF EDUCA-
TION IN THE SCHOOL'S RESIDUAL SERVICE
TO SOCIETY

CONTENTS xiii

Part One

THE SOURCES OF THE PHILOSOPHY
OF EDUCATION

CHAPTER
I

THE SCIENCE OF EDUCATION
AND
THE PHILOSOPHY OF EDUCATION

THE SCIENCE OF EDUCATION AND THE PHILOSOPHY OF EDUCATION

TWO CONFLICTING MEANINGS OF THE TERM "EDUCATION"

In educational theory and practice the term "education" has been used in the course of history with two fundamental and distinctive meanings.

The meaning that we shall first consider comprises two aspects, the demands of social heritage, on the one hand, and the demands of preparation for the individual struggle for existence, on the other. The demands of social heritage embrace the sum total of measures taken by qualified institutions and persons for the purpose of bringing the *educand* (the learner) up to standards of the good life that are cherished by the group (tribe, caste, religious organization, or nation) of which he is a member by birth or by adoption. The demands of preparation for the individual struggle for existence are controlled by the standards of competence set by the occupational group (trade, vocation, profession) of which the educand wishes to be a member. Such a conception of education may readily lead to an exaggerated degree of directed, prescribed learning and uniformity and may result also in insufficient adaptation of programs and methods of study to the individual needs and capacities of the educand. At the same time, this first meaning of the term "education" implies systematic, that is, sequential curricula (adequately covering the subject) and definite, distinctly shaped procedures or methods of study. It is, further, characterized by attention to fundamentals, such as the permanent moral values of humanity and the information, skills, aptitudes, and attitudes without which — in the judgment of educational authorities — neither the individual educand nor the group can achieve the good life.

The second important meaning of the term conceives education to be the sum total of measures taken by qualified institutions and persons to assist the educand toward as happy a life as is possible in a changing civilization. Such assistance consists in helping him to attain the satisfaction of his interests and inclinations, and to forward his development in the various aptitudes that are satisfying to him, and that are regarded by educational authorities as harmful neither to him nor to society. If education is conceived according to the second method, it may easily result in an educative process characterized by such negative features as exaggerated individualism and nonconformity, inadequate training in fundamentals, lack of balance in self-expression and insufficient self-control on the part of the learner, a dangerously large and self-defeating emphasis on the individual's right to happiness and a dangerously small emphasis upon his duty to contribute to the happiness of the group, an exaggerated egoism and hedonism or love of pleasure. At the same time, the second conception of education, if properly applied to the educative process, can produce the following positive results: the vitalization or vivid meaningfulness of school work, as a consequence of challenging and encouraging the individual interests and aptitudes of the learner; a more satisfying and consequently more retentive learning; a more cheerful outlook upon life, nourished by happy, unhampered growth.

These two fundamental conceptions of education — the "essentialist" and the "individualist-pragmatist" (see p. 139) — have repeatedly been in conflict during the course of history. Obviously, the ideal educative process would consist in combining the positive points of each conception of education and in eliminating the negative. It is the business of the science of education and of the philosophy of education to achieve the organization of such an ideal.

In order to understand the relationship between the science and the philosophy of education in this enterprise of building an ever more satisfactory educational system, it is necessary first to analyze the nature of the science of education. The analysis can profit from a consideration, however brief, of the place occupied by the science of education in the family of the sciences.

THE VARIOUS MEANINGS OF THE TERM "SCIENCE"

The term "science" is employed by educated people with more than one meaning. This is very natural because science or knowledge may have different degrees of reliability and exactitude. The Greeks, being well aware of this fact, created several words each meaning "science" or "a body of knowledge," but each designating a different degree of validity of each particular body of knowledge. Thus Plato used five different terms for which we have no other translation than the single word "science" or "knowledge." Our term "science" comes from the Latin word *scientia*. The Romans, who were the principal heirs to Greek civilization, were by temperament indifferent to verbal niceties, save legal ones. They therefore bequeathed to us from the wealth of Greek terms expressing the various degrees of reliability of knowledge or science just one general term, *scientia*. As a result, the word "science" is with us a sort of Jack-of-all-trades, a vague term which is frequently the source of confused thinking and of confusing discussion.

A medieval thinker has said that there is no variety of anything which cannot be classified. In accordance with this scholastic rule, which still holds, the variety of meanings in which the word " science " is employed can be reduced to two principal definite meanings.

First, the term " science " is employed in the sense of " science proper," an expression used by Kant. The philosopher meant by " science proper " a body of knowledge enabling the scientist to make exact predictions of the effects of certain given causes.[1] Such predictions are known as scientific laws. For example, the law of Guldberg and Waage, or the law of mass of action: " The chemical reaction of a chemical reacting substance is proportional to its active mass "; or the law of gravitation: " The force of attraction as exerted between two bodies is proportional to the product of the masses of the bodies, and inversely proportional to the square of their distance apart." The prediction is based upon a carefully observed and verified sequence of facts. A scientific law is defined as an affirmation of a constant relation between one fact of variation and some other fact of variation — for instance, between the warming of water to a certain degree and the formation of steam. The sciences dealing with matter (that is to say, with things extended in space and knowable by our five senses) have been increasingly successful in adding to such knowledge. These sciences are the mathematical sciences and the natural sciences. Their recent joint achievements have produced in the minds of some scholars, and with them in the mind of a considerable section of the general public, the tendency to monopolize the term " science " for the mathematical and the natural sciences and to refuse the dignity of a science to any body of knowledge which is unable to furnish exact predictions of the effects of given causes (or which does not occupy itself with such pre-

[1] *Metaphysische Anfangsgründe der Naturwissenschaften, herausgeg.* von Hofler, Leipzig, *Vorr., S.,* 190 ff.

Cf. also Aristotle, *Ethica Nicomachea,* VI, 3, 1139 b 31 (*Works,* Oxford, Clarendon Press, 1925, Vol. IX).

dictions). This seems to be an example of the ever-recurring arrogance of success.

Second, the term " science " may legitimately be taken in the sense in which Spinoza employed it when he spoke of science as correct reasoning about well observed facts.[2] In other words, science, in this second fundamental meaning of the term, is a body of information which presents a satisfactory degree of unity and validity and which is capable of bringing men who occupy themselves with the building or study of such a body of knowledge to certain concordant conclusions. The latter are the result neither of arbitrary, conventional opinions, nor of individual tastes and interests that those men have in common, but of objectively studied relations among the phenomena (facts, events, things) observed. Such relations are gradually detected and confirmed by methods of verification as definite as are humanly possible. This second meaning of the term " science " applies to the social sciences.[3]

THE FUNDAMENTAL DIFFERENCES BETWEEN THE MATHEMATICAL- NATURAL SCIENCES AND THE SOCIAL SCIENCES

These two groups of the sciences differ from one another as follows:

1. The mathematical sciences (such as geometry, trigonometry, algebra, the calculus) and the natural sciences (such as physics, chemistry, biology, geology, and the like) deal with

---

[2] *Ethica,* P. II, Scholium 2, Proposition 42 (" Reason or knowledge of the second kind ").

[3] Cf. Langlois, Charles V. and Seignobos, Ch., *Introduction to the Study of History,* Henry Holt, 1912 (esp. Authors' Preface, Ch. II, Conclusion), and Lacombe, P., *De l'Histoire Considérée Comme Science,* Paris, Librairie Philosophique J. Vrin, 1930 (esp. Ch. II: *Le Domaine de L'Histoire Science et Ses Limites*).

Cf. also Lalande, André, *Vocabulaire Technique et Critique de la Philosophie,* Paris, Félix Alcan, 1928, t. II, p. 735.

Cf. also Hume, D., *An Enquiry Concerning Human Understanding,* Section VIII: " *Its* [history's] * *chief use is only to discover the constant and universal principles of human nature.*"

* Bracketed remarks are added.

matter and its relationships. The social sciences (such as history, law, political science, economics, psychology — in the traditional meaning of the term — history of literature, and the like) deal, contrariwise, with human minds in their interrelationships; in other words, with the conflicting or concordant ideals, aspirations, inclinations, interests, and desires of men. Economics, for instance, searches for the best methods of stimulating and co-ordinating supply and demand.

2. The mathematical and natural sciences are more objective, that is to say, more capable of employing usefully the methods of exact measurement and of making exact predictions. The social sciences are less capable of detecting valid generalizations or scientific laws. The subject matter of the social sciences is the work and the reactions of the human mind. This subject matter has in it the confusing elements of warm blood and beating hearts, the co-operation or the clash of human wills, human passions, and human aspirations. In the behavior of men in so far as this behavior constitutes, in its various forms, the subject matter of the social sciences, we can frequently observe that the pressure of natural laws is there confronted by the self-determination, however restricted, of human reason and sentiment.[4] Man falls a victim to unwelcome physical necessity only when he is unable to defend himself against natural forces. Therefore, it is much more difficult — but also much more fascinating — to formulate scientific laws in the social sciences than it is to formulate such laws in the natural sciences.

Among human actions there are observable cases which, looked at through the eye of natural science, are not clearly and directly connected as causes and effects. For example, when it freezes, I shiver. Here we have a causative sequence of

[4] Cf. Davis, H. W. C., Regius Professor of Modern History in the University of Oxford. *The Study of History,* Clarendon Press, 1925, p. 15 f.

facts as natural science knows them. But what shall my conduct be in response to the sensation of shivering? Because I shiver, I can put on my overcoat or I can take some exercise. Mr. Pickwick would probably have fortified himself with alcoholic stimulants. Another man might do something else. Such reactions to the frosty weather can hardly be called effects in the sense in which natural science uses the term. They are, rather, purposeful acts of beings who deliberate and take choice among a number of possible expedients. No one can predict with exactitude, not even the individual himself, what any one person's conduct would be if some one fired a shot at him and wounded him.

Though it is difficult to formulate laws in the social sciences, it would be an error to think that the social sciences are incapable of formulating laws as exact as are those formulated by the natural sciences. For example, economics has a very exact law of diminishing return: " In any given stage of the arts an increase of labor or capital applied beyond a certain point in the cultivation of land causes less than a proportionate increase in the produce raised from a given area." As a simpler example (of a law formulated by a social science with an exactitude as nearly complete as that of the laws known to the natural sciences) there may be mentioned the economic law of inflated paper currency driving out of circulation coin or metallic currency. But this work of formulating laws, in the social sciences, seems to be possible only in the form of an intellectual " auscultation." [5] Auscultation is the method employed by the physician in order to establish a diagnosis of the condition of his patient. A talented and experienced physician arrives at correct diagnosis as a result of a general insight into the totality of the condition of the patient rather than as a consequence of the exact measurement of isolated symptoms,

[5] Cf. Bergson, Henri, *Introduction to Metaphysics*, G. P. Putnam's Sons, 1912, p. 36.

which measurement would be sadly inexact in proportion to the isolation of the symptoms. Similar " auscultation " of the complex social conditions which result from complex and conflicting interests and desires, ideals and aspirations of the individuals composing a social group, must be made by leaders both in the social sciences and in practical affairs of social leadership or government. The supreme application of social science is the art of statesmanship. This art consists in the ability of the statesman, assailed by conflicting public opinion and by conflicting demands and data concerning a problem, to perceive and to follow the correct or the best possible path.

It is important to remember in connection with this second difference between the mathematical-natural sciences and the social sciences that there is no serious reason why the latter should suffer from an inferiority complex in the presence of the former. The mathematical-natural sciences are themselves in reality much less objective than was claimed, prior to the formulation of the theory of relativity. In the apt words of H. Wildon Carr, it follows from Einstein's theory that " the nature we study is not independent of the mind which studies it. There is no absolute [objective] * physical reality which a mind may contemplate in its pure independence of the contemplator and the conditions of his contemplation. There is no universe common to all observers and private to none. The work of physical science is to co-ordinate the observations of observers." [6] Has not social science a similar goal?

In order to reduce to the right proportions our faith in and respect for the natural sciences — as compared with the social sciences — it is necessary to bear in mind that the history of those

---

* Bracketed remarks are added.

[6] Carr, H. Wildon, *The General Principle of Relativity and Its Philosophical and Historical Aspects*. By permission of The Macmillan Company, publishers, 1920, p. 20 ff.

sciences, even more than that of the social sciences, is a succession of errors which were abandoned and replaced by knowledge more correct and more dependable. The history of the sciences shows that one must be always ready to abandon a scientific " truth " for the sake of another truth. Not a few of the opinions of science which were believed in the past to be unquestionable truths have proved to be " enormous and even ridiculous errors," to quote a scientist.[7] To state it differently, many so-called scientific truths are not absolutely valid truths, but are truths in a degree, or relative truths. In February 1820, Duke de Berry, the grand-nephew of King Louis XVIII of France and the presumptive successor to the throne, was stabbed in the back by an assassin. The best physicians of France gathered around the bed of the wounded prince and applied all the medical truths of the time to save his life. Among other things, they bled the patient further by the application of leeches. Such a ministration in similar circumstances today would bring the physician to jail. Doubtless, more than one " scientific truth " of our own time will be regarded as a pitiful error by the successors of present-day specialists in the various natural sciences.

3. The mathematical and the natural sciences are more factual or matter-of-fact and less teleological, or purposive, than the social sciences. In other words, the unadulterated science of nature conceives of the universe as a fixed system of mechanical relationships between causes and effects. The unadulterated science of society, on the contrary, conceives of the world as a purposive system of adjustable relationships between means and ends, the latter including those of justice and happiness. As a philosopher has well expressed it, " there is no *ought* in the vocabulary of science [natural-mathematical science]; * only

---

* Bracketed remarks are added.

[7] Richet, Charles, " Réflexions sur la Science," *Revue des Deux Mondes,* 1er novembre 1931, p. 140.

is, was, or *will be,* in a universe of law, force, and matter." [8]
A chemist does not busy himself with musing as to what ought
to be the law presiding over the operation of this or that chemical reaction, but solely with the problem of what the law is. He
submits to the facts. A student in political science, on the other
hand, is interested, for example, not only in how the system of
popular representation in his country or in some other country
is organized and is functioning, but also in the problem of
how it ought to be organized, how it can be improved, and
what modifications ought to be made in it. He strives himself
to rise and to raise others above the existing conditions of
social life and to replace the existing facts with better facts.

4. Mathematics and the natural sciences possess definite, exact
terminology, while vague and inaccurate terminology is often
employed in the social sciences. When a mathematician or a
physicist says *angle, circumference,* or *calory,* the term has but
one meaning. But when students of social science discuss *democracy, progress, international law, freedom,* or the like, they
frequently debate on concepts whose definition they do not
take the trouble to establish, though each may associate with
the term a meaning widely different from that assigned to it
by his opponent.

WHAT THE MATHEMATICAL-NATURAL SCIENCES AND THE SOCIAL SCIENCES HAVE IN COMMON

The two fundamental groups of the sciences, different as
they are from each other, must possess some important feature
in common if the term " science " can legitimately be applied
to each. This important common feature is the scientific method.
Being scientific means investigating with order and clarity,
using devices of verification as precise and controllable as the

[8] Horne, Herman H., " An Idealistic Philosophy of Education," *The Kadelpian
Review,* November, 1932, p. 6.

subject matter of investigation may permit. To borrow from Professor John Dewey's *Sources of a Science of Education:*

There are those who would restrict the term [science] * to mathematics or to disciplines in which exact results can be determined by rigorous methods of demonstration. Such a conception limits even the claims of physics and chemistry to be sciences, for according to it, the only scientific portion of these subjects is the strictly mathematical. The position of what are ordinarily termed the biological sciences is even more dubious, while social subjects and psychology would hardly rank as sciences at all, when measured by this definition. Clearly we must take the idea of science with some latitude. The important thing is to discover those traits in virtue of which various fields are called scientific. When we raise the question in this way we are led to put emphasis upon methods of dealing with subject matter rather than to look for uniform objective traits in subject matter. From this point of view, science signifies, I take it, the existence of systematic methods of inquiry, which, when they are brought to bear on a range of facts, enable us to understand them better and to control them more intelligently, less haphazardly, and with less routine.[9]

THE PLACE OF EDUCATION IN THE FAMILY OF THE SCIENCES

Herbert Spencer has remarked, in *First Principles,* that " science means merely the family of the sciences — stands for nothing more than the sum of knowledge formed of their contributions." [10] This family seems to be fashioned upon the modern familial model. Past are the times of the patriarchal family of the sciences with theology at the head of the group and the rest considered as simply so many *ancillae theologiae,* maid-servants of theology. Family solidarity is not the strongest point of the contemporary family of the sciences. It is, rather,

* Bracketed remarks are added.

[9] Horace Liveright, 1929, p. 8 f.

[10] A. L. Burt, Publisher, 1880, p. 111.

a loosely connected heterogeneous assembly of individuals of different age and probably of varying respectability. In fact it is more a society than a family proper. This society is professed to be democratic, but not unlike many other democratic societies it is not free from tacitly maintained class distinctions. It has its " social climbers (*nouveaux riches*) " — the natural sciences — who have their retainers. It also has a somewhat frightened but outwardly composed aristocracy — the classics, the literary, artistic, and philosophic studies — which is, however, strong by breeding and finesse, and which contributes toward the ennobling and polishing of democracy. The family of the sciences has its secret and open jealousies, its rival coteries, its smart sets each pretending, secretly or openly, to dictate the rules of conduct and fashion for the rest of the crowd and to distribute unwritten licenses as to the rank of everybody who craves to be " on the inside."

What place does the science of education occupy in this family of the sciences? It occupies a peculiar place because it belongs by its different aspects, at one and the same time, to each of the two fundamental branches of the family of the sciences. For instance, the problems of educational organization and administration concerning the physical conditions of the educative process (such as lighting, ventilation, seating arrangements, and the problems of school architecture, in general) and, particularly, problems concerning the physiological aspects of the learning and teaching processes (such as the length and succession of study periods and recreational periods and other arrangements designed to offset the effects of fatigue, and similar problems) evidently relate the science of education to the natural sciences.

With regard to the problems of school hygiene, the science of education belongs in the province of natural science and, therefore, can and should profit by the methods of research and of control or verification employed in those sciences, namely, by laboratory and statistical methods. On the other hand, the solution of the problems of educational administration and organization raised by the various conflicting claims made by the individual educand, by the family, and by the various social, political, and economic organizations and institutions must, obviously, proceed through the method of insight or "auscultation" characteristic of social science. Similarly, the shaping of the educative process in accordance with the intricacies of the mental life of the learner, or educand, and with delicate shades of his reactions, in particular, the solution of problems regarding character education, are hardly susceptible to an accurate and conclusive treatment through quantitative methods of laboratory experimentation.

Such methods can deal more or less satisfactorily with isolated stimuli and responses but are still inadequate for fathoming a human personality which is a totality, a whole in which everything is inter-related with everything else. The Romans had a fortunate inspiration when they gave to the human personality the name *persona,* which means mask. As some one has well observed, the shades of the rainbow and the sounds of the seashore are not so numerous as are the subtle forms of thoughts and circumstances that determine our characters and our acts. The intellectual and moral life of the educand, as subject matter for the science of education, make it clearly related to those sciences which deal with the inter-relationship of human minds, in other words, to the social sciences. It is hardly necessary to enlarge upon the fact that educational objectives and the general method of education cannot be intelligently discussed and properly selected except in the light of the totality of the cultural, moral, political, and economic conditions, goals, and needs of a given country and of contemporary civilization. This light can be brought upon pertinent educational problems only in co-operation with, and through the methods of, the social sciences.

The twofold membership of the science of education in both the natural-science and the social-science branch of the family of the sciences has two important consequences, one negative, and one positive. The negative consequence is created by the fact that education is more a social science than it is a natural science because its more numerous, and its seemingly more important aspects, are akin to problems of the social sciences; hence the science of education is dominated more by the weak points of the social sciences than by the strong points of the natural sciences. As a result, many modern students of education have been influenced, somewhat unduly, by a sort of inferiority complex which has led them to believe that in order to be worthy of the denomination "scientists in education," they had no choice but to concentrate their effort upon investigations admitting of statistical treatment and demonstration. As a consequence of this neglect of the more important aspects — the social science aspects — of the science of education which are very fascinating and very enriching (but are not reducible to columns of figures, Sigmas, and radical signs) only too many Ph.D. dissertations in education have been produced which are merely statistical froth, neither nourishing nor stimulating, and which amply justify the cynical definition of educational research as "finding something that everybody knows and expressing it in language that no one understands."

In studying the science of education it is advisable never to lose sight of the fact that, taken as a whole, this science should be conceived in the light of the meaning given to the term

" science " by Plato. Science to Plato " means explanation and intelligibility; we ' know ' a truth when we can ' give account of ' it, and the way in which we can give account of it is by showing its necessary connection with wider and more independent truths. Progress in science is progress from isolated to connected thought." [11] Social science aspects of education include problems in the history of education, problems of financing education, training and selection of teachers, curricular problems, and the organization of tests, examinations, and the like. To the extent to which students of education, who occupy themselves with these social aspects, work with method, employ a definite and carefully organized procedure, bring to their tasks well-trained intelligence, and form no general views previous to patient and exhaustive investigation, they are scientists; their work is scientific even when it is entirely devoid of the formulae of correlation and deviation, of Sigmas and the radical signs.

The positive consequence of the twofold membership of the science of education in the two branches of the family of the sciences consists in the possibility, in fact, in the obligation to utilize, in the educative process, the enriching formative influence of both the natural and the social sciences. Educators, especially those responsible for the organization and administration of the educative process, should see to it that in the work of the educand at the pre-specialization stage of education, the curriculum should be balanced adequately between the mathematical and natural science method and content, on the one hand, and the social science method and content, on the other.

A teacher of geography presents a lesson on the trade routes between New York and Yokohama. This subject abounds in

[11] Abbott, E., *Hellenica,* Longmans, Green and Co., 1898, p. 136 (Also *Republic,* VI; *Theaetetus*).

difficult foreign names, and is not particularly appealing though not entirely outside the interests of the average student. Thanks to the double membership of the science of education in the sciences of physical facts and in those relative to the reactions of the human mind, a scientifically organized educative process would include in the experiences of the educand — designed to enrich his imagination and emotion — something about the highways of the sea that is quite different from the statistics and nomenclature of the routes of maritime transportation. Guided by a poet, the teacher and the class will try to penetrate the causes of the fascination of the sea for man.

They will muse with the poet:

Unlike the earth the sea does not bear the traces of human creation nor vestiges of human life. Nothing is permanently fixed on the sea. And what passes by it, does so in a transient manner. Think of vessels that traverse the sea. How swiftly vanishes the current produced in their wake! Hence that great purity of the sea which things terrestrial do not possess. The virgin water of the sea is also a much more delicate matter than the hard earth which cannot be handled without a pickaxe. . . . Pure is the sea as it was on the day of creation.

The sea has about it the charm of the things which break the dead silence of night and which promise to us that all will not be reduced to nothingness. Consequently, the sea is permission for agitated human life to go to rest. It is to us what the night lamp is to small children who feel less lonely when the light is on.

The sea is less separated from heaven than is the land. It is in constant harmony with the colors of the sky, and is aroused to the slightest gradation of light. It beams to the sun, and every evening seems to pass away together with the sun. In reality, when the sun has disappeared, the sea continues to mourn it and preserves some traces of its luminous passage.

The sea refreshes imagination because it does not remind us of the life of man. It delights our soul because, like the soul, it is an

infinite though ineffectual aspiration, a flight continually inter-
rupted by downfalls, an eternal regret and gentle complaint. The
sea enchants us as does music, which, unlike language, bears no
vestiges of things material, nor does it tell us anything about men
either, but reflects the movements of the soul. Our heart, while
mounting and falling with the waves, forgets its own failings, and
consoles itself in the intimate harmony between its own sadness and
that of the sea. . . .[12]

And they might reflect with another poet:

> There is a pleasure in the pathless woods,
> There is a rapture on the lonely shore,
> There is society, where none intrudes,
> By the deep Sea, and music in its roar:
> I love not Man the less, but Nature more,
> From these our interviews, in which I steal
> From all I may be, or have been before,
> To mingle with the Universe, and feel
> What I can ne'er express, yet can not all conceal.

> Roll on, thou deep and dark blue Ocean — roll!
> Ten thousand fleets sweep over thee in vain;
> Man marks the earth with ruin — his control
> Stops with the shore; upon the watery plain
> The wrecks are all thy deed, nor doth remain
> A shadow of man's ravage, save his own,
> When, for a moment, like a drop of rain,
> He sinks into thy depth with bubbling groan,
> Without a grave, unknell'd, uncoffin'd, and unknown.[13]

A curriculum scientifically organized and balanced in the
light of the twofold membership of the science of education in

[12] Proust, M., *Les Plaisirs et les Jours,* Paris, Editions de la Nouvelle Revue
Française, 1924, p. 235 ff. (*La Mer*).
[13] Byron, *Childe Harold's Pilgrimage,* Canto IV (CLXXVIII).

the family of the sciences, can and should contribute to the humanization of the mechanistic progress of our times. In the past quarter-century many educators have been overemphasizing the mathematical and natural sciences. To be sure, the sciences have not only purely utilitarian value, but they can also be of considerable cultural and moral value. Through them the student learns not to play hide-and-seek with himself; he is forearmed against false evidence and is inoculated against crises of credulity, unreflecting enthusiasm, and fanaticism. A sufficiently prolonged and properly conducted systematic training in the mathematical and natural sciences will develop in the student the taste for analysis, for classification and causal linking together of problems, as well as the aptitude for distinguishing truth from cant, and for seeing the full logical consequence of a fact. In particular, the natural sciences will accustom the student to discern things under words, to penetrate shams and appearances, to accept facts, not to shun the consequences of a true idea or a necessary action.

But the humanities (languages, literature, history, art, philosophy, etc.), on the other hand, are capable of as great contributions, in fact, of far greater contributions to the intellectual and moral development of the student. They also, like the sciences, occupy themselves with facts; but these are facts of the heart and the soul, if one may say so. Such facts are not less real than the facts of inanimate nature, but they touch us more deeply, and consequently are more essential to our spiritual growth and to our harmony with ourselves. And if the mind, while studying the humanities, has to face facts, its attitude toward them is different from that of the mind when it submits to facts studied in the natural and mathematical sciences. The humanities teach us to revolt against certain ugly facts and to apply ourselves to create new ones, more just and more beautiful. Thus it was that the great crusaders of justice and tolerance, of liberty and equality, treated the facts of injustice, oppression, and prejudice.

If the sciences and their practical application will furnish man the power infinitely to improve machinery and increase wealth, letters will help toward developing in him a heart capable of possessing wealth without becoming its slave, a mind capable of using machinery without becoming its victim, and will prevent him from becoming a tool of the tools created by man himself. If industrial organization, assisted by the development of the sciences, will enable one nation to dominate other nations, then the moral forces promoted by the study of the humanities will advise men to labor toward the organization of the world in accordance with the supreme moral conscience of humanity. In a word, while it would be wrong to negate the value, especially the potential value, of machinery for the increase of human comforts and probably of human happiness, yet it would be an error not to see that the progress of mechanical civilization in order to yield its potential good must be humanized, that is, corrected and tempered by human sympathy. Indeed, the humanities or *litterae humaniores* is a happy term given to the totality of the various patient, unsensational studies which do not seem to be conducive to an immediate utilitarian application, yet appear to be more valuable to mankind than are the sciences. The sciences devote themselves wholly to the acquisition of mere knowledge, while the humanities, taken in their ensemble, are consecrated to the pursuit of wisdom and sympathy.

In proportion as the school will engender in the students more and more real human wisdom and sympathy, which can be gained by the study of the experience of centuries, and in proportion as the school will diffuse in the world sympathy and understanding through the medium of properly humanized students, there will be more social harmony and more social efficiency despite the ever-changing and complex mechanistic aspects of our civilization.[14]

The twofold membership of the science of education in the family of the sciences, while it is a source of enrichment of the educative process, is also a cause of theoretical and practical controversy in education. To this inevitable conflict between the two sides of the science of education there is to be added the opposition between the various claims put on the school by the educand and by the various influences to which both the educand and school workers are subject. Such a set of conflicts and controversies, theoretical and practical, creates the necessity for a philosophy of education as a branch of the science of education. The purpose of the philosophy of education is to co-ordinate and reconcile those conflicting tendencies of educational theory and practice.

The employment of the term " philosophy " in this connection is legitimate, but needs explanation and clarification.

The term " philosophy " is employed in the conversation and writing of educated people with several different meanings.

1. Philosophy, in its academic-historic sense, that is, philosophy considered as a subject traditionally studied in the higher institutions of learning, means a critical outlook upon life's real values and upon human conduct. In other words, the fundamental problem of philosophy, in the traditional academic meaning of the term, is relative to the task of fitting human conduct with a critically worked out scale of values. The technical name for this traditional fundamental problem of philosophy is " ethics." The various solutions of the problem which are found in the history of philosophy are worked out in the light of the answer

[14] Cf. Vial, F., *Questions de Pédagogie Inactuelle*, Paris, Delgrave, 1933.

to two questions: (a) What is the ultimate reality? (b) How much can we know about it — how valid is this human knowledge? Answers to the first of these questions are considered in that division of philosophy which is called " metaphysics " or " ontology." Answers to the second question constitute that aspect of philosophy known as " epistemology." Thus philosophy, in the academic-historic sense of the term, presents three aspects: ethical, metaphysical, and epistemological. Ruling out a few instances where philosophers have been indifferent to the problem of providing a scale of values by which to judge human conduct, in other words, indifferent to ethics, philosophy has been a threefold search (metaphysical or ontological, epistemological, and ethical) for an answer to the fundamental questions of the ultimate sense of all existence and, in particular, of human existence. Philosophy, then, with regard to the various sciences, has the function of a clearing house. In the light of a clear, critical evaluation, it strives to build a general outlook upon life, to decide what, if anything, has become certain scientifically; to decide also what remains scientifically uncertain, with relation to the knowledge of the first cause and final end of human existence.

2. The term " philosophy " is also employed in the sense of the ensemble of guiding principles of conduct derivable from any highly specialized and advanced knowledge or studies. Hence, we hear people speak of the philosophy of history, the philosophy of law, the philosophy of mathematics, etc. It is one of the noble tendencies of the human mind not to live in vain, but to work at something that has permanent value. Therefore a scholar who is really devoted to his calling sooner or later experiences the need of drawing from his special knowledge some lessons which may be generally useful in life. An astronomer, a mathematician, an historian strives to relate for the benefit of humanity how the universe in general and human

life in particular look to him, in the light of his special studies, and what is the ultimate purpose of life, according to his special information and his reflection over this special information. The philosophy of history, for instance, is an attempt to formulate, in the light of historic certainty, some general suggestions as to worthy individual conduct, more especially, worthy social and political conduct.

3. The connotation given to the term "philosophy" by popular usage seems to be "the general hang of things," that is to say, the general outlook upon life which shows how everything is related in life to everything else. Philosophy so conceived is the kind of knowledge which Sophie Charlotte, the Queen-Philosopher of Prussia, sought when she wanted to know, according to Leibniz, not only the why of a thing, but also the why of the why.[15] Hence, being a philosopher or taking life philosophically means, in the popular usage of these expressions, the disposition to look at things and events from the point of view of the eternal "general hang of things"; in other words, from a plane rising above our personal individual interests and beyond the accidents of our individual or national life. When achieved, this disposition of mind brings us to bear with serenity our bad luck, and to accept with humility and calm our good luck. This, of course, is not saying that anyone who bears calmly the vicissitudes of life is to be called a philosopher in the popular usage of the term. The title "philosopher" is not intended for a man who is merely dull and insensitive. It is properly used only in the case of the man whose calm in the face of violent changes in his personal life is the result (though it may be a subconscious result) of the conviction — however inarticulate — that the universe taken as a whole is reasonable.

4. Philosophy, finally, is employed in the sense given it by Voltaire, a restatement, with some modifications, of the mean-

[15] Cf. G. G. Leibnitii Epistola ad Guilielmum Wottonum, *Opera Omnia*, Genevae, MDCCLXVIII, Apud Fratres De Tournes, Vol. VI, P. II, p. 217.

ing in which Socrates employed the term. In his celebrated article, *The Philosopher,* contributed to the Encyclopedia, Voltaire says:

> The philosopher forms and bases his principles upon an infinite number of observations. For the purpose of increasing their store of knowledge and enriching their ideas, philosophers study men of the past and men of today. And here is advice for those who want to be philosophers: " Spread yourselves like so many honey-bees in the world past and present, and then return to our beehive to compose your honey! " The philosophic turn of mind is the one characterized by observation and analysis, which put things in their right proportions and relations.[16]

Philosophy so conceived — as an appraisal of values — will make the philosopher who practices it a person very different from the conventional philosopher, whom Rembrandt has represented as sitting in a dark niche of a gloomy cloister and looking absently before him into the distance, above and beyond earthly life. The philosopher, if he fosters the practical attitude in philosophizing, will put himself beyond the resounding criticism against philosophers formulated by La Rochefoucauld when he said in his *Maxims:* " Philosophers can triumph over the evils of the past and the future, but present evils triumph over philosophers." [17]

Philosophy, then, can be conceived as a critical search for the rules of general conduct in life. These rules are determined in the light of the evaluation of values in which men are guided by a critically built general outlook upon life and its ends — a kind of clearing house for the evaluation of values.

The philosophy of education seeks, precisely, to be a sort of clearing house where the relative values in education and the relative validity of different claims on the school are weighed.

[16] *Le Grand Dictionnaire Encyclopédique,* t. VII.
[17] *Réflexions, Sentences et Maximes Morales,* Paris, Garnier Fréres, p. 18 (XXII).

To draw a suggestion from the parallelogram of forces in physics, the purpose of the philosophy of education is to work out the "resultant" that determines the general educational policy. Each individual, each family, each community or country has just so much — or rather so little — energy, time, and money to put into the education of the oncoming generations. How much of that time and money and energy is to be devoted to the various educational objectives which the educand himself, his family, and the various social and political agencies consider desirable or even indispensable? What method or methods should be employed to attain an educational objective? Such and similar are the problems on which, naturally, much disagreement exists and will exist within the teaching profession and among educational authorities as well as in the public mind. As suggested above, the purpose and task of the philosophy of education, as a branch of the science of education, is to examine critically and then seek to co-ordinate and to reconcile the conflicting but worthy points of view relative to educational objectives, curricula, courses of study, training and selection of teachers, classification of students, methods of teaching, and the like — and the corresponding problems of educational administration and finance. An intelligently purposeful organization and administration of a school system, as well as of a class period, presupposes a philosophy of education.

In order to realize how much a philosophic clearing house is needed for the evaluation of conflicting claims upon the school budget, it is sufficient to attend just a few committee meetings of any school board when the funds to finance the various educational objectives and activities are being apportioned. A properly balanced school system which reasonably satisfies the legitimate needs of the individual educand and of the community is hardly to be attained without such a philosophic clearing house.

To perform such a necessary and useful work as that of a clearing house in educational theory and practice, other branches of the science of education do not suffice, for the simple reason that they conflict with one another. For example, educational psychology is absorbed in the individual learner. It is primarily interested in shaping the educative process in such a manner that the educand may remain his own self, so to speak. It strives to help the individual " to harmonize with himself," as the Greeks would say. In fact, certain schools of thought in modern educational psychology go further than the Greek sage who advised the individual, " Know thyself." Such schools of thought advise the individual, " Be thyself." But an educational administrator who represents the educational authority financing the school is advised by the philosophy of education to object: " Yes, you can be yourself, and follow in your school work your own not undesirable inclinations, but you can do this only on the condition that you do not neglect preparation for any of your duties toward your community and your nation." The educational administrator should co-ordinate and direct the work of the school according to these principles of educational philosophy.

THE PHILOSOPHY OF EDUCATION AS A GUIDE IN EDUCATIONAL " STRATEGY "

It is said that life is a struggle. It would probably be more accurate to say that all activity is a struggle. Even such peaceful, unaggressive, and spontaneous activity as artistic creation is a struggle. Is not art, indeed, a relentless struggle of the artist — sculptor, painter, musician, poet — toward expression of his emotions and ideas through the medium of unyielding, unwilling matter, be that clay, color, tonal instrument, or vocabulary? Similarly, is not public education, taken as a whole, a struggle toward a better human society, toward a worthier, more beautiful life for all? Is not this goal to be promoted through the right development of the individual toward the ideal of the good, the just, and the beautiful as over and against various forces, individual and social, adverse to such an ideal?

The organization of a struggle or of an activity of any kind can profit, perhaps, from the suggestion which the organization of military struggle — the supreme form of human struggle for existence — seems to offer. In the conduct of warfare, the organization of the activities of the fighting forces by the General Staff must follow two lines. The first, relative to the correct selection of objectives toward which the effort must be directed, is called strategy. The second, concerning the technique to be used for the attainment of the objectives, is called tactics. Those armies have been successful which have had, other conditions being equal, in commanding positions generals who were good strategists and who knew how to select their objectives and to adjust their tactics to those objectives.

Recent educational developments probably have been characterized by an exaggerated emphasis upon educational "tactics"; that is, methods of teaching various subjects, or time-table "plans," such as the Gary Plan, Dalton Plan, Winnetka Plan, and the like. On the other hand, there has been not nearly enough attention given or effort made with regard to the building of a critically evaluated scale of values in education. Such a scale of values should issue from a critical outlook upon life and upon its goals. It should be harmonized with a sufficiently complete picture of the ideals and potentialities (moral, intellectual, and aesthetic) offered by the realities and possibilities (political, economic, and cultural) of the community, the nation, and humanity at large.

To put it differently, educational leaders in recent decades have been more intent upon "tactics" than upon "strategy" in education. Yet the latter alone can furnish the background against which all the various little " plans " must be projected in order that their worth may be properly weighed. If, for instance, a " plan " implies merely an educational method which aims at a happy carefree time for the children in school, and fails to develop in them a stern sense of duty, the ability of persistent effort, and other similar qualities of character — as if the overwhelming majority of students were not going to be tried severely in the harsh school of adult life in which success is normally conditioned upon much perseverance — such a " plan," clearly, is to be rejected or substantially modified. Sound realistic educational " strategy " condemns unsound educational " tactics," however spectacular or however new such " tactics " may appear.

An educational administrator engrossed in the " tactics " of school activity and yet inattentive or unenlightened with regard to educational " strategy " would resemble a general who uses up his time and the fighting means at his disposal in figuring out and playing with the niceties of tactics (such as application of one or another kind of arms), but sends his troops into a strategical hole, to the destruction of those troops and of his nation. The interests of both the educand and society recommend that actual and future teachers, as well as educational executives, give sufficient attention to the problems of educational " strategy." Research and analysis relative to these problems constitute the subject matter of the philosophy of education and also its justification as a branch of the science of education. To fulfill its role in the development of educational theory and practice, the philosophy of education draws its data from two principal sources: (a) the information derived from other — factual — branches of the science of education; (b) the guidance and inspiration received from a general outlook upon life and its values formulated in the doctrines of philosophy.

SUGGESTIONS FOR READING

Dampier, Whetham, W. C. D., *A History of Science* (Cambridge University Press)

Dewey, John, *The Sources of a Science of Education* (Horace Liveright)

Millikan, Robert A., *Science and the New Civilization* (Charles Scribner's Sons)

CHAPTER
II

PHILOSOPHIES OF EDUCATION AND PHILOSOPHY

CHAPTER II

PHILOSOPHIES OF EDUCATION AND PHILOSOPHY

WHY PHILOSOPHY?

In order that a man may be a reformer, a leader of men, he must know, or at least be convinced that he knows, the way to a better state of things toward which he wants to lead others. He must not only believe passionately that his goal and his way to it are right, but he must be able also to spread a contagious belief that his is the only right and good goal and way. To succeed in creating among his followers a sufficiently lasting impression of knowing the new truth, the reformer must be possessed of some sort of ultimate certainty as to the ultimate end of life; in other words, a well-rhymed general philosophy of life, and a definite scale of values. Small wonder, then, that many social and educational reformers draw their inspiration from the leading philosophic thought of their time.

Leading philosophers, in the academic-historic sense of the term (see p. 24), have differed in temperament and in point of view, but they have never differed in the substance of their philosophic search. Some of them were men eager to exercise an immediate influence upon the society in which they lived or upon humanity as a whole. Others were men who sought an explanation of the origin and final goals of the universe for the sake of knowledge itself. But all philosophers who have exercised a lasting influence upon contemporaneous and subsequent philosophic thought have invariably striven to work out a reasoned, self-critical, ultimate certainty as to the primary cause and the ultimate end of all existence.

An educational reformer cannot exercise an enduring influence unless his plan of educational reform issues from and is supported (a) by a solid philosophic foundation made of religious faith, or a rationally founded conviction, or both, relative to the ultimate certainty, (b) by a scale of values based on that certainty and relative to the good life in accordance with those values. Therefore the thought of significant educational leaders, past and present, cannot be properly understood except in connection with the philosophic system to which they adhered; neither can the history of education be properly studied in abstraction from at least certain chapters of the history of philosophy.

Thus the educational philosophy of Rousseau (which appeared new in its time) in order to be rightly evaluated must be considered not only in the light of the contemporary rationalistic educational philosophy against which Rousseau militated (see p. 370) but also in the light of a philosophy of life such as was professed, for instance, by Antisthenes (d. 365 B.C.), the head of the Cynics. The Cynics were so named for three reasons. First, the headquarters of their philosophic society was located in the village named Cynosarges, or the White Dog's Village, a suburb of Athens. It derived its name from a white dog (κύων ἀργός, cyon — or kyon — argos), which according to tradition snatched away a part of the victim when Diomus was sacrificing to Heracles. Second, the Cynics were insistent and unceremonious in teaching their puritan morals as a good watchdog (dog in Greek is κύων, kyon or cyon) is in guarding his master's property and person. Third, some Cynics carried their practice of simple life to the point where the comforts of their dwellings did not exceed those of a dog's kennel. According to tradition, the celebrated Cynic, Diogenes of Sinope (d. 323 B.C.), actually lived in a dog's barrel. Among his few belongings was a clay water-cup. He discarded it as an unnecessary article of luxury after he had seen a rabbit drink directly from the stream. When Alexander the Great called on Diogenes and asked what he could do for the philosopher, Diogenes, seated in the dog's barrel, answered: " Kindly don't stand between me and the sun." The Cynics, consequently, were anything but cynical, in the modern sense of the term. They were early Greek puritans who thought that virtue was the only good. They denounced the corruptions resulting from the artificialities and abuses of civilization and recommended a return to the frugality and simplicity of life. This theme reappeared several times in the history of philosophic thought before Rousseau brilliantly restated it in the eighteenth century and based on it his philosophy of education.

Similarly, Froebel's educational philosophy cannot be understood in abstraction from his romantic pantheism, a poetical paraphrasing of Spinoza's (d. 1677) theory of substance and Schelling's (d. 1854) theory of " Self (*Ich, i.e.,* God)," or the " World-Soul " — the Being that comprises in Itself all reality. Froebel believed that the universe in its totality and in all its manifestations was the realization of the Divine Unity, or the Absolute; that God and the universe were one and the same thing. The component parts of the physical universe, such as celestial bodies (the sun, the stars, the moon, the earth, and the planets) as well as all forms of plant and animal life, also all forms of the social universe (the various forms and stages of group life and civilization) — all and everything that exists — are but various forms and stages through which the Absolute realizes itself.

Among those various forms of the realization of the Absolute, man occupies, according to Froebel, a privileged place because it is through man that the Absolute realizes itself as a moral being. Man is, so to speak, the spokesman of the Absolute on the question of good and evil, and the artisan in the service of the moral idea of the Absolute. Consequently, the child, the maturing spokesman of the Absolute, should develop in accordance with his natural tendencies, which are the inner, inborn laws of his nature such as the Absolute wishes them to be. The child, according to Froebel, is a channel "through which heaven floweth."

It is the destiny and life-work of all things to unfold their essence, hence their divine being, and, therefore, the Divine Unity itself — to reveal God in their external and transient being. It is the special destiny and life-work of man, as an intelligent and rational being, to become fully, vividly, and clearly conscious of his essence, of the divine effluence in him, and, therefore, of God; to become fully, vividly, and clearly conscious of his destiny and life-work; and to accomplish this, to render it (his essence) active, to reveal it in his own life with self-determination and freedom.

Education consists in leading man, as a thinking, intelligent being, growing into self-consciousness, to a pure and unsullied, conscious and free representation of the inner Law of Divine Unity, and in teaching him ways and means thereto.

. . . Therefore, education in instruction and training . . . in its first principles, should necessarily be passive, following (only guarding and protecting), not prescriptive, categorical, interfering.

Indeed, in its very essence, education should have these characteristics; for the undisturbed operation of the Divine Unity is necessarily good — can not be otherwise than good. This necessity implies that the young human being — as it were, still in process of creation — would seek, although still unconsciously, as a product of nature, yet decidedly and surely, that which is in itself best; and, moreover, in a form wholly adapted to his condition, as well as to his disposition, his powers, and means.

. . . In accordance with the laws of divine influence, and in view of the original soundness and wholeness of man, all arbitrary (active), prescriptive and categorical, interfering education in instruction and training must, of necessity, annihilate, hinder, and destroy.[1]

[1] Froebel, Friedrich, *The Education of Man*, Appleton, 1887, pp. 2, 7, 8, 9.

Froebel advised that direct instruction and discipline, coming, as it were, " from outside in," is the wrong method of education because it is contrary to the intention of the Absolute. The Absolute has deposited in the child powers and tendencies which must develop through free inner growth from " inside out." Froebel believed that educational procedure which interferes with such free growth defeats its own real aim, precisely because it puts obstacles in the path of the child's free growth. The true purpose of educational procedure is, according to Froebel, to put the child into an environment where such obstacles would have no place. This service of the school to the child, and indirectly to the Absolute, cannot begin too early. Therefore, as soon as the child can leave his nursery, he must be placed in a kindergarten, which Froebel conceived as a select environment best adapted for assisting the child's nature toward free growth.[2]

Such is, in substance, the educational philosophy of Froebel. Common sense easily detects in it certain absurdities. Among other things, Froebel's doctrine overlooks the child's undesirable natural tendencies and does not provide for their correction and elimination. Whatever may be the absurdities of Froebel's educational philosophy, they are less absurd than those now

[2] It may be mentioned that Froebel was much more sober in practice than he was in theory. Colonel Hermann von Arnswald, an alumnus of the celebrated Froebel School at Keilhau, to whom Froebel wrote several letters, says in his reminiscences:

" In the domestic life of the institution strict order had to be observed. Every pupil was supplied with the necessary facilities for the cleansing of the body and clothes. New-comers were minutely examined every morning before breakfast to ascertain their personal cleanliness. Whoever was found negligent in this respect, had his allowance of milk for breakfast stopped, receiving nothing but a piece of bread. In fact, there were hardly any other penalties than reductions in the regular meals. Whoever deserved punishment, found at dinner or supper a piece of bread on his plate, which meant to say that he had to pass by all other dishes without tasting of them. It was exceedingly rare that any punishment had to be inflicted. But, on the other hand, it was an inevitable rule that the penalty followed in the footsteps of the evil deed, as the following occurrence may prove. Large dishes of strawberries were standing ready for supper, when I, passing through the room, yielded to the temptation of tasting a strawberry. Froebel had seen me; and when we took our seats for supper, I found on my plate — the ominous piece of bread. " (*Froebel's Letters to his Wife and Others*, edited by Arnold H. Heinemann, Boston, Lee and Shepard, 1893, pp. 12–13.)

professed by his disciples who have adopted his pedagogical conclusions without adopting his philosophic premises.

Similarly, the theory relative to interest, or significance, which is the central point of Herbart's educational philosophy, cannot be properly understood except in connection with his metaphysical doctrine of monads — a modification of the monadology of Leibniz (d. 1716) (see p. 73). The starting point of the metaphysical speculation of Herbart was the question he asked himself: Why is it that our concepts of things and of changes in things are full of contradictions? The answer at which he arrived was to the effect that such contradictions are the result of the fact that various qualities of things are, in reality, made of simple units independent of one another — units which are monads " absolute in themselves," or " reals."

The " reals " are the true reality. The mind, or soul, is also a " real," or " self." The way through which the " extra-self " world can come to the knowledge of a " self," or a " real," or a mind, is that of apperception. Other " reals " seek to penetrate the " real " which is your or my mind. Hence the " disturbances (*Störungen*)," sensations, and ideas, which one " self," or " real," can send to another " self," or " real." But they can actually penetrate into the mind and become our new " presentations," or our new experiences, only via apperception. The occurrence of the latter presupposes the fulfillment of two conditions: (a) our receptivity for or interest in a " disturbance," that is, a sense-impression or an idea, must function; (b) the new experience which seeks admission to our " self " must adapt itself to or be organized in terms of our past experience. Only then, when a " disturbance " has found the password to the " self," which password is interest, or significance, and has adjusted itself to " the apperceiving mass of ideas," *i.e.,* our past experience, can it become our new experience and one of the " apperceived mass of ideas " residing in our minds. Hence,

Herbart's belief that the true task of philosophy is the clarification and crystallization of concepts. ♩

The metaphysics of Herbart — with the corresponding epistemology and ethics — was the source of inspiration for his pedagogy. It was his doctrine relative to the nature of the "reals" that led him to organize his celebrated general method of teaching and learning around the problem of "many-sided interest," or significance, concentration, reflection, and the well-known "steps": preparation (analysis), presentation (synthesis), association, systematization, and application.[3]

So, too, Dewey's educational philosophy is a logical issue of his agnostic-pragmatic "instrumentalism" (see p. 112), and Lenin's educational philosophy is the result of his Marxian historic materialism (see pp. 51–52).

To say it again, a powerful leader and reformer in any sphere of life can scarcely be conceived apart from his or her more or less definite scale of values which presupposes some sort of ultimate certainty as to the primary cause and final end of all life and all endeavor.

Each teacher, irrespective of the level of his school, and still more each educational administrator, is a leader whether he wishes to be or not, and his leadership is either positive or negative. Therefore, for the sake of the proper discharge of his duties, every teacher and each school executive must possess a definite philosophy of education based upon and supported by a general philosophy of life. An old schoolmaster dedicated his book to all his old pupils, at whose expense, he said, he had learned everything he knew about education. This is either a case of exaggerated modesty or it is a belated confession of incompetence. It is necessary to distinguish strictly between broadmindedness and ignorance.

---

[3] Herbart, J. F., *The Science of Education*, D. C. Heath, 1869, p. 122 ff. *Outlines of Educational Doctrine*, Macmillan, 1901, Ch. III.

In the attempt to build for himself or herself a definite philosophy of education supported by a general philosophic foundation made of a critical outlook upon life, the student of education can be greatly assisted by acquaintance with the fundamental theses and arguments of the history of philosophy. A philosophy of education devoid of such foundation can hardly be — spectacular and sensational as it may appear — anything more than a groundless, hazardous, irresponsible theorizing. Besides, while trying to master any realm of human knowledge, it is only fair to suppose that there were clever people before us, and it is sound economy to try to learn from their relevant basic experiences.

TWO FUNDAMENTAL FACTS ABOUT THE HISTORY OF PHILOSOPHY

The history of philosophy is the history of the more important doctrines or systems of thought relative to the problem of the ultimate reality which have influenced men's general outlook upon life and their scale of values. Considered from the point of view of its educational implications, the history of philosophy presents two basic facts.

First, the center of gravity of the philosophic search has always lain in the search of the ultimate reality. This problem constitutes the subject matter of metaphysics or ontology, which thus constitutes the principal aspect of philosophy. Metaphysics is the real support of ethics, or theory of the good life and right conduct. It is clear that one's conduct in important life situations depends upon one's scale of values, itself depending upon one's idea of the ultimate reality. The general outlook upon life and the conduct of a man who believes that there is no future life, no eternal moral values and moral duties, nor anything superior in value to man's own pleasure or immediate needs and wants can readily be vastly different from the general outlook upon life and the conduct of a man who holds the opposite view upon the ultimate certainty. In addition to these two aspects of the philosophic search — metaphysics and ethics — there is, it will be recalled, the third one, epistemology, or the theory of the validity and limits of human knowledge. A philosopher's epistemology, however, is merely an argument in support of his metaphysical or ontological position (relative to the ultimate, true reality or "things-in-themselves" as over and against phenomena or things as they appear to be).

The certainty which philosophy seeks is a rationally established certainty. This distinguishes the philosophic search recorded in the history of philosophy not only from theology, which treats of the revealed truth and appeals to our faith, but also from experimental science. Science — in the sense of experimental science or "science proper" — is interested in knowing facts, their immediate origin, their fruits and consequences. It controls and verifies its own knowledge only within the realm of those facts. Experimental science does not study — nor can it study — the first causes and last ends of all existence. Those things cannot, on account of their very nature, be demonstrated in a laboratory. Similarly, experimental science is not concerned with the problem of the last foundations of all knowledge, of the validity of knowledge in general. In the fitting words of a keen student of philosophy:

Science accepts its data as it "finds" them in experience and carries its analysis only so far as is necessary for its immediate purposes. Philosophy never accepts the data as given in experience, but endeavors to carry them back to some ultimate foundations, to the so-called "last analysis." Philosophy is interested in the reduction of every individual datum of experience to some ultimate principle upon which, in the totality of knowledge, every individual depends. . . . The principles of science are the beginnings of science with which it takes its start, the foundations which it utilizes in establishing its structure. Science does not investigate the origin of these foundations any more than the carpenter performs the work of the stone mason who has laid the foundation of a given house; and it does not establish the validity of the foundation any more than the upper stories of a building actually support the foundations of the house. The foundation of science now is this or that *philosophical* theory, consciously or unconsciously accepted. . . .[4]

All told, experimental science on account of its very nature, resulting from its method of investigation and verification, cannot penetrate below the surface of phenomena or the reality as it appears to be. But humanity clamors for an answer to the question as to what is the ultimate sense of all existence. The history of philosophy, in its metaphysical or ontological doctrines, presents a series of answers for the benefit of all who wish to be assisted in their quest for a rational ultimate certainty by the proved findings and suggestions of great philosophers. Such is the first fundamental fact about the history of philosophy.

Its second basic fact is that in their noble effort to give a critical, in other words, a rationally founded solution to the problem of the ultimate certainty, the philosophers have advanced and restated, in the course of history, just four or five fundamental theses, which are so many keys to the apparently confusing intricacies of philosophy. " New " philosophic doctrines have their roots in anterior doctrines, and there is continuity of rotation of the basic themes.

THE BASIC THESES OF THE HISTORY OF PHILOSOPHY

Man somewhat closely resembles other animals of the genus to which he belongs biologically. He is born and dies like the animals. Like them he is engrossed in practical preoccupations

---

[4] Sanborn, Herbert C., " Democracy, Science, and Philosophy," *Journal of Tennessee Academy of Science*, *Vol. VI*, No. 3, p. 123.

upon which depends his survival. Not unlike the animals, his interests and his anxieties are centered around the problem, what he shall do to insure his existence and make it more pleasurable; what he shall do to protect and promote his progeny. But man alone among the animals seems from his earliest historic existence to have been visited (amidst and beyond his practical problems) also with a problem and anxiety of a very different kind. He alone asks himself the questions: Where do I come from? Whither do I go?

With the exception of man, no being wonders at its own existence; but it is to them so much a matter of course that they do not observe it. Its (nature's) wonder however is the more serious as it here stands for the first time consciously in the presence of death, and besides the finiteness of all existence, the vanity of all effort forces itself upon it. With this reflection and this wonder there arises therefore for man alone the need for a metaphysic; he is accordingly an *animal metaphysicum*. At the beginning of his consciousness certainly he also accepts himself as a matter of course, but very early, with the first dawn of reflection, that wonder appears which is some day to become the mother of metaphysics. . . . By metaphysics I understand all knowledge that pretends to transcend nature or the given phenomenal appearance of things, in order to give an explanation of that by which, in some sense or other, this experience of nature is conditioned, or, to speak in popular language, of that which is behind nature and makes it possible.[5]

Man early began to reflect upon the fact that whenever he made anything, a tool, a piece of clothing, or planted a seed, he had a plan, that is he intended his action to produce a certain result, to serve a certain purpose. This is why he manufactured those objects and conducted his action in a certain manner rather than in any other manner.

In the words of Marcus Aurelius:

[5] Schopenhauer, A., *World as Will and Idea*, II, xvii.

Everything exists for some end, a horse, a vine. Even the sun will say, I am for some purpose, and the rest of the celestial deities will say the same. For what purpose then art thou? [6]

Hence the question presented itself to man's mind as to the plan and purpose back of his own existence. What am I for? What is the purpose of all things that exist? What is the goal of the universe? Why should there be a universe rather than nothing?

Man early began also to wonder at the fact that while asleep we have dreams and nightmares. Sometimes even when we are awake, we have hallucinations. While in any such condition, we take for objective or tangible realities things which disappear when the hallucination ceases. They then become intangible, and at best simply images. We know they were merely phantoms and illusions, yet there is a striking resemblance between the images we had on the occasions in question and the perception of certain objects which we have when awake and in a normal, healthy condition. Hence man raised the question: Is anything truly real? Is there a true reality — the reality beyond all doubt? If there is one, what is its true, intimate nature? What are " things-in-themselves " in distinction from their appearances or phenomena? (See p. 43.)

Man also saw that men live and then die. Anything that lives, a plant, an animal, dies. As a result, man asked himself, What is death? Is it the dissolution of a being once and for ever, for eternity? Or, on the contrary, after an individual's visible death does his life continue in an invisible way, in an invisible world? In the latter case, what is that world, and where is it? The problem of death is the mysterious door sealed with more than seven seals in front of which men spend most anxious hours of their philosophic speculation.

[6] *Meditations,* VIII, 19.

Many wonders there be, but naught more wondrous than man;
Over the surging sea, with a whitening south wind wan,
Through the foam of the firth, man makes his perilous way;
And the eldest of deities, Earth, that knows not toil nor decay
Ever he furrows and scores . . .
Master of cunning he: the savage bull, and the hart
Who roams the mountains free, are tamed by his infinite art . . .
Speech and the wind-swift speed of counsel and civic wit,
He hath learnt for himself, all these . . .
He hath provision for all: fell plague he hath learnt to endure;
Safe whate'er may befall: yet for death he hath found no cure . . .[7]

Finally, and again very early in his historic, that is to say, his recorded existence, man was brought by his anxious curiosity to face the problem which is, in a sense, superimposed upon all the others: Is man's thinking power capable of answering the anxious questions relative to the ultimate reality which knock at the door of the reflective human mind? Is it not possible that he raises them in vain and quibbles in the void? Is not the human mind by reason of its very structure and properties condemned to remain in front of those problems, panting and vainly struggling to find for them a solution which man is never to attain?[8] Or as Kant has expressed it:

" What can I know?
What ought I to do?
What may I hope? "[9]

MONISM

Among the theses which the philosophers have worked out in the way of solution of the problem of the ultimate certainty,

[7] Sophocles, *Antigone*, Chorus 340–350. (Translated by F. Storr, Loeb Classical Library, Harvard University Press, 1924, pp. 341–342.)

[8] Cf. Cresson. A. *Les Systèmes Philosophiques*, Paris, Librairie Armand Colin, 1929, pp. 7–9 (Les Problèmes de la Métaphysique).

[9] *Critique of Pure Reason*, The Canon of Pure Reason, Second Section.

the most powerful, because the most appealing to men's need for certainty, and consequently the most frequently recurrent, is the thesis which answers in the affirmative the question as to the knowableness of the ultimate reality. This theme is sometimes called absolutism or dogmatism. More often, however, this theme is called monism — from the Greek word *monos* (μόνος), single — because it asserts that the ultimate reality has just one form, is just one in number. But what is this one or sole reality? At this point the monistic theme branches out into two schools of thought, materialism or " naturalism," and idealism or spiritualism.

MATERIALISM

Materialism, or " naturalism " — as it is sometimes timidly or hypocritically called — asserts that the variety of things composing the universe is reducible to just one principle, to one fundamental datum, which constitutes the ultimate reality. This principal datum and this ultimate reality is matter — in other words something extended in space. Its motion and its transformations resulting from motion are governed by the mechanical laws inherent in the properties of matter itself. The grand total which man seeks to discover is not anything different from nature as known to our senses, nor anything more sensational than the various bodies and their properties found in nature. Those bodies, however subtle, and those properties and their relationships, however intricate, are simply the various combinations and functions of just one and the same basic material reality. As to what, exactly, this sole and only material basic substance is, materialism or " naturalism " has, in detail but not in principle, several times changed its answer in accordance with the advancement of natural science.

The earliest outstanding forerunner of the present-day evolutionistic materialist, Democritus of Abdera, was born around

460 B.C. The first philosopher in western civilization to present a systematic materialistic doctrine, Democritus taught that the basic material reality was composed of atoms, a term derived from the Greek word *atomos* (ἄτομος), meaning uncuttable, indivisible — that is to say, an infinitely small unit or corpuscle. From combinations of these atoms produced by blind, mechanical movement (*i.e.,* not designed or directed by anybody but resulting from the inherent properties of matter such as weight, etc.) — there arise the various compound bodies of nature. What is called death or destruction is simply separation of the atoms whose temporary combination produced a body. After such separation the atoms return into the infinite whirl of atoms from which continually arises the formation and dissolution of the various bodies of matter, which is the only thing that exists and has existed eternally.

The present-day materialism or materialistic "naturalism" has substituted for atoms the units of positive and negative electricity (electrons and protons), but it professes the same fundamental metaphysical or ontological positions as did Democritus himself and his ancient disciples. As of old, the materialistic ontology of our own days negates the creation of the world by a Supreme Being, and also the very existence of such a Being. According to materialism, there is no such thing as spirit or soul. Materialism teaches that the belief in the existence of spirit is the result of ignorance, of fear, or of more or less voluntary self-deception. What is called thought or imagery is merely a subtle form of the working of the cerebral tissue and nerves in response to the various physical stimuli and is wholly dependent upon our physiological structure.

Materialism or materialistic "naturalism," it may be mentioned parenthetically, is sometimes called by the confusing name of realism. This is a rather loose employment of the term and is justly deprecated by the better modern philosophic usage in the interest of a more rigorous clarity. Materialism or materialistic " naturalism " may properly be called realism only with the understanding that the term " realism " stresses the original meaning of the Latin substantive *res* which originally denoted only material things knowable by, or tangible to, our senses.

The materialistic or " naturalistic " doctrine of the ultimate reality (in other words, the materialistic or "naturalistic" metaphysics or ontology) is empiricism (or sensationalism), epistemologically, that is to say when considered from the point of view of the problem as to the basic method of attaining the true knowledge. The empirical or *a posteriori* epistemology asserts that the knowledge of truth must be based on the experience of our senses, and is posterior to it; all knowledge originates in the experience of our senses and there is no *a priori* knowledge prior to such experience, neither are there any innate concepts or principles which constitute the foundation of all knowledge.

Ethically, that is to say with regard to the motives or springs of human conduct, materialism is determinism. It asserts (and when it does not do so openly for whatever reasons, the assertion is implied in its basic metaphysical position) that men's conduct is determined by mechanical natural laws, *i.e.,* laws resulting from the inherent properties of matter. Freedom of the will is an illusion resulting from our ignorance of the particular natural mechanical cause or chain of causes which has produced any given human action. Every act is nothing but an operation of addition of causes, on the one hand, and of effects, on the other. To say that an act is free is the same as to say that there is in a sum total something that was not in the elements added up. This is as absurd in psychology as it would be in arithmetic. Freedom of the will is as nonexistent as is the Supreme Impartial Judge and eternal justice. It follows, then, concludes the materialist, that there is no good or evil. Neither is there a moral responsibility — in rigorous logic, which, fortunately, not all adherents of materialism follow. Man is what the combination of blind mechanical factors makes him. He does what the blind play of mechanical causes and effects brings him to do.

Logically enough, consistent or orthodox adherents to the materialistic or " naturalistic " doctrine would be in their daily conduct egotistical hedonists or pleasure seekers. It does not follow, however, that every materialist, be he even an orthodox materialist, is a person who is guided in his conduct by a more or less frank, a more or less subtle pursuit of personal pleasure. Human nature has many intricacies and inconsistencies. One of them is that a materialist and determinist disbelieving in any eternal moral laws or an absolute moral responsibility can be a very fine fellow, considerate and even self-sacrificing, not only in regard to his family and close friends but also in regard to other men and humanity at large. In such cases, the possible effect of materialistic and atheistic determinism is restricted or entirely counteracted by a sense of the beautiful and the ugly in conduct or by habit implanted through the family, the school, or tradition.

The most impressive picture (impressive in magnitude and far-reaching consequences) of the ethical implications of materialism, in the practice of government and education, is furnished by the communist or Bolshevist or Soviet philosophy of life and government. The communist or Bolshevist doctrine, at least as represented by its leaders, has its roots in an ultimate certainty. The latter is provided by the Marxian theory of historic materialism. According to this theory formulated by Karl Marx (d. 1883) and inherited from him by Lenin (d. 1924), history has been shaped not by any spiritual factors, which do not exist, but by the struggle for possession, power, and enjoyment; first, the anarchical, unorganized struggle of individuals, and next an organized struggle of groups and of social classes. Needless to say, the doctrine of historic materialism conveniently overlooks many historic facts relative to the motives of unselfishness, sympathy, and sacrifice, which are responsible for many important events of history. Likewise it neglects to take into consideration certain great historic movements caused and sustained by the ideal of service to God or by some other form of religious emotion.

It is important that educators should clearly realize the fact that though not every adherent of materialism or of materialistic " naturalism " is a ruthless collectivist, communism has its roots, philosophically, in the Marxian materialistic ultimate certainty, propounded in the doctrine of historic materialism.

IDEALISM

Materialism, or materialistic " naturalism," has had its day several times in the history of philosophic thought. Each time as the development of natural science would make a great stride, materialism or materialistic " naturalism " would reappear to present its claim as the only true doctrine of the ultimate reality, which would be, of course, a material entity described in the terms of some latest impressive discovery of natural science. (This does not at all suggest that the development of natural science inevitably has such an effect on the mind of each and every scientist, of whom a fair proportion have been spiritualists.) Each time, however, materialism was sooner or later forced at least to share the stage with the opposite doctrine, idealism — when it was not entirely retired into the darker parts of the stage. Why? Not wholly because of men's craving for variety. The principal cause for supplanting materialism with idealism probably is that the materialistic analysis of the ultimate reality is inevitably reduced to the nature of an autopsy. And autopsy inevitably remains on the surface of life's intimate secrets. This is why materialism or "naturalism" has never been able to establish its final dominion over humanity's philosophic search for certainty. Sooner or later, but invariably after the first excitement over the new scientific discoveries was spent, man would begin to clamor: "Give me truths; for I am weary of surfaces, and die of inanition."

When, in the effort to prove his position, a materialistic scientist (believing that the very principle of life is something mechanical, something mechanically self-made) works upon the living cell, he kills the cell, and his analysis is reduced to an autopsy, inescapably inconclusive. When the materialistic philosopher tries to explain the historic process by the mere play of human possessive and hedonistic appetites, and all human actions by the mechanical laws of physiology, his work again leads to a kind of autopsy, an intellectual autopsy. By explaining away heroism, pure, spontaneous human sympathy, unadulterated attachment and loyalty, and the like, the materialist-determinist can readily kill the very impetus to life and activity in many of those who would accept the materialistic ultimate certainty. As William James put it in a letter to Shadworth H. Hodgson, determinism "leaves the world *unheimlich,*[10] reptilian, and foreign to man."[11] This is why the sound human instinct would always send Faust, aged and devitalized in the depressing atmosphere of the materialistic "scientism" or "scientific" materialism, away from it and toward the refreshing dream and sentiment nourished by some kind of spiritualistic ultimate certainty. Even though it may not be any more able rationally to establish the ultimate certainty than materialism is, idealism, with its flights of imagination, has

[10] Uncanny.
[11] *Letters of William James,* Atlantic Monthly Press, 1920, Vol. I, p. 257.

always been the unconquerable opponent of the materialistic autopsy. In the words of the poet:

> Thru the midnight star-lit sky once came
> An angel, singing of the Groves of Paradise
> And of the bliss of those ethereal ones
> Who there their solace and their comfort find
> In singing God Almighty's praises true.
> Within his arms a tender soul he brought
> To this our world of sorrow and of tears,
> Within whom echoed beatific songs,
> Born from that realm of happiness supreme;
> But soon within the young and tender soul,
> There welled a wondrous grief; then first he felt
> A strange nostalgic urge for his first sphere
> And surcease and repose from mortal cares;
> Nor might the strange cacophonies of Earth
> Silence within his being the heaven-born rhapsodies.[12]

Idealism or spiritualism asserts that the ultimate reality is spiritual or immaterial; that it is something like our thought or images, something unextended in space. When you say to your class, "Germany has a population of sixty-five millions," no Germans are put into the space of your classroom. In other words, the thought about sixty-five millions of Germans does not crowd anything in space, it is unextended in space, does not occupy place in space.

The term "idealism" is of Greek origin and is derived from the metaphysical doctrine of Plato (d. 347 B.C.) who taught that the ultimate reality consists of pure forms or Ideas, of which things observable or "sensible" — phenomena of the universe which are accessible to our senses — are merely imperfect reflections or shadows. Hence, it would have been more appropriate to call the Platonic doctrine *idea-ism* rather

[12] *Angel* by Mikhail Lermontov.

than ideal-ism. The consonant *l* serves merely the purpose of euphony.* The usage of the term " idealism " is protected by long philosophic tradition. This does not, however, make the term less unfortunate or less confusing. Among other things, it suggests, on the surface of things, that materialism or materialistic "naturalism" is devoid of all and any ideal, which is certainly not the case. Besides the ideal of working out a perfect materialistic explanation of the universe, a materialistic or "naturalistic" philosopher may well have high ideals of social justice, disinterested service, etc., only in his case such ethical ideals will inevitably be somewhat inconsistent with his basic metaphysical doctrine of materialism.

The idealistic metaphysical doctrine is conjugated, epistemologically, with rationalism or apriorism or intuitivism. If the true reality is spiritual, if it is in the nature of thought or imagery, then our senses, which work only in conjunction with material stimuli addressing themselves to our physiological organs, cannot be the channel through which the true reality can be reached. The senses themselves are, according to the idealistic epistemology, merely confused ideas, and our problem is not to fit our perceptions to the world, but the world to our perceptions, because there exists nothing except what exists in the Absolute Mind and in our finite minds which partake, to a degree, of the Absolute Mind. What mind projects into the world is reality and the only reality there is. The external world is nothing but a landscape painted by our minds or spirits.

According to the idealist, our reason possesses the inborn capacity of classifying or molding the indications of our senses, which are in themselves confusing. Why can a child, at the very beginning of his conscious life and with very few sensory experiences to guide him, understand the conceptions of *more*

---

* This euphonic operation was performed upon the Platonic term " Idea " (ἰδέα) by the Romans who created the adjective *idealis,* " existing in Idea, or pattern "; "pertaining to Platonic Ideas."

and *less,* and distinguish between *better* and *farther?* Because — answers the idealist — the child's mind possesses the inborn power of classifying his sensory impressions as relative, for instance, to either quantity or quality. Without the pre-existing (or existing *a priori,* prior to receiving any sensory impressions) power of molding or classifying the sense impressions the child could not have consciousness or awareness of anything because he would not know of what he is aware; he could have had but a confusing and confused flow of sensations. The true method of obtaining knowledge of the true reality is the speculation of our reason, that is, mental or spiritual vision. The supreme form of speculation is intuition. In the words of Henri Bergson:

By intuition is meant the kind of *intellectual sympathy* by which one places oneself within an object in order to coincide with what is unique in it and consequently inexpressible. Analysis, on the contrary, is the operation which reduces the object to elements already known, that is, to elements common both to it and to other objects. . . . Consider a character whose adventures are related in a novel. The author may multiply the traits of his hero, may make him speak and act as he pleases, but all this can never be equivalent to the simple and indivisible feeling which I should experience if I were able for an instant to identify myself with the person of the hero himself. Out of that indivisible feeling, as from a spring, all the words, gestures, and actions of the man would flow naturally . . . All the things I am told about the man provide me with so many points of view from which I can observe him. All the traits which describe him, and which can make him known to me only by so many comparisons with persons or things I know already, are signs by which he is expressed more or less symbolically. Symbols and points of view, therefore, place me outside him; they give me only what he has in common with others, and not what belongs to him alone. But that which is properly himself, that which constitutes his essence, cannot be perceived from without, being internal by definition, nor be expressed by symbols, being incommensurable with everything else. Description, history, and analysis leave me here in the relative. Coincidence with the person himself would alone give me the absolute.[13]

Ethically, idealism is "indeterminism," which according to William James, "is the only way to *break* the world into good parts and into bad, and to stand by the former as against the latter." [14] Idealism asserts that freedom of the will exists. In his choices and decisions man can defy adverse external mechanical factors, and naturally wishes to do so. What is still more important, man is capable of inner freedom. A tyrannous political power or a slave driver can by torture or by menace of it force the subject or the slave to do almost anything against his will, and appear cheerful and pleased in doing it; but the oppressed and mistreated ones cannot be forced to enjoy in their heart of hearts their abject condition or to believe the oppressor a good man.

SKEPTICISM

If materialism melts the spiritual in the physical, idealism melts the physical in the spiritual by negating to the material the status of a true reality. Its anti-empirical speculative method of inquiry into the "thing-in-itself" readily puts idealism into many difficulties. Contrary to the assertions of the extreme idealists relative to the unreality of matter, matter has shown itself as real enough by subjecting man to material needs from which he cannot normally escape and which he must satisfy. Metaphysical speculation of the rationalists and intuitivists has remained of limited value in helping man toward a solution of the practical problems of his material well-being, individual and social; while natural or positive science dealing with tangible things has, through its discoveries and mechani-

[13] *Introduction to Metaphysics,* G. P. Putnam's Sons, 1912, pp. 3, 4, 5, 7.
[14] *Letters of William James, cit.,* Vol. I, p. 245.

cal inventions based upon those scientific discoveries, profoundly and in many respects apparently favorably changed the material condition of man's earthly life. Hence, many thinkers have refused to accept the idealistic doctrine of the ultimate reality.

Moreover, some thinkers have been unable to accept the doctrine of the ultimate certainty of either of the two monistic schools of thought, that is to say, either of materialism or of idealism. Not seeing any other issue from such a difficulty, in fact, from the impasse, some thinkers have professed skepticism. Skepticism, in philosophy, is the negation of metaphysical or ontological knowledge. It is the doctrine according to which the human mind is incapable of attaining to any degree of certainty relative to the ultimate reality.

According to the skeptic, our minds are so constituted that we can never know what are things-in-themselves. All that we can perceive are phenomena, that is, things as they appear to be, and their apparent relations. It is easy to see how little dependable are our means of knowledge, reasons the skeptic. What are they? They are our senses and ideas. But is it not right that all things appear yellow to a person suffering from the jaundice? They are blue to us, says Shakespeare, " when gripping grief the heart doth wound, and doleful dumps the mind oppress." [15] Those things which seemed tasty and desirable to a man in his youth or while he was in good health may seem distasteful to him when he is sick or after he has attained an advanced age. One and the same object appears to us smaller or larger depending upon the distance and the position from which we perceive it. Bodies are lighter in water than in the air. It is plain, the skeptic concludes, from such and similar facts (relative to information given to us by our senses) that no sensation is pure, epistemologically. No sensation gives

[15] *Romeo and Juliet,* Act IV, Scene 5.

us an exact and universally valid, in other words, an absolute knowledge of the thing about which it is a sensation. Our ideas are not any more dependable than are our sensations as a source of knowledge about things-in-themselves. Is it not true that Jupiter, whom his believers thought the true god, was thought by the worshipers of Jehovah a mere idol? Similarly, has not the traditional idea of the rotation of the sun around the earth been proved wrong?

It may be mentioned that skepticism as an epistemological theory must not be confused with skepticism as a method in logic. Doubt may be a fruitful method for purging our experience of its contradictory, untrue notions, and therefore a help toward attaining truth. It is useful also to remember that the milder form of epistemological skepticism is called agnosticism — the doctrine which holds that although absolute knowledge about anything is impossible, we can have workable hypotheses.

DUALISM AND PLURALISM

Skepticism has never held dominion in the history of the philosophic debate for any great length of time. It is barren, without issue, and contrary to the instinctive desire of humanity for an ultimate certainty as well as to man's instinctive belief in the possibility of attaining such certainty. Therefore, the plaintive, pessimistic airs of skepticism, born usually from the apparently irreconcilable conflict between materialistic monism and idealistic monism, have usually given way to the voice of moderation, conciliation, and encouragement speaking through some dualistic or pluralistic metaphysical doctrine.

Dualism is characterized by the assertion that the ultimate reality is twofold, that it is both spiritual and material. Consequently, dualism is, metaphysically, both idealistic and materialistic. Epistemologically, it is rationalistic and empirical.

Ethically, it is characterized by the belief in freedom of the will and in its limitations resulting from mechanical laws of nature.

Pluralism — or, as it might be more plainly called, multiplism [16] — consists in the belief that the true reality is more than two in number, that it is multiple. Pluralism opposes not only the view that beings which compose the universe must be considered as mere modifications of one absolute reality, as the monistic doctrines, materialism and idealism, assert; pluralism also refuses to accept the dualistic view which reduces the variety of things found in the universe to just two fundamental principles, spirit and matter. The pluralist sees in the universe more than one or two fundamental realities. To him, among such realities are found not only the dualistic pairs like physical and mental, good and evil, constant and variable, but also multiple combinations such as identity, similarity, difference; events, quantities, relations. Pluralism, however, as the philosopher, R. H. Lotze,[17] has rightly observed, inevitably ends in a monism, which is more satisfactory to the human craving for simplicity and clarity, however deceptive.

But such seems to be also the fate of dualism. Dualism has found support among the greatest giants of philosophic thought. Aristotle (d. 322 B.C.), Descartes (d. 1650), and Kant (d. 1804) were dualistic philosophers. Yet the domination of dualism each time it appeared in the history of philosophy was sooner or later displaced by a monistic doctrine of the ultimate reality. One of the reasons why it should be so is that the dualistic doctrines (which, it will be recalled, seek to reconcile the monistic doctrines of materialism and idealism) never divide the true reality fifty-fifty, so to speak, between matter and

[16] The Latin word " *pluralis* " means " relating to more than one." Dualism therefore is also, strictly speaking, a version of pluralism. In fact, Eisler (*Wörterbuch der Philosophischen Begriffe*, S. 464.) uses the expression " dualistic pluralism (*der dualistische Pluralismus*)." It would be useful to replace the term " pluralism " with " multiplism."

[17] Bréhier, Emile, *Histoire de la Philosophie*, Paris, Félix Alcan, 1932, t. 2⁴, p. 995.

spirit, but usually lean in the direction of idealism. As a result, among disciples of dualistic philosophers there soon develop purely monistic idealistic tendencies. Next, idealistic extremism calls forth, by opposition, materialistic monistic extremism, and the cycle of the fundamental philosophic themes begins again, in the effort to find a rationally proved ultimate reality. The effort in all probability is doomed to remain futile so far as the final result is concerned, but the search is enriching and useful in many regards, or at least inevitable. Man's proud intellect is unwilling to accept truths unanalyzed by itself. Nothing except religious intuitive faith can perhaps ever bring us to behold the ultimate reality. But man's irrepressible tendency to view life and its problems rationally and yet in the light of the eternal or ultimate reality, *sub specie aeternitatis,* seems to account for more of his nobler actions than his purely practical-utilitarian tendencies can account for. Even an embittered, disillusioned person who is no longer capable of finding in the normal occupations and preoccupations of life sufficient motivation for further effort and for disinterested service to others can still readily find such motivation in a philosophic point of view similar to that of the writer who said:

Man is not interesting, important, worthy of being revered for himself; what inclines mankind to progress . . . is precisely that mankind does not consider itself as an end — nor its comfort, nor its satisfactions, nor its rest — but indeed as a means by which, and through which, something which is higher can be performed and brought about.[18]

Though no philosopher has had the last word, and none is likely to have, the search for a rationally demonstrable ultimate certainty is not likely to cease, neither is the influence of

[18] *Académie Française, Recueil des Discours, 1900–1909, Discours de M. Francis Charmes dans la séance publique du 7 janvier 1909 en venant prendre séance à la place de M. Marcelin Berthelot.*

great philosophers upon men and women busy in the various other pursuits of life, especially in education, likely to become a matter of the past. This is particularly true of social and educational reformers and would-be reformers.

THE PHILOSOPHIC PERSPECTIVE AND PHILOSOPHIES OF EDUCATION

May we here recapitulate the foregoing thesis? Reformers' theories and proposals of reform invariably have roots, whether visible or not, in a philosophy of life and life's values traceable to one of the briefly summed-up fundamental themes — or theses — of philosophy, learned or independently arrived at. The variety and rotation of the themes known to the history of philosophy account in a great degree for the variety and rotation of the philosophies of education. These philosophies have their foundation in some old philosophic theme, though the latter may be concealed under a layer of new or quasi-new technical educational terms. As a result, it seems advisable that a student of education wishing to visualize for himself the logical consequences, in practice, of a philosophy of education, should probe into the philosophic sub-soil from which such philosophy of education springs and which is among the principal sources of each thorough-going theory of education.

One of the indispensable qualifications for intelligent planning and reforming in any sphere of human activity is the historic perspective. It alone can protect us from giving exaggerated weight to a reformatory proposal whose principal claim for trial is, as frequently happens, the assertion that it is a new scheme never before proposed and never tried. Educators are now constantly confronted with the various schemes of " new education." The latter are connected with the various supposedly new, but actually more often than not, very old philosophies of life. It appears that, for the purpose of real independence of judgment in the elaboration of their own working philosophy of education, students of education would be well advised to view those various, frequently conflicting, educational philosophies and the philosophic doctrines in which they have their roots (open or covert) in the light of the perspective of the history of philosophy — to be exact, in the light of the rotation of the fundamental philosophic themes.

SUGGESTIONS FOR READING

Cunningham, G. W., *The Idealistic Argument in Recent British and American Philosophy* (Century)
Davis, H. T., *Philosophy and Modern Science* (Principia Press)
Eckardt, Hans, *Russia* (Knopf)
Haldane, J., *Science and Philosophy* (Doubleday Doran)
Havre, Franz de, *Philosophy and Education* (Benziger)
Jeans, Sir James, *The Mysterious Universe* (Macmillan)
Krutch, J. W., *The Modern Temper* (Harcourt)
Lange, F. A., *History of Materialism* (Truebner)
Maritain, J., and others, *Essays on Order* (Macmillan)
Ward, J., *Naturalism and Agnosticism* (Macmillan)
Weber, A., and Perry, R., *History of Philosophy* (Scribner's)

CHAPTER
III

CONTEMPORARY EDUCATIONAL PHILOSOPHIES
VIEWED IN THE PERSPECTIVE OF THE
HISTORY OF PHILOSOPHY

CONTEMPORARY EDUCATIONAL PHILOSOPHIES VIEWED IN THE PERSPECTIVE OF THE HISTORY OF PHILOSOPHY [1]

THE TRANSITION FROM SCHOLASTICISM TO MODERN PHILOSOPHY

In our attempt to trace historically the philosophic sources or antecedents of contemporary philosophies of education, we shall confine ourselves to a very brief review of modern philosophic doctrines. It is important to remember that the modern period in the history of philosophy is divided from the medieval or scholastic period by the establishment, in modern times, of the independence of metaphysics, separating it from theology to which philosophy was in the Middle Ages merely an *ancilla,* a maid-servant. The task of philosophy in the Middle Ages was to deduce, from the sacred texts and the theology which interpreted them, all the knowledge that man possessed, as a revealed knowledge. The spirit of scholastic philosophy, that is of the philosophy taught in the Middle Ages by the schoolmen controlled by the church, is best expressed in the celebrated statement of St. Anselm of Canterbury (d. 1109): " I do not seek to understand in order that I may believe; but I believe that I may understand. For this, too, I believe, that unless I first believe, I shall not understand." [2]

---

[1] Cf. Ueberwegs, Friedrich, *Grundriss der Geschichte der Philosophie,* Elfte Auflage, E. S. Mittler & Sohn, Berlin, 1928, Bd. II–V.

Bréhier, Emile, *Histoire de la Philosophie,* Félix Alcan, Paris, 1928–1932, t. 1^3, 2^1, 2^2, 2^3, 2^4.

[2] *Neque enim quaero intellegere ut credam, sed credo ut intelligam. Nam et hoc credo, quia, nisi credidero, non intelligam. Proslogium I.*

The official medieval philosophy of the schoolmen was a monistic idealism in the service of theology. It was a rationalization, ingenious but very guarded and restrained, of theological dogmas. The result of such subservient employment of reason was skepticism. Francis Bacon has well described the situation by pointing out that in speculation (*i.e.,* rational and not empirical or experimental demonstration of a truth), if one begins by certainty, he will end in doubt; but if one begins by doubt, and if one can bear it patiently for a time, one will arrive at certitude.[3] Alfred Weber also analyzed well the spirit of the transition period in philosophy from scholasticism to modern times when he said: " Christian thought hemmed in by the law of the church resembled a river confined between two steep banks; the narrower the bed, the deeper the stream. Being unable to escape from the dogma encompassing it, it endeavored to penetrate it, and eventually undermined it." [4]

The scientific discoveries made by some gifted, curious, and industrious minds during the period of the Renaissance or revival of Greco-Roman learning (the thirteenth through the sixteenth centuries) following the Crusades, created an uncontrollable general intellectual movement toward investigation, criticism, and reform. A notable issue of this spirit of rational investigation and criticism in philosophy was the skepticism (see p. 58) of the French philosopher, Montaigne (d. 1592). Objective truth, or true reality, is inaccessible to the human mind, thought Montaigne. The human mind, he believed, is doomed to remain the prisoner of its own subjectivity, errors, illusions. The only thing that is left to man in the way of improving his knowledge is to try to bring as much order as possible into his thinking. However imperfect our knowledge may be even then with regard to the true reality, it will be less im-

---

[3] *Novum Organum,* I.
[4] Weber, Alfred, *History of Philosophy,* revised edition, Scribner's, 1925, p. 156.

perfect because it will at least be consistent, free from self-contradictions.

The English philosopher, Francis Bacon (d. 1626), supplied a method insuring not only logical consistency but also practical fertility of knowledge. This is the experimental method. The mind is not equal to the subtlety of the true or ultimate reality of nature. Then it is necessary to inquire of nature itself in order to know anything at all about it. Thus Bacon revived the tradition of the experimental knowledge of nature which had been fructified in the work of Aristotle and which never totally disappeared from the field of philosophy, even during the Middle Ages, as is evidenced by the doctrine of Roger Bacon, the *Doctor Mirabilis* of Oxford (d. 1294), though in the Middle Ages the experimental method led a retired and precarious existence.

Metaphysically (see p. 42), Francis Bacon was, in a sense, a forerunner of the positivists of the nineteenth century of the school of Auguste Comte (d. 1857) and of the agnostic pragmatists of the school of John Dewey in our own time (see p. 112). He subordinated philosophy to positive science, that is, to science dealing with the properties of tangible things and their invariable relations. Philosophy is assigned by him and his followers the role of bookkeeper for the ensemble of the positive sciences. Its task is to balance the accounts of those sciences. Francis Bacon excluded from philosophy inquiry into first causes and final ends because he held them unknowable, and he excluded as futile all metaphysics separate from positive science.

THE DUALISM OF DESCARTES

The attitude of doubt relative to the medieval doctrine of the ultimate reality, which attitude had resulted in the case of Montaigne in skepticism and in that of Bacon in agnosticism, led René Descartes to a very impressive dualistic system of philosophy (see p. 59). It is usually known as Cartesianism because of the Latinized name of Descartes — Cartesius. Cartesianism is generally regarded as the true beginning of modern philosophy.

Impressed with the fact that the knowledge which we obtain through our senses and from tradition is often deceptive and plainly false, Descartes decided that the only way to purge our knowledge of false notions was to subject everything to doubt and inquiry. But then if we should be justified in doubting the existence of everything else before we can prove such existence, we cannot doubt the existence of our doubt, consequently our own existence as thinking beings. Hence the celebrated formula of Descartes, *Cogito ergo sum* — if I doubt, then it follows that I think and that I exist.

Having thus established beyond all doubt his own existence as a thinking being, Descartes ingeniously deduced from it the existence of God. If I doubt, then it follows that I am lacking something, I desire something, I am imperfect, I do not have perfect knowledge. But how could I have all these sensations of inferiority if I did not have any idea of a perfect being in comparison with which I cannot but feel myself imperfect. This idea, however vague, of something infinite, perfect, and perfectly true, I could not have produced myself. There cannot be less reality in the cause than there is in the effect; consequently, only a perfect being can be the cause of my idea of a perfect being — the effect. But neither can there be more perfection in the effect of a cause than there is in the cause itself. Then it follows that the cause of my idea of a perfect being must have at least as much objective, *i.e.,* real perfection, as there is in my idea of this perfect being. Consequently, I, as a limited and imperfect being, could not have been the author of the idea of a perfect being. Nobody but the perfect being itself could be its author. There must exist a being possessing the perfections of which I have an idea though I do not possess them myself.

It follows next that I, as the species, cannot conceive myself the author of my own being; because if I had the power to create myself then I should have had also the power to give myself all perfection. It is demonstrated, then, that I am an imperfect, limited being, and consequently not the author of my own being. Who is? No one else can be but the perfect being which alone is *causa sui, i.e.,* its own cause.

Two indubitable truths, then, are demonstrated: my own existence as a thinking being, and the existence of God's perfect Being, concludes Descartes. From the latter truth it results, according to him, that my clear and distinct ideas correspond to reality; that things exist of which I have clear and distinct ideas. The existence of God as the perfect, infinite, and infinitely good Being and my Creator is the guarantee that I am not deceived by my clear and distinct ideas. If we have erroneous ideas the reason is not the failure of our reason but of our will power. Our reason is, to be sure, not unlimited in its power. The fact is that it may have, side by side with clear and distinctly truthful ideas, also obscure and confused ideas. But our liberty is unlimited in accepting or rejecting the ideas arising in our understanding. Hence, it follows that my soul exists, because I can have a clear idea of myself as a thinking being without making any feature or property of my body enter into this idea.

I am thus assured that my soul exists and is distinct from my body, which, as my clear and distinct idea tells me, exists also. The substantial characteristic of my body is that it is extended in space; in other words, it occupies a place in space. But I still ignore, or rather have not proved to myself, that other bodies also exist. Indeed, nothing but a very strong natural inclination to believe in the real existence of bodies which seem to me to exist is the proof of their existence. But then the perfect Being, in Its goodness, could not let our natural inclination deceive us, declares Descartes.

This is the first important rift in the Cartesian reasoning. Descartes has found himself forced to attribute to "the natural inclination" the validity which he would not previously grant to anything but indubitably clear and distinct ideas. The next important difficulty into which his dualism involved Descartes was the explanation of the relationship between body and soul. Body and soul are, in the logic of dualism, two absolutely distinct and unrelated realities. Soul is everything that body is not, and vice versa. Body is absolutely soulless and soul is absolutely bodyless, *i.e.*, immaterial or incorporeal. As a result, there can be no relationship of cause and effect between soul and body. To be sure, sensations appear to consist in an action of the body upon the soul, and our voluntary motions seem to be an action of the soul upon the body. But these are deceptive impressions, taught Descartes. The relationship between the body and the soul is never one of cause and effect, but merely one of occasion. All its sensations, or, better, sensible ideas, the soul receives, according to Cartesianism, from its own nature on the occasion of certain corresponding sensory "excitations" occurring in the body. The body, on the other hand, is in itself a mere automaton. Its movements are mechanically produced on the occasion of some volitional ideas of the soul.

IDEALISTIC MONISM IN THE SEVENTEENTH AND EIGHTEENTH CENTURIES

In philosophy as elsewhere it is impossible to serve equally well two masters. Cartesian dualism was decidedly pro-idealistic or pro-spiritualistic. Descartes' certainty relative to the existence of matter is based on his certainty that spirit exists. As a result, there soon developed among his successors an irresistible tendency toward idealistic monism (see p. 54). Spinoza (d. 1677), in particular, taught that body and soul, matter and spirit, though they are distinct elements, are inseparable because they are the elements of one and the same universe, two manifestations or attributes of one and the same substance, God. Idealistic monism of the seventeenth and eighteenth centuries reached its extreme point in the doctrines of Leibniz (d. 1716) and Berkeley (d. 1753).

Leibniz believed that no substance can be real unless it contains in itself, though in its own manner, the infinity of the universe and reflects in itself the traces of all the past of the universe and the germs of all its future. His " infinitism " led Leibniz to conceive the universe as consisting of monads, which are simple, indivisible, and infinite centers of activity, independent of one another, maintaining no communication with one another, but all viewing eternally the same universe. They all develop eternally while reflecting eternally the universe which is the same to all monads, thanks to the harmonious process planned or pre-established by God, the Monad of Monads. The only true reality is, then, one that a monad perceives by looking into itself.

According to Berkeley, the only true existences are the minds which perceive ideas and the ideas perceived by them. Nature does not exist independently from the mind which perceives it. Neither is nature, as some pagan philosophers imagined, something distinct from God. It is merely the language through which God speaks to us.

MATERIALISTIC MONISM IN THE SEVENTEENTH AND EIGHTEENTH CENTURIES

As at each of its previous recurrences, idealistic monism was in the seventeenth and eighteenth centuries opposed by materialistic monism (see p. 49). Already Hobbes (d. 1679), a contemporary of Descartes, had asserted that sensation is the source of all knowledge, and that science is entirely derived from this source. What is sensation? It is, Hobbes explained, the modification produced in our bodies by a movement which is itself produced in surrounding matter by some other body. This movement is communicated to the brain and from it to the heart. Thought as something distinct from sensation and independent of it does not exist. What is called mind, or spirit, or thought, is simply the brain or nervous system in action. Every act of man is determined by mechanical laws. Good is something that is agreeable, and bad is identical with the disagreeable. The supreme judge in morals and the supreme guide in life in general is interest, that is to say, the desire to have an agreeable experience and to avoid the unpleasant.

Hobbes did not formulate any metaphysical doctrine, though his theory of knowledge or epistemology as well as his ethics showed a plain materialistic trend. The epistemology of Hobbes received further development in the doctrine of Locke (d. 1704) whose metaphysics, however, was idealistic or spiritualistic, somewhat inconsistently. Locke believed in the existence of God and attributed to Him the origin of our power of understanding, and therefore believed Him also the creator of matter: since God is the author of man's power of understanding, He is also the author of matter, which is something much simpler than our power of understanding and, consequently, the easier to create. But as to the nature of our understanding, there are no innate or *a priori* ideas or truths in it. It contains nothing that has not come through sensations, that is, through indications of our senses and through reflection about them. The inductive method, or the method of experience, is the only way to attain truth. It is not by closing one's eyes and stopping one's ears in order to look into one's own speculative reason, as the idealists-rationalists do, that true knowledge can be gained, but by the inductive method, the method of proceeding from the simple to the complex, from the individual to the general.

Though Locke believed thought to be a continuation of sensation and dependent upon it, he distinguished between thought and sensation. This dualism disappears in the doctrine of La Mettrie (d. 1751), author of *Man-Machine,* according to whom man's understanding, sensibility, volition, or will power are all animal functions developed to a high degree; they are not produced by soul or spirit any more than are similar functions of animals.

But where, according to materialism, does man, this highly developed animal, come from? How has he come to be? The answer was furnished by the evolutionistic or transformistic doctrine formulated by Diderot (d. 1784) many decades before Lamarck's and Darwin's theory of evolution. To borrow from the excellent summary of Diderot's doctrine by Alfred Weber:

This developed animal did not fall from the clouds ready-made, nor did it arise from the bowels of the earth. It is not the work of a supernatural creator, the realization of an idea: it owes its origin to a natural evolution which gradually evolves more and more perfect forms from lower forms of the elementary organisms. The human species is no more a separate creation than the other animal and vegetable species; its present form has been evolved from lower animal forms, slowly and by progressive stages. . . . According to Diderot, the entire universe is an endless fermentation, a ceaseless interchange of substances, a perpetual circulation of life. . . . Animals have not always been what they are now. In the animal and vegetable kingdoms, individuals arise, grow, decline, and die. Can we not say the same for entire species? Now there is an affinity, and perhaps identity, between kingdoms, just as between species. Thus, who can ever exactly determine the boundaries between plants and animals? . . . We speak of three kingdoms, but why should not one emanate from the other, and why should not the animal and vegetable kingdoms emanate from universal heterogeneous matter? The evolution is wholly mechanical.[5]

[5] Weber, Alfred, *History of Philosophy,* revised edition, Charles Scribner's Sons. p. 334 f.

There is nothing mysterious about man's mental life, asserted Cabanis (d. 1808). It is the product of man's brain and the nervous system which produce thought in exactly the same manner as liver secretes bile. When food is introduced into the stomach, the digestive function begins. When sense impressions reach the brain through the medium of the nervous system, the brain " digests " them, and secretes images and ideas. In his intellectual and moral experiences, just as in his physical life, man is subject to natural laws.

The ethical implications of this revived materialistic monism were frankly and fearlessly drawn by Helvetius and Baron d'Holbach. In substance there was nothing really new in the materialistic ethics of the eighteenth-century materialists in comparison with the doctrine of Leucippus, Democritus, Epicurus, and Lucretius, any more than the materialistic ontology or metaphysics of the seventeenth and eighteenth centuries was new in comparison with the ancient materialistic ontology of the philosophers just mentioned. Helvetius declared self-interest or egoism the true and only motive of our acts. Baron d'Holbach, who thought that there was no soul and that matter alone existed eternally, negated also freedom of the will as an absurdity: the universe is governed by mechanical laws, in other words, by the properties of matter (see p. 49).

THE SKEPTICISM OF HUME AND THE DUALISM OF KANT

Hume (d. 1776) accepted the materialistic-empirical doctrine, according to which sensations are the only source of knowledge, and so-called ideas are merely weak, half-extinguished sensations. Next, logically enough, he raised the question: What is the proof that things about which we have sensations really exist, and that their reality is such as our sensations picture? Logically enough, he answered this question in the negative and said that such proof cannot be obtained. If sensation is the only source of knowledge, then knowledge is necessarily subjective, and the knowledge of true reality is unattainable. One group of our sensations can control and verify another group; for instance, our visual sensations can verify our auditory or our olfactory sensations. But our senses as a whole, as a class, cannot verify themselves. To do that, they would have to step out of themselves, so to say, and look at themselves from the outside. This is, however, impossible by definition, because our senses would still continue to be *our* senses, and not an external, independent, and impartial observer whose judgment might be objective.

The skepticism of Hume challenged the critical thought of Kant (d. 1804), who, not unlike Descartes, decided to draw up an inventory of the power and content of his mind, in order to attain certainty. Not unlike Descartes, though by a different method, he found in the structure and functioning of the human mind sufficient bases for science and morals. Though he came to the conclusion that the ultimate reality, the *thing-in-itself,* escapes our reason, the latter possesses in its very constitution all the resources necessary for the realization of the good life.

Kant interpreted the Socratic motto, "Know thyself," as meaning that before launching itself upon the search for the ultimate certainty our reason should critically investigate its own powers. As a result of such an investigation, Kant agreed with the empiricists or sensationalists (see p. 50) that all our knowledge begins with our sense impressions. On the other hand, though he admitted that no purely *a priori* (see p. 50) knowledge exists, he was convinced that there is no purely *a posteriori* (see p. 50) knowledge either. According to Kant, all our ideas — their subject matter being necessarily furnished by sensations — contain an element which does not come from sensations, an *a priori* element. This element consists in the intuitions of pure reason, that is, of reason as it is constituted prior to our receiving any sensations. Kant calls two of these intuitions of pure reason, namely, space and time, "pure forms of sensuous intuition"; he calls the other twelve intuitions "categories" of pure reason, or the "pure conceptions of the understanding," or the "series of universal ideas": [6] unity, plurality, totality (the categories of quantity); reality, negation, limitation (the categories of quality); inherence-subsistence, causality-dependence, community (the categories of relation); possibility-impossibility, existence-non-existence, necessity-contingence (the categories of modality). Consider, for instance, the "two pure forms of sensuous intuition," space and time. They are molds into which our sensations are classified as soon as they enter our minds, and without which no knowledge would be possible. Our minds would be submerged with the chaos of sensations unattached to a place in space or to a moment in time. Nothing in nature, for instance, tells us about time; no voice reaches the child when he begins to receive his first sensations saying, " I am something that was here *yesterday, before,* and shall be here *tomorrow, afterwards.*" The conception of time is a gift that the child's reason brings with it into the world of objects and sensations about those objects. Similarly, the child's mind possesses the intuition or pure form or category of unity or universality. It is thanks to this category or intuition of pure reason that the child can understand such expressions as " All men are mortal," though he has not seen *all men* nor found out through the medium of sensation that they are all mortal. In general, the child could not come otherwise, *i.e.,* without the help of the category of universality, to have a language — language being made of symbols which universally stand each for the class of things of which the word is a symbol. That is why the child rapidly comes to designate with the oral

[6] *Critique of Pure Reason,* Introduction: Of the Difference Between Pure and Empirical Knowledge, Colonial Press, 1900, p. 22 f.

or written symbol *tree* any kind of tree — actual or pictorial or imaginary — before he has made personal acquaintance with all the trees existing in the universe, which kind of investigation is obviously out of the question.

In the words of Kant:

That all our knowledge begins with experience there can be no doubt. . . .

But, though all our knowledge begins with experience, it by no means follows that all arises out of experience. For, on the contrary, it is quite possible that our empirical knowledge is a compound of that which we receive through impressions, and that which the faculty of cognition supplies from itself (sensuous impressions giving merely the *occasion*), an addition which we cannot distinguish from the original element given by sense, till long practice has made us attentive to, and skilful in separating it. It is, therefore, a question which requires close investigation, and is not to be answered at first sight — whether there exists a knowledge altogether independent of experience, and even of all sensuous impressions? Knowledge of this kind is called *a priori,* in contradistinction to empirical knowledge, which has its sources *a posteriori,* that is, in experience.

. . . That which in the phenomenon corresponds to the sensation I term its *matter;* but that which effects that the content of the phenomenon can be arranged under certain relations I call its *form.* But that in which our sensations are merely arranged, and by which they are susceptible of assuming a certain form, cannot be itself sensation. It is, then, the matter of all phenomena that is given to us *a posteriori;* the form must lie ready *a priori* for them in the mind, and consequently can be regarded separately from all sensation.

I call all representations *pure,* in the transcendental meaning of the word, wherein nothing is met with that belongs to sensation. . . .[7]

Kant's epistemology or the theory of the validity of knowledge is, then, dualistic. It is both empirical and speculative or rationalistic. His metaphysics and his ethics are likewise dualis-

---

[7] *Op. cit.,* pp. 1, 21.

tic. Kant admitted the real existence of both matter and pure reason. He did not believe in the possibility of a rationally demonstrable knowledge of the ultimate reality. He deduced, however, the existence of God from what he called the categorical imperative, *i.e.,* the irresistible sentiment of moral duty, which commands us to " act as if the maxim of your will were to become by your adopting it a universal law of nature." From the categorical imperative follow two consequences, Kant thought. First, there must exist God, the supreme Judge of good and evil. Second, freedom of the will exists also. " I must " necessitates " I can." My inner voice tells me that I must do something. This would be absolutely absurd if I did not have free will, that is, freedom of choice of actions, side by side with my inevitable obedience to certain inescapable laws of nature. As to metaphysics or ontology, any and every metaphysical or ontological assertion, Kant thought, is at one and the same time undemonstrable and irrefutable through a direct rational analysis.

IDEALISTIC AND MATERIALISTIC MONISM IN THE NINETEENTH AND TWENTIETH CENTURIES

The Kantian dualistic doctrine, though supported by the great might of the philosopher's intellectual power and overwhelmingly vast learning, went the way of the dualistic doctrines of the past. Out of it grew the idealistic monism of the nineteenth century whose leading representatives were Fichte (d. 1814), Schelling (d. 1854), Hegel (d. 1831), Herbart (d. 1841), and Schopenhauer (d. 1860). Kant's disciples, some of whom he lived to denounce as false, seized upon his theory of pure reason. They drew from it the conclusion that no true reality exists outside the mind. It is pure reason that gives to things a place in space and in time, argued the idealists. It is pure reason again that transforms the chaos of sensations into a cosmos of thoughts by clothing them with time, space, quantity, quality, and the other intuitions or categories of pure reason. Where then does the thing-in-itself exist? It cannot exist in an independent space and time, because the only space and time there are exist in the mind as the intuitions of space and time. Neither can a thing-in-itself have any properties except those with which the mind, again, guided by its intuitions, endows it. Yes, concluded the monistic idealists, the so-called thing-in-itself is, like time and space, identical with the subject that conceives it and there is no true reality except the Spirit realizing Itself in the universe; and of this Spirit our minds partake.

The extremes of idealistic monism in the nineteenth century were soon to be displaced by the extremes of evolutionistic materialistic monism. Promoted by Lamarck (d. 1829), Ludwig Feuerbach (d. 1872), Darwin (d. 1882), Karl Marx (d. 1883), Moleschott (d. 1893), Thomas Huxley (d. 1895), Büchner (d. 1899), Herbert Spencer (d. 1903), Haeckel (d. 1919), Peter Kropotkin (d. 1921), Bertrand Russell, and others, evolutionistic materialism or " naturalism " reaches with its powerful influence into our own days. Side by side with it grew an agnostic pragmatism or "instrumentalism," authoritatively represented by Professor John Dewey. It is precisely these two philosophic movements — evolutionistic materialism, or " naturalism," and instrumentalism — that have furnished inspiration for the educational movement variously known as " Progressive Education," " The Activity School," " The New Education," " The Project Method," " The Child-Centered School," and the like.

THE FUNDAMENTAL POSITIONS OF EVOLUTIONISM [8]

The evolutionists of the nineteenth and twentieth centuries revived the ancient atomistic doctrine and the doctrine of evolution or transformation formulated by Diderot (see p. 75).

[8] The discussion of evolutionism presented in this volume has the purpose of analyzing the educational implications of the doctrine. The term " evolutionism " is used in its current sense, that is to say, materialistic evolutionism. This remark seems

They have made, however, a very important addition to the doctrines of their predecessors. Those doctrines have left unexplained the purposiveness or adaptation shown by the structure of living beings, the fact that the various organisms seem to be perfectly adapted to the conditions under which they have to live and to find their subsistence. Thus the animals which are to live on fish can swim and dive; those which have to find subsistence by grazing in high mountains possess tireless muscular legs, etc.

As the result of a prolonged, keen, and ingenious observation and study of plants and animals by Charles Darwin, evolutionism has worked out a principle which it considers a satisfactory explanation of the moving force underlying the evolution or transformation of animals and plants. The principle is twofold: (a) the competition of living beings for means of subsistence, or the struggle for existence; (b) the survival of the fittest and the corresponding elimination of the unfit. As of old, contemporary evolutionism is, ontologically, materialistic monism. It negates the existence of God, and of anything that is not matter, of which all things existing — the evolutionist teaches — are made under mechanical laws, *i.e.,* laws resulting from the very properties of matter.

Evolutionism teaches that it is the mechanical laws of nature — nature designating the sum total of material things — that have very slowly and gradually transformed original homogeneous indeterminate matter into a variety of things, among which the most wondrous, apparently, are living beings. In this

---

to be necessitated by the publication of the excellent volume of Professor William C. Bagley, *Education and Emergent Man,* Thomas Nelson and Sons, 1934. The philosophic conclusions which Bagley reads from the history of emergent man are spiritualistic and heroic (p. 221 ff.) and are distinctly opposed to the materialistic and deterministic conventional philosophy of the evolutionists. Bagley defines evolution as " a progressive series of integrations which reveal a clear-cut continuity of structures and an equally clear-cut discontinuity of qualities, properties, and in a certain sense of the term, functions " (p. 1). To Bagley the history of evolution affords a rational escape from the fetters of a mechanistic materialism and determinism (p. 65 ff.).

process of transformation of the forms of life, nature very slowly and gradually performs a work similar to that of the breeder of pigeons who saw that one of his male pigeons happened to be born to have several more tail feathers than the other pigeons. The breeder found a female which also possessed the same characteristic and coupled the two. The result was that the off-spring of the pair had even a larger number of extra tail feathers than the parents. There is, however, a very important difference, maintains evolutionism, between the work of the breeder of pigeons and that of nature. The difference is that the breeder purposely applies himself or plans to exploit the happy accident of the birth of the original pigeons with more tail feathers than are found in other pigeons. Nature does no planning. Its mechanical laws, such as the law of the survival of the fittest, do the trick.

Thus the palmate foot of the duck has not been planned or created by a creator, the evolutionist holds. The pre-duck, which was not created either, lived, like our own duck, by paddling muddy water. It did not have the web or membrane uniting its toes. How has the web come to be? It possesses two clear characteristics: it is inherited, and it is adapted for the functions it performs. Yet, it is simply the result of a happy accident, or, better still, of a happy monstrosity. Among the pre-ducks individuals appeared that were fitted out with the web, which the others of the species did not possess. It was, then, a monstrosity. This monstrosity, however, soon proved itself a happy accident, a felicitous monstrosity, for the pre-ducks possessing the palmate feet by accident were able to outdistance the pre-ducks not possessing the web in the competition for food and in escaping from enemies. The progeny of the palmate ducks having inherited the happy monstrosity of the web were surviving in the struggle for existence much better than the progeny of the non-palmate pre-ducks. In the course of time, the latter came to be entirely extinct. Thus, according to the evolutionist, the palmate foot of the duck has come from an accidental characteristic under the pressure of the mechanical law of the struggle for existence (or "natural selection," or "the survival of the fittest"), that is to say, the survival of such forms of animal and plant life as are best adjusted to the conditions under which they have to live. Similarly, the pre-cows that by happy accident possessed the happy monstrosity of rudimentary horns not found on other pre-cows and thanks to which they succeeded better than hornless "regular cows" in maintaining themselves in life, in defending themselves and their progeny, gave origin to the horned cow that we know.

Man, with all the wondrous intricacies of his nature, no more than the palmate duck or the horned bull is an issue of the romantic miracle of creation, concludes the evolutionist. Man is of simian origin, that is, descended from the same stock as the anthropoid ape, developed into what is called humanity. This development proceeded under the same prosaic law of natural selection that accounts for the present-day form of the duck and the cow. The substance of man has nothing spiritual about it, affirms the evolutionist. It is material, namely, "electrological"; in other words, a kind of electrochemical energy.[9]

Evolutionism has undoubtedly succeeded in explaining many

[9] Cf.

Darwin, Charles, *On the Origin of Species by Means of Natural Selection*, Appleton, 1887.

Darwin, Francis, *Life and Letters of Charles Darwin*, Appleton, 1887.

Haeckel, E., *Evolution of Man*, Appleton, 1887. *History of Creation: The Development of the Earth and Its Inhabitants by the Action of Natural Causes*, Appleton, 2 vols., 1875. *Riddle of the Universe at the Close of the Nineteenth Century*, Harper's, 1900.

Kellogg, Vernon L., *Evolution*, Appleton, 1924.

McDougall, W., *Modern Materialism and Emergent Evolution*, D. Van Nostrand Co., 1929.

Osborn, H. F., *From the Greeks to Darwin*, Scribner's.

Romanes, G. J., *Darwin and After Darwin*, Open Court, 1892.

Russell, B., *Analysis of Matter*, Harcourt, Brace and Co., 1927. *Free Man's Worship*, Longmans, Green and Co., 1921.

Spencer, Herbert, *Principles of Biology*, Appleton, 1891.

important details of animal and plant life in terms of mechanistic materialism. Yet, it is a theory to which applies the Voltairean summary of the difficulties which a scientific theory encounters when it seeks to be the only true final basis of the ultimate certainty and of a philosophy of life resulting from such certainty. " Theory," said Voltaire, " is like the mouse. It can pass nine holes, but the tenth hole will catch it." [10] Evolutionism is not unlike other scientific theories which seek scientifically, *i.e.,* in terms of the mechanical laws of nature experimentally founded, to give an answer to the problem of the ultimate reality. This problem bears upon something which, by definition, is not demonstrable experimentally. Evolutionism can pass many obstacles which formerly were considered impassable, but it does not seem able to pass at least three fundamental impasses and is therefore disqualified for the role of keeper of the secret of the ultimate reality.

The three impasses in question are created by common sense, intellectual and moral. This judge * is quite competent to take issue with the scientist when the latter presumes to hand out decisions relative to the ultimate reality, that is to say, relative to the first cause and final goal of all existence. By definition, those problems are outside the legitimate sphere of science, which is that of tangible demonstrable actuality and not of the origin of all origins or of the end of all ends.

The three obstacles which seem to be insurmountable in terms of evolutionistic-materialistic (or " naturalistic ") ontology are as follows: First, it seems that entirely too many happy monstrosities or happy accidents are presupposed by the evolutionistic theory of the mechanistic transformation of life.[11] Second,

---

* Cf. the French saying, *Le sens commun est le génie de l'humanité.*

[10] *L'Académie des Sciences. Un Coup d'Oeil sur l'Histoire des Sciences et des Théories Physiques. Discours de M. Emile Picard (du 17 décembre 1929).*

[11] Cf. Bergson, Henri, *Creative Evolution,* Henry Holt, 1928, pp. 56–57, 70:

The Darwinian idea of adaptation by automatic elimination of the unadapted is a simple and clear idea. But, just because it attributes to the outer cause which controls

even though certain biochemical processes in our bodies are the
necessary concomitant and at least partially the cause of our
thoughts and emotions, it does not follow that such chemical
combinations are the only real goal and end of all human life.
How, indeed, can one admit that to produce the very mediocre
amount of warmth, of water, and of carbonic acid which constitute the human body, nature has so patiently worked upon
the construction of the complex and delicate physiological apparatus that is man, with his most intricate, almost miraculous,
power of intelligence? Third, admitting that certain transformations of the various forms of life are the result of mechanical
adjustment of organisms to mechanical laws of nature in the
process of the struggle for survival, it remains undemonstrated,
indeed, scientifically undemonstrable, how and why from the
original matter there grew the principle of life, that is to say,
spontaneous movement of the living cell.

---

evolution a merely negative influence, it has great difficulty in accounting for the
progressive and, so to say, rectilinear development of complex apparatus. . . . How
much greater will this difficulty be in the case of the similar structure of two extremely
complex organs on two entirely different lines of evolution! An accidental variation,
however minute, implies the working of a great number of small physical and chemical
causes. An accumulation of accidental variations, such as would be necessary to produce a complex structure, requires therefore the concurrence of an almost infinite
number of infinitesimal causes. Why should these causes, entirely accidental, recur
the same, and in the same order, at different points of space and time? . . . The
struggle for life and natural selection can be of no use to us in solving this part of
the problem, for we are not concerned here with what has perished, we have to do
only with what has survived. Now, we see that identical structures have been formed
on independent lines of evolution by a gradual accumulation of effects. How can
accidental causes, occurring in an accidental order, be supposed to have repeatedly come
to the same result, the causes being infinitely numerous and the effect infinitely
complicated?

The principle of mechanism is that " the same causes produce the same effects."
This principle, of course, does not always imply that the same effects have the same
causes; but it does involve this consequence in the particular case in which the causes
remain visible in the effect that they produce and are indeed its constitutive elements.
That two walkers starting from different points and wandering at random should
finally meet, is no great wonder. But that, throughout their walk, they should describe
two identical curves exactly superposable on each other, is altogether unlikely. The
improbability will be the greater, the more complicated the routes; and it will become
impossibility, if the zigzags are infinitely complicated. Now, what is this complexity
of zigzags as compared with that of an organ in which thousands of different cells,
each being itself a kind of organism, are arranged in a definite order?

EVOLUTIONISM AND BEHAVIORISM

Evolutionism is a monistic materialistic doctrine, metaphysically or ontologically. Ethically, it is determinism as much as any other monistic materialistic doctrine of the past (see p. 48). Its epistemology, naturally, is empirical or sensationalistic. In other words, it maintains that all so-called psychological or mental phenomena are in truth physiological, and that there is no other source of knowledge than sensations. How has man come to have what in the language of idealistic or spiritualistic (see p. 54) psychology is called insight and foresight, the power of generalization, *i.e.,* of correct prediction of events and the like? Exactly in the same manner, answers evolutionism, as the duck has come to have the palmate foot, that is to say, through happy accident and its utility in the struggle for existence. Those among our most distant ancestors who by happy chance possessed the rudiments of the power of higher, *i.e.,* subtler, more elastic forms of adaptation which are called superior mental ability, have survived and transmitted to their progeny that power by way of the physiological structure or the physiological endowment of the progeny. Man's ideas as well as his muscles are made of one and the same and the only existing substance, matter. The celebrated evolutionistic philosopher and psychologist of the latter part of the nineteenth century and beginning of the twentieth, Herbert Spencer, reviving the doctrine of Thomas Hobbes, declared that ideas are simply " secondary feelings," that is to say, fainter revivals of " primary feelings " or sensations and emotions proper. At the bottom of psychic life there is nothing, according to Spencer, but instinct (that is, the sum total of inborn tendencies to feel and act in certain ways).[12] From this simple unlearned mechanical basis more complex data grow; these, however, are not any more spiritual than is

[12] Cf. Thorndike, E. L., *Animal Intelligence,* Macmillan, 1911, p. 294.

instinct, which consists in mechanical adaptation to environment. "Intelligence" and "consciousness" are nothing mysterious; they are just certain forms of adaptation to environment.

This general outline of evolutionistic psychology, in other words, psychology corresponding to the evolutionistic doctrine of the ultimate reality, was, however, too general and too vague to play the role of systematic evolutionistic psychology. This role fell to the school of psychological thought known as behaviorism.

What is behaviorism? [13] It is the doctrine according to which all so-called psychic processes or states of consciousness (awareness) are purely physiological in their origin and functioning, or behavior. Behaviorism is opposed to the traditional or idealistic or spiritualistic or introspectionist, or " mentalistic " psychology. It declares that there is no such thing as mind or consciousness, or *psyche* (ψυχή), as the Greeks called it, that is, something distinct from the sensory organs, the brain, and the nervous system. The totality of so-called psychic life consists, according to behaviorism, in physiological responses to stimuli, or

[13] Cf.

Holt, Edwin B., " Response and Cognition," *The Journal of Philosophy*, Vol. 12, pp. 365–373, 393–409.

Hunter, W. S., " The Problem of Consciousness," *The Psychological Review*, Vol. 31, pp. 1–31. " The Symbolic Process," *Ibid.*, Vol. 31, pp. 478–497. " The Subject's Report," *Ibid.*, Vol. 32, pp. 153–170. " General Anthroponomy and Its Systematic Problems," *The American Journal of Psychology*, Vol. 36, pp. 286–302.

Lashley, K. S., " The Behavioristic Interpretation of Consciousness," *The Psychological Review*, Vol. 30, pp. 237–272, 329–353.

Tolman, E. C., " Nerve Process and Cognition," *The Psychological Review*, Vol. 25, pp. 423–442. " Instinct and Purpose," *Ibid.*, Vol. 27, pp. 217–233. " A New Formula of Behaviorism," *Ibid.*, Vol. 29, pp. 44–53. " Concerning the Sensation of Quality: A Behavioristic Account," *Ibid.*, pp. 140–145. " A Behavioristic Account of the Emotions," *Ibid.*, Vol. 30, pp. 217–227. " A Behavioristic Theory of Ideas," *Ibid.*, Vol. 33, pp. 352–369. " A Behavioristic Definition of Consciousness," *Ibid.*, Vol. 34, pp. 433–439.

Watson, John B., *Behavior: An Introduction to Comparative Psychology*, H. Holt, 1914. *Psychology from the Standpoint of a Behaviorist*, J. B. Lippincott, 1924. *Psychological Care of Infant and Child*, W. W. Norton and Co., 1928. *The Ways of Behaviorism*, Harper's, 1928.

to sensory excitations, which are transmitted by neural paths, through the medium of the brain, to muscles and glands. " Consciousness," or " awareness of content," and " knowledge " are, according to behaviorism, merely so many misleading names for the simple fact of certain action of the nervous system, muscles, and glands in response to stimuli. There is nothing back of " consciousness " but S-R bonds, a receptor-conductor-effector mechanism. There is no mysterious " psychic " life, talked about by " mentalists," but just the body and its functions caused by the various stimuli, material like the body and its functions, so behaviorism asserts.

The subject matter of behavioristic psychology is, then, the old doctrine of Democritus and Lucretius, " The nature of the mind and soul is bodily." In fact, behavioristic " psychology " is a misnomer, and the behavioristic doctrine should rather be called, as Professor E. B. Titchener rightly suggested, biological psychology or psychobiology.[14]

If the doctrine of behaviorism is a very old one, the method of investigation it employs presents many important novel features. In the search for evidence relative to their claim that all so-called psychic processes are merely physiological processes traceable to the various functions of the nervous system, muscles, and glands, and are consequently mathematically measurable (the S-R bond doctrine), the behaviorists had, of course, to employ the experimental or laboratory method as over and against the traditional method of introspection based upon a description of mental processes by one who experiences them and who, so to say, looks into his inner self and tells what he sees or has seen there. Moreover, behaviorism has applied the experimental method with ingenuity and skill equaled only by its enthusiasm.

[14] Titchener, E. B., " Psychology as the Behaviorist Views It," *Proceedings of the American Philosophical Society*, Vol. LIII, p. 14 ff.

The foundation of the behavioristic method of investigation of states of consciousness, or psychic processes, has been furnished by the research of two scholars. These two men began their investigations, one in psychology, the other in physiology, at approximately the same time, in the nineties, and for a long time worked toward the same goal without knowledge of each other's findings. These scholars are the American psychologist, Professor E. L. Thorndike, who published in 1898 the work entitled *Animal Intelligence: An Associative Process in Animals,* and the Russian physiologist, Professor Ivan Pavlov, author of the theory of conditioned reflexes, which was presented in various publications in Russian and a summary of which is given in English in the volumes entitled *Conditioned Reflexes* and *Lectures on Conditioned Reflexes.* Later on Professor Thorndike devoted the major share of his effort and attention to the pedagogical implications of psychology, in other words, to educational psychology, while Professor Pavlov uninterruptedly continued his research on conditioned reflexes. His work may be considered the principal present support of the behavioristic doctrine. Pavlov's theory of conditioned reflexes is, briefly, as follows:

At the basis of all learning or knowledge there are instinctive adaptations or, as Pavlov prefers to call them, unconditioned reflexes. When an animal is hungry and food is put into its mouth, the mouth waters, or, in the technical language of physiological psychology, the salivary reflex takes place. The flow of saliva in response to the presence of food in the mouth of a hungry animal is something that the animal was not taught and did not have to learn. It occurs automatically. Similar are the acts of the infant such as stretching, sucking, and the like. Those unlearned bodily movements, responding to certain needs of the body, are unconditioned (inherited) reflexes.

The hungry pup which at first would respond by the flow of saliva only to the presence of food in its mouth, later learns to respond in the same manner to the sight or smell of food. And when it does so, this is not the case of any mysterious " mental insight " into the situation, Pavlov holds, but that of a reflex. It is not, however, any longer a direct or unconditioned reflex, as is the case of the salivary flow in response to the actual presence of food in the dog's mouth, but a conditioned (acquired) reflex, a reflex or response produced by a symbol of the direct and authentic natural stimulus which has in the past called forth the unconditioned reflex.

If, next, you sound a bell each time just before you give meat to the hungry dog, and repeat this operation a sufficient number of times, the dog's mouth will water on the sounding of the bell even though no food is in sight. More than this, Pavlov has shown, if a tuning fork is sounded simultaneously with the placing of a definite quantity of powdered meat on the dog's tongue, and the procedure is repeated over and over again, sooner or later the tuning fork alone, without the meat, will call forth, not only the flow of saliva, but in exactly the same quantity as was originally produced by the placing of meat in the dog's mouth. To say it in Pavlov's own words:

Any sound whatever, odor, etc., may become a stimulus, and it will call out the activity of the salivary glands as definitely as does food at a distance. . . . What, then, are these conditions under which anything can become a stimulus to the salivary glands? The basic prerequisite is *coincidence in time*. The experiment proceeds in this way: We take, for example, a sound, no matter what, which has no relation to salivary glands. The sound acts on the dog, and he at the same time is fed, or acid is put into his mouth. After several repetitions of such a procedure the sound itself without either food or acid will stimulate the salivary glands.[15]

[15] *Lectures on Conditioned Reflexes*, International Publishers, 1928, p. 265 f.

Furthermore, if the amplitude of the tuning fork (or the tone of it, depending upon the number of vibrations per second) is changed after the dog has learned to respond to it by the flow of saliva, and if the food is actually given to the dog each time upon sounding the tone of 1,000 vibrations and is withheld each time in connection with a higher tone, the dog soon will cease to respond to the tone which is higher than the food-bringing tone of 1,000 vibrations. In this manner he will learn to distinguish as insignificant an elevation of tone as .012 (twelve thousandths), and no salivary response will follow.

Does this mean that the dog has a musical " consciousness " or " insight " ? Not at all, Professor Pavlov thinks. This proves only that upon the basis of unconditioned reflexes, most complex conditioned reflexes can be built, which have the appearance of mysterious " psychic " processes. Professor Pavlov does not, however, pretend that his experiment upon the building of conditioned reflexes in dogs is the key to all the " states of consciousness " of man. In a guarded statement found in the concluding chapter of *Conditioned Reflexes,* he says:

. . . In applying to man the results of investigation of the functions of the heart, digestive tract, and other organs in the higher animals, allied as these organs are to the human in structure, great reserve must be exercised and the validity of comparisons must be verified at every step. Obviously even greater caution must be used in attempting similarly to apply our recently acquired knowledge concerning the higher nervous activity in the dog — the more so since the incomparably greater development of the cerebral cortex in man is preëminently that factor which has raised man to his dominant position in the animal world. It would be the height of presumption to regard these first steps in elucidating the physiology of the cortex as solving the intricate problems of the higher psychic activities in man, when in fact at the present stage of our work no detailed application of its results to man is yet permissible.[16]

[16] Oxford University Press, 1927, p. 395.

This " height of presumption " was braved by Professor John Watson, the mechanistic physiological psychologist, and his school. The behaviorists' belief as voiced by K. S. Lashley is that " the study of man will reveal nothing except what is adequately describable in the concepts of mechanics and chemistry." [17]

Behaviorism considers, logically enough, as its goal the experimental explanation of the higher psychic activities of man. Behavioristic experimentation is, however, inevitably confined very largely to the study of animal behavior. Yet behaviorism seeks to explain, in the mechanistic terms of conditioned reflexes, the capacity for planning or insight observable in man's behavior, his emotions, language, and thinking, by reducing these functions to the purely physiological working, or behavior, of a bundle of nerves, muscles, and glands capable of a complex but none the less physiological function in the form of conditioned reflexes. According to Edward Chace Tolman, who echoes La Mettrie's *Man-Machine* (see p. 75), man is similar to a slot-machine, except that responses of " the human machine " are more variable than those of a slot-machine.[18]

The working of conditioned reflexes is traceable, the behaviorists are convinced, to two classes of " drives." The one is made of the various " hungers " that form the soil from which spring the stimuli or sensory excitations: " food-hunger, sex-hunger, shelter-demands, excretion-demands, fatigue-demands, and aesthetic-demands." These are the " ultimate *appetites,* or drives toward quiescences." The other class of " drives " is constituted by fear and pugnacity, the " ultimate *aversions,* or drives from disturbances." [19]

In other words, behaviorism maintains that there is nothing in man's behavior which is not explicable in terms of man's

[17] " The Behavioristic Interpretation of Consciousness," *Psychological Review,* Vol. 30, p. 244.
[18] " Instinct and Purpose," *Psychological Review,* Vol. 27, p. 217 f.
[19] " A Behavioristic Theory of Ideas." *Ibid.,* Vol. 33, p. 357.

physiological tendency to procure pleasures and to avoid annoyances, and a series of conditioned reflexes, more or less complex, built upon this simple basis.

For example, a hungry cat is shut in a cage. Food is placed near the barred door of the cage, but out of reach of the imprisoned animal. The door of the cage is fastened by means of some very simple mechanism, such as "a hanging loop of wire which required but the slightest clawing, or a wooden latch easily lifted by the nose." [20] The cat in its random movement sooner or later turns the latch, the door falls open, and the cat goes out and gets the food. After this experiment has been repeated several times, any cat learns to turn the latch without much delay and promptly to secure the food.

The cat that is clawing all over the box in her impulsive struggle will probably claw the string or loop or button so as to open the door. And gradually all the other non-successful impulses will be stamped out and the particular impulse leading to the successful act will be stamped in by the resulting pleasure, until, after many trials, the cat will, when put in the box, immediately claw the button or loop in a definite way.[21]

Now, what is the basic spring of this learning? Is it the power of insight and foresight, of planning or "bringing the future into the present," on the part of the cat? Not at all, answers behaviorism. At the basis of the entire process is food-hunger and instinctive or "determining" adjustment — clawing about the cage in which the cat is held and which separates it from the food. The cat's learning how to escape from the box is simply a conditioned reflex built into its nervous system through the medium of (a) the factor of satisfaction and annoyance (or

[20] Tolman, Edward Chace, "Instinct and Purpose," *Psychological Review*, Vol. 27, p. 225.
[21] Thorndike, E. L., *Animal Intelligence*, p. 36. By permission of The Macmillan Company, publishers.

pleasantness and unpleasantness) and (b) the frequency or repetition of the hunger situation and the annoyance and satisfaction involved in the trial and error process of escaping from the puzzle-box and getting the food. The " intelligence " the cat shows in learning how to escape promptly from the box is simply a physiological adaptation in the form of conditioned reflexes, concludes the behaviorist.

When a man tries to escape from a burning hotel, again we have a case of instinctive adaptation, or unconditioned reflexes, or " determining adjustment," perhaps intermingled with " thinking," or conditioned reflexes.

Imagine a man trapped in a burning hotel. He *may* rush madly about in the same blind fashion as does the cat in the cage. If so, his behavior and that of the cat would seem to be entirely identical. It may happen, however, that instead of thus rushing blindly he stops to *think*. If such be the case, he does not attack all the exits of his trap indiscriminately, but only some one which is apparently suggested by his " thoughts." . . . What, now, we may ask, is this thought and when and how does it occur? [22]

Thinking, according to behaviorism, means nothing other than performing " thoughts-of-acts "; in other words, undergoing a complex case of conditioned reflexes:

. . . thoughts, or at least the kind of thought with which we are here concerned, can be conceived from an objective point of view as consisting in internal presentations to the organism (on a basis of memory and association) of stimuli not actually present but which would be present, if some hypothesized action were carried out. Such a definition says nothing about the subjective " immediate-feel " side of thoughts as such. . . .

What is this stopping to think in behavioristic terms? It consists, I would assert, in what may well be called, not random subordinate

[22] Tolman, Edward Chace, " Instinct and Purpose," *Psychological Review*, Vol. 27, p. 229.

acts, but random subordinate *thoughts-of-acts.* . . . As a result of each successive response the cat was automatically provided with a stimulus for another response. How now in the case of the man? He sees a door but instead of actually responding, he merely thinks of responding. He hypothesizes a response and on the basis of this hypothesized response he achieves mentally a new stimulus, *i.e.,* the mental image of what is beyond the door.[23]

Thinking, behaviorism maintains, may be a very complex combination of conditioned reflexes, but it is nothing else. It is a symbolic response or series of responses to symbolic stimuli. Every effort of the cat to get out of the cage, or every inquiring look that a man casts at the street cars in order to find one which will take him home, is nothing but a trial and error process repeated until the purpose is attained. As a result, a conditioned reflex is built incidentally and without the cat's or the man's being conscious of it. Next time, at the sight of a car bearing the number of his destination, the man will take it without delay and will reach home in due time — just as one of Pavlov's dogs is prepared to be fed upon the sounding of the bell or even of the tuning fork of a certain amplitude. A conditioned reflex has been built.

Man's language is also nothing more mysterious in substance, though decidedly more complicated, than is the salivary reaction of Pavlov's dog to the bell, or the dog's " understanding of the meaning " of the bell — thus runs the argument. Language, in its genesis, consists merely of a combination of conditioned reflexes, that is, selective responses to stimuli or to their substitutes or symbols, in the form of words spoken by others or of written words. The selective responses are built on the basis of unconditioned reflexes or instinctive responses to stimuli. Indeed, how does the child learn to say the word *milk,* or *bottle,*

[23] Tolman, Edward Chace, " Instinct and Purpose," *Psychological Review,* Vol. 27, pp. 229, 230.

for instance? When he is hungry and some milk is given him from the milk bottle he is satisfied. Food has been actually put into his mouth and his hunger has been stilled. This is the case of an unconditioned reflex. Next, he learns to recognize the milk bottle as the satisfier. He expresses his joy at seeing it, and his impatient desire to have the milk served him. This is already the case of a conditioned reflex — response to a symbolic stimulus — but still a simple or simultaneous conditioned reflex.

Now the child has an instinctive endowment or ability for an unconditioned reflex whereby sounds arouse in him a desire to imitate them. As a result, when he hears his nurse say, " Yes, this is your *milk bottle*," or the like, with emphasis upon the words, *milk bottle*, he imitates, among other sounds, these words. After several trials and errors in which he receives the help of the nurse and of his admiring parents, the child succeeds in reproducing the words well enough to have his food served to him more promptly. As a result, his annoyance from hunger is shortened and his satisfaction comes more quickly. What, then, is the substance and the source of the child's knowledge of the words, *milk, bottle*? What, in other words, is the " meaning " of these words to the child? There is no mysterious " meaning " there, but simply a conditioned reflex, answers the behaviorist. Our " purposes " and " attitudes," our " thinking " in general, that is our ability to operate with ideas and to respond to ideas, is not any mystic " inner " experience, but merely covert talking, " implicit " speech operation, a muscular or " motor " activity, and, originally, a combination of selective or conditioned responses, behaviorism advises.

The study of emotions made by behaviorism has allied it with Freudism, or psychoanalysis. This school in psychology, or, to be exact, in psychopathy, made well known through the work of Sigmund Freud, a Viennese psychiatrist, stresses the importance of sex-hunger and sexual inhibitions in the unriddling of many forms of behavior, in particular, in explaining "complexes" or emotional disturbances resulting from a set of ideas — fixed ideas, as the French called them long before Freud — dominating the mind of the person so afflicted. For example, a person who is painfully diffident of his or her mental powers, or physical attraction, or social position, has in the terms of Freudism an "inferiority complex." (In reality what the Freudians call complex is simply a milder form of mania.) In its extreme version, Freudism attributes most of the emotions of man or of child, even such emotions as filial piety and religious faith, to sex-hunger and conditioned reflexes built upon such hunger. The method of psychoanalysis is, however, much more in the nature of the traditional introspective method. It is the *Aussage* or *Ausfragemethode,* or " talking-out " method; in other words, the method or procedure consists in making the subject talk about night dreams and other intimate experiences.[24]

Such, briefly, is the substance of the behavioristic doctrine, because a doctrine it must be called since it claims more than it can prove, or at least more than it has proved.

SOME DOUBTS ABOUT BEHAVIORISM AS A PSYCHOLOGICAL DOCTRINE

Behavioristic psychology has rendered appreciable scientific services in the capacity of a " co-ordinating science." It is, indeed, a kind of *liaison* or contact study as between physiology and psychology.[25] It is undoubtedly capable of further similar services, provided, however, that a tug — to paraphrase A. A. Roback, the author of *Behaviorism and Psychology* — does not try to assume the proportions of a man-of-war.[26] Among other

---

[24] Boring, E. G., *A History of Experimental Psychology,* The Century Co., 1929. Murphy, Gardner, *An Historical Introduction to Modern Psychology,* Harcourt Brace and Co., 1929.

[25] Cf. Roback, A. A., *Behaviorism and Psychology,* The University Bookstore, Cambridge, Mass., 1923, p. 201.

[26] *Ibid.*

things, it is well that behaviorism should challenge introspective psychology and force it to put to a reasonable use the method of quantitative experimental observation where and when such a method is appropriate. On the other hand, human personality is very largely a deep sea of qualitative facts, such as general values, faith, ideals, aspirations, and passions, non-measurable quantitatively. Despite all the ingenious behavioristic laboratory measurements, Leibniz' words still hold: " When I came to meditate on the union of the soul with the body, I was as if cast back into the open sea." Or, as Shakespeare said:

> There are more things in heaven and earth, Horatio,
> Than are dreamt of in your philosophy.[27]

May we add, " or in your psychology " ? Not unlike other " isms," behaviorism shares in the fate of the Voltairean " theoretical mouse " (see p. 85) and though it has passed several holes, there are such as it cannot pass.

Behaviorism may well claim that it has emancipated itself from the reign of abstract concepts. Still it is unexplained in terms of S-R bonds or in those of conditioned reflexes — unless by the dogmatic wholesale statement that concept is a conditioned reflex — why and how the child very early in life comes to understand that not only two apples and two apples make four apples, but that two and two of anything make four of that same thing. The quantity " category " or intuition of pure reason still seems to offer the best explanation of this phenomenon (see p. 78).

Behaviorism may further repeat incessantly that consciousness is nothing but the mechanical functioning of the environment and the reaction system, in other words, the S-R system. Too many things about our consciousness or awareness of content remain unaccounted for to accept behaviorism as the basis for

[27] *Hamlet*, Act I, Scene V.

a philosophy of life or of education. In the words of Professor Edwin Boring, a historian of experimental psychology and a behaviorist himself:

As behaviorism began to absorb most of the content of the older psychology, and to expand to include social psychology, the word *stimulus* began to lose much of its precision. It came often to be used for any initial term in the relation that ended in response. Thus a stimulus, instead of having an exact physiological meaning, was often a situation or an involved object with meaning encrusted upon it. A chair, a dinner-table, a symphony, a loved person, a piece of conversation might be called a ' stimulus.'

So it came about that the very adaptability of behaviorism tended to defeat the original purpose of Watson in ' founding ' it. With hypothesized implicit responses admitted, with any kind of situation or mass-object playing the role of stimulus, with all uttered words counting as responses, much of the original precision of physiological method was lost.[28]

May we observe that this was inevitable because behaviorism is too simplistic a doctrine, while the realities of our psychic life are complex and subtle? Seemingly, many of those realities are something more than mere mechanical physiological processes. Therefore, behaviorism has not only found itself forced to employ with dogmatic, vague, and quite subjective latitude the word " stimulus," but it has been forced also to employ other basic terms which are very slightly physiological, such as " substitute stimuli " or " symbolic stimuli " or " symbolic process," without ever having explained how it happens that we can have symbols and respond to them, and what is the purely physiological mechanism of a symbol if there is such a mechanism — which appears subject to very legitimate doubt.

Behaviorists may indulge — with more dogmatic finality than

[28] From *A History of Experimental Psychology,* p. 586. By Edwin Boring. Used by permission of D. Appleton-Century Company, Publishers, New York, N. Y.

true scientific sobriety — in a derisive employment of the word *psychic* and regard it merely as a physiologist's pleasantry. The mystery of imaginative artistic creation in music, literature, and other fine arts is still as complete (in abstraction from idealistic ontology and introspective psychology corresponding to it) as it was before Pavlov's theory of conditioned reflexes had been formulated and the evolutionistic simplistic S-R physiological psychology was "founded" by Professor John Watson and his school. It will be remembered that behaviorism is, in substance, at least as old as the Democritian atomistic psychology; and it appears legitimate not to attach to the present-day behavioristic doctrine, in working out one's philosophy of education, any more finality than can reasonably be attached to what is described by such an able and devoted promoter of behaviorism as Professor Pavlov in the following words:

In this domain [physiological research] * there will for long remain an immense breadth of unchartered ocean with small patches of the known.[29]

Thomas Huxley, the English biologist and evolutionistic philosopher, declared that "six monkeys, set to strum unintelligently on typewriters for millions of millions of years, would be bound in time to write all the books in the British Museum." [30] In the meantime, until this has happened, it seems quite justifiable not to accept from the behavioristic and evolutionistic doctrines more philosophic implications, pedagogically or generally, than can be satisfactorily proved. Furthermore, the objectivity, in other words, demonstrability and universal validity of the behavioristic theory (to the effect that intelligent adaptation is, at its origin, nothing but a random process of trial and error which brings the animal to a satisfactory learning or in-

* Bracketed remarks are added.
[29] *Conditioned Reflexes, cit.*, p. 394.
[30] Jeans, Sir James, *The Mysterious Universe*, Macmillan, 1930, p. 4.

telligent adaptation, only as the result of a happy conjunction of bodily movements occurring accidentally among many such movements) may be seriously questioned even on behaviorism's own ground — animal learning.

Professor Wolfgang Köhler of Berlin, for instance, has shown as a result of his study of chimpanzees that they are capable of insight — the ability to see a situation in the totality of relationships involved in it — and foresight — the ability to visualize in the mind or imagination the solution of a problem involving bodily movements without random movements or hitting about.[31] Besides, is not the objectivity of the observation, for example, of the behavior of the hungry cat imprisoned in a puzzle-box vitiated by the artificiality of the situation? In normal conditions of life cats do not live imprisoned in puzzle-boxes. Was Thorndike's cat caged in a puzzle-box still the " cat-in-itself "? Imagine a cat, spoiled by the children and the mistress of the house, a sleek heart-killer of the cat community (in fact, any cat not born in the captivity of a puzzle-box, which origin would disqualify it for the experiment) thrown into a narrow, dingy puzzle-box! Small wonder that he would hit about and otherwise behave unintelligently, that he would be overcome, so to speak, with indignation and probably with fear.[32] A man, whom we know as a perfectly intelligent person

[31] *Mentality of Apes*, Harcourt, Brace and Co., 1926.

[32] This idea occurred to us, by a ricochet, while reading the following passage in *Animal Intelligence*, p. 35 (quoted by permission of The Macmillan Company, publishers):

" In these various boxes were put cats from among the following. I give approximately their ages while under experiment.

" No. 1. 8–10 months	No. 7. 3– 5 months
No. 2. 5– 7 months	No. 8. 6– 6½ months
No. 3. 5–11 months	No. 10. 4– 8 months
No. 4. 5– 8 months	No. 11. 7– 8 months
No. 5. 5– 7 months	No. 12. 4– 6 months
No. 6. 3– 5 months	No. 13. 18–19 months

" The behavior of all but No. 11 and No. 13 was practically the same. When put into the box the cat would show evident signs of discomfort and of an impulse to escape from confinement. It tries to squeeze through any opening; it claws and bites at the bars or wire; it thrusts its paws out through any opening and claws at everything

capable of rapid and correct decisions, is dumfounded for some time when subjected to a sudden, unprovoked offense. In general, animals are fond of privacy, of the privacy of their natural ways, except when they have companionship of their own choice. They are upset and never any longer themselves when put into the unnatural conditions of laboratory observation. An animal is not an unfeeling piece of chemical. The laboratory study of animal behavior can be objective and convincing in a very limited degree only, even with relation to animal psychology proper, though it may be entirely sufficient for the purpose of discovering the laws of animal physiology.

Theodore Roosevelt wrote, fittingly, in his paper, "The Search for Truth in a Reverent Spirit " : " There is superstition in science quite as much as there is superstition in theology, and it is all the more dangerous because those suffering from it are profoundly convinced that they are freeing themselves from all superstition." [33] The behaviorists readily accuse the traditional introspective psychology of " the neglect of all data con-

---

it reaches; it continues its efforts when it strikes anything loose and shaky; it may claw at things within the box. It does not pay very much attention to the food outside, but seems simply to strive instinctively to escape from confinement. The vigor with which it struggles is extraordinary. For eight or ten minutes it will claw and bite and squeeze incessantly. With No. 13, an old cat [?],* and No. 11, an uncommonly sluggish cat [What were the proofs?],* the behavior was different. They did not struggle vigorously or continually. On some occasions they did not struggle at all. It was therefore necessary to let them out of the box a few times, feeding them each time. After they thus associate climbing out of the box with getting food, they will try to get out whenever put in. They did not, even then, struggle so vigorously or get so excited as the rest."

Were not these two cats, No. 11 and No. 13, the most intelligent of the lot? Curiously enough, Dr. Thorndike in the course of his study depicts the behavior of his cats in rather general, vague terms, while he describes the architecture of each of the cage-boxes and the way they work with great care for detail. Lack of certain fundamental details relative to the behavior of the cats makes it impossible to analyze epistemologically, as it were, his analysis of their behavior. For instance, it is not clear from Dr. Thorndike's account when and how, exactly, the factor of observation and imitation was permitted to play its role in the behavior of each of the cats. It may be mentioned, also, that it is not clear in what sense Dr. Thorndike calls No. 13 " an old cat." " Twelve years appear to be the usual length of [a cat's] * life, though eighteen may be reached," says the *Riverside Natural History*, Vol. V, p. 458.

* Bracketed remarks are added.

[33] *The Outlook,* December, 1911.

cerning the human individual which cannot be interpreted as evidence for the existence of some type of psychic process." Yet, in the appropriate words of A. A. Roback, " The new movement was consistently dodging the issues raised by the opposite side; and busy with their loud protestations, its representatives did not deign to lend an ear to those who in their turn were voicing their protests against the unheeding *doctrinaires*. It is easier to frame a theory than to defend it." [34]

Professor Watson would give the grade " zero " in psychology to the celebrated German dualistic psychologist and philosopher, Wilhelm Wundt, who founded about 1879 the first psychological laboratory. " The psychology begun by Wundt," declares Mr. Watson with as complete subjectivity as can be found in any extreme introspectivist, " has thus failed to become a science and has still more deplorably failed in contributing anything of a scientifically usable kind to human nature — in helping people to understand why they behave as they do and how to modify their behavior. . . ." [35] The behaviorists may claim for themselves the monopoly of being scientific and may deny the honor, arbitrarily enough, to any other psychologists. It is none the less true that a comprehensive view of human life still finds room for both consciousness and behavior (or mechanical physiological adaptation to stimuli); in other words, for both subjective or introspective and objective or experimental methods of studying human conduct.

> Soul and body, close and yet separate, alas!
> Will be a twin wanderer, as long as the world shall last. . . . [36]

As Wundt has admirably summarized the problem, all psychology begins with introspection and the latter disposes of

---

[34] *Behaviorism and Psychology, cit.,* p. 70.
[35] *Psychology from the Standpoint of a Behaviorist, cit.,* p. 3.
[36] Musset, Alfred, *Namouna (Conte Oriental),* Chant I, XLIX.

two auxiliaries (*Hilfsmittel*): experiment and the history of mankind.[37]

Plato, whose colossal scholarship and prodigiously fertile mind anticipated many subsequent " new " theories, political, philosophic, and psychological, also anticipated the epistemological truth and falsity of behaviorism.

In one of his earlier dialogues, Plato professed enthusiasm for " the art of measurement " as a road to true knowledge:

. . . But the art of measurement would do away with the effect of appearances, and, showing the truth, would fain teach the soul at last to find rest in the truth, and would thus save our life.[38]

As he progressed, however, in the maturity of his philosophic thought, Plato came to understand that one can " find rest in the truth " with the help of " the art of measurement " only in relation to limited and, on the whole, secondary problems of knowledge. His next reference to the epistemological significance of the art in question was made in more guarded and restricted terms:

The art of measuring and numbering and weighing came to the rescue of the human understanding — there is the beauty of it — and the apparent greater or less or more or heavier no longer have the mastery over us, but give way before calculation and measure and weight.[39]

" The art of measuring " can, then, furnish the reassuring truth with regard to the question of whether or not a thing is " greater or less or more or heavier " than some other thing, and the like. There alone can " calculation and measure and weight " successfully operate. But there are other and more

[37] *Beiträge zur Theorie der Sinneswahrnehmung*, Leipzig-Heidelberg, 1862.
[38] *Protagoras*, 356.
Note: This and all other citations from Plato used in this volume are taken from the translation of the *Dialogues* by Benjamin Jowett, Oxford, Clarendon Press, 1871–1895.   [39] *Republic*, 10, 602.

poignant problems that haunt the mind of man; above all, the problem of the true " essence " of his own being and of all being. Sensual-mechanistic and quantitative methods of probing into the human mind will not yield the desired knowledge and " teach the soul at last to find rest in the truth." Other means and other methods are necessary. What are they? They are not sensual-mechanistic and quantitative, but are spiritual-qualitative. Anticipating Bergson's remarkable theory of intuition as the method of perfect knowledge (see p. 56), Plato reasons in the *Phaedo* in a direction away from the earlier unrestricted enthusiasm for the epistemological value of the senses and of " the art of measurement " based upon the senses:

What again shall we say of the actual acquirement of knowledge? Is the body, if invited to share in the inquiry, a hinderer or a helper? I mean to say, have sight and hearing any truth in them? Are they not as the poets are always telling us, inaccurate witnesses? And yet, if even they are inaccurate and indistinct, what is to be said of the other senses — for you will allow that they are the best of them?

Certainly, he replied.

Then when does the soul attain truth? — for in attempting to consider anything in company with the body she is obviously deceived.

Yes, that is true.

Then must not existence [true existence, the thing-in-itself] * be revealed to her in thought, if at all?

Yes.

And thought is best when the mind is gathered into herself and none of these things trouble her — neither sounds nor sights nor pain nor pleasure — when she has as little as possible to do with the body.[40]

Is that idea or essence, which in the dialectical process we define as essence or true existence — whether essence of equality, beauty,

---

* Bracketed remarks are added.

[40] *Phaedo*, 65.

or anything else — are those essences, I say, liable at times to some degree of change? Or are they, each of them, always what they are, having the same simple self — existent and unchanging forms, and not admitting of variation at all, or in any way, or at any time?

They must always be the same, Socrates, replied Cebes.

And what would you say of the many beautiful things — whether men or horses or garments or any other things which may be called equal or beautiful, — are they all unchanging and the same always, or quite the reverse? May they not rather be described as almost always changing and hardly ever the same, either with themselves or with one another?

The latter, replied Cebes, they are always in the state of change.

And these you can touch and see and perceive with the senses, but the unchanging things you can only perceive with the mind. . . .[41]

PRAGMATISM

Side by side with evolutionistic "naturalism" or materialism is another school of philosophic thought which has exercised a profound influence upon the New Education. It is pragmatism, or the philosophy of the immediate (versus the deferred) and of action. The origin of the term "pragmatism," as is true of most philosophic terms, is Greek. Its root is the word *pragma* (πρᾶγμα), which means a thing done, business, effective action. The first occurrence of the term in a philosophic sense seems to be the expression "the pragmatic history" found in the Greek historian Polybius (d. 123 B.C.). By the term Polybius means, as he himself explains, that his historical study has the purpose of investigating facts of the past in order to draw from those facts practical lessons useful for guiding posterity in its conduct — in other words, in its actions.[42] This application of the term "pragmatic" found favor with French historians in the seventeenth and eighteenth centuries, some of whom were fond

[41] *Ibid.,* 78–79.
[42] *Histories,* Book IV, 1–2.

of the type of historical study designated "reasoned history (*l'histoire raisonnée*)." Kant also employed the term "pragmatic" in this sense. In the *Metaphysics of Morals*,[43] Kant says: "A history is composed pragmatically when it makes one wise, when it teaches *prudence, i.e.,* instructs the world how it can provide for its interests better, or at least as well as the men of former time."

Kant employed, however, the term "pragmatic" also in an epistemological meaning. This latter usage of the term in the philosophy of Kant played only a secondary role and related to some minor positions of the Kantian doctrine. But the term was destined to become the name of a whole philosophic school and the banner of a new philosophic battle.

In the latter part of the nineteenth century the term "pragmatism" was given currency, though the substance of the philosophic doctrine involved was not new. This is well indicated by the subtitle of William James's volume on *Pragmatism*. The subtitle is: "A New Name for Some Old Ways of Thinking — Popular Lectures on Philosophy."

There are found in the course of the history of philosophy several recurrences of the thought that the only true origin and the only worthy purpose of the knowledge of reality can be found in a tangible, practical application of knowledge, or in the use of it in action (as over and against the speculative or contemplative curiosity and the search of knowledge for its own sake in complete aloofness from the practical problems of life). Those schools of thought which professed a practical conception of the origin and value of knowledge were not, however, called pragmatic, though they were antecedents of the present-day pragmatic school of thought. The latest recurrence of the pragmatic point of view under a different name, prior to the pragmatism of the end of the nineteenth and beginning of

[43] Longmans, Green and Company, 1927, Second Section (41), p. 34, *note*.

the twentieth century, was the positivistic philosophy of Auguste Comte (d. 1857). The revival of the term " pragmatism " as the name for a philosophy of action is due to the American scholar and thinker, Charles S. Peirce, who published in *Popular Science Monthly,* January 1878, a paper entitled: "How to Make Our Ideas Clear." It is from this paper of Peirce that William James (d. 1910) dates the beginning of the pragmatist school of philosophic thought in this country.

According to Professor Dewey,[44] Peirce drew his inspiration from the Kantian meaning of the term " pragmatic," found in the *Metaphysics of Morals.* In this work, while discussing the "imperatives" (or "rules characterized by 'shall,' which expresses the objective necessitation of action "),[45] Kant distinguishes three kinds of imperatives. One of these he calls "pragmatic": "We might also call the first kind of imperatives *technical* (belonging to art), the second *pragmatic* (to welfare), the third *moral* (belonging to free conduct generally, that is, to morals)." [46]

[44] *Philosophy and Civilization,* Minton, Balch and Co., 1931, p. 13 f.

[45] *Op. cit.,* p. 106.

[46] *Ibid.,* pp. 33, 34.

Note: It is quite possible that Peirce was still more impressed by the meaning in which the term " pragmatic " is employed by Kant in a passage in the *Critique of Pure Reason.* The latter employment of the term by Kant seems to be much closer to the basic position taken by Peirce than is the meaning given in the passage in the *Metaphysics of Morals* to which Professor Dewey refers. The passage in the *Critique of Pure Reason* is as follows:

"Happiness is the satisfaction of all our desires; *extensive,* in regard to their multiplicity; *intensive,* in regard to their degree; and *protensive,* in regard to their duration. The practical law based on the motive of *happiness,* I term a pragmatical law (or prudential rule); but that law, assuming such to exist, which has no other motive than the *worthiness of being happy,* I term a moral or ethical law. The first law tells us what we have to do, if we wish to become possessed of happiness; the second dictates how we ought to act, in order to deserve happiness. The first is based upon empirical principles; for it is only by experience that I can learn either what inclinations exist which desire satisfaction, or what are the natural means of satisfying them. The second takes no account of our desires or the means of satisfying them, and regards only the freedom of a rational being, and the necessary conditions under which alone this freedom can harmonize with the distribution of happiness according to principles. This second law may therefore rest upon mere ideas of pure reason, and may be cognized *a priori.*" (*Critique of Pure Reason,* George Bell and Sons, London, 1890, pp. 488–489: The Canon of Pure Reason, Section Second.)

The fundamental position of pragmatism as formulated by Peirce is as follows: " Consider what effects that might conceivably have practical bearings we conceive the object of our conception to have. Then our conception of these effects is the whole of our conception of the object." In other words, the truth of a proposition is measured by its efficiency, by what it can do as a guide in action. To know means the ability to get something, to have something done. In the words of James, pragmatism is " the attitude of looking away from first things, principles, ' categories,' supposed necessities, and of looking toward last things, fruits, consequences, facts." [47]

But if the truth and value of a proposition are measured by its efficiency, this is, plainly, not yet a certainty sufficient for all cases and capable of giving men all the certitude and guidance they need in their life conduct. What is the criterion of efficiency? Clearly, people differ in their points of view regarding efficiency. What to a communist is a perfectly efficient communistic scheme of government is an absurdly ruinous proposition to one who does not adhere to the communistic principles of life and government. In vain does pragmatism try to look " away from first things, principles, ' categories,' supposed necessities." Those are disturbing factors, to be sure, and difficult to handle, but they cannot be ruled out, pragmatism or no pragmatism. The human mind is so constituted that it needs some sort of final certainty, final criteria and standards, and will not be satisfied with anything that has no finality.

It is said sometimes by the pragmatists that the criterion of the efficiency of action and conduct is the good life. But, again, what is the good life? What is its criterion? The criterion of the good life is to be found in some kind of ultimate certainty. Therefore, the materialist's conception of the good life, and consequently his conception of efficient conduct, is — when he

[47] *Pragmatism*, Longmans, Green and Co., 1908, pp. 54–55.

rigorously follows the logic of the doctrine — diametrically opposite to that of the idealist-spiritualist. In building a general outlook upon life the pragmatists cannot, any more than others, escape the problem of the ultimate criterion, the ultimate certainty. This fact is responsible for at least three principal trends of pragmatism, trends dependent upon what is, avowed or unavowed, the philosopher's ultimate criterion of efficiency; in other words, his conception of the ultimate certainty.

There is hedonistic pragmatism such as was preached, for instance, in Italy at the beginning of this century, through the medium of the magazine *Leonardo*. The fundamental position of the *Leonardo* version of pragmatism was to the effect that the criterion of efficient human conduct is personal success and personal pleasure. In other words, it revived the sophistic doctrine of Protagoras of Abdera, according to whom, it will be remembered, man as an individual is the measure of all things (see p. 132). What he, as an individual, thinks good, is good; what he thinks bad, is bad.

To another school of pragmatism, that of William James, the criterion of efficient conduct and the good life is a spontaneous consensus of opinion, something verified by facts observed in common. Among those facts verified in common James placed the religious-metaphysical ultimate certainty, the existence of God and His laws relative to moral conduct. James was deeply influenced by the teaching of Professor Louis Agassiz, the zoologist, who advised his students to go to nature herself, take her facts into their own hands and examine them in person. Hence, James was distrustful of the idealistic speculative method. He believed in the value of the empirical method. But his empiricism did not develop into materialism, because James was the son of Henry James, Sr., the mystic, and he belonged to the theological race of Emerson, the race which was in its true substance Puritan and Calvinist. James, in his empiricism, accepted religion as a fundamental experience. According to James, religious experience, taken in its real fullness such as is seen in saints and mystics, is an experience bringing satisfaction and joy and security, and is productive of moral initiative. The pragmatism of James is at the basis of the pragmatic " humanism " of F. C. S. Schiller of Oxford.

The third and most influential version and one that has deeply influenced Progressive Education is the " instrumentalism " of John Dewey. His doctrine is developed in the following principal works: *Darwin's Influence on Philosophy and Other Essays, Studies in Logical Theory, Essays in Experimental Logic, Democracy and Education, Creative Intelligence: Essays in the Pragmatic Attitude, Reconstruction in Philosophy, Human Nature and Conduct, Experience and Nature, The Quest for Certainty, Philosophy and Civilization, Art as Experience.* The general outline of his doctrine is as follows: Man seeks certainty. Where can true certainty be found? It can be found in such an adjustment between the organism and the environment in which the organism finds itself as will lead to the most satisfactory adjustment between the exigencies, possibilities, and limitations of nature, on the one hand, and man's social life, on the other. What is the way to certainty? It is knowledge. But what is knowledge? It is experience. True experience, and consequently true knowledge, is functional. Its function consists in devising means, or tools, or instruments, with the help of which we can meet situations demanding adjustments and solve problems as they arise. In other words, knowledge or experience is functional as to its origin, its purpose, and the process of its growth. The final goal of its function is the reconstruction of society in the sense of betterment or " amelioration." Consequently, " social " is synonymous with " moral," and truth is the quality ascribed to a hypothesis which sufficiently stands the test of action.

The doctrine of Dewey is, in substance, an extension and perfection of the doctrine of Auguste Comte and his school. This influential doctrine is to the effect " that only the knowledge of facts is fertile because certain; that the standards of certainty are furnished by the experimental sciences; that in order to avoid getting lost in empty verbalism, the human mind must limit its work to the experience derivable from tangible things, and must renounce all attempt at building knowledge upon an *a priori* foundation; that things-in-themselves are inaccessible to the human mind, which must, therefore, confine its effort to the study of their relations and of the laws governing these relations." [48]

A pragmatist or instrumentalist, epistemologically, and a volitionist or indeterminist, ethically (see p. 57), because he admits the possibility of improvement, of the reconstruction of society through the social effort of men, Dewey is an agnostic metaphysically or ontologically. According to him, philosophy should abandon as useless all search for the ultimate reality:

To abandon the search for absolute and immutable reality and value may seem like a sacrifice. But this renunciation is the condition of entering upon a vocation of greater vitality. The search for values to be secured and shared by all, because buttressed in the foundations of social life, is a quest in which philosophy would have no rivals but coadjutors in men of good will.[49]

Dewey identifies religion with superstition when he says that religion originated in man's fear and his effort to safeguard himself in every way possible against unknown and uncontrollable forces and changes:

Being unable to cope with the world in which he lived, he sought some way to come to terms with the universe as a whole. Religion was in its origin an expression of this endeavor. . . . As a drown-

---

[48] Lalande, André, *op. cit.,* p. 599.
[49] *The Quest for Certainty*, p. 311. Courtesy of Minton Balch and Co., Publishers, New York.

ing man is said to grasp at a straw, so men who lacked the instruments and skills developed in later days snatched at whatever, by any stretch of imagination, could be regarded as a source of help in time of trouble. . . . In such an atmosphere primitive religion was born and fostered. Rather this atmosphere *was* the religious disposition.[50]

Dewey's position relative to the origin and nature of religious experience practically places him outside of agnosticism and into materialism. The position he takes is, indeed, very close to that of Karl Marx, for instance, who said: " Religion is the sighing of a creature oppressed by misfortune, it is the ' soul ' of the world that has no heart, as it is the intelligence of an unintelligent epoch. It is opium for the people." [51] This is not the time or place to go into a detailed exposition of the disagreement between many facts in the history of the religious experience of humanity and the point of view of Marx or Dewey upon the origin and growth of religion. It may be mentioned, however, that religion in reality serves what seems to be an inherent and ineradicable need of man for the ultimate certainty. Neither science nor philosophy satisfies this need. It is precisely after he has solved satisfactorily the more poignant problems

[50] *The Quest for Certainty,* p. 10. Courtesy of Minton, Balch and Co., Publishers, New York.

Cf. also *Experience and Nature,* Open Court Publishing Co., p. 41:

". . . Man finds himself living in an aleatory world; his existence involves, to put it baldly, a gamble. The world is a scene of risk; it is uncertain, unstable, uncannily unstable. Its dangers are irregular, inconstant, not to be counted upon as to their times and seasons. Although persistent, they are sporadic, episodic. It is darkest just before dawn; pride goes before a fall; the moment of greatest prosperity is the moment most charged with ill-omen, most opportune for the evil eye. Plague, famine, failure of crops, disease, death, defeat in battle, are always just around the corner, and so are abundance, strength, victory, festival and song. Luck is proverbially both good and bad in its distributions. . . .

" Anthropologists have shown incontrovertibly the part played by the precarious aspect of the world in generating religion with its ceremonies, rites, cults, myths, magic. . . ."

[51] *Contribution to the Critique of the Philosophy of Right by Hegel,* J. Molitor, p. 84.

The last sentence of the Marxian definition of religion has become the slogan of the Bolshevist propaganda against religion.

and mysteries arising out of the relationship between man and his material environment that man is more than ever pervaded with the wondrous longing to know the ultimate truth and the ultimate Being, and to find in such knowledge repose and guidance. Maeterlinck has well said that " there is a notable difference between the mystery which comes before our ignorance is dissipated and the mystery which comes after we have learned." [52]

Science cannot, on account of its very nature, lift from the mind of man the multiple burden made of uncertainties and blind alleys which weighs him down in his anxious quest for the comprehension of the ultimate meaning of his own life and of the universe. Science cannot, therefore, nor can anything else, replace the solace of religion. The great secret of the vitality of religion seems best revealed in these words of Christ: " Come unto me, all ye that labour and are heavy laden, and I will give you rest." (Matthew xi:28).

Doubtless religion will survive the agnostic instrumentalism of Dewey, as it has survived many schools of philosophic thought which sought to rule it out as a vital force, or to sneer it out of existence, for the simple reason that religion proposes to give man something that he needs most even when he has obtained all other things. This is, to repeat it, the ultimate certainty which neither science nor philosophy can supply.[53]

Dewey's conception of the origin and growth of religion can, therefore, justly be regarded as one-sided and narrow, though it undoubtedly explains satisfactorily some forms and cases of religious experience. Similarly narrow and one-sided is his instrumentalistic conception of the origin and growth of knowledge. He says:

[52] Cf. Dewey, *Characters and Events,* Henry Holt, 1929, Vol. I, p. 34.

[53] In so far as one can gather from Dr. Dewey's pamphlet, *A Common Faith* (Yale University Press, 1934, pp. 87), his attitude toward religious faith has somewhat changed in the direction of a more sympathetic understanding. He maintains, however, intact his rigorous negation of the supernatural.

If one looks at the history of knowledge, it is plain that at the beginning men tried to know because they had to do so in order to live. . . . The desire for intellectual or cognitive understanding had no meaning except as a means of obtaining greater security as to the issues of action.[54]

Again, this utilitarian conception of the origin and growth of knowledge explains many things relative to the origin and growth of knowledge, but not everything by far.

Why, for instance, did the earliest Greeks, living in a poor, primitive environment with very limited leisure, where a man had to procure by his own direct labor everything that he and his progeny needed — why did such men trouble themselves about the true substance of which the universe is made, and the relationship between the sun and the earth? Whatever the ultimate substance of the universe may be, man had to get immediately somehow and somewhere some substance that would feed him. No matter whether the universe is basically made of air, or water, or fire, as the various early thinkers believed, man could not — and he knew it — satisfy his physical hunger through such knowledge. His physical hunger demanded the consumption of vegetables, cereals, meats, and fish, just as his physical thirst demanded water, milk, fruit-juices, and the like. Regardless of what was man's solution concerning the problem of the ultimate basic substance of which the universe is made, it could not solve his problem of breakfast or dinner for himself or his family. Yet many a primitive man worried himself, to no material advantage, about those ultimate things, and there were always many people eager to learn from him about them. Whether the earth was round or not, and whether the sun slept in the sea at night or elsewhere, there were clearly to be nights and days, and the fisherman must go out to fish, the hunter to hunt, and the shepherd to tend his sheep. In all these

[54] *The Quest for Certainty*, p. 38. Courtesy of Minton, Balch and Co., Publishers, New York.

and similar questions which motivated man's scientific and philosophic search — which was primarily a disinterested search, materially, and often only indirectly, indeed unwittingly, a source of utilitarian knowledge — there was nothing in the nature of " a means of obtaining greater security as to the issues of action." There was behind those problems something very real, though undreamt of in the instrumentalistic philosophy.

Now that the fundamental positions of the doctrine of materialistic evolutionism, or evolutionistic materialism, and of instrumentalism, which have influenced the New Education, or Progressive Education, have been studied, and the historic antecedents of these philosophic doctrines have been outlined, let us summarize the tenets of this important present-day educational movement before attempting an analysis of its connections with the philosophic doctrines of evolutionistic materialism and instrumentalism.

THE PRINCIPAL TENDENCIES OF PROGRESSIVE EDUCATION [55]

During the past twenty-five years, and in particular since the end of the World War, many important and fruitful changes have been worked out in democratic countries in the organization, administration, and financing of education. Some of these innovations are of real significance and are destined to influence the future of democracy. Not only were they unknown to ancient civilization, but a few decades ago they would hardly have been thought feasible. Consequently, they can justly be called new.

One would expect Progressive Education — as its promoters have named it — to be the collective name for theories and practices relative to those truly new things. Yet the titles " Progressive Education " and " New Education " are practically

[55] Cf. among the various publications of the progressives *The Thirty-third Yearbook of the National Society for the Study of Education, Part II: Activity Movement.*

monopolized — with much inexactitude, historically — by certain theories and practices regarding the general method of education. The principal tenets of the Progressive Education or New Education theory, as represented by the official doctrine of the Progressive Education Association and the New Education Fellowship, seem to be in substance as follows:

1. Schools should discontinue feeding children on bookish facts and should abandon formal discipline. The old pedagogical menus could not fail, it is asserted, to make children anemic, physically and mentally. If their latent possibilities are to be realized, vital activity must take the place of mechanical memorizing; and learning by doing, by experiencing and experimenting, must be substituted for learning by listening and sitting still. The school, it is claimed, must be converted into a living creative influence, producing self-directing citizens and not stultified masses of graduates. To that end, the detrimental characteristic features of the orthodox education, such as coercive discipline and dogmatic instruction on the part of the teacher, and automatic obedience and passive receptivity on the part of the child, must be banished from the school. They must be supplanted by free and joyous activity determined by the child's interest, and based on his environment. All indoctrination should be eliminated.

2. That the school may be true to real life, it must, it is pleaded, be the scene of physical activity, of handling things on the part of the child. Allowing for individual differences, there are certain cravings inherent in natural youth, we are reminded. Among these the insatiable hunger of the young for making things, for being active, is of great educational value. While working with their hands, children accumulate firsthand knowledge of the world of things. Learning by merely looking at or hearing about these things is necessarily of lesser value to the student; only life can teach life. The new school

will take children away from sickly, barren intellectualism — which is alleged to be the greatest curse of the conventional education. To save the wits of children from getting as worn out as their elbows, their inventive powers and creative instincts are to be set free in workshops. It is held that manifold advantage will result from the method advocated, in particular that children will " find themselves " vocationally.

3. The customary method of directed learning, it is further argued, fails chiefly because it does not develop in the child the ability to meet new situations, to attack problems which constantly crop up in real life, to make the adjustments necessary in a changing economic, social, and political order. The break between the passive, unwilling learning in the familiar school and the active work of life must be avoided. How? By the simple device of leaving the child free to choose and execute his tasks. This will make the child happy and will eliminate the hurtful divorce between school and life.

4. Learning and thinking, it is still further stressed, are superlatively stimulated and fructified when the student recognizes the purpose of learning, when he takes up the problem as his own and works at it independently. Those who are not convinced have but to watch the child at play. Indeed, all school work should be permeated by the spirit of play, we are counseled. By busying himself with problems which he envisages as his own real problems and by overcoming obstructions similarly envisaged the student will develop a consciousness of the need of the three R's and, by implication, proficiency in them. Besides, the *what* of school work is less important than the *how*.

5. The traditional teaching by chalk and talk, guided by official regulations instead of the child's interests, we are told, is particularly wrong because it ignores the fact that children want to learn each in his or her own way and each at his or

her own rate of speed. Once give a child the chance to work as he likes, and you will be surprised at what he can accomplish. In guaranteeing the child his freedom the school must go, it is demanded, unflinchingly all the length of the new road. The school must not be discouraged at the sight of a pupil breaking away from the task he has undertaken or at other irregularities. Some among the advocates of the New Education insist upon holding sacred every desire and feeling of the child. Dissipative as the new method may seem, it is helpful, they affirm, to the growth of the learner. Desultory, scrappy, haphazard learning, though not free from shortcomings, is decidedly less faulty than the tyranny of established programs of study and rigid time schedules.

6. Artificial stimulation of interest on the part of the learner, we are counseled, must be abandoned. In place of the more or less cunning application of a system of rewards and punishments, the interests that are already present of their own accord are to be permitted full play.

7. Since pupils should be permitted and encouraged to discover and to acquire instructional material by their own efforts, it is only logical, we are admonished, to depart from the artificial splitting and chopping of subject matter characteristic of the old school. Integrated instruction, or the project method, which dispenses with time schedules and separate subjects, has to be made the order of the day. Students must be given the liberty to swim right in the stream of life, which is a living unit. Then they will learn how to swim well. Furthermore, it is reasoned, the child has his roots in the home environment. Accordingly, the school can derive its maximum strength from laying the foundation of education on the native soil of the home locality or region.

8. It is further emphasized that the self-activity school presupposes a kind of teacher vastly different from that of the old

school. In the new school, which is the school of free, spontaneous experience and experimentation, the teacher is not to rule
supreme, an incessantly talking dictator. He is there to listen
and to aid rather than to command and to contract a throat
disease. Every child being a self-activist, his teacher's job is to
provide a setting, a suggestive environment where the free creative spirit of the student can operate.

9. Finally, it is contended, the method of education that
would carry into effect these principles would constitute the
only natural way of educating the young. It would be calculated
to promote social progress amidst our changing civilization.

In substance, then, Progressive Education seems to be characterized by two fundamental features. The first is its opposition 1.
to the general method of education which places emphasis
upon sequential curricula. In place of such a general educational method, the Activity movement recommends as the only
sound method of learning and teaching that of joyous, spontaneous activity on the part of the educand. A measure of
sequential study may enter into the educative process under the
Activity method only in so far as such study is invoked by and
is compatible with the joyful interest of the educand, motivated by tangible, immediate purpose. The second fundamental 2.
feature of the Progressive Education doctrine is that it condemns, on the ground of opposition to all indoctrination, all
direct systematic effort of the traditional school toward inculcating in the young even the moral values, traditionally considered fundamental (see p. 352), and is, at best, indifferent to
teaching the metaphysical truth relative to the ultimate reality.

It appears that the limitations of our human species and the
particular place we seem to occupy in the scheme of things
necessitate the reverse educative process; in other words, at each
level of education above the kindergarten, and in each type of
school, the general educational method should be permeated

with an effort on the part of the school to bring the educand to master an appropriate sequential curriculum. This effort seems to be demanded by the responsibility of the school toward the individual and toward the national commonwealth, as well as by indubitable lessons from the history of civilization regarding the achievements and failures of humanity. Spontaneous activity of the educand as a method of education, it appears, should enter the educative process only in so far as such activity is in harmony with and is conducive to the sequential study of an appropriate curriculum, aiming at the development of desirable attitudes as well as skills and information. It seems to be impossible to accept the fundamental positions of the doctrine of Progressive Education, or the New Education, because it is difficult to accept the major premises of this doctrine. More will be said about this in Parts II and III.

Our purpose at present is to show the connections between the Progressive Education doctrine, on the one hand, and the doctrines of evolution and instrumentalism, on the other. Before doing this, however, it may be repeated that when Progressive Education (which is a term more vague and presumptuous than precise or modest) is given also the title of New Education, a gross historic inaccuracy is committed. There is nothing essentially new in the New Education, as any attentive student of the history of education knows. It is not only that the chief positions advocated by the New Education relative to the Activity method are found in sum and substance, sometimes even textually, in the ancient and modern authors who in their time were the advocates of new educational methods. Omitting less known writers, such thinkers as Rousseau, Pestalozzi, Froebel, and Tolstoy [56] can be remembered in this connection.

[56] The philosophic roots of the pedagogical doctrines of these forerunners of present-day activists were, however, very different from the philosophic roots of the New Education. The above-mentioned forerunners of the New Education adhered to some form of idealism, or spiritualism.

The New Education is not new for reasons other than those given in *Ecclesiastes* where it is said, with some exaggeration, that " there is no new thing under the sun." Something which is nearer to us historically than the very general conservative formula of *Ecclesiastes* makes the New Education not so novel. Many things written on its banners have been practiced long since by good teachers the world over, but in a form moderated by experience and sobered by the conditions of actual class teaching. Motivated learning or purposeful activity, as the phraseology of the New Education has it, individual and group self-activity, even integrated instruction itself, to mention only these, are vistas by no means new. Only, says *Ecclesiastes* again: " There is no remembrance of the former things."

One of the devices employed by orators and dialecticians in ancient Greece consisted in using two adjectives to denote a single quality. The moderns, on the contrary, often include in one word two quite different meanings. Thus, the adjective *new* stands simultaneously for itself and for the adjective *good*. Therefore, to avoid all misunderstanding, it must be expressly stated that the denial of originality and newness in the main positions of the New Education should not be taken as a wholesale, outright condemnation of the movement.

The confusion between novelty and desirability, between changing and improving, should, of course, be vigilantly avoided in education as much as in other human matters, or perhaps even more so. On the other hand, suggestions for reform and the invitation to review the existing educational situation, when prompted by a sincere and solid quest for social good, should be welcomed. For the school should not be " a single individual who talks to himself for a hundred years, and takes an extraordinary pleasure in his own being, however foolish and silly it may be," [57] as Goethe exaggerated a condi-

[57] *Maxims and Reflections*, German Classics, J. B. Lyon Co., Vol. II, p. 386.

tion that should not be permitted to exist. Things educational, like any others, should not be left to rule unquestioned, except, of course, such as have proved their worth beyond all doubt.

The Progressive Education movement is a renewed challenge to traditional methods. Its proposals and criticisms are set forth very pointedly, which may be to the advantage of its supporters and of its critics alike. For, as Socrates told one of his disciples, " If we are bold we shall gain one of two advantages: either we shall find that which we seek, or we shall be less likely to think that we know what we do not know — and this, surely, is no mean reward." [58]

Let us now turn to the study, however brief, of the connections between the fundamental tenets of the New Education, or Progressive Education, and the philosophic sources and antecedents of these positions. The sources and antecedents in question are materialistic evolutionism — in particular, behaviorism, which is an evolutionistic psychological doctrine in support of the evolutionistic epistemology — and pragmatic instrumentalism. The connections between the philosophy of Progressive Education and general modern philosophy are acknowledged by few supporters of the Progressive doctrine, while many do not even suspect that such connections exist. The Progressive movement owes its influence largely to the supposed novelty of its educational philosophy, so, naturally, the leaders of the movement seem to avoid all emphasis upon the doctrines of their predecessors either in pedagogy or in philosophy.[59] So much the more is it important, then, that the future teacher and the future educational administrator should not only be acquainted with the historic connections between the philosophy of Progressive Education and modern philosophy generally, but should also endeavor to perceive for themselves

[58] *Theaetetus,* 187.
[59] Cf. Knight, Edgar W., *Education in the United States,* Ginn and Co., 1934, Preface.

the far-reaching consequences, positive and negative (such as can be gathered from the working of previous similar doctrines), of the philosophic "lining" of the doctrine of Progressive Education.

Evolutionistic ontology and behavioristic psychology (the latter being very largely a chapter in the monistic materialistic and evolutionistic epistemology) have exercised a profound influence upon Progressive Education. This influence has been both positive and negative. On the positive side, evolutionism and its epistemological concomitant, behaviorism, emphasize the possibility of change and, consequently, of betterment and may inspire one with an optimistic outlook upon the future.

Behaviorism has challenged traditional objectives and methods of education in so far as they are unsupported by objective measurable data. It has forced the educational philosophy of essentials, based upon the belief in certain eternal unchanging human values and certain permanently valid methods of education toward those values, to restate its position. This procedure has resulted in essentialists' finding in the history of humanity new proofs in support of certain fundamental educational objectives and methods. An attempt to present some of these restated positions and the proofs supporting them will be made in Parts II and III of this volume.

The physiological conception of mental life, characteristic of behaviorism, has contributed to the promotion of research concerning the various aspects of physical education and school hygiene, particularly concerning the measures preventive of fatigue. It has contributed also to the improvement of the teaching of reading and writing by assisting in the discovery of the physical conditions which insure the proper movements of the eye and which are in general conducive to the formation of proper working habits in the processes of reading and writing. The research on tests and measurements accompanying the growth of behaviorism has contributed directly or indirectly (by forcing the traditional method of examination to prune itself of its weaker points of procedure) to the increase of objectivity in the control of school work and to the more homogeneous classification of students on the basis of intelligence, or mental age, and of achievement. Indeed, students can be somewhat more objectively judged when the judgment of the teacher and of the examining committee is fortified by scaled tests than when such judgment stands alone.

The Freudian or psychoanalytical theory of inhibitions and "complexes" resulting from inhibitions has called the attention of parents and educators to the fact that an individual is a *continuum,* that his earliest experiences are not immaterial from the point of view of the sanity of the individual throughout his or her life. Furthermore, it has taught educators the value and necessity of elasticity in the educative process, as well as enriched and perhaps also burdened the educational vocabulary with such terms as "complex," "rationalization," "defence-mechanism," "projection," and the like.

On the negative side, evolutionism has led Progressive Education to minimize the permanent, unchanging standards and objectives of education (see p. 351). Therefore, not infrequently "progressive" schools are characterized by the chaos of "curriculumless curriculums." Behaviorism, with its supposedly omnipotent mechanics of stimuli and responses, can also not illogically result in a kind of revolutionary fanatical credulity, such, for instance, as is shown by certain aspects of the communistic theory and practice in education in Soviet Russia. There behaviorism has furnished the "scientific" basis for the communistic educational objectives relative to eliminating from life the factors of private property, religious faith, and the individual family life. If it is scientifically true that everything in animal and human life is changing and changeable, as evolutionistic materialism and behavioristic psychology teach; if it is further true that one can produce through the mechanics of conditioned reflexes any kind of responses in the subject, provided that one knows how to supply the right kind of stimuli; then the communistic educational theory and practice which seek to exclude from the life of the child all religious experiences, and which teach atheism from childhood on, and contempt for the institution of marriage and for the "bourgeois" family morals generally, are scientific.

The physiological conception of the mental life of the child is responsible for the exaggerated stress that Progressive Education places upon the physical, the muscular activities of the child. There may be mentioned, also, among the negative influences of behaviorism on Progressive Education that the latter seems inclined to the abuse of experimentation upon children. Further, the movement of tests and measurements has been not a little vitiated by the deterministic attitude which is characteristic of evolutionism and behaviorism. The exaggerations involved in this attitude were foreseen and admirably analyzed many years ago by that clear-sighted thinker, Professor William C. Bagley, who stressed the importance of the student's will power and character for success in school and life side by side with his or her I.Q.[60] These and similar pedagogical exaggerations rooted in evolutionism and behaviorism have already harmed Progressive Education and, as many indications predict, may discredit it still further and thus, unfortunately, may interfere with the working of its more desirable features. But even more significant, negatively, are the ethical implications of evolutionism and behaviorism.

If everything changes, and if, consequently, there are no

[60] *Determinism in Education,* Warwick and York, 1925.

permanent moral values or moral standards; if there is no freedom of the will and, consequently, no good or bad act of man but merely a mechanically produced combination of stimuli and responses; then there is no moral responsibility. If this be true, there are no good men or bad men, no heroes and honest men, on the one hand, and no scoundrels, on the other; but simply mechanically produced " cases " of certain S-R combinations which persons unenlightened through the only scientific psychology, behaviorism, persist in calling morally good or bad men and actions.

The dividing line between the positive and the negative influence of behaviorism upon the theory and practices of Progressive Education is constituted by the philosophic implications of behaviorism. As long as behaviorism remains a purely genetic psychophysiological investigation — the science of the facts or phenomena of self — seeking to describe and explain certain phenomena found in the vast field of human nature, by trying to derive the more complex from the simple, behaviorism is a perfectly legitimate branch of psychology and is capable of rendering valuable services to educational psychology. Such has been, for example, the work of Professor E. L. Thorndike, who may be regarded as standing apart from the present-day behaviorists, as a class in himself, and who may be designated a " connectionist " pure and simple. His research seems to gravitate around the idea that learning consists in establishing new connections in the nervous system. Though one of the two real founders of modern behaviorism — the other being Professor Ivan Pavlov — Professor Thorndike has refrained, with the prudence of a cautious and disciplined scientific mind, from venturing, unless privately, into the equalitarian realm of metaphysics, where the scientist has no more authoritative entree than any layman (see p. 44). This prudence and true scientific reserve have not, unfortunately, been among the qualifications of some of his less disciplined and less cautious though able disciples, who have been carried away by the desire — not unnatural but certainly not scientifically unimpeachable — to build up a sort of behavioristic ultimate certainty and to propagate behaviorism as the only true foundation for the right outlook upon life.

As soon as the behaviorist raises the question, What is the ultimate source and basis of all the phenomena observable in the field of human nature? in other words, What is the ultimate reality? he is by definition no longer in the field of science but is in that of philosophy; to be exact, in the field of ontology or metaphysics, and he can no longer be considered a scientist. His " psychology " then is the epistemology by means of which he seeks to validate or to justify his metaphysics, open or covert. If the behaviorist still persists in claiming scientific value for his doctrine of the ultimate reality, he acts on a false premise whether or not he is aware of the fact.

The tendency to philosophic generalization is a noble and irresistible natural tendency of all keen intellects. A behaviorist is as much entitled to it as anyone else, provided he does not still claim to be a scientist. A leading behaviorist, Professor John Watson, who, in the words of Boring, " had little patience for philosophical niceties " [61] and who willingly announces in his *Psychology from the Standpoint of a Behaviorist* his contempt for philosophy, says himself, though perhaps not quite in agreement with himself: " Every human individual needs the data and laws of behaviorism for organizing his daily life and conduct." [62] In other words, Professor Watson recommends behaviorism as the basis for a philosophy of life and as the guiding principle of conduct.

When the behaviorist negates the existence of any incorporeal reality in the life of man, and asserts (without being in

[61] *Op. cit.,* p. 582.　　　　[62] Pp. 8–9.

a position to demonstrate scientifically such ultimate things) that there is no mind as an entity whose functions are distinct from the functions of the body, he is working simply at a chapter in materialistic epistemology and in support of evolutionistic monistic materialism or materialistic "naturalism" (see p. 48). It would have been better for all concerned if all behaviorists had heeded the advice of the philosopher, Professor John Dewey — who is a moderate behaviorist in psychology [63] — given in the preface to his *Psychology* published in 1886. Professor Dewey stressed the fact that an exposition of psychology inescapably presupposes certain philosophic assumptions which should be made explicit and out in the open rather than used with the pretense that they are not there:

On the other hand, there are books which attempt to leave behind all purely philosophic considerations, and confine themselves to the facts of scientific psychology. Such books certainly have the advantage of abandoning — or at least the opportunity of abandoning — a mass of material which has no part nor lot in psychology, and which should long ago have been relegated to the history of metaphysics. But one can hardly avoid raising the question whether such surrender of philosophic principles be possible. No writer can create nor recreate his material, and it is quite likely that the philosophic implications embedded in the very heart of psychology are not got rid of when they are kept out of sight. Some opinion regarding the nature of the mind and its relation to reality will show itself on almost every page, and the fact that this opinion is introduced with-

[63] Cf. Dewey, J., *Experience and Nature, cit.,* p. 285:
". . . In the hyphenated phrase body-mind, ' body ' designates the continued and conserved, the registered and cumulative operation of factors continuous with the rest of nature, inanimate as well as animate; while ' mind ' designates the characters and consequences which are differential, indicative of features which emerge when ' body ' is engaged in a wider, more complex and interdependent situation. . . ."
In other words, " mind is what body does."
See also *Philosophy and Civilization, cit.,* p. 27:
". . . The psychological tendencies which have exerted an influence on instrumentalism are of a biological rather than a physiological nature. They are, more or less, closely related to the important movement whose promoter in psychology has been Doctor John Watson and to which he has given the name of Behaviorism. . . ."

out the conscious intention of the writer may serve to confuse both the author and his reader.[64]

Behaviorism of the school of Professor John Watson and the educational theories inspired by it cannot escape the ethical implications of the ontology, for which their doctrine in psychology is an epistemological support, as man cannot escape his own shadow.

When a behavioristic psychologist or an educator inspired by behaviorism does not for one reason or another bring " out in the open " the inevitable philosophical consequences (or rather implications) of the psychological doctrine which he professes, his brighter students will. What are those consequences or implications? They are the old materialistic ethics of the ancient atomists which were re-formulated by modern forerunners of the present-day evolutionistic materialists, for example by Diderot and D'Alembert (see p. 75). Diderot, an evolutionistic materialist or " naturalist " of the eighteenth century, said: " The real goal of life consists in the enjoyments it can furnish. Drinking good wines, eating delicate foods, resting in soft beds, this is what constitutes the sense of life. The rest is nothing but vain emptiness." D'Alembert corroborated this philosophy by saying: " Oh, vanity of our thought! Oh, poverty of our glory! Oh, smallness of our outlook! There is nothing really solid or tangible but drinking, eating, loving, and sleeping." [65]

Mr. Edwin B. Holt declares triumphantly: ". . . behaviorism can rest unperturbed while the sad procession of Spirits, Ghost-Souls, transcendental Egos, and what not, passes by and vanishes in its own vapor." [66] The truth is, however, that in

---

[64] *Psychology,* American Book Co., 1898, Third Revised Edition, pp. iii–iv.
[65] Quoted in Doumic, René, *Etudes sur la Littérature Française,* Paris, Perrin, t. I, p. 148 ff.
[66] " Response and Cognition," *Journal of Philosophy,* Vol. 12, p. 405.

more cases than not where such a procession really takes place·
the departed spirits leave behind a gaping emptiness which
devours the very source from which new creation was expected to issue, as the Titans, the children of Cronus, devoured
their own father.

Professor John Watson claims that behavioristic psychology
is " a scientifically usable kind . . . in helping people to understand why they behave as they do and how to modify their behavior; and how to bring up the youth in their charge to act in
such a way that the youth can live, move, and have their being
in society, and not have their own individuality swamped and
flattened out by society." [67] This is certainly a praiseworthy
ideal. But the history of education as well as the political history
of the Western world, beginning with the Greco-Roman times,
has abundantly shown, it appears, beyond any need of costly
new experiments on human beings, that the materialistic-evolu-
tionistic recipe for happiness and for education toward the good
life can at best lead to sophistic-nihilistic individualism, when
it does not lead to a crushing single-handed or oligarchic dictatorship. Such sophistic-nihilistic individualism has several
times reappeared as a strong movement in the history of the
Western world, each time in connection with an exhausting
war and new strides in the development of natural science. The
latter was encouraged in order that its discoveries might assist
in the organization of the material side of warfare. The shortest
statement of the philosophy of life underlying this unhealthy
kind of individualism is given by Protagoras of Abdera, the outstanding sophist of the fifth century: " Man [as an individual] *
is the measure of all things, of the existence of things that are,
and of the non-existence of things that are not." [68]

---

* Bracketed remarks are added.

[67] *Psychology from the Standpoint of a Behaviorist*, J. B. Lippincott, 1924, p. 3.
[68] *Theaetetus*, 152.

The sophistic movement spread in Greece in connection with the devastating Greco-Persian wars which were accompanied by a skeptical reappraisal of values. This reappraisal, together with the enlargement of the scientific horizon of the Greeks which occurred during the Greco-Persian wars, gave impetus to an intellectual movement based upon and inspired by the doctrine negating the existence of any stable reality and asserting that there are no permanent values; that the goal of knowledge is not an immutable truth, which does not exist (because everything changes), but simply practical success.

This doctrine was propagated by fashionable wandering teachers who came to be known under the name of sophists. Originally sophist ($\sigma o \phi \iota \sigma \tau \acute{\eta} s$) meant expert. An expert in anything was called a sophist, whether the man was an expert in blacksmithing or in grammar. Next, since people not unnaturally desired to have their children trained by such experts, the term " sophist " came to designate an expert teacher. Then some smart individuals, using to their personal advantage the doctrine of change, saw that with some dialectic skill they could teach without studying hard or knowing anything definitely themselves. They declared that there cannot be any fixed subject matter. It is the method of presenting a proposition or attacking a problem that really matters. The bolder and more successful sophists announced that they would teach the method of presenting successfully any proposition to the mass of citizenry; how to prove by means of skillful verbal jugglery, first that black is white and then that white is black. This irresponsible activity of the sophists was, indirectly, the cause of the death sentence returned by the Athenian jury against Socrates, whom his personal enemies accused, untruthfully, of being a dangerous sophist, of corrupting the youth and undermining the religion of the land. The well-intentioned but uninformed citizenry was enraged against the sophists and was inclined to show no mercy to any popular teacher brought before the jury on accusation of subversive sophistic activity.

The sophistic movement that flourished in Greece from the latter part of the fifth century, B.C., to the middle of the fourth century, B.C., and that undermined the moral fibre of the Greek people, was among the important contributing causes to the downfall of Greek independence and the decadence of Greek civilization. This sophistic movement has been paralleled in subsequent centuries by several neo-sophistic movements usually following in the wake of long and arduous wars. One of these neo-sophistic movements was visited upon Rome at the end of the Punic Wars about the middle of the second century, B.C., and its dissolving effect upon the moral fibre of Rome is instructively analyzed by an eye-witness, the historian Polybius, in Books XXI and XXXIX of his *Histories*. The next notable revival of sophism was about the middle of the seventeenth century, after the wars of the later Renaissance period which culminated in the Thirty Years' War; the next was in connection with the wars of the French Revolution, 1791–1814; the next, in connection with the wars of 1850–1871; and the next is the one of our own day. Each time sophistic-nihilistic individualism, when it reached its height, led to some sort of Cæsarism and played into the hand of a strong, ruthless, shrewd, or fanatical man, be he Alexander of Macedon, or Octavius Augustus, the first of the Hohenzollerns, or Louis XIV, or Napoleon, or any one of the dictators of our own day (see p. 429).

Sophistic nihilism is readily conducive to spiritual suicide, moral dissolution, and sordid emptiness of life. It creates in the masses of people the longing for a leader who says that he knows the truth and will make it triumph by crushing the heretics and dissenters. Violent abuse, when it does not kill, calls forth a violent cure.

THE EDUCATIONAL IMPLICATIONS OF INSTRUMENTALISM

Considered as an educational influence, the pragmatism, or instrumentalism, of Dewey — " Dewey's powerful stuff," as James characterized his work in a letter to F. C. S. Schiller [69] — has been the source of both worth-while and negative inspiration for the progressives. On the positive side, instrumentalism is conducive to emphasis upon the immediately practical, usable studies, which emphasis has sometimes been insufficiently developed either as a method of motivation or subject matter in the conventional theory and practice of education. Instrumentalism has exercised some positive educational influence also in another direction, notably, by its position to the effect that the real universe is the one that corresponds to our needs, that it is transformable by our action. Such an attitude of mind may, however, be the inspiration for robust and lastingly fruitful action only when the ultimate goal of all our effort and the criterion of our values have a sufficient finality. This the instrumentalist cannot give, because instrumentalism is agnosticism, ontologically.

On the negative side, to instrumentalism may be traced, first, the narrow conception of interest and experience which is characteristic of Progressive Education. The progressives condemn all deferred values as a means of motivation in the educative process. Interest is, to the progressives, a tension toward a goal or aim immediately foreseen, and experience is knowledge acquired for the solution and by the solution of an immediate problem (see p. 118).

Second, instrumentalism has influenced Progressive Education away from definite and exacting standards. In its disbelief in any fixed reality, instrumentalism is opposed to fixed standards. This is, perhaps, why Dewey himself not infrequently lapses in his writings into vague, nebulous sentences like the following:

In effect, its [philosophy's] * function would be to facilitate the fruitful interaction of our cognitive beliefs, our beliefs resting upon the most dependable methods of inquiry, with our practical beliefs about the values, the ends and purposes, that should control human action in the things of large and liberal human import.[70]

But what is this " large and liberal human import " ? It is incomprehensible unless in terms of some final stable criterion of values; that is, in terms of something that Dewey scornfully excludes from the truly philosophic quest. " The essence of pragmatic instrumentalism is to conceive of *both* knowledge and practice as means of making goods — excellencies of all kinds — secure in experienced existence," teaches Professor Dewey.[71] But unless there is some definite scale of values by which to judge the actions of men, " excellencies of all kinds " are bound to remain vague to the point of an empty phrase. Nothing is excellent except that which, in the light of some definite scale of values, is the best among the better. In his Inglis Lecture, *The Way Out of Educational Confusion,* Professor Dewey, while deploring the confusion weighing upon the present-day educational thinking in this country, correctly states that the " confusion is due ultimately to aimlessness." [72] The future historian in all probability will attribute a considerable share of responsibility for the confusion in question to Dewey's influential pragmatic instrumentalism. At all events, his disciples among the " progressive " educators (precisely on account of the fact that their leader has failed to supply them with

---

* Bracketed remarks are added.

[70] From *The Quest for Certainty,* by John Dewey, pp. 36–37. Courtesy of Minton, Balch & Co., Publishers, New York.

[71] *Ibid.,* p. 37.

[72] Harvard University Press, p. 40.

definite and stable standards of social values) made, in connection with the short-lived doctrine of technocracy, a very instructive, negatively, *volte-face*. This change of front was subjected to penetrating analysis in the well-known paper of Professor I. L. Kandel, "Education and Social Disorder":

The most curious phenomenon in this new movement is that the new standard has been raised by the same leaders who for the past twenty years have been the most vociferous advocates of individualism, the new freedom, the child-centered school, and the sanctity of the child's ego—in a word, of laissez faire in education. The two major organizations, the Progressive Education Association and the New Education Fellowship, which for nearly two decades have been the loudest in decrying the evils of authoritarianism and of imposition from above, have preached far and wide the gospel of the individual and of the child-centered school, have consistently refused to define goals or ends in advance, and have relied on the magic of growth, self-expression, and development from within, have suddenly, in response to the social crisis . . . assumed the leadership in a new direction—social reconstruction through the school with an emphasis on planning, co-operation, and collective will. . . . Having broadcast one slogan for twenty years, the progressives have adroitly refrained from considering its consequences. It would, indeed, be inconvenient to be compelled to square the position recently assumed with that which is beginning to be discarded. . . . Hence new slogans. . . . Exploitation, the competitive spirit, every individual for himself, the cult of selfish self-centered interests and purposes have been responsible for the crisis which is upon us. . . .

The cynic may be pardoned if he seeks to prick the bubble of the new enthusiasm for social reconstruction by posing a few questions. What is the difference between individual selfishness and a philosophy which has been preaching the gospel of individual satisfactions as the mainspring of education and conduct, and which has made that which works synonymous with truth? What is the difference between exploitation and a philosophy which has found a moral sanction in the gospel of success, confirmed to the satisfaction of its exponents by a mechanistic psychology? Those who are loudest in denouncing the profit motive and the competitive spirit are fortunately able to forget that they ever propagated the theory that every child has the inherent right to ask " *Cui bono?*" [What is this good for?].* . . .

The progressives have apparently seen the light, although in their surprised discovery of the causes of social disorder they do not seem to link the principles of their own philosophy with these causes. Undirected growth, with nothing fixed in advance, is now to be replaced by social planning; personal gain is to be surrendered for the welfare of the whole; and co-operation is to be substituted for the competitive spirit. As Kilpatrick, who would have nothing fixed in advance or set out to be learned, and who has for so long protested against indoctrination and authoritarianism, now insists in his *Education and the Social Crisis,* " man has worked best when lost in common tribal causes, giving up any possible personal gain for the welfare of the whole." If this does not mean that education must grow out of and be guided consciously and not incidentally by an accepted culture, by ideals and convictions, if this does not mean that society is prior to the individual; if this does not mean that the function of education is indoctrination (in the good sense, if it must be qualified to distinguish it from indoctrination in the bad sense), then Kilpatrick's acceptance of the statement quoted is meaningless. And further, its acceptance implies that objects of social allegiance must be fixed in advance and set out to be learned.[73]

The essentialists, then, whom the progressives accuse, often *in absentia* and sometimes by contumely, of the capital crime of non-progressiveness, seem to be fully entitled to a repartee like the following, made by Socrates:

See now, most excellent Callicles, how different my charge against you is from that which you bring against me, for you reproach me with always saying the same; but I reproach you with never saying

* Bracketed remarks are added.
[73] *Teachers College Record,* February, 1933, pp. 359–364.

the same about the same thing. I wish, my good friend, that you would tell me, once for all, whom you affirm to be the better and superior, and in what particular.[74]

This oscillation on the part of the progressives from one pole of political and social theory to its opposite is due, in part at least, to the lack in their pragmatic philosophy of a stable, permanent criterion of values. They have no yardstick with which to measure social or political values. Similarly, the progressives are not in a position to offer a clear criterion by which to measure the progress of their own progressive education. They speak of the growth of the learner as the criterion of educational progress. When asked how they measure growth, they usually answer, "By further growth," or "By the leading-on" effect of the educative process. But it is plain that the doctrine of growth and "leading-on" is an empty slogan unless it means development in a desirable direction; in other words, development toward the attainment of a standard. To borrow from Professor Herman H. Horne's lucid discussion of the point in question, found in his *Democratic Philosophy of Education:*

The trio of famous statements, "Education is life," "life is growth," "education is growth," all sound well and awaken pleasurable emotional states, but they do not tell us what to do next. The trouble is we have growths as well as growth; there is a wrong way to grow as well as a right way; there is abnormal growth as well as normal growth; there are schools of crime. . . . and criteria of right growth must be set up. . . . Teachers must be able to tell when they are directing growth in the right way. . . . The very definition of growth proposed [by the progressives]* is not clear: "This cumulative movement of action toward a later result is what is meant by growth." Is there any action without a later result? What is the "movement of an action"? . . . But the difficulty lies deeper.

* Bracketed remarks are added.
[74] *Gorgias,* 491.

Growth aims at more growth, and education is subordinate only to education. This is the theory. Its weakness is, growth needs a goal.[75]

As in the case of evolutionism and behaviorism, so also in that of instrumentalism, the dividing line between the positive and negative influences of instrumentalism upon education is, in the last analysis, its ontological, or metaphysical, position. By denying the possibility and necessity of education for the ultimate certainty, instrumentalism becomes much more a source of harmful educational influence than of positive influence.

If only instrumentalism were more consistent with itself, it would encourage the inclusion of some provision for introducing at least the keener and intellectually more mature adolescents and youths to the metaphysical speculations of great thinkers, lay and religious. Education, according to instrumentalism, should occupy itself with immediate problems and needs. Indeed, the need of the ultimate certainty is to many, very early in life, and to every one — save insignificantly few exceptions — at some time in life, the problem than which there is none more immediate nor more urgent. " As soon as thought begins to seek the ' ends ' or ' aims ' to which life is subservient, it has already confessed its inability to achieve that animal acceptance of life for life's sake which is responsible for the most determinate efforts to live." [76]

The pragmatist may bid " the absolute to bury the absolute." [77] But, as Kant rightly points out in the Preface to the First Edition of the *Critique of Pure Reason:*

Human reason, in one sphere of its cognition, is called upon to consider questions, which it cannot decline, as they are presented

[75] From *Democratic Philosophy of Education,* by Herman H. Horne. By permission of The Macmillan Company, Publishers. pp. 52–53.
[76] Krutch, Joseph Wood, *The Modern Temper,* Harcourt, Brace and Co., 1929, p. 234.   [77] James, *Pluralistic Universe, cit.,* p. 129.

by its own nature, but which it cannot answer [rationally]*, as they transcend every faculty of the mind.[78]

Besides our reason's having the peculiar fate to be so constituted that it searches for reasons which it cannot evolve, " man's emotions are not satisfied when hemmed in by the order of experience; man wants to worship, to pray, and to praise. And still further, man must act and live. He prefers to do so *sub specie aeternitatis* [motivation from permanent values and truths].* Deny him this outlook, keep him *sub specie generationis* [immediate, transient motivation] and his impulses to act are not so broadly motivated as they might be." " We want a philosophy of education," concludes Professor Horne, " that will relate our work to man's transcendent as well as his social relationship. And this conclusion may well be based on the nature of man himself and the kind of world in which he lives and must live. . . . If speculation satisfies an interest of man, it is not good pragmatism to reject it." [79]

Our contemporaries are as much in need of, or in fact in quest of the ultimate certainty as people have always been. Some of them may advertise their contempt for anything that does not pay in the most metallic sense of the word. Others may appear little appreciative of the effort that certain minds make to acquire more clarity in a general outlook upon life, greater mental vigor, and especially greater spiritual elevation. To arrest our glance on the great problems of our destiny may seem to some a bizarre remnant of the past. And yet man remains man. Announce in any town of even medium size a lecture on the mystery of death, on the future of science, and do not worry about the size of the crowd; you will have enough people to

* Bracketed remarks are added.

[78] *Op. cit.*, p. xvii.

[79] From *Democratic Philosophy of Education*, by Herman H. Horne. By permission of The Macmillan Company, Publishers. p. 4.

speak before. Or establish an exotic secret sect requiring an elaborate initiation and promising the marvels of a perfect super-physical lucidity of vision; you will not lack disciples. Put forth a plan of social organization promising to make men and women better and happier; they will listen to you with an attention nourished by great hopes. Put into any newspaper an advertisement saying that you wish to correspond with some-body who is interested in the great problems of religion and morality; you will be overwhelmed by your epistolary obli-gations. Despite many a wave and vogue of materialism and paganism known to history, man inevitably remains an animal that thinks, or at least has the urge to think. Whether thought is a divine imprint or an hereditary defect, man continues to be a creature that has a remembrance of God; man still is accursed Prometheus devoured by the hawk of metaphysical anxiety. He has not the force to suppress the profound echo evoked in him by the drama of the world in which he participates. Spirit-ual suicides are hard to live through. Our souls have a hard life nowadays, to be sure, but whoever wills cannot stifle it.[80]

To our time, despite all its indulgence in pragmatism and scientism and communism and cynicism and other " isms," the analysis of man's anxiety for the metaphysical or ultimate cer-tainty which Charles Morgan put into the mouth of one of his characters, still fully applies:

Do you remember how, in Italy, early in the fifteenth century, the infusion of the Greek into the Christian vision changed the eye of certain painters, so that in the faces they painted, in the faces of

[80] Adapted from the *Revue Universitaire*, March 1931, p. 206.

Cf. Dr. Rusk of Scotland speaking at the Conference on Examinations, 1931:

". . . at the end of each session I say to my classes: ' You know what has been inflicted on you. What do you think ought to be inflicted on the next year's students? ' . . . Each year these students call for more philosophy of education and of life; and that, I think, shows that there is a conscious need of a wider culture than they acquire in their university training." (Monroe, Paul, Editor, *Conference on Examina-tions*, International Institute, 1931, Teachers College, Columbia University, p. 67.)

Botticelli, for example, there appeared always a sadness which seemed to spring from a desire to participate in two separate and opposed existences? The women of Botticelli are beings of divided mind, or, I would rather say, of divided spirit. Into their knowledge of earth, their love of it, their wish to cling to its sensible beauty, there enters the disturbing breath of aspiration. They are aware of it, but dare not accept their kinship with the angels who whisper to them; and with reluctance, but under necessity, they turn away their heads. They are saddened by visible beauty, even while they rejoice in it, because they perceive, shining distantly through it, another and absolute beauty calling to them, but by them unattainable. In the same way the infusion of the heavenly into the earthly vision changes the eye of him that experiences it, and he sees men and women, not as empty vanities, as some of spiritual pretensions have claimed, nor as self-sufficient and responsible in reason, as the materialists will have it, but as beings whose dominating character is uncertainty — uncertainty of where they are and what may be their true relation to their surroundings. . . .[81]

To assist the maturing educand in any way possible in the acquisition of the ultimate certainty seems to be one of the noblest and most important tasks of the educator. This assistance cannot be fully given through the study of natural science or through the scientific (experimental) method. The young must be brought up to seek moral sustenance in metaphysical faith when science is powerless to provide this sustenance and is too proud or too ignorant frankly to acknowledge its own epistemological insufficiency. To borrow from a statement made by Signor Guglielmo Marconi before the International Congress of Electro-Radio-Biology in September, 1934, at Venice:

The mystery of life is certainly the most persistent problem ever placed before the thought of man. There is no doubt that from the

---

[81] Reprinted from *The Fountain*, p. 382, by Charles Morgan, by permission of and special arrangement with Alfred A. Knopf, Inc., authorized publishers.

time humanity began to think it has occupied itself with the problem of its origin and its future — which undoubtedly is the problem of life. The inability of science to solve it is absolute. This would be truly frightening were it not for faith. . . .

If we consider what science already has enabled men to know — the immensity of space, the fantastic philosophy of the stars, the infinite smallness of the composition of atoms, the macrocosm and microcosm whereby we succeed only in creating outlines and translating a measure into numbers without our minds being able to form any concrete idea of it — we remain astounded by the enormous machinery of the universe.

If, then, we pass toward the consideration of the phenomena of life, this sentiment is accentuated. The complexity of the different organs which all work out in co-ordinated and determinate functions, the constant preoccupation for the conservation of the species, man's marvelous adaptation of his constitution to surroundings, the transmission of instincts, the mechanism of thought and reasoning, and, lastly, the specter of death, place man, who wishes to explain the tormenting mystery, before a book closed with seven seals.[82]

The future educational executive and the future teacher should make themselves sufficiently acquainted with the significant historic precedents of conflict between religious faith and certain leaders in the so-called positive science, as well as with the political and social implications of such conflicts known to history. This students in education can best learn in the calm and serene atmosphere of the historic perspective of the history of philosophy, which, therefore, can be legitimately regarded as a worthy source of one's working philosophy of education. They will then be in a position to speak with confidence to their inquisitive pupils about those cases of conflict, choosing for this information an appropriate place in the educative process and an appropriate form. They will also be able to impress upon their pupils the fact that humanity has heard

[82] Associated Press Dispatch, September 11, 1934.

many brilliant and sincere atheists and agnostics before our own. It has not, however, abandoned religious faith, but has carried it through all doubts and hesitations, probably helped somewhat by the fact that many brilliant and sincere scientists and philosophers have been humble believers and worshipers of the Divine Mind. This and similar historic truths which the maturing pupil may not hear elsewhere, while he may hear atheistic preachments, will at least teach him the wisdom of a suspension of judgment in the presence of doubtful data, even when such data come from most " advanced," fashionable sources. He will then remain free to hear the inner voice of his moral conscience, as well as of his common sense, and of tradition in so far as the latter represents the cumulative common sense of mankind.

Left to their own immature lights, the young pupils may give more credit and attribute more finality than the historic experience of humanity has proved wise to the various agnostic and atheistic doctrines, especially to those presented or endorsed by men who have won distinction in the field of experimental science, who are surrounded with the glamour of success, and who have in some cases made outstanding disinterested contributions to the satisfaction of the fundamental material needs of humanity. The pupil should be made to understand, above all, the simple and indubitable truth that, great as he may be in his sphere of knowledge, no scientist has any scientific authority to decide questions regarding the problem of the ultimate reality, for the simple reason that the problem of the beginning and end of all things lies, by definition, outside the realm of experimental evidence and of the " science proper " based upon it. Unassisted by properly trained teachers and educational administrators possessing a sufficiently clear and balanced philosophy of life and education, the pupil may only too readily draw from the widely spread materialistic and agnostic doctrines at best the viewpoint which Bertrand Russell, distinguished and candid contemporary exponent of materialistic "naturalism," describes as follows:

That man is the product of causes which had no prevision of the end they were achieving; that his origin, his growth, his hopes, are but the outcome of accidental collocations of atoms; that no fire, no heroism, no intensity of thought and feeling, can preserve an individual life beyond the grave; that all the labors of the ages, all the noon-day brightness of human genius, are destined to extinction in the vast death of the solar system; and that the whole temple of man's achievement must inevitably be buried beneath the débris of a universe in ruins — all these things, if not quite beyond dispute, are yet so nearly certain that no philosophy which rejects them can hope to stand. Only within the scaffolding of these truths, only on the firm foundation of unyielding despair, can the soul's habitation henceforth be safely built.[83]

We may humbly observe that "these truths" seem to lack the first and in a large measure the only qualification of a truth — the proof. As to the building "within the scaffolding of these truths . . . the soul's habitation," we submit that, according to the historic experience, the only possible kind of habitation of the soul on such a foundation is, in the final analysis, a society characterized by a more or less general hedonistic self-seeking, an almost equally subversive indifference.

Fortunately enough, the evolutionistic-materialistic "scaffolding" of supposed truths is not the only one that humanity has at its disposal. It has another set of blueprints, tools, and building material, which it actually puts to use in its brighter moments of enlightened liberalism and spiritualistic socialness. It is the duty of the school to equip the maturing man with such blueprints, tools, and building materials.

[83] *Mysticism and Life and Other Essays,* Longmans, Green and Co., 1921, p. 47 f.

In building a foundation for their own working philosophy of education and in subjecting to the searching light of their own philosophic clearing house the relative values of the various philosophies of education, the future educational administrator and teacher, while naturally attracted by the new or supposedly new theories of education, should not overlook as one of the possible sources of their own philosophy of education the school of educational thought which may be designated as " essentialist." This school of thought, among whose distinguished veteran representatives in this country are William C. Bagley, Thomas H. Briggs, Herman H. Horne, I. L. Kandel, Paul Monroe, Dean James E. Russell, Frank E. Spaulding, and George D. Strayer, insists upon the duty of educators to develop in the young fundamental attitudes, appreciations, skills, and information, the value of which has stood the test of the history of civilization and which therefore can be regarded as constant, unchanging fundamentals in the education of man, citizen, and world inhabitant.

In the presence of the neo-sophistic movement in education (see p. 134) sponsored by the Progressive Education Association and the New Education Fellowship, to the educational philosophy of constant essentials falls a task similar to that which Socrates and the Socratic schools of thought strove to carry out in connection with the sophistic movement in Greece subsequent to the Greco-Persian War. Socrates and the Socratics strove to bring the people — excited and befuddled by the hedonistic doctrine of change preached by the sophists — back to the simple unsensational truth formulated by Socrates in his counter-sophistic doctrine. This doctrine was, in substance, to the effect that there are permanent, unchanging, moral values; that not man as an individual but the consensus of opinion of humanity is the criterion of moral values and of the good life for which man should be formed by careful, systematic training. The role of the essentialists in education in our own days is very similar to that of Socrates and the Socratic philosophic schools.

As over and against evolutionistic-behavioristic determinism, the essentialists are inspired with a belief in the moral responsibility of man for his actions. Their thought is further characterized by faith in the efficacy of human will power, in the nobility of the free human personality, which, if properly developed and educated, can, in the mind of the essentialists, measure itself successfully against the blind forces of nature and the miseries of humanity resulting from those forces. The political ideal of the essentialists is in the direction of liberal-individualist democracy of the type embodied in the American Constitution. As over and against the instrumentalists' negation of permanent criteria and stable standards in life and in education, the essentialists are animated with the conviction that the history of civilization, in its cumulative experience, indicates clearly enough certain permanent criteria and standards of achievement, moral, intellectual, aesthetic, and material, and of the proper balance of those standards. They would shape the curricula, the training and selection of teachers, and the methods of teaching accordingly.

The philosophic roots of the educational philosophy of constant fundamentals reach well back into the teaching of Socrates and the Socratics, as the philosophic roots of evolutionism and behaviorism reach into the teaching of Democritus and Heraclitus. Among the recent philosophic allies of the educational philosophy of constant fundamentals may be mentioned the neo-Kantian philosophers, such as Heinrich Rickert, Wilhelm Dilthey, Rudolph Eucken, Georg Simmel, and Eduard Spranger, who have profoundly influenced the German — and

the Continental — educational philosophy of constant fundamentals. The growing influence of Henri Bergson's doctrine of
dualistic vitalism will in all probability prove to be the most
powerful ally of the essentialists.

THE DUALISTIC VITALISM OF BERGSON

The doctrine of M. Henri Bergson (1859–1941), of the
Académie Française, is set forth in his principal works: *Time
and Free Will, Matter and Memory, Introduction to Metaphysics, Creative Evolution, The Two Sources of Morality and
Religion.* Very briefly, the doctrine of Bergson (which James in
a letter of June 13, 1907, called " a real marvel, a real wonder
in the history of philosophy, making [sic!] an entirely new
era ") [84] is as follows:

Not unlike his predecessor and peer, Descartes (see p. 70),
Bergson descended into himself to search in the inner life, in
consciousness, for indications as to what true reality is. " The
existence of which we are most assured and which we know best
is our own, for of every other object we have notions which may
be considered external and superficial, whereas, of ourselves, our
perception is internal and profound." [85] The contemplation of
his inward life has convinced Bergson that

Every psychical state, simply because it belongs to a person, reflects
the whole of a personality. Every feeling, however simple it may
be, contains virtually within it the whole past and present of the
being experiencing it, and, consequently, can only be separated and
constituted into a " state " by an effort of abstraction or of analysis. . . . [86] There is no consciousness without memory, and no continuation of a state without the addition, to the present feeling, of
the memory of past moments. It is this which constitutes duration.
Inner duration is the continuous life of a memory which prolongs

[84] *Letters of William James, cit.,* Vol. II, pp. 290–291.
[85] *Creative Evolution, cit.,* p. 1.
[86] *Introduction to Metaphysics, cit.,* p. 25.

the past into the present, the present either containing within it in a distinct form, the ceaselessly growing image of the past, or, more probably, showing by its continual change of quality the heavier and still heavier load we drag behind us as we grow older. Without this survival of the past into the present there would be no duration, but only instantaneity.[87]

Man's consciousness is nothing but awareness of his "undivided continuity," or of "the constitutive duration of his own being."[88] The "inner duration" is, then, the true reality of our inner life. The only reliable method of perfectly knowing this reality, consists in seizing it directly without the intermediary of any symbols, concepts, or words — in seeing it intuitively.

The intuition of inner duration is a simple, *i.e.*, not a compound act (see p. 56). It is "an inner absolute knowledge of the duration of the self by the self,"[89] a direct seeing of a whole by a whole. Similar internal, direct, intimate knowledge of all reality is, according to Bergson, the real object of true metaphysics, which in that way would become at last its true self, namely, the perfect science of reality, "a serious occupation of the mind" and not any longer a "play of ideas."[90] Metaphysics, to Bergson, "is the science which claims to dispense with symbols."[91] It is the crowning point of true philosophizing. The office of philosophy is, then, a methodical organization and accumulation of the intuition of duration.[92]

All true reality is like that of our inner life. It is inner duration, or the mobility of unity. As with the inner duration of our consciousness, the present of all reality implies the past. Therefore, "we do not obtain an intuition from reality . . . unless we have won its confidence by a long fellowship with its external manifestations. . . . A mass of facts must be accumu-

[87] *Ibid.*, pp. 44–45.   [88] *Ibid.*, pp. 15–16.
[89] *Ibid.*, p. 24.   [90] *Ibid.*, p. 21.
[91] *Ibid.*, p. 9; *Matière et Mémoire*, p. iii.
[92] Cf. *Introduction to Metaphysics, cit.*, pp. 74–75.

lated and fused together. . . ." [93] The simplicity of the act of intuition, or " a direct taking possession " of reality, presupposes a great effort and a great complexity of preparation. In the words of Bergson, to picture intuition as something consisting " in watching oneself merely live, ' as a sleepy shepherd watches the water flow,' . . . would be to misconceive the singular nature of duration, and at the same time the essentially active, I might almost say violent, character of metaphysical intuition." [94]

Being of that simplicity which is preceded by a great complexity, the intuition of duration is not a mysterious faculty possessed by supermen, Bergson reassures us. [95]

But then the following question arises: If man's consciousness is awareness of his " undivided continuity," or of " the constitutive duration of his own being," how can forgetfulness be explained? Bergson gives the following explanation. If we were purely spiritual, incorporeal beings, unmixed with matter, then the awareness of all our past at any moment of our present would be complete and unfailing. But we are not purely spiritual beings; we have body as well as spirit. The body must respond to external impressions by certain adapted reactions. Power of attention is, as a result, spread or scattered in the present and distracted by it and cannot envelop our past states of consciousness like a current running freely about the whole of our past. We cannot maintain life without constant attention to the present because this attention brings about the adaptation of our bodies to external conditions without which adaptation we should perish. The body is not, however, a curse to our spiritual life. If it were not for the body, man would be an idle dreamer. The body is the ballast which prevents the mind from losing itself in aimless digressions. More than this, the body is a sort of instrument of selection which forces man to choose

[93] *Ibid.*, p. 91.　　[94] *Ibid.*, pp. 55–56.　　[95] *Ibid.*, pp. 89, 90, 91, 92.

from among the images of the past such as permit him to inter-
pret and utilize the present. Consequently, it is the principle
of utility that produces, in the last analysis, the discontinuity of
memory.

It is, then, our intelligence, or power of comprehension, that
incessantly introduces discontinuity into our view of things and
of ourselves, in other words, of the external and of the inner
world. What is the true nature of our intelligence? Intelligence,
according to Bergson, is a function of life. But what is life? Life
is a twofold movement: (a) of " procession," " spreading," or
" externalization; " and (b) of " tenseness," or " conversion," or
" concentration." Life is something that strives to organize matter in living beings by accumulating on certain points reservoirs
of energy capable of spending themselves suddenly. We cannot
grasp the twofold movement or the dual principle of life except
in the form of the *élan vital,* vital impetus, *i.e.,* impetus toward
a more complete life in plants, animals, men. We cannot seize
the dual principle of life except as an effort which the vital
impetus makes to liberate itself from the matter which it ani-
mates and in which it loses itself, so to say, in order to come into
a fuller possession of itself.

The vital impetus employs two instruments, instinct and intelligence. Instinct is a perfect tool but of limited application. Instinct finds its supreme realization in the perfect and perfectly
stable societies of the *hymenoptera,* like ants, bees, wasps. Instinct furnishes a perfect knowledge of the object with which it
occupies itself, but of that object only. Intelligence, on the other
hand, though imperfect, is perfectible or progressive, and finds
its application in human societies which, like intelligence itself,
are imperfect but also progressive, *i.e.,* capable of improvement.

So if the ants, for instance, have a language, the signs which compose it must be very limited in number, and each of them, once the
species is formed, must remain invariably attached to a certain op-

eration: the sign is adherent to the thing signified. In human society, on the contrary, fabrication and action are of variable form, and, moreover, each individual must learn his part, because he is not pre-ordained to it by his structure. So a language is required which makes it possible to be always passing from what is known to what is yet to be known. . . . *The instinctive sign is* adherent, *the intelligent sign is* mobile.[96]

The crowning point of the work of intelligence consists in liberating spirit from servitude to matter by preparing for the spirit a road to intuition, that is, to the perfect way of knowledge of the true reality. Intelligence is, then, a "procession" or "spreading" which prepares the way for "conversion" or "tenseness" of intuition, the supreme form of which is religion as it comes to birth in prophets, saints, and mystics, which tears man away from and raises him beyond the limitations of human societies.

In short, the fundamental reality of life is twofold or dual. It is "spreading" or "externalization" or "procession" which goes the way of materiality, but it is also "tenseness," "concentration," "conversion," which goes the way of spirituality. The supreme unity is found in God, the eternal Being and the Creator, whose being is characterized by fully and perfectly concentrated inner duration. The path for penetrating into the substance of the true reality is furnished by intuition. Consequently, the metaphysics born of the intuition of inner duration is a science of high practical value, in distinction from the traditional metaphysics of the purely speculative nature distant from life.

THE PEDAGOGY OF BERGSON

Count Keyserling, in his *Creative Understanding,* deplores the tendency of present-day culture to be what he calls the

[96] Bergson, Henri, *Creative Evolution*, pp. 157–158. Henry Holt and Company.

culture of making all things easy.[97] This tendency seems to be translated to education, in places, by so conceiving educational method as if all things in civilization were or could really be made easy without anyone's ever having exercised an effort to produce them. Indeed, it is not altogether without foundation that ever more frequently " cubism " in education is lamented by thoughtful teachers and parents. Bergson, also, dissuades us from trying to preserve the existing civilization or to build a more satisfactory one by the method of " taking it easy."

It appears that two important suggestions relative to educational method are implied in Bergson's theory of knowledge. The first is to the effect that the simplicity of perfect knowledge presupposes the complexity of preliminary concentrated study.

To be sure, there is as little virtue in making studies harder than good systematic studies inevitably are as there would be in making people go long distances on foot and carry burdens on their backs while there are means of motor transportation available. But it is of importance that pupils be duly impressed with the fact that the various devices facilitating our lives have come to be, not by playing ball or dancing jazz or otherwise idling, but by hard study and systematic application on the part of somebody. Something very important educationally is missed when school children are not shown — to continue our simile — that many people have worked very hard to build the means of transportation which make our locomotion an easy process.

When a king asked Euclid, the mathematician, if he could explain his art to him in a more compendious manner, the scholar answered that there was no royal road to geometry. Nothing has changed in this respect since the days of Euclid. In consequence, Bergson teaches that there are no short cuts to perfect knowledge.

The second important suggestion of Bergson relative to edu-

[97] Harper & Brothers, 1929, pp. 75–81.

cational method is to the effect that all true understanding is creative. This seems a most valuable suggestion as compared with the doctrine of Progressive Education to the effect that nothing except free, *i.e.,* undirected activity (however erratic!) and self-nourished thinking (however meagre in content!) are means of satisfying and developing the creative impulses of the child.

To illustrate his thought, Bergson says:

Can we follow a mathematical calculation presented by somebody if we are not continually doing it over in our own mind for our own sake? Can we understand the solution of a problem given by somebody unless we solve the problem, in turn, ourselves? To be sure, the calculation is presented on the blackboard and the solution is printed in our text or exposed by the teacher *viva voce.* But the figures we see are merely so many way-posts to which we are looking back in order not to deviate from the route we have to make; the sentences we read or hear would not have their complete meaning to us were we not capable of finding that meaning by re-creating it, so to say, in our own mind and by our own effort, while express-ing, in our turn, the mathematical truth that those sentences contain and develop.[98]

That effort be strong and methodical, that quality be pursued in intellectual work, are the basic principles of Bergson's pedagogy.

THE RESIDUAL FUNCTIONS OF THE PHILOSOPHY OF EDUCATION

In working out his or her own philosophy of education, the future educational administrator and the future teacher may well be guided by the idea of the residual function of the school. It is rightly said that the function of the school in the service of the individual and of society is residual. In other words, the school must strive to develop in the pupils worth-while atti-

[98] *Revue Philosophique,* janvier 1902, p. 12.

tudes, appreciations, aptitudes, information, and skills, such as neither the individual pupil himself nor social agencies other than the school — for instance, the family, or religious, scientific, political, economic, or recreational organizations — are in a position to develop or seek to develop. Hence many important details of school work change from one stage of civilization to another and even from one community to another in the same civilization.

Take a very simple example. In a school whose clientele comes very largely from families poor economically and backward culturally, one of the several residual tasks of the teacher will be to teach the children the elementary habits of cleanliness and elementary manners demanded in a civilized society. On the other hand, the teacher, whose pupils are very largely the children of families possessing hereditary wealth, should consider it as one of the residual tasks to implant in the pupils certain valuable attitudes (which the family may totally fail to develop in the children, or may never even try to develop), such as earnestness, or the attitude of respect and sympathy for the honest labor of those less fortunate economically.

Similarly, at a time pervaded by radical revolutionary tendencies, it would be the duty of the teacher tactfully but firmly to call the attention of the students to the dangers and absurdities of violent social revolutions as shown by history. Contrariwise, in a conservative community composed of the privileged, it would be proper to acquaint the students with the dangers and moral injustice of the abuse of power and influence on the part of the privileged as abundantly demonstrated in the fall of the insensitive ruling classes in the various countries of the world.

The task of the philosophy of education is likewise a residual task. The philosophy of education must contribute, to the consideration of educational objectives and methods, a " strategical " point of view which is unlikely to be sufficiently heeded by other branches of pedagogy, not unnaturally occupied with the various problems of educational " tactics " (see p. 30).

The purpose of the future educational administrator or the future teacher in studying the philosophy of education is, then, in the last analysis, to work out his own practical philosophy of education, and to build up a philosophic clearing house. In such a clearing house, conflicting claims upon the educand and upon the teaching process presented by various social and private factors, by the various branches of the science of education and various philosophies of education, can be gathered for critical " strategical " evaluation.

In the attainment of this purpose of study in the field of the philosophy of education, the student of education should, it seems, let his or her thought find a tenable orientation between the basic polarities of all human relationship: the *ego,* or the individual, and the *alter,* or the social — man being at one and the same time an egotistic and an altruistic creature. As is the nature of polarities, the basic polarities of all human relationship limit and expand, attract and repel each other. But the degree of harmony between the basic polarities of human relationship is not pre-established in a fixed form. It is, as history shows, subject to alteration, positive or negative in its results, by man's wisdom or lack of it.

Through studies in philosophy, as well as in the various branches of pedagogy, the future teacher or administrator is preparing for a residual service both to the individual and to society, which service should consist in contributing to the strength of this harmony in the nation, and among mankind in general. He can profit, it seems, by organizing his thought further in connection with what appears to be the fundamental residual educational problems — three in number — gravitating around the polarity of the *ego,* or the individual, and three fundamental residual educational problems gravitating around the polarity of the *alter,* or the social.

The three problems of the first group appear to be: (a) assisting the educand toward general orientation amidst the facts of the animate and inanimate world and the interdependence of these two worlds, by training him in the most fertile methods possible relative to the acquisition of a working store of facts, that is to say, experience; (b) assisting the educand toward an analysis, as correct as is humanly possible, of the facts of experience, by training him in intellectual discipline; (c) assisting the educand toward translating the meaning of experiences into the right disposition and into the right action, by developing in him a good character. The three fundamental residual educational problems of the second group appear to be: (a) training the educand toward an intelligent participation in the advancement of social progress; (b) training the educand toward an intelligent participation in the organization of relations between his nation and other nations; (c) training the educand toward an intelligent participation in the promotion of leadership within the nation.

In the chapters that follow, these fundamental problems of education will be considered in the light of the residual services of the school to the individual and society, and of the residual function of the philosophy of education within the science of education. On the other hand, such worth-while things as the individual educand is likely to learn satisfactorily of his own accord, or which the various legitimate social agencies can satisfactorily teach him or guide him toward doing, will be omitted from the scope of our analysis and meditation. Similarly, pedagogical problems relative to educational objectives and methods which constitute a definite sphere of action and influence of the various definite specialized branches of the science of education — such as physical education, or vocational education — in which sphere those branches of education are alone competent, are not included in the discussion that follows.

SUGGESTIONS FOR READING

Adams, Sir John, *Educational Theories* (Ernest Benn)

Bagley, William C., *Education and Emergent Man* (Thomas Nelson)

Bode, B. H., *Modern Educational Theories* (Macmillan)

Boring, E. G., *A History of Experimental Psychology* (Century)

Bréhier, E., *Histoire de la Philosophie* (Félix Alcan)

Burtt, E. A., *Metaphysical Foundations of Modern Science* (Harcourt, Brace)

Cresson, A., *Les Systèmes Philosophiques* (Armand Colin)

Dewey, John, *The Quest for Certainty: A Study of the Revolution of Knowledge and Action* (Minton, Balch)

Eddington, A. J., *The Nature of the Physical World* (Macmillan)

Edman, J., *The Contemporary and His Soul* (Cape and Smith)

Horne, H. H., *The Democratic Philosophy of Education* (Macmillan)

Joad, C. E. M., *Essays in Common Sense Philosophy* (Allen and Unwin)

Kandel, I. L., *The Philosophy Underlying the System of Education in the United States* (Educational Yearbook, 1929, Bureau of Publications, Teachers College, Columbia University)

Murphy, G., *A Historical Introduction to Modern Psychology* (Harcourt, Brace)

Roback, A. A., *Behaviorism and Psychology* (The University Bookstore, Cambridge, Mass.)

Part Two

THE FUNCTIONING OF THE PHILOSOPHY OF EDUCATION IN THE SCHOOL'S RESIDUAL SERVICE TO THE INDIVIDUAL

CHAPTER
IV

EXPERIENCE AND EXPERIMENT
AS METHODS OF LEARNING

EXPERIENCE AND EXPERIMENT AS METHODS OF EDUCATION

THE THREEFOLD RESIDUAL FUNCTION OF THE SCHOOL IN DEVELOPING A HUMAN PERSONALITY

Among the residual functions of the school there are three fundamental services to the individual which, when it is properly conceived and organized, the school alone can render. Those functions are relative to the training of the individual educand in the methods of accumulation and verification of experience and of action in accordance with experience. To use technical pedagogical terms, the three fundamental residual services of the school to the individual which will be studied in the second part of the present volume bear upon (a) experience and experiment as methods of learning, (b) intellectual training, (c) character formation.

To be sure, individual educands normally help themselves much toward the development of their experience, intellectual efficiency, and character. It is also true that besides the school the various other social agencies, public and private, like the family, the church, clubs, the press, the radio, and films may and usually do exercise influence upon the educand with relation to each of the three educational objectives stated above. Such self-help and such external influence may be direct or indirect, intentional or casual. The role and the responsibility of the school concerning the growth and pruning of the maturing individual's experience, his or her ability to verify and crystallize experience, and to translate it into worthy conduct retains, nevertheless, the character of a fundamental service and responsibility.

The individual educand has, normally, adverse as well as favorable tendencies and inclinations relative to the building of a worth-while experience and of intellectual and moral discipline. The educand must, therefore, be assisted by the school toward the triumph of the better self. The various other social agencies and organizations, private or public, are not necessarily as well equipped as is the school, for the intellectual and moral training of the maturing individual toward the good life; neither is any other institution so fully and directly entrusted with the task, by the family and the nation. The work of the school is supplementary to the work done by other organizations and agencies — working in the same direction — when they are competent, well-intentioned, and their work is good. When this is not the case, the work of the school must be, in so far as possible, corrective, and above all, preventive of the pupil's own shortcomings and of injurious influences upon the experience, the intellectual training, or the character of the maturing individual, irrespective of the sources from which such undesirable influences come. These three, experience, intellectual training, and character, are intimately interrelated and form a threefold basis for the development of human personality, and therefore a threefold educational objective. But the problem of experience seems to be primary in the genesis of the human personality as over and against bestiality. It will, therefore, be studied first.

WHAT IS EXPERIENCE?

"Experience" is a highly fascinating term. No one can be more conscious of its market value than the young educator without experience when in competition with another who can boast the "required" two years. In the words of the Greek sage, "Experience makes the days of men proceed according to art, and inexperience according to chance." [1]

Experience is defined in philosophy as the fact of being affected not by something that is a transitory, fleeting, fugacious impression which leaves no vestige or trace in the sum total of our knowledge and thought, but by something which broadens and enriches our minds. It may also be defined as the ensemble of modifications produced by life (in other words, by the functioning of our mental and physical powers) in the adaptability, insight, and foresight of an individual and of the species as a whole.

The Aristotelian definition of experience appears to have prevailed throughout the subsequent history of philosophy, including modern times:

Now from memory experience is produced in men; for the several memories of the same thing produce finally the capacity for a single experience. And experience seems pretty much like science and art, but really science and art come to man *through* experience; for "experience made art," as Polus says, "but inexperience luck." But yet we think that *knowledge* and understanding belong to art [an analytical knowledge] * rather than to experience [unanalyzed or only partially analyzed sense impressions] *, and we suppose artists ["masterworkers" or experts] * to be wiser than men of experience [which implies that Wisdom depends in all cases rather on knowledge] *; and this because the former know the cause, but the latter do not. For men of experience know that the thing is so, but do not know why, while the others know the "why" and the cause. [2]

Our everyday language combines these definitions of experience. Any kind of knowledge that we possess, or that we think we possess, which rightly or wrongly teaches us how best to

---

* Bracketed remarks are added.
[1] *Gorgias*, 448.
[2] *Metaphysica*, 980^b, 981^a (*Works*, Oxford, Clarendon Press, 1928, Vol. VIII).

act in a situation with which we are confronted in actuality or in our imagination, is called experience. Moreover, such knowledge is our own experience in so far as it is preserved in our memory and in the measure that we can summon it to assist us when we need its aid in facing a new situation. It is immaterial from the standpoint of the result of the application of an experience whether we have acquired it by personal doing, undergoing, and analysis of our doing and undergoing, or whether we have borrowed it from the personal experience of others. The vital factor is the degree of helpfulness of an experience in solving a problem. One man knows from his personal trial-and-error experience in the capacity of a responsible officer of the treasury of the State that the progressive income tax is a wholesome form of taxation. Another man may have formed the same idea from what was taught him in school and from subsequent reading. When the problem of income tax comes up in an electoral campaign, they presumably vote identically in the light of the conclusion which they have in common, though each has arrived at it in a different way. One has reached his conclusion by the processes of first-hand experience, the other by the means of indirect or second-hand experience.

FIRST-HAND EXPERIENCE AND SECOND-HAND EXPERIENCE CONTRASTED

The difference in practical value between one experience and another is determined by the accuracy of the conclusion which we can draw from it and by the ingenuity of the application which we can make of it. Our information may be first-hand or second-hand, but its value as experience depends on what we can do with it. Schiller never saw the " Switzerland, of which his *William Tell* contains such vivid descriptions "; neither did he see the falls of the Rhine pictured in the beautiful verses of *The Diver*.

Any one who has ever stood by the Falls of the Rhine will involuntarily recall, at the sight, the beautiful strophe in *The Diver* in which this confusing tumult of waters, that so captivates the eye, is depicted; and yet no personal view of these rapids had served as the basis for Schiller's description.

But whatever Schiller did acquire from his own experience he grasped with a clearness which also brought distinctly before him what he learned from the description of others. Besides, he never neglected to prepare himself for every subject by exhaustive reading. Anything that might prove to be of use, even if discovered accidentally, fixed itself firmly in his memory; and his tirelessly-working imagination, which, with constant liveliness, elaborated now this now that part of the material collected from every source, filled out the deficiencies of such second-hand information.[3]

In a manner quite similar he made the spirit of Greek poetry his own, although his knowledge of it was gained exclusively from translations. In this connection he spared himself no pains. Similar methods of acquiring new experience and of completing and perfecting our own previously gained experience are, fortunately, within the reach of all of us in the measure of our intelligence and effort.

This is not, however, an attempt to minimize the importance of first-hand experience, but rather to warn against the disparagement of so-called second-hand or vicarious experience. To be sure, all other conditions being equal, a direct experience impresses us more vividly and leaves deeper traces in our memory than one indirectly gained by hearing or reading about the direct or first-hand experiences of other people. Yet the former is not necessarily more valuable for future reference than the latter. To have experienced much does not mean that much experience is gained. As Carlyle has observed, "In every object there is inexhaustible meaning; the eye sees in it what the eye

[3] Humboldt, Wilhelm von, *Schiller and the Process of His Intellectual Development*, German Classics, J. B. Lyon Co., Vol. IV, pp. 42–43.

brings the means to see." [4] Some eye-witnesses have proved unreliable. A first-hand experience is not necessarily an experience of first-rate value; neither is a second-hand experience necessarily of second-rate significance. In serious matters of health, for instance, we seek the advice of a good physician, and thus get a second-hand experience which helps us to meet the unpleasant situation called illness rather than be guided by our own lights and be assisted by our own clumsy findings. We give then the preference to a second-hand rather than to a first-hand experience.

SECOND-HAND EXPERIENCE AND DEMOCRACY

The worth-while experience of others, embodied in the spoken, written, or printed word, is common mental or spiritual wealth. Among the birthrights of the child is the right to culture; in other words, the right to share in the accumulated experience of humanity. This right of the child seems to be the basis of all the fundamental rights and duties of a man and citizen in a democracy.

Indeed, a democratic form of government is very largely based on vicarious experience. If the average voter could not be guided on subjects such as the tariff, free trade, and protectionism by knowledge based largely on the recorded worth-while direct experience of others, how could he vote intelligently on such issues? How can the average citizen, on the other hand, acquire first-hand experience sufficient to enable him to see his way clearly concerning the problems mentioned or similarly difficult problems, for example, currency inflation, naval armaments, and the like?

In a word, the practical civic issue involved in the educational problem of experience building seems to be this: either people can, and the public school should, help them to gain adequate

[4] *The French Revolution*, P. F. Collier, 1900, Vol. I, p. 6.

experience about many important things without actually handling them, and thus acquiring a first-hand experience about them, or democracy is a contradiction in terms and is doomed to be displaced by the rule of bureaucrats who have acquired their expert knowledge through first-hand experience, through the method of doing.

Much has been written lately about the trial of democracy. It would certainly be a very unfair trial if the public school should fail to arm the maturing citizen with the largest possible amount of what the progressives somewhat disdainfully call second-hand experience. In a democracy the school, in order to fulfill its duty, must send out into the adult community youths who have appropriated by means of second-hand experience, *i.e.,* primarily through book learning, as much of the existing wealth of human experience as is compatible with the satisfaction of other legitimate needs of the young and of other legitimate aims of education. But, first and foremost, the school must arm the growing citizen with the tools needed to facilitate his access to the wealth of the collective experience of civilization and to assist him or her in the selection of the best of the recorded pertinent experience. It is evident that these tools are reading and well-disciplined reasoning.

Of course, if boys and girls on leaving school cannot make a better use of their book learning than slowly and faultily to read comic cuts and mural scribblings, then they would better have spent more of their time at school in gardening, bricklaying, sewing, and the like. But there is no reason to think that properly conducted schools cannot achieve better results than those just described unless the intelligence of the student prohibits it. " No torch, though lit from Heaven, illumes the blind! " says the poet.[5] On the other hand, it is not impossible for the school to train the young to " Read not to contradict and confute, not

[5] Schiller, *The Lay of the Bell*, German Classics, *cit.,* Vol. III, p. 66.

to believe and take for granted, nor to find talk and discourse, but to weigh and consider. Reading maketh a full man; conference a ready man; and writing an exact man." [6]

To be sure, bookishness such as was criticized by Francis Bacon in his discussion of purely verbal and verbose "delicate learning" is not the most desirable result of learning from books, but neither is it the only possible result. It is possible to educate the normal child to weigh and consider what he reads and to habituate him not to separate books from life, but to look on a good book as a record of impressions, observations, and reflections of persons who are more wise and more sensible than the average man and to whom it is interesting and profitable to listen. It is not at all inevitable that book learning should make bookworms of our students. It is entirely within the limits of the possible to train our students to be, rather, book interlocutors who, in the words of Bacon, " read . . . to weigh and consider."

Naturally, the individual aptitudes and endowment of the students have to be taken into account as far as possible in the arrangement of book studies. To one student, history may be nothing but dull records of remote and irrelevant events, the study of which is an annoying and hateful imposition. The whole thing is to him merely so many empty words. To another, it is a delightful open book in which he can read the sentiments, passions, and thoughts of the past. A literary discourse to one student is a ravishing excursion full of beautiful sights and excitingly hard climbing. The same discourse to one who does not understand the subjects treated is a nuisance and a waste of time.

The average student, however, can develop under proper school conditions a sufficiently strong taste for worth-while book learning. Purely mental work — in a reasonable measure

[6] Bacon, Francis, *Of Studies,* Oxford, Clarendon Press, 1890, p. 342.

— done while sitting still, may be an acceptable form of activity to every normal child at any time of his school life. He needs only to be properly stimulated and to have the work periods rightly placed in a round of well-directed and varied activities. The validity of the idea that children like to be constantly on the move, and cannot bear book learning and sitting still, is open to question. Yes, children want to be active; but this means simply that their minds must be occupied. There is nothing predetermined as to the nature of the occupation. It may come from and through motor and muscular activity, or it may consist in so-called purely mental work in which a very small part is played by muscular movements. Reading an interesting book is an activity which stimulates the appetite as good foods do. Furthermore, a good book can, in the case of every normal boy or girl, fulfill the important functions of which an object lesson and direct participation in a stimulating activity are capable. It awakens thought and sends it into new channels, promotes inquiry, imagination, and reflection, and increases the desire for further knowledge, to say nothing of the fact that the book is the sublime and supreme democratic tool of civilization that extends the life of the reader in time and space by bringing to him something that a rich man could not buy for all his wealth, before the spread of the art of writing and printing, notably, the experiences of many lives, or — as the poet expressed it — " the slow results of swiftly flowing life." [7] It is not a bizarre exaggeration to say that the moment a child discovers for himself the joy of reading, his real education is accelerated. And how infinitely pleasant is that wandering in the immense world of thought and deed, where at every turn each little Columbus may discover beautiful new lands full of lovely pictures, heroic deeds, and great adventures!

[7] Pushkin, Alexander, *Boris Godunov: A Drama in Verse*, Kegan Paul, London, p. 48.

MAN'S MEMORY AND CIVILIZATION

In the words of Sophocles, a wise man is wise because, from observing the experiences of the past, he " anticipates what the future will bring." [8] This is especially true with regard to the wisdom necessary in the conduct of the relationships of men — in other words, in politics, taking the term in its honorable meaning as defined by Aristotle. His definition is to the effect that politics is the art and science of leading human groups in pursuit of "the highest good," that is, of the good of all.[9] In problems relative to the subject matter of the natural sciences, the wise man is the one who is familiar with and knows how to use the latest discoveries of the sciences; in problems relative to the subject matter of the social sciences, that is to say, concerning human minds in their inter-relationship, the necessary wisdom cannot well be secured just by reading the latest copies of the leading magazines treating of social problems, or even by studying a few of the latest college textbooks — though they be good ones — in sociology, politics, and economics. In addition to good will and a good mind, a long experience of men, their passions, ideals, aspirations, and failings is a necessary pre-condition for wise political action as well as for wise discrimination between forgotten mistakes and truly new and fertile ideas. Such experience cannot be sufficiently gained unless we extend our limited life, both in space and in time, by being present, so to speak, in all lands and in all times whose political history is recorded in reliable documents. History can render its full service when it is remembered not only by students in politics but also — in a reasonable degree — by the public at large.

It is unfortunate, therefore, that in recent times many mem-

[8] *Oedipus the King*, 916 f.
[9] Cf. Aristotle, *Ethica Nicomachea*, 1180e-1181a, *Works*, Oxford, Clarendon Press, 1925, Vol. IX; *Politica*, 1252c, *Ibid.*, Vol. X.

bers of the teaching profession have regarded the deprecation of memory work a necessary qualification for the title of progressive educator. The truth of the matter is that memory is one of the most important and valuable intellectual possessions of man as an individual and as a species. Napoleon has well expressed this when he said that a head without memory is like a fortress without a garrison. It is well said, also, that man is man because he remembers. The collective memory of humanity is the primary secret of its kingly superiority over other creatures. For example, it is due to his collective memory, or tradition, and to his civilization conditioned on the cumulative memory, that man is still hunting elephants even more successfully than centuries ago; while the elephant, though the oldest and one of the brightest inhabitants of earth, is ever easy game for man because of the absence of cumulative memory in the mental equipment of the species.

The New Education or the Activity Movement seems to be committing a gross historic error when it places great stress upon learning by doing and is disdainful of systematic memory work. Learning by doing is a very old method, and when proposed as the method of learning and teaching, is as much of an anachronism as is the frontier type of civilization to which it was naturally suited. It can be suited only in a very limited degree to our complex and congested modern life, which demands, for the continuity and improvement of civilization, men and women of broad culture and accurate knowledge, who are capable of intensive, systematic, sustained, and correct thinking on the basis of data as multiple and as exact as possible. If it is the lot of humanity, as it seems to be, to advance at the price of costly errors, then common sense demands that those errors should not be repeated. Learning by doing, and gaining experience at first hand by trial-and-error, must not degenerate into trying old errors under the name of new and revolutionizing

ideas. The knowledge of any significant error of their predecessors, in their own land or in other lands, will, in the case of
leaders and citizens of good faith and satisfactory intelligence,
increase their civic competence by adding to their native five
senses a new sense, as it were, from each important error committed by other leaders and other communities under similar
circumstances.

No one would assert that people ought not to put into their mode
of life, and into the conduct of their concerns, any impress whatever
of their own judgment, or of their own individual character. On
the other hand, it would be absurd to pretend that people ought to
live as if nothing whatever had been known in the world before they
came into it; as if experience had as yet done nothing towards showing that one mode of existence, or of conduct, is preferable to
another.[10]

It is not only that the quantity of the personal capital of experience of each of us, whether acquired at first hand or at
second hand, depends considerably upon our memory; the
quality of our experience depends much upon the cumulative
memory of humanity. We are assisted in the proper evaluation
and further perfection of our own and other people's creations
by our recollection, however subconscious, of the highest examples of precision, clarity, and depth of the intellectual work
of great minds, and by our remembrance of beauty in great
works of art.

It is also useful to bear in mind that in addition to the intellectual and artistic geniuses of humanity, there are also what
may be called moral geniuses — in other words, men and
women who have given the noblest manifestations of the purer,
higher side of human nature. Inasmuch as direct contact with
genius, intellectual or moral, is necessarily the privilege of very
few persons, an indirect contact through our study of the crea-

[10] Mill, J. S., *On Liberty,* The Harvard Classics, Vol. 25, p. 262.

tion of genius is the only opportunity afforded the majority of us to learn from them. For enriching and stimulating the educand's intellectual experience, indirect mental contact with outstanding minds is of indisputable value to the young (see p. 231). Memory, consequently, should be developed and perfected in the child as fully as is compatible with satisfying other legitimate educational objectives. In the words of Hegel:

> The true significance of the admonition, "Know thyself," lies not as much in the psychological self-knowledge of the individual gained through introspection as in the historical knowledge about man. The psychological self-knowledge of the individual and his faculties is in reality nothing but an abstract partial knowledge, something subordinate to a higher knowledge which is the knowledge of the aptitudes and powers of human nature as they have revealed themselves in both the physical and the spiritual realm amidst forces, influences, and circumstances in the various latitudes and longitudes. It is in such knowledge that the real man can be found, and such knowledge is the only veritable knowledge of man, *i.e.,* of human nature.[11]

Such is one of the meanings of the saying, "Man is man because he remembers."

FIRST-HAND EXPERIENCE AS THE BASIS FOR SECOND-HAND EXPERIENCE

Assuredly, a certain amount of first-hand experience is necessary in order to enable us to share in the experience of others, to understand what they are talking about, to capitalize their experience, as it were. No one can learn from Edison's discoveries in electricity without having seen with his own eyes the functioning of at least a dynamo machine. Socrates asked with good reason: "How can a man understand the name of that of which he does not know the nature?"[12] A certain capital of percep-

[11] *The Philosophy of Religion,* French edition, Véra, Vol. II, Chap. II, p. 6.
[12] *Theaetetus,* 147.

tions, of root meanings, is necessary to start our mental operations toward building and enriching our experience. The more we have of such capital, the better. All increase of it is beneficial to our mental operations relative to experience building, just as increase of financial capital is beneficial to business.

As educators, however, we have always to consider the limitations of time and space which restrict the quantity as well as quality of our first-hand experience. If one may say so, a pound of first-hand experience of mediocre quality should not be acquired at the expense of missing ten pounds of more valuable second-hand experience.

Our students then should be encouraged, within reasonable limits, to make personal acquaintance of things and to learn their properties by actual handling. These limits should be determined by carefully and judiciously balancing the various legitimate but often conflicting claims upon education in a democracy. We must never lose from sight, in this operation of co-ordination and balancing, the two following considerations:

First, one great menace to the stability and efficiency of democracies is the ignorance of indispensable fundamentals of the various aspects of social and political life — from lack of schooling or from poor schooling — on the part of the citizens. An ancient Greek thinker, a man familiar with the ways of democracies, has rightly said: " There is nothing more daring or more pernicious than ignorance." [13] Another thinker, who witnessed the coming of the French Revolution and of its abuses, made many sad reflections upon " ignorance, properly called, which is almost always presumptuous, which decides, approves, and condemns with the same degree of temerity." [14] It is, usually, political ignorance on the part of the masses of the citizenry that permits selfish or fanatical individuals to

[13] Menander, *Fragments.*
[14] La Chalotois, Louis René de, *Essay on National Education,* Edward Arnold Co., London, 1934, p. 34.

transform the enthusiastic popular movement toward honest popular government into the tyranny of dictators.

Second, there is much valuable knowledge which the child is unlikely to gain by way of doing, but which is vital for worthy democratic citizenship, in fact for any form of ordered social life. For instance, by participation in a well-organized and properly guided student government, the boy can gain elementary knowledge of the *externa* of governing — that is, of the elements of the machinery of government. It is much less probable that students, with the exception of those very gifted, will acquire by the method of doing a sufficiently clear picture of the historic foundations, basic principles, and vital characteristics of the legal and social institutions of their country.

Every graduate of a public school must have certain lessons of the past solidly packed in his baggage of experience. In the interest of the health of the community, all the members are obliged to observe certain rules of hygiene. No community will knowingly permit a house visited by a dangerous contagious disease to neglect the observance of certain rules of quarantine, because everyone knows, or should know, though perhaps by way of second-hand experience, what will happen if the book-learned advice of medicine is ignored. Similarly, members of enlightened communities should be aware of what will follow, for example, when order is dislodged by anarchy:

> Behold the red Destruction come!
> When rages strength that has no reason,
> There breaks the mold before the season;
> When numbers burst what bound before,
> Woe to the State that thrives no more! [15]

History contains eloquent and convincing lessons on the subject. Communities familiar with these lessons will not be disposed complacently to let anyone tamper with the fundamental

[15] Schiller, F., *The Lay of the Bell*, German Classics, *cit.*, Vol. III, p. 65.

mainstays of social organization, or experiment with them. They need not learn the results by first-hand experience — experience they might never survive. Bernard de Fontenelle, in the *Dialogues of the Dead,* makes Montaigne and Socrates exchange the following reflections:

Montaigne: Be assur'd that men's manners are at present a large subject of lamentation, and that all things degenerate daily.

Socrates: Is't posible? I thought in my time things went as pervertly as could be, and was in hopes at last they would fall into more reasonable train.

Montaigne: Alas! What regard have they to experience? Like silly birds they suffer themselves to be taken in the same nets that have caught a hundred thousand of their kind already. There is not one but enters a perfect novice upon the stage of life, the follies of the fathers are lost upon their children, and do not serve to instruct them at all.[16]

In the time of either Socrates or Montaigne there was no free obligatory public education to enlighten the people. May our public education escape the disgrace of having zero as the balance of its work for leadership and citizenship when the present generations are viewed impartially by a future historian and a future philosopher!

An interesting discussion of the principles of education was conducted some time ago in a leading European newspaper. Among other problems considered was that of the liberation of the young from the authority and tutelage of the family. This kind of emancipation sometimes goes under the name of " democratization of the home." A contributor to the paper pointedly remarked that " homeless, or hotel-like, family " was a more probable result of the new familial ways than " the home democratized." [17]

[16] Translated from the French, London, 1708, p. 71 f.
[17] *Le Temps,* 26 août, 1927, " Sociologie Primaire."

Similarly, to be a democratic commonwealth, it is necessary first to be a nation. And what makes a nation? Primarily the things spiritual make it. The blood of twenty races may flow in the veins of a people, yet in the presence of its customs, manners, beliefs, and ideals, bodily differences may fade into insignificance. A nation is a nation in proportion as it is a spiritually homogeneous group; that is, a group united in a community of memories, customs, sentiments, ideals, and interests. These factors give nations their unity and significance. The wealth of national traditions and historical reminiscences has to be assimilated by the young, or else a nation, by definition, cannot continue to hold together. Obviously very little of national integration can be effected by the method of doing, and by the actual handling of things. Vicarious experience, in particular the study of national history and literature, is a more dependable means of inculcating what Schiller has named " The Instinct of the Fatherland." [18]

The way to the treasures of past experience lies often through difficult reading. The school must, therefore, accustom the student to do and to appreciate such reading. The development of the technique of reading and sense-getting must hold one of the foremost places among the primary devices regarding experience building.

THE ABANDONMENT OF " PROGRESSIVE " METHODS OF TEACHING
BY THE SOVIET SCHOOLS

It may be permissible to interrupt here our analysis of the problem of experience in order to study briefly the condemnation by the Soviet government of the method of learning by doing — project method, and the like " progressive " devices for experience building.

When in November, 1917 (in October, according to the old

[18] *The Lay of the Bell, cit.,* p. 64.

Russian calendar), the Communist group, under the leadership of Lenin, overthrew the democratic Kerensky government and established the Communist dictatorship of the Soviets, Lenin himself and his principal lieutenants had more on their hands than they could do. Absorbed entirely with economic, political, and international issues of the first magnitude, they were preoccupied with the survival of the Communist regime through the critical initial phase. Lenin, who had understood and handled well several other problems vital to the consolidation of the Communist dictatorship, erroneously expected that a world Communist revolution was imminent and that its advent could be considerably hastened by an impressive and spectacular demolition of as many as possible of the mainstays and vestiges of the capitalist order in public and private life in Russia. The Communist officials, out of a surplus of ardor and scarcity of real generalship, opened an orgy of upside-downism in everything, including education, art, and even the standard use of the Russian language.

In education, the history of the Communist regime opened with the abolition (in 1918) of the traditional secondary school disconnected from the elementary school. The common school was now established under the name of the United Activity School (*Edinaya Troodovaya Shkola*), and special facilities were created in the form of the Labor College (*Rabochyi Fakultet,* in abbreviation, *Rabfak*) for the Communist and pro-Communist youth. In addition to, in fact in distortion of, the instructions of the Central Executive Committee of the Communist Party, the " minor gods (*dii minores*)" from among the Communist " old guard " placed in charge of education indulged, as is the nature of " minor gods," in many forms of upside-downism, unnecessary and in fact harmful even to the Communist cause itself. Every new, or supposedly new, extravagant method of teaching was welcome, simply on the strength of its being different from the traditional ways. The proponents of such extravagances in other countries came one after another to Soviet Russia to receive from the Communist officials the homage that was not to be obtained at home or elsewhere in the world, where a fair degree of normalçy still obtained at the time. One sixth of the globe was gained for the experiment with the " progressive " methods.

The orgy of gratuitous upside-downism in education was permitted, for various reasons, to continue undisturbed by the supreme Soviet authorities much longer than was a similar tendency in some other spheres of life and work. In the latter, for example, in the army and the navy, standardization and the rigorous elimination — within the limits of the Bolshevist conception of life and government — of " ballyhoo " took place immediately after the installation of Joseph Stalin in the role of supreme leader of the Communist group in 1927. Stalin, though like Lenin and other leading Communists a staunch believer in the mission of the Communist Soviets to bring about the world Bolshevist revolution, correctly sensed that the glamour of the demolition of capitalism in Russia and of world propaganda by word had spent itself. The walls of the capitalist Jericho refused to crumble before the mere sounds of the Communist trumpet, though the rapping of that trumpet on the capitalist walls, and the rebound from the Bolshevist blows dealt to capitalism in Russia produced a few cracks here and there and minor damages in the outside world.

Hence the plan to concentrate on world propaganda by deed, by the building in Russia of a model Communist state, producing all the comforts of which the capitalistic industry is capable, and yet free from all the actual and supposed evils of capitalism; hence the laying out of the plans for the *piatiletka,* or the five-year plan — the corner stone of the future Communist paradise. Hence arose the various forms of restoration of standards and tested methods of organization of industry, among others the restoration of the executive authority of experts (*spetzialist,* in abbreviation, *spetz*), even of non-Communists, over the Communist workers' committees.

But it was only after the plans for the *piatiletka* were laid out and started on the way to execution that Stalin began to lend his ear to the many voices of the better educated and the more sensible Communist educators, who were demanding that an end should be put to the wasteful chaos created by the *svistopliaska* (" the whistling witch-sabbath ") in education, resulting from the shallow ostentatiousness of the " new methods " inimical to all solid systematic training in anything. As the adolescents, who were babies or small children at the moment of the establishment of the Communist regime and who had received their entire preliminary training in the Soviet schools (under the centralized system of Soviet administration), began to arrive before the examining committees of the higher educational institutions, the appalling ignorance of the fundamentals of the sciences and letters on the part of the Soviet alumni became evident beyond all possibility of doubt or camouflage. Rich collections of " boners " rapidly accumulated and the ridicule of the product began seriously to threaten the Communist functionaries responsible for the Soviet educational reforms. Finally, the criticism gathered sufficient momentum to cause the Central Executive Committee to decree, in September, 1931, that the schools should apply themselves to the task of doing more thorough work.

This was merely the first and lighter thunder, which cost the life of the Dalton Plan, found wasteful of the forces of the better teachers and conducive to farcical play with the " contracts " on the part of many average students who proved, however, teachable under the plan of systematic class instruction. The more drastic measures toward the abolition of the chaotic

" method of projects " and the restoration of educational standards and of the systematic, sequential educative process were soon to follow.

On August 25, 1932, the Communist Central Executive Committee issued a long decree ordering the reorganization of the entire educational system in Soviet Russia. The part concerning educational method and the restoration of standards was expounded by the Soviet Commissary for Public Instruction in his address before the convention of the regional Commissaries and local superintendents of education on December 9, 1932, as follows:

The first thing which I wish to impress upon you is that our next task is to re-establish discipline in the schools. Without planned discipline properly imparted to the students there will never be a real Soviet education. The decree of the Central Executive Committee of August 25, 1932, stresses " the fact that the Soviet school is characterized by weak discipline and even in places by the complete absence of all discipline." During the present school year we must not only talk about discipline and order, but must finally establish them. The information I have received leads me to the conclusion that the problem of discipline is not yet given the attention that should be given to it. And yet, the efforts toward re-establishing discipline must be regarded as our first and foremost present task. I know cases where the organization and maintenance of discipline is shoveled over to the student government. In such disciplinary " schemes " the teacher is assigned a passive role or even none at all. But in order to attack the problem of discipline concretely, practically, and to transfer it from the plane of empty discussion to that of reality, it is necessary to set in motion all the levers that the school has and without which it is impossible to accomplish order and discipline in the school. First among these levers are the school principal and the teachers. . . .[19]

[19] *Kommunisticheskoye Vospitanye* (The Communist Education), No. 2, 1933, p. 67.

Let me also remind you of the decree of the Central Executive Committee of August 25, Article 2, Paragraph C. Be good enough to bear it in mind constantly and to carry it out unflinchingly. And this is, you will recall, the text of the paragraph: " The teacher shall systematically and consecutively present the subject he teaches and shall train the children in systematic work, whether they are working with textbooks and reference books, or at themes and compositions, or at experiments in the physical and chemical laboratory, or at tasks in the workshop." [20]

In 1920, in the third year of the Soviet regime, Professor Kapterev, a liberal of the old school, wrote in the *Vestnik Vospitania* (The Educational Review):

Two great misfortunes have befallen Russian education. One is the establishment of the Common Activity School and the elimination of all serious work that followed in the wake of this reform, and the other is the elimination of discipline from the school.

The Communist officials, promoters of the " new education," then raised a great outcry against the " reactionary, tzarist professor." Twelve brief years passed and the Communist Central Executive Committee, in the decree " On Textbooks for the Elementary and Secondary School " of February 12, 1933, employs very much the tone that Professor Kapterev used in his condemnation of the error of the " new " ways:

In its decrees on education of September 5, 1931, and August 25, 1932, the Central Executive Committee stressed the fact that the fundamental defect of our elementary and secondary education is that " school instruction fails to impart a sufficient grounding in general culture and in the sciences and as a result it unsatisfactorily fulfills its task of sending to the technicums [vocational schools on the secondary level] * and the higher institutions of learning persons fully literate and possessed of the fundamentals of knowledge (physics, chemistry, mathematics, literatures, geography, etc.)."

---

* Bracketed remarks are added.   [20] *Ibid.*, p. 75.

The necessary precondition for the realization of the above decrees of the Central Executive Committee relative to both the removal of the fundamental defect stated and to the switching of the educative process over to new [in reality, old] * stable and standard programs and method lies in the availability of stable and standard textbooks, which must put an end to the method of an endless making of "project syllabi."

It is to be noted that as a result of the erroneous policy of the Commissariat for Public Instruction and its organs in the past, not only does the Soviet school not possess at the present time any stable and standard textbooks, but this defect and gap has been regarded by the leading resorts of the Commissariat for Public Instruction as a landmark of the "revolutionary achievements."

The Central Executive Committee considers such a state of affairs absolutely intolerable and therefore decrees:

1. The policy of the Commissariat of Public Instruction relative to textbooks is condemned.

2. The following ordinances and other documents are condemned and revoked as contrary to the decrees of the Central Executive Committee:

   (a) The Circular Letter of the Common School Division of the Commissariat for Public Instruction of August 8, 1918, advising its subordinate organs that "textbooks should generally be banished from the school."

   (b) The Ordinance of the Commissariat for Public Instruction of March 28, 1930, declaring it "impossible at the present time to adhere to the idea of standardization of textbooks."

   (c) The Resolution of the United States-Soviet Russia Conference on Textbooks of May 16, 1930, approved by the Commissariat for Public Instruction and circularized by it to the regional offices of education on June 30, 1930, and containing the following passage: "Textbooks under no circumstances should be standardized. The Conference decidedly rejects the idea of standardization of textbooks."

   (d) The Resolution of the Central Committee of the Union of

* Bracketed remarks are added.

Public Instruction Workers of March 3, 1932, opposing the idea of standardization of textbooks and declaring the idea of three-year validity of standard textbooks " wrong and politically injurious."

3. The publication of all so-called " project-work-books " and " loose-leaf-textbooks " is to be stopped at once because these are a poor substitute for real textbooks and do not impart systematic knowledge of the subjects of the curricula.

The Commissariat for Public Instruction and the State Publishing Board will proceed at once with the publication of standard textbooks designed to serve the school for a number of years, the printing to be finished by July, 1933, so that the textbooks may be in actual use beginning September 1, 1933.

4. The rule is hereby established that each textbook be approved for publication by the Commissariat for Public Instruction after a careful analysis and no changes in the text may be made in subsequent editions without the express approval of the Commissariat.

5. The existing practice of the independent publishing of textbooks by the regions and autonomous republics is hereby abolished. Each region or autonomous republic may, however, publish, subject to the approval of the Commissariat for Public Instruction, regional source books for the elementary school intended for home-locality study.[21]

The school year 1933–34, as Mr. Ralph W. Barnes, the Moscow correspondent of *The New York Herald Tribune,* correctly reported from Moscow on September 2, 1933, opened under the sign of abandonment of the wasteful and chaotic " project-method " or " complex-method " and the return to standards and system in education.

Moscow, Sept. 2. — When 25,000,000 Soviet children and youths began or resumed their studies this week in the 200,000 " little red schools " of the U.S.S.R., they found the educational revolution

[21] *Pravda,* February 13, 1933.

[an educational counter-revolution] * which had been in progress for the last twelve months advanced by several new stages. Radical innovations [restorations!] * in the system began just a year ago with the scrapping of the so-called " brigade system " [the system of working-squads, under a modified Dalton Plan] * and the " project method " and the restoration of the teacher to the time-honored position as disciplinarian.

The seven-year school has changed to the ten-year school, and in general there is a new emphasis on the rudiments of human knowledge including the traditional three " R's " and the relegation of secondary matter to secondary importance.

For the first time in a long period written examinations were held at the end of the last school year. Meanwhile, it was decided that textbooks, properly so called, should be substituted for the frequently changed pamphlets and the manuals hitherto in use in the schools, and it is these brand new school books, prepared by Soviet scholars in a six-month period of feverish labor, which the pupils found waiting for them when they began their classes this week.

Under the new system such subjects as history and geography, which had been lost in the maze of " conferences " and " projects," are definitely differentiated, with the result that among the new texts histories and geographies make their appearance for the first time [under the Soviet regime].* . . .

After a fifteen-year autocratic experiment with the " progressive " methods of experience-building, the plan has been abandoned, and one sixth of the globe has revoked the " progressive " methods of teaching and learning.

BOOK LEARNING AS A VEHICLE AND SAFEGUARD OF DEMOCRACY

A method of education which neglects fully to realize the significance of systematic study with the help of book learning, and which was condemned even by the dictatorial Communist Soviets, certainly is little in accord with the best interests of

* Bracketed remarks are added.

democracy. Among other contributions to the preservation and betterment of democracy, appropriate systematic reading can render a great service by lighting up in the children " the ardor to resemble not one another, but each to resemble the highest." [22] Their minds, however unconsciously, will then be colored by the great examples of civic achievement, as men walking in the sun have their faces browned without knowing it. Democratic communities are often reproached by their critics for neglecting and for even deliberately keeping down men of superior intellect and character.

A situation similar to the one described in a Heraclitean fragment, " The Ephesians," will not so readily occur in a democratic community where the young are educated through the study of the past to understand great truths and to appreciate the exponents of them. The fragment runs:

> Every grown man of them would do well to hang himself and leave the city to beardless youths, for they have cast out Hermodoros, the best man among them, saying, " We will have none who is best among us; if there be any such, let him be so elsewhere and among others." [23]

Much can also be said with respect to the role of the printing press in the democratization of pleasurable experiences and in the worthy use of leisure. If the taste for good books is imparted to the public school population, then reading will rapidly enough become the greatest public source of pleasure — a pleasure that is sanitary, uplifting, and restorative from the effects of drudgery, as against carnal enjoyments sold at the market of thrills, costly and wasteful in every respect. What Cicero said of the pleasure of reading, or, as he put it, of " literary studies," still remains true:

[22] Schiller, *Gedichte,* Votivtafeln: Aufgabe.
[23] Burnet, John, *Early Greek Philosophy,* Adam and Charles Black, London and Edinburgh, 1892, p. 141 (Fragment 114).

Even if there were no such great advantage to be reaped from them, and if it were only pleasure that is sought from their studies, still I imagine you would consider them a most reasonable and liberal employment of the mind; for other occupations are not suited to every time, nor to every age or place; but these studies are the food of youth, the delight of old age; the ornament of prosperity, the refuge and comfort of adversity, a delight at home and no hindrance abroad; these are companions by night and in travel, and in the country.[24]

All told, the printing press is among the most important safeguards of sound democracy. The printing press has served as a powerful agent of intellectual democratization and, by implication, of political and social democracy. It has accelerated the dissemination of knowledge as the steam engine and electricity have accelerated industry and trade. It has reduced time and distance to their lowest terms in the mental commerce of men. Truly, like all good things in this world, the printed word can be, and has been, abused. On the whole, however, democracy is much indebted to the printed symbols of thoughts and facts. Men no longer have to make weary and costly pilgrimages to the homes of learning. Knowledge of the best that has been thought and discovered and achieved in the world, for which Solon sought on his long and arduous travels, can be brought right to the door of the inquisitive boy in any civilized community. Millions are taught by the pen of a great teacher where only a very few were taught by his voice. The history of many beneficial reforms, religious, political, social, and economic, exhibits tangible evidence of the irresistible influence exercised by book learning and of the invaluable service of experience gained through it. It is not without reason that despots and dictators of modern times have carefully suppressed the circulation of printed matter except that approved by them. One

[24] *Pro Archia Poeta*, VII.

of the deadliest weapons of oppression employed by modern tyranny is arbitrary censorship of the press.

BOOK LEARNING AND CREATIVE ORIGINALITY

"We grant you," it may be objected, "that capitalization by the school of the experience of humanity in social, moral, and political matters, in natural science, in religion, and in philosophy, etc., is desirable. But is it not still true pedagogically, in the light of relative values, that the attention to be given to what is, after all, second-hand experience will inevitably lead to an inadequate preparation of the young for attacking the problems constantly raised by our changing civilization? Is it not true that second-hand experience, to be gained through memory work, is likely to stultify the average student rather than develop his creative powers?" The answer would be that the objection in question is based on a misconception of the nature of understanding. Whatever we understand in the thought or work of others, we create, as it were, over again for ourselves. This is true of a theorem as it is true of a piece of art, of a political plan, of an economic scheme, or what not (see p. 155).

Some members of our profession may hold that book learning is an unnatural method of learning, being the "outside-in" method, while the natural growth of the mind of the child is that of "inside-out" development. This opinion is rooted, again, in a misconception of the nature of all growth. There is no growth entirely "from inside-out," but all growth, physical or mental, is the result of the process of food-reception from the outside by the food-assimilating organism. Nothing is actual food to me except that which my organism has digested and assimilated of the potential food received from the outside. Nothing can mechanically become a part of my mind unless my mind has absorbed it; this the mind cannot do without working, and, consequently, without growing. There is much sense in the old motto adopted by the School for Scientific Police at the *Palais de Justice* in Paris: " The eye sees in things what it looks for, and it looks for what is already in the mind."

It may be of interest to read the reference to his mental growth made by Goethe in the *Conversations With Eckermann:*

We are indeed born with faculties; but we owe our development to a thousand influences of the great world, from which we appropriate what we can and what is suitable. I owe much to the Greeks, and to the French; I am infinitely indebted to Shakespeare, Sterne, and Goldsmith; but in saying this I do not show the sources of my culture — that would be an endless as well as an unnecessary task. What is important is to have a soul that loves truth and assimilates it wherever found.

Besides, the world is now so old, so many eminent men have lived and thought for thousands of years, that there is little new to be discovered or expressed. Even my theory of colours is not entirely new. Plato, Leonardo da Vinci, and many other excellent men have before me found and expressed the same thing in a detached form; my merit is that I have found it also, that I have said it again, and that I have striven to bring the truth once more into a confused world.

The truth must be repeated over and over again; because error is repeatedly preached among us, not only by individuals, but by the masses. In periodicals and cyclopaedias, in schools and universities — everywhere, in fact, error prevails, and is quite easy in the feeling that it has a decided majority on its side.[25]

From a very natural reaction to the mechanical, unintelligent cramming served out as education in some conventional schools, some of the " new educators," in reality repeating the old ideas of Rousseau, of Pestalozzi, or of Tolstoy, preach (under the name of education by first-hand experience, learning by doing, or education for initiative and originality, for attacking prob-

[25] E. P. Dutton Co., 1930, p. 253 f.

lems, for independent thinking, and the like) warfare upon memory work and book learning.

Independent thinking is a very good thing. But it is socially valuable under normal conditions only when it is not independent of the findings of experience or of logic. The old Chinese sage, Confucius, expressed this idea briefly and effectively as follows: "Learning without thought is labor lost; thought without learning is perilous," [26] especially in our complex civilization, it may be added. Independent thinking should be independent only of the interpretation placed by others on relationships between facts or between causes and effects. It is the business of mental training to help the individual to evaluate for himself the meaning of facts as well as to read the minds of those who offer him interpretations of facts (see p. 247). But the fundamental historical facts as well as the fundamental contemporary events he obviously must know before he can form any judgment about those facts. Genius, let us remember, does not consist in having no library, or in not reading books, newspapers, and magazines.

"People are always talking about originality," Goethe rightly complains, "but what do they mean? As soon as we are born, the world begins to work upon us, and this goes on to the end. What can we call our own except energy, strength, and will? If I could give an account of all that I owe to great predecessors and contemporaries, there would be but a small balance in my favor." [27]

Professor E. L. Thorndike, in his paper on *Education for Initiative and Originality,* emphasized well the fact that true initiative does not mean jumping forth blindfolded, nor that originality mean a deliberate ignorance of the achievements or errors of others in the direction that interests us; but that both

[26] *Analects,* II, XV, quoted in Dawson, M. M., *The Ethics of Confucius,* G. P. Putnam's, 1912, p. 20.   [27] *Ibid.,* p. 115.

mean a step forward in the light of those and an improvement upon the work of others who faced the same or similar conditions. " The truly independent mind," he says, " does not make less use of other men's ideas than does the servile thinker, but more. For a man whose every thought was original we should have to go to our hospitals for the insane."

An imitative creature is man. Benjamin Franklin's prose style is taken as worthy of imitation by school children over the land. Yet he says in his *Autobiography* that he achieved whatever style he had by imitation — at first very close — of Addison.

. . . At this time [in 1717, at the age of 11] * I met with an odd volume of the " Spectator." I had never before seen any of them. I bought it, read it over and over, and was much delighted with it. I thought the writing excellent, and wished if possible to imitate it. With that view I took some of the papers, and making short hints of the sentiments in each sentence, laid them by a few days, and then, without looking at the book, tried to complete the papers again, by expressing each hinted sentiment at length, and as fully as it had been expressed before, in any suitable words that should occur to me. Then I compared my " Spectator " with the original, discovered some of my faults, and corrected them. But I found I wanted a stock of words or a readiness in recollecting and using them, which I thought I should have acquired before that time if I had gone on making verses; since the continual search for words of the same import, but of different length to suit the measure or of different sound for the rhyme, would have laid me under a constant necessity of searching for variety, and also have tended to fix that variety in my mind and make me master of it. Therefore I took some of the tales in the " Spectator " and turned them into verse; and after a time, when I had pretty well forgotten the prose, turned them back again.

I also sometimes jumbled my collection of hints into confusion, and after some weeks endeavored to reduce them into the best order

* Bracketed remarks are added.

before I began to form the full sentences and complete the subject. This was to teach me method in the arrangement of the thoughts. By comparing my work with the original, I discovered many faults and corrected them; but I sometimes had the pleasure to fancy that in certain particulars of small consequence I had been fortunate enough to improve the method or the language, and this encouraged me to think that I might in time come to be a tolerable English writer, of which I was extremely ambitious. The time I allotted for writing exercises and for reading was at night, or before work began in the morning, or on Sundays, when I contrived to be in the printing-house, avoiding as much as I could the constant attendance at public worship which my father used to exact of me when I was under his care, and which I still continued to consider a duty, though I could not afford time to practice it. . . . I continued this method some few years.[28]

True originality seems to be best achieved after careful study and imitation of masters in the particular field — by surpassing the great masters.

Only a very few minds are gifted enough to read directly and correctly from what Schopenhauer called the " Book of the World." [29] Therefore, it is correct to say, with a thinker, that " there would have been a gap, a hole in the world, if certain books had not been written." [30] And it was good advice that a university teacher gave his students when he told them, " In the accumulation of knowledge, as of other forms of wealth, saving must follow earning. So among the offices of a university we find the conservation of experience . . . the fulcrum of historic knowledge." [31]

[28] Franklin, Benjamin, Autobiography, New York, The Perkins Book Company, 1902, pp. 16–17, 19.
[29] Parerga und Paralipomena, II, §§ 257, 258.
[30] Brunner, Constantin, Die Lehre von dem Geistigen und dem Volk, 2 Aufl., G. Kiepenheuer, Potsdam, 1927, 1119.
[31] Gilman, D. C., " The Characteristics of a University," Modern Eloquence, Vol. VI, p. 215.

POLITICAL EXPERIENCE AND THE " ALGEBRA " OF CIVICS

It will be agreed that school education in a democracy should help the maturing citizen toward taking an intelligent, constructively critical attitude with reference to political problems of the day. This presupposes political experience. But how can it be gained? Not only direct sharing in the solution of political problems on the part of the legally immature, of whom the school population is composed, is out of the question, but even indirect sharing on the part of school students by the method of discussion and analysis of current politics in class is to be very restricted, if not altogether excluded from the school. It will be agreed that partisan politics must be kept as much as possible out of the school in a democratic community. Such a policy is one of the fundamental safeguards of democratic education in distinction from the school regime under dictatorships and oligarchies, where schools are obliged to teach the political doctrine favorable to the dictator.

True friends of true democracy wisely deprecate the wish of conflicting political parties to "steal the hearts of youths through their ears." [32] Slight effort of thought is necessary to see that very few matters relative to the community's current political or business issues can be appropriately discussed at a public school. Questions of that nature are controversial. Academic freedom seems inevitably to be limited, at least in the case of elementary and secondary schools, by the private susceptibilities of young students and their families — among other factors — to say nothing of the authorities of the hour. The school cannot very well be turned into a "mutual laundry" shop, to borrow the expression of an inventive Chinese laundry manager in New York. A common human infirmity makes people think themselves right and honest even when, to the

[32] *Sophist*, 234.

best knowledge and belief of some of their fellow men, they are not. " When honesty is in question," says Plato, " or some other political virtue, even if they know that he is dishonest, yet, if the man comes publicly forward and tells the truth about his dishonesty, in this case they deem that to be madness which in the other case was held by them to be good sense. They say that men ought to profess honesty whether they are honest or not. . . ."[33] Besides, as another ancient political thinker has said, " People are apt to deem an attack upon vices akin to their own to be an attack upon themselves."[34]

The case in point is not a specific defect of public men and politicians. Scientists and philosophers themselves sometimes drop their serene broadmindedness and abandon their benevolent tolerance abruptly enough when their own doctrines are questioned. People are more readily sincere than impartial. Socrates in vain assures us: " I am one of those who are very willing to be refuted if I say anything which is not true, and just as ready to be refuted as to refute."[35] Everyone who has read the dialogues of Plato can judge for himself that the calmness and fairness of Socrates showed considerable limitations when his interlocutor drove him hard.

Of all social institutions, the public school seems to be most clearly indicated as the one in which maturing citizens should receive as disinterested, impartial, unadulterated, and sound initiation into the puzzles of politics as is humanly possible. Tacitus, the Roman historian profoundly conversant with political arts, has observed, " For but few have wisdom enough of their own to distinguish what is honourable from what is base, the expedient from the hurtful; most men have to learn these things from the experiences of others."[36]

---

[33] *Protagoras*, 323.
[34] Tacitus, *The Annals*, IV, 34 (From an English Translation by G. G. Ramsay, London, John Murray, 1904).
[35] *Gorgias*, 458.   [36] Tacitus, *The Annals, Ibid.*

If, in the discharge of its vital residual function relative to the building of the educand's political experience, the school cannot always directly and freely discuss in its classes the problems and methods of daily political life, it can arrange for a sound political education in an indirect way by guiding pupils in their reading of history, more remote and less remote, in addition to the cultivation of their intellectual efficiency. Reading is rightly said to be as free as breathing.

History is regarded here in the sense of social human history — that is, the story of the relations of men or of groups of men with each other. Properly organized reading in history would constitute a sort of algebra of civics. Algebra proper is a generalization and extension of arithmetic operated through the replacement of the varying concrete figures with symbols or letters. Similarly, the typical combinations and conflicts of higher human aspirations and lower passions, of virtues and vices, of errors and truths, and the consequences of such combinations and conflicts known to history, can serve as a kind of serene political algebra supplanting, in the civic training of the educand, the delicate slippery ground of political arithmetic dealing with the concrete political personalities active in the community today.

The historian is said to be a prophet looking backward.[37] Without letting the dead bury the living, history properly taught at school will help the student to comprehend the present in the light of the past. With regard to the psychology of politics, it is no doubt true that, as a student in the classics has said, " If one reads the ancients only, one is sure of always remaining modern." [38] Napoleon, on April 17, 1821 convinced of the near end dictated to Bertrand the instructions as to what he and the

[37] Schlegel, F., *The Lyceum and the Athenaeum*, German Classics, *cit.*, Vol. IV, p. 176.
[38] Ebner-Eschenbach, Marie von, *Aphorisms*, German Classics, *cit.*, Vol. XIII, p. 432.

other executors of Napoleon's will should tell his son, the captive King of Rome, when they see the young boy. In this supreme message of a dying father, who was among the most brilliant minds of his time, Napoleon said: " My son shall often read history and meditate upon it. History contains the only veritable philosophy." [39]

We can make of our students sufficiently enlightened modern citizens if we take the trouble to know how to do and to do what Tacitus — a realistic political thinker and a man of great experience in politics — long ago suggested as a practical method of political education, *i.e.,* that we teach our pupils by selecting proper instances as examples or as warnings.

Democracy is no new thing. All high sacrifices and noble services to the cause of democracy that may in our own days be registered here and there, as well as base machinations and outrages that are committed in its name by selfish or ignorant men, have their precedents in the history of times gone by.

A community may happen to have in its midst accommodating individuals who stand in readiness to oblige any rising politician without being apparently troubled by any consideration for the good of the community as a whole. These persons and their activities cannot be conveniently discussed by the teacher and pilloried before the students. But the teacher can well enlighten the students by substituting the disturbing " arithmetic " of concrete political personalities with a lesson from the historic " algebra " of political types and typical political abuses of demagogues and dishonest voters. For instance, the teacher can acquaint the students with pages of the history of Rome which tell about professionally organized political agents nicknamed *Laudicaeni* [40] from their eagerness to applaud anybody and anything for the sake of getting a square meal, or

[39] Abry, Octave, " Les derniers Jours de Napoleon," *Revue des Deux Mondes,* 15 décembre 1934, p. 803.
[40] Literally, " table-flatterers." Pliny, *Letters,* II, XIV.

more. Their Athenian forerunners went under the equally picturesque name of *Kothornos* (κόθορνος), *i.e.,* " shoe that would
fit both feet." [41]

Your students may hear and read of political extremists who
lavishly throw into crowds all sorts of alluring though unreliable promises of economic and political millennium, as well
as venomous accusations against the existing order and against
moderate political leaders. Have the students read Aristophanes
and they will see for themselves that many a slogan employed
by the selfish, vote-hunting " friends of the humble and oppressed " has already been used by the Athenian demagogues.
Your students may be fascinated by propagandists of a violent
social revolution, the new self-styled " Attorney Generals of
Truth." These orators broadcast fiery manifestoes to the " little
and humble folks " and call them to rise in revolt against the
established social order, to demand that the community of all
goods, and consequently the real domination of the majority
for the benefit of this same majority, may be erected on the
ruins of the destroyed minority. Again, read in the history of
social revolutions, ancient and modern, and you will invariably
find that once in power the revolutionary extremists became a
new privileged minority, usually worse than the one over-
thrown. They showed the invariable tendency of forgetting
their promises, and as soon as they could manage it, shackled
the majority composed of " the little and the humble." " Pay
well your soldiers and don't care a straw for the rest," an ancient tyrant counselled his sons. The advice is not lost on modern dictators who have arisen to power as champions of " liberty for the oppressed."

Indeed, does not the best and sometimes the only way open
to the public school to contribute to the political enlightenment
of the students consist in inoculating the maturing citizens,

[41] Xenophon, *Hellenica,* II, 3, 30–31.

through the medium of the algebra of civics, with a kind of mental serum against the venom of deceitful propaganda and political cheating? If and when there comes a time in a community when no one " has the hardihood to say what is just " [42] and from whom the young might learn, then the past experience recorded in history can very largely supply the want.

For example, imagine yourself in a democratic community much agitated by communistic preachments which, for whatever reasons, cannot be directly analyzed and pricked through by the teacher before his students. Would it not be useful if the students read a dialogue, imaginary and yet realistic, between two citizens on the introduction of the Communist regime in their city-state: It may be entitled, " Communism for Others."

Chorus: * Do you not intend to pay them (your goods) in?

Citizen: I'll take care not to, till I see what the people determine on.

Chorus: Why, what else than that they are ready to carry their property?

Citizen: Well, I'd believe, if I saw.

Chorus: At any rate, they talk of it in the streets.

Citizen: Why, they *will* talk of it.

Chorus: And they say they will take them up and carry them.

Citizen: Do you think any of them who has sense will carry *his* property? For this is not a natural custom; but, by Jove, we ought only to receive.

Chorus: You will kill me with disbelieving everything. . . .

Crier: O all ye, citizens — for so this now — come, hasten straight to our Princess-President in order that chance may point out to you, drawing lots man by man where you shall dine; for the tables are piled up and furnished with all good things, and the couches are heaped with goatskins and carpets. . . . Wherefore come! for he who carries the barley-cakes is standing. Come, open your mouths!

---

* In Greek drama, the chorus, or a company of singers or chanters, acting as a unit, represents a collective personality, a body of men united in a purpose or in a conviction.   [42] Aristophanes, *The Acharnians,* 643 ff.

Citizen: Therefore I will certainly go. For why do I keep standing here, when these things have been decreed by the State?

Chorus: Why, whither will you go, if you have not paid in your property?

Citizen: To dinner.

Chorus: Certainly not if there be any sense in them, until you *deliver in your property.*

Citizen: Well I will deliver it in.

Chorus: When?

Citizen: I shall not be a hindrance, my good sir.

Chorus: How, pray?

Citizen: I assert that others will deliver in *their property* still later than I.

Chorus: But will you go to dinner notwithstanding?

Citizen: Why, What must I do? for it behooves those who have right understanding to assist the State to the best of their ability. (To himself) By Jove, of a truth I have need of some contrivance so that I may retain the property I have, and may somehow partake in common with these of the things which are kneading. It seems to me to be just.[43]

But the question may be asked whether the "algebra" of civics is not superfluous, and whether it is not true that the civic "arithmetic" of the daily press — where things and people are called with sufficient clearness by their names — is not adequate for the purpose. The answer, it seems, should be in the

[43] Aristophanes, *The Ecclesiazusae,* 7684. (Translated by W. J. Nickie, London, Bell and Daldy, 1869).

The economic difficulties of Soviet Russia — a country two and a half times as large as the United States and rich in natural resources — which seem to be on the increase as the "collectivization" and bolshevization of Russia increases, are a modern echo of the witty dialogue of the *Ecclesiazusae.* In fact, the rather general attitude prevalent at the "*sovkhoz*" and "*kolkhoz,*" or the "collectivized" farms, which well explains the lingering famine in Soviet Russia, is very much like the reasoning of an inmate in an institution for defectives. A visiting patroness of the institution was pleased to see the squads of boys working in the fields. When she came upon a husky fellow comfortably stretched out in the shade, she asked him: "What are you doing here?" — "Why, I am one of the crazy boys." — "Why are you not working, then? Look, those boys in the field are crazy, too, but they are working!" — "Well, lady, I am not as crazy as that."

negative for several reasons which the scope of the present volume does not allow us fully to discuss. Some of the principal reasons seem to be as follows:

Modern newspapers perform three functions: (1) They supply the public with news; (2) they are an advertising agency; (3) they furnish opinions and comment on affairs of public importance. The third function is, however, the weakest and is utterly dominated by the other two. The success of a newspaper is measured by its circulation, and upon the circulation the advertising value depends. A large newspaper is an expensive commercial enterprise, involving immense capital. It must succeed financially, must yield the dividends which the shareholders think satisfactory, or else it will cease to exist. Therefore, the thing in which the manager is mainly interested is the circulation chart. He thinks in terms of circulation; it is the curve of the circulation that advises him whether the political line he has adopted on a burning question is the right one, and he changes it in accordance with what he reads, or thinks he reads, in his circulation chart. To say nothing of the possibilities of direct pressure and corruption, a costly newspaper cannot afford to indulge in championing an unpopular cause, however just. Neither can it, in general, occupy itself primarily with the problem of the disinterested enlightenment of citizens. The manager's first and foremost task is to make his paper a first-class seller and thus to secure the best paying advertisements. The most successful newspaperman is he who can offer what will please the largest number of people. Therefore, he is tempted to exert himself in amusing his readers with verbal stunts, to thrill them with sensational headlines and with similar devices that can make " bright copy." With regard to the interpretation of current political issues, he is tempted to try, as best he can, to give the public what he thinks it is asking for.[44]

[44] See Spender, J. A., *The Public Life*. Stokes, 1925, Vol. II, p. 107 ff.

Apparently, when all is said, the "arithmetic" of civics offers a precarious enough method of sound political education for the students. In contradistinction to the familiar succession of mathematical subjects, the political "algebra" must precede the political "arithmetic" and must be used in every school which earnestly strives to educate the youth for the privileges and responsibilities of democracy.

But is the knowledge of political history and the algebra of civics based upon such knowledge a reliable guide in the discharge of their duties and the enjoyment of their rights on the part of honest, well-intentioned citizens of a democratic community? It is decidedly more reliable than ignorance, even though the political history of humanity, like other branches of history, is not free from obscurities and falsifications. The following reflection of a contemporary student of politics seems to illustrate the point under consideration:

The testimonies of history are contradictory at times because based upon a narrow interpretation of facts made on the spur of the moment. Despite this, I honor Knowledge before and above all. Books, which are the continuous record of the genius for observation proper to each race of men, are the marvelous key for the opening of our power of comprehension. They demonstrate to us, when we read the records of the past in the light of present-day events, how each nation has forged its chain of effort toward civilization. And also they show how much this effort has in common with that of other nations. As a result, any one who is not blind will see from the record of the past the right place and the right proportion of things.[45]

EXPERIMENT AS A METHOD OF LEARNING AND TEACHING

According to Christian Wolff (d. 1755), a great master of definitions who wrote in Latin the earliest modern definition of the term, experiment is " an experience bearing upon such facts

---

[45] Margueritte, V., *Non! Roman d'une Conscience,* Flammarion, 1931, p. 106.

(or phenomena) of nature as would remain unknown unless uncovered by us." [46]

Wundt (d. 1920) defines experiment as " observation under the conditions of purposive control by the observer of the rise and course of the phenomena observed. *Observation,* in the narrower sense of the term, is the investigation of phenomena without such control, the occurrences being accepted just as they are naturally presented to the observer in the course of experience.[47] Experiment is observation accompanied by deliberate interventions on the part of the observer into the behavior of the object under observation." [48]

Professor Hugo Dingler, author of the noteworthy work *Das Experiment,* says, " Experiment in the full meaning of the term embraces all the actions on the part of the observer which are employed to bring forth unknown and untouched forces or properties of nature." [49]

In broad everyday language, experiment means (a) proof by measurable, tangible demonstration; (b) doing things which one does not at first know exactly how to do right. It has been glorified in recent years because of the service it has rendered in the field of natural science. The term " experiment " has become a fascinating and formidable term. Many sensible school principals and school superintendents have found themselves forced against their better judgment to open the doors of their classrooms to dubious and even frankly foolish educational experiments for fear that some influential member of the community might otherwise pass on the word, " Mr. Jones is getting old; he is so terribly old-fashioned and unprogressive. He will not experiment with any new ideas in education. We want to

[46] *Psychologia Empirica,* 1732, § 456, quoted in Dingler, Hugo, *Das Experiment: Sein Wesen und seine Geschichte,* München, E. Reinhardt, 1928, S. 51.

[47] *Outlines of Psychology,* Third Revised English Edition, Leipzig, Wilhelm Englemann, 1907, pp. 22–23.

[48] *Logik,* Stuttgart, Ferdinand Enke, 1921, B. II, S. 364.

[49] *Op. cit.,* S. 51.

be a progressive community and we should have a more progressive man to run our schools."

The late President Woodrow Wilson, while pondering over the fact that science is capable of doing great disservice as well as great service, made the following penetrating observation:

No man more heartily admires, more gladly welcomes, more approvingly reckons the gain and the enlightenment that have come to the world through the extraordinary advances in physical science which this great age has witnessed. He would be a barbarian and a lover of darkness who should grudge that great study any part of its triumph. But I am a student of society and should deem myself unworthy of the comradeship of great men of science should I not speak the plain truth with regard to what I see happening under my own eyes. I have no laboratory but the world of books and men in which I live; but I am much mistaken if the scientific spirit of the age is not doing us a great disservice, working in us a certain great degeneracy. Science has bred in us a spirit of experiment and a contempt for the past. It has made us credulous of quick improvement, hopeful of discovering panaceas, confident of success in every new thing.[50]

With regard to the employment of experiment as a method of learning and teaching, education suffers from the double membership of the science of education in the family of the sciences. Education is primarily a social science, but it belongs, in some of its aspects, to the group of the natural and mathematical sciences as well. (See p. 16).

In the latter group experiment deservedly holds a high place. It has recently been of great assistance in working out many astounding scientific discoveries, some of which added more

[50] Wilson, Woodrow, *Selected Literary and Political Papers and Addresses of Woodrow Wilson,* 3 Vols., New York, Grosset & Dunlap, 1926. Extract taken from vol. 1, pp. 67–68. The individual paper is entitled " Princeton in the Nation's Service " (pp. 40–72). It was " An Oration Delivered at the Princeton Sesqui-Centennial Celebration, October 21, 1896." It was printed in " The Forum," December 1896, vol. XXII, pp. 447–466.

to the sum total of scientific knowledge and technical arts than all that had been previously accomplished since the days of Archimedes. Yet, it appears that many of the most valuable and surprising things which the natural sciences have done for civilization would never have been performed had not each branch of knowledge been guided by purely mental, speculative vision.

From the history of civilization we know that a signal advance in one sphere of research starts a parallel sympathetic current running in several others. Harvey's discovery of the circulation of the blood was echoed in the field of political economy by the doctrine of the circulation of wealth, advocated by the physiocrats. Similarly, happy formulae or watchwords are usually borrowed far and wide. It is, therefore, not astonishing that the success of experiment in the natural science part of pedagogy (well attested, for example, by several valuable discoveries of educational psychology) should open to it the doors also of that part of the science of education which is destined by its very nature to be first and foremost in harmony with the social sciences and to employ their best methods of research.

The two branches of the science family and the two corresponding aspects of the science of education are quite unequally situated with regard to experiment. The first could rightly take as its motto the saying of Lessing: " How many things would have appeared impossible in theory if genius had not succeeded in proving them to be the contrary in practice." [51] As to the second, Schiller's warning observation, " Illusion is brief, but Repentance is long," [52] seems to apply to it best.

A settlement of the annoying inconclusiveness of economic, political, and ethical controversies and educational disputes cannot always be sought, without infinite damage, in testing out

[51] *Laokoön*, IV.
[52] *The Lay of the Bell, cit.*, p. 58.

discordant theories by means of actual experiments on the living man. Fortunately enough, this is not always necessary, because we have other tools with which to work.

When can experiment be legitimately employed in social matters, that is, in matters bearing upon the welfare of men? The answer is: Not before a careful preliminary study and only after mental experimentation on a given problem. Only when a thorough mental search for the best solution of a social problem has brought into evidence points insoluble by way of mental experiment alone, and has reasonably shown that the experiment to be undertaken promises good results justifying the inevitable risks to be run, only then is a social experiment legitimate. Of all social experiments, special precautions should be taken in the case of educational experiments, the school being a trustee of the young as well as one of the guardians of the spiritual heritage of the nation. As the proverb says, " Measure seven times before you cut."

It would be for the common good if the young and the adult alike would look upon the method of experiment as upon a tool that should be used with great moderation in social matters, and only after careful preparation. A nation so minded will be spared the utter misery and appalling disasters that, as a rule, fall upon all concerned (with the exception, perhaps, of the malicious or foolish experimenters themselves) when a social experiment is undertaken which cannot stand the preliminary test of a thorough mental experimentation. The examples are abundant nowadays. The school in a democratic country should teach the prospective citizen to appreciate properly the fact that there are immutable, though sometimes unwritten, economic and moral laws which always reassert themselves and yield to no power or force. When unwise or vicious governments try to violate them, it is not the laws but the happiness and lives of the governed that are broken as a result.

We must teach our students that worth-while initiative and solid progress do not mean a bold leap into the unknown, but a step forward that is made in the light of all accumulated knowledge, however commonplace. It is said that many a truth is the result of an error. That may be correct, but the trial and error process, as far as is humanly possible, should be performed in the mind. On the other hand, children should be permitted, or even induced, in a degree which is justified by careful balancing of all fundamental objectives of school education, to fend for themselves and to learn by actual experimenting. Indeed, the situation is pedagogically not quite commendable when Max, in Schiller's *The Death of Wallenstein,* speaks to his trustee as follows:

My General, this day thou makest me of age to speak in my own right and person. For till this day I have been spared the trouble to find out my own road. Thee have I followed with most implicit unconditional faith, sure of the right path if I followed thee. Today, for the first time, dost thou refer me to myself.[53]

EXPERIMENT AS A SOURCE OF EXPERIENCE

What is the real significance of experiment as a source of experience and a method of learning?

A parallel between acquiring experience in general and learning our mother tongue in particular may throw some light on the problem. It appears that the notions to be acquired by the actual handling of things and thus experimenting with them bear, normally, to the whole volume of one's knowledge and reasoning very much the same quantitative relation which the names of things, of their qualities and relations, that we have learned directly, bear to our entire mastery of language. In fact, what we have to learn to know personally, as it were, is the *etyma* or roots of the meanings embodied in a language. For

[53] Act II, Scene II, German Classics, *cit.,* Vol. III, p. 113.

the rest, the ability of an individual to express himself, or to understand linguistic expressions of others using the same tongue, comes from perspicacity as to derivations, from fidelity of generalizations, fertility of comparisons, and accuracy of analogies. The higher the position an individual holds in the scale of intelligence the more he makes of what he has acquired through immediate linguistic experience; in other words, through personal, concrete, and direct introduction to the meaning of a word.

It goes without saying that anyone suffering from color blindness (Daltonism) cannot very well make use of meanings derived from or depending upon terms describing color. In order that we may be in a position to determine rightly our conduct with regard to a thing or set of things, it is necessary to have gained certain notions related thereto by means of actual or experimental experience; in other words, by undergoing, enduring, trying out, or testing in action. On the other hand, a very significant part of human creative activity undoubtedly is planned and worked out through mental experimenting, or toying, as the case may be, with the root meanings we have gained from our sensory-motor impressions and their verbal symbols. It is through our mental manipulations, through thinking with imagination and with visualization, that our disconnected doings and undergoings and sufferings are brought to fruition. This ability of man to execute in his mind experiments based on remembering, preserving and recording his experiences, constitutes an important difference between bestiality and humanity, between culture and raw, crude, undeveloped mental endowment.

To underestimate this human gift and power would be a gross error in education. The employment in our teaching of the motor-sensory learning and motor-sensory trial and error to excess would be merely a reversion to the methods of our remote ancestors. True enough, there are people who can reach accurate knowledge and arrive at accurate deduction only by way of muscular handling of subject matter. Such was the case of Professor Rignano's peasant landlady from the Alps. She could not subtract seven francs owed her by her boarder from twelve francs that had been given her to hand to him, otherwise than by laying down upon the table twelve one-franc pieces and putting aside, one by one, the seven francs. Only then did she think it safe to agree to the separation from the five francs.[54] But that and like cases are unfortunate examples of very limited native endowment or of completely uncouth, untrained minds, which, when found in schools, should be treated in special classes.

Of course, we must not forget that there is no way of demonstrating certain truths other than by actual experiment. Beyond all doubt, it is necessary to educate the race to have proper regard for experimental investigation. But it is not less important that people see and separate experimental truth from experimental falsities and fallacies. Schools should make provision for an appropriate amount and adequate distribution of experimentation, of handling things by the students themselves. It is natural, however, that only a very small percentage of them are likely to execute really fruitful and significant experiments. This necessarily limited proportion of gifted experimenters among the school population must be given all encouragement and help in original research. The rest, with reasonable individual gradation, should be trained rather for aptitude and skill in reading an experiment, *i.e.,* for critical examination of findings or designs put forth before the public by qualified scholars, inventors, and more especially by would-be political and social reformers.

[54] Rignano, E., *The Psychology of Reasoning,* Harcourt, Brace & Co., 1923, p. 72.

MENTAL EXPERIMENTATION AS A GREAT DEVICE IN THE BUILDING OF EXPERIENCE

It is not prescribed by the psychology of learning that tragedy should be the school of men. Intelligent leaders of nations can learn from their own and other people's past tragedies by experiencing them mentally. A poet says:

> I ask not a year of sunshine bright,
> Nor for golden crops I importune.
> Kind Fate, let the blazing thunderbolt smite
> My people with years of misfortune!
> Yea, smite us and lash us into one
> And the bluest of springs will follow.[55]

But that poet's wish appears to be of questionable prudence. The renaissance he promises may or may not follow; for many it certainly will not. Such a ruinously expensive method of learning is not absolutely necessary either. There is a better way that is less costly and, in the end, more reliable, the way of mental experimentation through reasoning and imagination, conducted in the light of the lessons of history. In the fitting words found in Professor Eugenio Rignano's *Psychology of Reasoning:*

It [reasoning] * would seem to be nothing else than a series of operations or experiments simply thought of, that is to say, operations or experiments that we imagine performed on one or several objects in which we are particularly interested, and that we do not perform actually because, by a series of similar experiments which have been really accomplished in the past, we already know their respective results. And the final experimental result " observed with the mind's eye," to which a similarly connected series of mental ex-

---

* Bracketed remarks are added.
[55] Heidenstam, Werner von, "Invocation and Promise," *Anthology of Swedish Lyrics,* The American-Scandinavian Foundation, 1917, p. 167.

periments leads, constitutes precisely the "result of the demonstration," the "conclusion of reasoning." [56]

Whatever disadvantages may be found in mental experimentation as against sensory-motor experimentation, it has many and valuable properties. "We deal more easily and conveniently with the representations of our imaginations than with physical acts. We experiment, so to speak, on our own thoughts with smaller cost." [57]

Moreover, as Professor Rignano rightly contends, "the much greater facility and promptitude with which experiments can be thought of as compared with the difficulty and delay in their actual performance enables reasoning to attempt again and again in rapid succession the most varied combinations and connections of experiments and thus to increase largely the probability of new discoveries. So that reasoning is eventually much more fruitful than actual experimenting, pure and simple." [58] This contention appears to have been borne out by many momentous scientific discoveries, from Galileo's law of two falling bodies to Einstein's theory of relativity. It seems right to say also that great technical inventors come upon their discoveries largely by testing and retesting, mentally, their own and other men's actual experimental combinations, and perfecting in its smallest details each new combination adopted. Biographies of Watt, Stephenson, Edison, Marconi, Ford, and many others well illustrate this.

MANUAL TRAINING AS A DEVICE IN BUILDING FIRST-HAND EXPERIENCE

"I do not know," said Anatole France, "whether the men who cut and polish ideas have not more merit than other

---

[56] Rignano, E., *The Psychology of Reasoning*, Harcourt, Brace & Co., p. 81 f.
[57] Mach, Ernst, *Erkenntnis und Irrtum*, Leipzig, 1917, p. 187, quoted in Rignano, *op. cit.*, pp. 83–84.
[58] *Ibid.*

mortals. . . . In many ways they make life better for everybody. In his laboratory from his quiet courtyard, the frail,
bespectacled man of science reshapes the world." [59] Some present-day educators seem to hold an opinion to the contrary, and
demand a large place for manual work at the expense of the
so-called academic or mental work. The demand is based, substantially, on three points: (a) the formative value of manual
work as an excellent device for learning by doing; (b) the
economic significance of manual training; (c) the moral or
social value of manual training as an instrument for social integration and social peace. The problem is evidently one which
can be equitably considered only in the light of relative values
in education.

THE FORMATIVE VALUE OF MANUAL TRAINING

Defenders of manual work as a basic school occupation claim
that handicraft, nourished by the child's instinct for activity, not
only makes his hand skilled and sure, sharpens his eye, refines
his taste, and develops his feeling for form and space relationships, but also furnishes excellent training in thinking and self-
discipline. It presupposes the overcoming of obstacles and
involves the necessity of doing real and accurate work, we are
told.

All these good things may very well happen, under the right
conditions, in the case of children who are intended by their
native endowment to profit from utilitarian, immediately usable
information rather than from abstract or " bookish " subjects.
There are, however, children who do not like manual work and
whose desire for activity finds expression in what may be called
purely mental occupations. Every pumpkin in the field very
probably goes through every point of pumpkin history. It is different with the child. From what we know about the children of

[59] Motto to *The Aspirations of Jean Servien*, London, John Lane.

higher intelligence, it is precisely this socially valuable group who would be likely to resent too much tabouret-making as some other children hate algebra or Latin. Even when they play, they prefer intellectual, sedentary games to field games. The child who, by obedience to school regulations, takes part, as all children certainly should, in gymnastics or games, but gives a sigh of relief when he can go back to his books or maps or diagrams, is neither an imaginary individual nor horribly unnatural. He simply belongs to a restricted yet large enough and quite lovely section of the young who are similarly constituted by nature. Wordsworth made himself their spokesman when he said:

> And when thereafter to my father's house
> The holidays returned me, there to find
> That golden store of books which I had left
> What joy was mine! How often in the course
> Of those glad respites, though a soft west wind
> Ruffled the waters to the angler's wish,
> For a whole day together, have I lain
> Down by thy side, O Derwent! murmuring stream,
> On the hot stones and in the glaring sun,
> And there have read, devouring as I read. . . .[60]

Misplaced and exaggerated manual instruction is as little desirable as is exaggerated and misplaced intellectual instruction. " Manualism " and " intellectualism " employ the same Procrustean bed. The difference between the two is that, in the first case, the legs of the victim are cut off, while in the second, they are broken by stretching, so as in each case to adapt the victim to the length of the bed. With regard to the significance of manual training for acquisition by the child of desirable habits, attitudes, skill, and information, it would be superfluous to argue that manual arts do not possess a monopoly of the gen-

[60] *Prelude*, V, 476 ff.

eral transfer of learning in any greater degree than does each of the other subjects of instruction (see p. 228). The progressives who are enthusiastic promoters of "manualism" ought to be more logical, and, after having protested against the old theory of formal discipline, they ought not to create a new theory of formal discipline with tabouret-making in place of Latin and Greek. As a general proposition, tire-mending can safely be declared a less transferable kind of learning than rapid and careful silent reading.

In this connection, the following statement by President Pritchett of the Carnegie Foundation for the Advancement of Teaching, found in the eighteenth report of the Foundation, is of interest:

The public school makes its greatest contribution to training in the crafts when it teaches boys and girls in the elementary school to do such work there as will give them the discipline of mind and the accuracy of knowledge necessary to enter a skilled craft. The greatest service the elementary school can do for the boy who wants to be a carpenter, or a mason, or a machinist, or an electrician, or a plumber, or a glazier will not be accomplished by trying to teach him something about any of these skilled trades. It will do the greatest possible service for him if it sees to it that he knows the English language well, that he can reason in terms of his elementary mathematics, with sharpness and accuracy, that he understands the fundamental principles upon which his government rests; and that he has acquired in the process of his elementary education that thoroughness in these simple subjects and that ability to turn his mind to one problem or another which will qualify him to go into a trade-school and to do the work so well that the trade-school will not have to teach him English and elementary mathematics.

M. André Siegfried, well-known authority on economic geography, advises, in the essay *On the Nature of French Exports,* that if a community wishes to produce real craftsmen, it should create in its schools an atmosphere of fine taste and broad culture by teaching well literature and history of art.[61]

It appears, indeed, that both in the interest of competence in manual arts and in that of civic education of all but very few children, handwork should be refused precedence or preponderance over " academic " studies. Manual training is devoid of the miraculous power of Moses' staff. The extraordinary capacity of manual work as a means for generating or prompting the general creative ability of the child is imaginary rather than actual.

On the other hand, it is true that under the guidance of an extraordinarily gifted and competent teacher, manual work can serve as the starting point for the student's ultimate mastery of many valuable and transferable notions and attitudes. Such was the case of Francesco, the little favorite of the great Leonardo da Vinci, in whose workshop the boy spent many ravishing hours, as pictured in the delightful novel of Merezhkovsky, *The Romance of Leonardo da Vinci.*

Timid and shy as a girl, the boy at first stood in great awe of the painter; one day, however, he came into his room at a moment when Leonardo, studying the laws of color, was experimenting with colored glass. He pleased the child by letting him look through the different pieces, yellow, blue, purple, or green, which gave a fairy aspect to familiar objects and made the world seem now smiling, now frowning, according to the color of the glass. Another of Leonardo's inventions proved very attractive. This was the *camera obscura,* by means of which living pictures appeared on a sheet of white paper; and Francesco saw the turning of the mill-wheel, the swallows circling round the church, the woodcutter's grey donkey, with his load of fagots, stepping daintily along the road while the poplars bowed their heads under the breeze. Still more fascinating was the weather gauge . . . a copper ring, a small stick like the beam

[61] Juvenel, H. de *et alii, Notre Diplomatie Économique,* Paris, Félix Alcan, 1925. p. 205 ff.

of a balance, and two little balls, the one covered with wax, the other with wadding. When the air was saturated with moisture, the wadding grew heavy and the little ball, falling down, inclined the beam till it touched one or other of the divisions marked on the copper ring. The degree of damp could thus be accurately measured and the weather predicted for two or three days. The little boy constructed a similar apparatus for himself, and was jubilant when the prophecies were fulfilled which he had deduced from its variations. Francesco went to the village school where he was taught by the old prior of the neighboring convent. The dog-eared Latin grammar and arithmetic primer were odious to him, and he learned but slackly. Leonardo's lore was of a new sort, pleasant to the child as a fairy tale. The instruments for the study of optics, acoustics, hydraulics, were to him new and magical toys, nor was he ever tired of hearing the painter's talk.[62]

Similarly, every intelligent lad who was lucky enough to be helping Socrates when the philosopher busied himself with sculptural work or basket making could learn any number of valuable things besides the crafts themselves. The same could happen to an apprentice in grinding lenses for optical instruments who had Spinoza for his master. But what we can reasonably hope for as a result of a boy's studying carpentry with an ordinary teacher of carpentering is a more or less adequate competence in carpentry.

In a word, the claim for a large place to be given to manual training over " academic " studies in the public school does not seem to be justifiable by any special formative effects of handwork, that is, on the ground of educational psychology.

THE ECONOMIC SIGNIFICANCE OF MANUAL TRAINING

The next point to be examined briefly is the question whether or not the ascendency of manual work over intellectual work or

[62] G. P. Putnam's Sons, 1902, p. 288 f.

simply the equality of the former to the latter in the public compulsory school can be defended on the ground of economics.

It appears that it cannot be justified except in certain emergency cases, for example, in a country ruined by war or a cosmic catastrophe, where every pair of hands which can be recruited has, naturally, to be set to work for the housing and feeding of the population, and should be trained for the work as rapidly as possible. Under normal conditions, however, the economics which would come to the support of the pedagogical theory advocating the ascendency of manual arts over mental work or merely the equality of manual work with intellectual work, in the public compulsory school could justly be called bad economics. It would be bad economics, in the first place, because of unfair competition to the unemployed adult workman — robbing Peter in order to help Paul.

Furthermore, manufactured monstrosities and botched products of the manual work of school children can perhaps be consumed by the school itself, but to produce marketable goods, painstaking craftsmanship or highly specialized division of labor is necessary. Both can readily mean physical work and boredom much in excess of what would be wise to impose upon most children. A premature overburdening of the child with monotonous handwork, even though it be the construction of school paraphernalia, has certainly no virtue whatsoever over choking him with Latin. A " production school " would be little compatible with the principle of reasonably joyful activity or with the general physical and mental welfare of the young generation. May we remind the progressives that the " production school " excludes, by definition, an arrangement permitting the students to work when they please, as they please, and if they please?

The economics of the " production school " is bad economics also because there can be no sound economic development of a nation without social peace. Social peace presupposes, among other things, sufficient economic intelligence on the part of the people. It presupposes the capitalist who knows that he owes his fortune as much to social order and organization as to his own or his ancestors' efforts and vision, and who realizes that wealth, like a fertilizer, is most useful when it is properly spread. It also presupposes the worker who knows how far he can go in his fight for the improvement of his economic condition without destroying the tree of whose fruits he desires to have a larger portion.

It is true that the boy destined to practice a craft cannot begin too soon, so that he may make it a part of himself while his muscular sense is easily impressed. But it is also true that he must learn a number of things of an intellectual nature in order that he may become an enlightened worker and citizen. Consequently, the school should help him to develop his mind, which is, in the end, the supreme tool. The World War has abundantly shown that the working class consists of men of very slight skill. Even many of the so-called skilled men when called for service were easily replaced by admittedly unskilled men, or simply by shop girls and domestic servants. There is no ground for fear that the " academic " school is antagonistic to the future industrial fitness of the majority of children; they can very well, and rapidly enough, learn at the factory itself how to perform the simple mechanical function to which they may be assigned. It is much less certain that outside the school, and after they have left it, they will acquire the habit of careful, correct reasoning, or sound fundamental notions regarding the organization and functioning of national and world economy.

The factory system of industry, deadening in the monotony of minute jobs, can scarcely be changed back to the craftsmanship of the time of guilds and home industry. But the working hours can be gradually reduced; wages can be increased and popular recreations and hobbies can, be made not only the source of invigorating rest, but also the provider of agreeable thoughts to occupy the worker's mind afterwards and thus help him to carry on through the drudgery of machine tending or similarly unattractive daily work. Lasting improvements of the existing economic order cannot be realized, except through the co-operation of an enlightened working class with enlightened national leaders in industry, commerce, and government.

Contrary to the belief of an enthusiastic advocate of the " production school " and the supremacy of manual arts, the beautiful medieval domes do not owe their existence entirely to handworkers.[63] Still less, probably, can there be erected by hand alone, or largely by it, the dome of democracy, in particular what is described as economic democracy, *i.e.,* the economic system based on the participation of workers in the administration of industry. Nothing but ruinous anarchy could result from an unintelligent meddling with the financing of industry and the marketing of its products. An intelligent participation in the conduct of business on the part of workers through the medium of their delegates can be gradually realized, however, on condition that the rank and file of workers have, in addition to sufficient native intelligence, a sufficient general education. It is interesting to see that the representatives of workers on the Committee on Adult Education appointed by the Minister of Reconstruction in Great Britain at the close of the World War joined in the recommendation that adult education. promote " deliberate efforts by which men and women attempt to satisfy their thirst for knowledge, to equip themselves for their responsibilities as citizens and members of society, or to find opportunities for self-expression." [64] The Committee found a wide and pressing demand among adults for education, a consider-

---

[63] *Reichsschulkonferenz* 1920, Amtlicher Bericht, S. 540.

[64] Kandel, I. L., *Education in Great Britain and Ireland,* U. S. Bureau of Education, No. 9, p. 67 f.

able suspicion of " technical education " and a desire to become "better fitted for the responsibilities of membership in political, social, and industrial organizations." [65]

To say it with Monsieur Servien, the old bookbinder, in a novel of Anatole France, " Ah, it is a famous tool, is a workman's hand! But an educated man's brain is a far more wonderful thing still." [66]

THE SOCIALIZING INFLUENCE OF MANUAL WORK

Can manual work at school be regarded as a dependable method of integrating the young toward a united, national, classless community? Can that integration, by means of handwork at school, be made strong enough to counteract the disuniting influences, social and economic, among families and social groups from which school children come and to which they will return?

The answer should hardly be in the affirmative. It appears little advisable, sociologically, to demand of all students more manual work than is necessary in order to teach them to fend for themselves in simple domestic needs, and to impart to them reasonable sympathy and understanding for the occupations based on handwork, and at the same time to furnish them with proper change from intellectual school work.

It seems that the civics of the " production school," like its economic theory, rest upon a certain confusion of ideas. The confusion is between what is called in sociology " community," in the sense of lasting alliance (*Lebensgemeinschaft*) on the one hand, and a community for the occasion (*Bedarfsgemeinschaft*), on the other. The mere fact that a certain group of workers is engaged in a certain industrial undertaking, or in the same line of industry, does not socialize or integrate them beyond the degree to which the wage-earning interest brings

[65] *Ibid.*   [66] *The Aspirations of Jean Servien, cit.,* p. 83.

them together. Karl Marx has erroneously considered them a solidly welded mass, free from stratification. On the contrary, they are vocationally divided into levels, or strata, and within a level. There is no miraculous integrating power in factory labor, still less is the school shop such a miracle worker. Other means have to be employed. As Paul Nathorp, neo-Kantianer and pedagogue, expressed it, *Sozial-Idealismus,* that is the spirit of self-abnegation in the interest of social service, is the necessary cement for durable socialization or integration of men.[67]

To increase appreciably co-operation and friendliness in the world at large, or even within a nation, warm-hearted companionship practised in school life surely is a welcome ally, but it is only an auxiliary force. The making of a tabouret at the school shop as between the future director of a corporation and the future street-sweeper is not enough to insure a reasonable understanding and civic co-operation between the actual corporation director and the actual street-sweeper. To achieve a reasonable victory over antisocial, egotistical tendencies of men, there has to be brought into action the main force, stronger than romantic tenderness or fugacious amiability and other similar auxiliaries. This force cannot be generated without careful systematic work on the part of the school for the intellectual and moral enlightenment of the maturing citizens.

SUGGESTIONS FOR READING

Childs, J. L., *Education and the Philosophy of Experimentalism.* (Century)

Dewey, John, *Experience and Nature.* (Open Court)

Follett, M. P., *Creative Experience.* (Longmans, Green)

Rignano, E., *The Psychology of Reasoning.* (Harcourt, Brace)

Wallas, G., *Our Social Heritage.* (Yale University Press)

[67] Nathorp, Paul, *Sozial-Idealismus: Neuen Richtlinien Sozialer Erziehung,* Berlin, J. Springer, 1920.

CHAPTER
V

INTELLECTUAL TRAINING

INTELLECTUAL TRAINING

Among the various confusions of technical pedagogical terms there is one which is particularly apt to cause wrong ideas regarding the fundamentals of the educative process. The confusion in question is between formal discipline and intellectual training. It is usually aggravated by vagueness and disagreement in the opinions of educational psychologists concerning the working of the transfer of learning.

The theory of formal discipline holds that the study of a single " hard " subject can form the mind of the student, that is, can develop in it such qualities and powers as to prepare the student successfully to meet situations of life demanding adaptability, inventiveness, and elasticity. Two groups of school subjects have for a long time disputed the monopoly of formal discipline: the classical languages and mathematics. The other subjects with secret jealousy or loudly, but in vain, claimed, each for itself, the distinction. The controversy is of old date, indeed. Plato, in the *Republic,* expressed the opinion that " those who have a natural talent for calculation are generally quick at every other kind of knowledge; and even the dull, if they have had an arithmetical training, although they may derive no other benefit from it, always become much sharper than they would otherwise have been. . . .[1] And in all departments of knowledge, as experience proves, any one who has studied geometry is infinitely quicker of apprehension than one who has not." [2] Vol-

---

[1] *Republic,* VII, 526. [2] *Ibid.,* 527.

taire, on the other hand, used to say: " I have always remarked that geometry leaves the mind just where it found it." [3] Educational psychology offers no ground on which to intervene, on principle, in favor of the monopoly of either mathematics or the classics. On the other hand, no competent student in educational psychology has ever doubted either the feasibility or the utility of intellectual training.

Educational psychology has shown that transfer of learning is possible with regard to information only in the case of a situation similar wholly or in part to that under which certain learning was acquired. For instance, take an American adolescent born in Japan and partly educated there. Among other things, he has learned the Japanese syntax to meet the need of getting the exact sense of Japanese sentences. There was not any, or infinitely little, transfer of information from his study of the Japanese syntax to his ability to meet the situation of correctly handling the problems of the geography of America. On the contrary, there was considerable transfer of information from his learning the Latin syntax to his learning the French idiom and vice versa. No transfer whatsoever occurred on the information side between the young American's study of the Japanese syntax and of Greco-Roman history, or between his study of geometry and of American history.

But, on the side of mental habits, after our scholar has been sufficiently impressed in the course of his study of the Japanese language — probably not by the beauty of the language alone — with the idea that one should never be satisfied with an expression unless it is clear and conforms to the rules of grammar and logic, he demands of himself and of others, possibly not always with complete success, a certain degree of clarity and precision of expression. That mental habit, once formed, is with him no

---

[3] Quoted in Goethe's letter to Zelter of February 28, 1811, *Goethes Briefe,* Weimar, Hermann Böhlau's Nachfolger, 1901, 22 Bd., S. 49.

matter whether he is preparing his classes or listening to a radio talk or to dinner speeches. Normally, it is with him under all circumstances and in very dissimilar situations.

The following distinction between the theory of formal discipline and that of intellectual training might probably be convenient. The formal discipline theory says: There are certain valuable mental habits — such as concentration, clarity, precision, perseverance in thinking — which should be inculcated in pupils and which can be developed only (or best of all) through studying the classical languages (or mathematical subjects or statistics, as the case may be).

The theory of intellectual training says: Yes, there are certain valuable mental habits which must be inculcated as thoroughly as possible in the school population; their development depends, however, not so much upon what is studied, but upon how it is studied, though the study of subjects of richer content and complexity is a better means for intellectual training than studies of the opposite type.

Intellectual training is, then, the development of the habit of accurately retaining our experiences and of accurately reasoning about our experiences whether first-hand or second-hand, in other words, whether direct or borrowed from the experiences of others and learned by the spoken and written word or by means of any other symbols. Intellectual training is the development of the ability to get new and clearer meanings from our experiences, whether acquired at first hand or second hand. It is the development of such habits of mind as would make thinking accurate and fertile to the highest possible degree. As Socrates has expressed it, " Knowledge does not consist in impressions of sense, but in reasoning about them; in that only, and not in the mere impression, truth and being can be obtained." [4]

<hr>

[4] *Theaetetus*, 186.

Accurate thinking, thinking critical of itself as well as of the thoughts of other people, is a thing that has to be learned. In the very fitting words of John Dewey found in *How We Think:*

> While it is not the business of education to prove every statement made, any more than to teach every possible item of information, it is its business to cultivate deep-seated and effective habits of discriminating tested beliefs from mere assertions, guesses, and opinions, to develop a lively, sincere, and open-minded preference for conclusions that are properly grounded, and to ingrain into the individual's working habits methods of inquiry and reasoning appropriate to the various problems that present themselves. . . . And since these habits are not a gift of nature (no matter how strong the aptitude for acquiring them); and since, moreover, the casual circumstances of the natural and social environment are not enough to compel their acquisition, the main office of education is to supply conditions that make for their cultivation. The formation of these habits is the training of mind.[5]

The way to the acquisition of those habits of mind lies through the arduous road of careful, relentless training, the result of watchful effort on the part of the teacher never to leave uncriticized and uncorrected the reasoning process of the pupils unless it shows a satisfactory degree of precision and sequence. Inculcating mental efficiency in the young is not at all incompatible with reasonably joyous co-operation on their part. Long ago Shaftesbury observed that " it is the habit of reasoning which can make a reasoner. And men can never be better invited to the habit than when they find a pleasure in it. A freedom in rallying, a liberty in decent language to question everything and an allowance of unravelling or refuting any argu-

[5] Dewey, J., *How We Think,* p. 27 f. Reprinted by special permission of D. C. Heath and Company.

ment without offense to the arguer, are the only terms which can render such speculative conversations any way agreeable." [6] It is not at all impossible to develop in pupils a craftsmanship, as it were, in reasoning. To this end a properly guided apprenticeship in the school of the great masters of thought is invaluable.

Humanity has become civilized very largely by imitation, to be exact, by imitating its best sons. The highest form of imitation is emulation. Let your young reasoners imitate and emulate the art of thinking developed by the greatest minds of all times and of all lands. Young reasoners not unlike young musicians and young painters should be " tuned up " to the harmony created by great or classical masters. The term " classics " not infrequently is somewhat vaguely and loosely used. Its real meaning is twofold: (a) classical in the sense of pertaining to Greco-Roman antiquity; (b) classical in the sense of universally valid, *i.e.,* valid or appealing to men of all times and all nations, as is the case of certain undying creations in statesmanship, literature, music, the pictorial and plastic arts, and philosophy. While seeking to inculcate in your students the habits of fertile and exact thinking, apprentice them to classics, to the greatest masters of thought — ancient and modern — that humanity has known.

Not only is it true to say that if certain books had not been written there would have been many more gaps in the structure of our civilization; it is also true that anyone's life and development is incomplete who has not read certain books. Education is never finished as long as man's intellect lives and is active. The task of the school is not to give the students a finished education but to equip them with a sort of life directory in the form of fundamental information, ideals, and habits

---

[6] Cf. Baldwin, Stanley, *On England and Other Addresses,* London, Philip Allan, 1926, p. 97 ff.

which will make it possible for them to grow intellectually as long as they live and preserve their physical and mental capacities. Do not permit the lost paradise to be twice lost in the life of your students, first when their biblical ancestors lost it and again when the young themselves miss the great creations in which the lost paradise of beauty and moral and intellectual grandeur is, at least partially, recovered by genius. When they have beheld the vision of paradise regained they will never be satisfied with lowly ways of thinking and the productions of inferior men, and thus the general tone of life, moral and intellectual, of the community will be improved and elevated.

A keen student of books and of their destinies has written, not without sadness:

In almost everything vast opportunities and gigantic means of multiplying our products bring with them new perils and troubles which are often at first neglected. Our huge cities, where wealth is piled up and the requirements and appliances of life extended beyond the dreams of our forefathers, seem to breed in themselves new forms of squalor, disease, blights, or risks to life such as we are yet unable to master. So the enormous multiplicity of modern books is not altogether favorable to the knowing of the best. I listen with mixed satisfaction to the paeans that they chant over the works which issue from the press each day; how the books poured forth from Paternoster Row might in a few years be built into a pyramid that would fill the dome of St. Paul's. How in this mountain of literature am I to find the really useful book? How, when I have found it, and found its value, am I to get others to read it? How am I to keep my head clear in the torrent and din of works, all of which distract my attention, most of which promise me something, whilst so few fulfill that promise? The Nile is the source of the Egyptian's bread, and without it he perishes of hunger. But the Nile may be rather too liberal in his flood, and then the Egyptian runs imminent risk of drowning.

And thus there never was a time, at least during the last two hundred years, when the difficulties in the way of making an efficient use of books were greater than they are today, when obstacles were more real between readers and the right books to read, when it was practically so troublesome to find out that which it is of vital importance to know; and that not by the dearth, but by the plethora of printed matter. For it comes to nearly the same thing whether we are actually debarred by physical impossibility from getting the right book into our hands, or whether we are choked off from the right book by the obtrusive crowd of the wrong books; so that it needs a strong character and a resolute system of reading to keep the head cool in the storm of literature around us. We read nowadays in the market-place — I would rather say in some large steam factory of letter-press, where damp sheets of new prints whirl around us perpetually — if it be not rather some noisy book-fair where literary showmen tempt us with performing dolls, and the gongs of rival booths are stunning our ears from morn till night.

Contrast with this pandemonium of Leipsic and Paternoster Row the sublime picture of our Milton in his early retirement at Horton, when, musing over his coming flight to the epic heaven, practicing his pinions, as he tells Diodati, he consumed five years of solitude in the reading of the ancient writers.[7]

Obviously, it is not in our power as teachers to do anything about the pandemonium of the book-fair except — and this would be sufficient materially to check the pandemonium — to train the school population through the inculcation of the right mental habits in general and through the companionship of the classics as defined above in particular, toward knowing a good book from a bad or mediocre one at first sight, so to say. The result will not be less gratifying than is the result of training in music appreciation through the hearing of classical music in the school and in the home. The children so trained can safely be left to hear radio music; they will not acquire bad

[7] Harrison, F., " The Choice of Books " (1878), *Modern Eloquence*. 1923, pp. 239–240.

taste in music. As soon as a savage performance, instrumental or vocal, floats into the air, they will shut it off. If and when more of them do this, the advertiser will demand and obtain better music with which to endear his merchandise to the radio listeners.

Apprenticeship to classical examples of clear, precise, and fertile thinking can be made a sufficiently effective and pleasurable source of stimulation for the student to exercise himself or herself in careful, finished thinking. But, clearly, the constant attention of the teacher to the accuracy of the reasoning of students, systematic effort on his part to make correct, careful thinking a sort of good form which the pupils must observe in all they say or write, is the foremost dependable way of developing intellectual craftsmanship in the young. This kind of work has to be done, however, with as much tact as firmness. Goethe has justly observed:

> We more readily confess to errors, mistakes, and shortcomings in our conduct than in our thought. . . . And the reason is that the conscience is humble and even takes a pleasure in being ashamed. But the intellect is proud, and if forced to recant is driven to despair.[8]

This is true of young learners as much if not more than of adult persons. At all events, intellectual training can only be properly considered as attained when it has acquired with the student the character of a habit. The literature of the New Education, or the Activity School, abounds in statements to the effect that one of the invaluable results of the method of free activity is the aptness of the latter in imparting to the child methods of attacking problems. But a method of attack, like any kind of method, must be a habit. To attain the rank of firm habit it must accomplish all the qualifications required. Among these, systematic training through intensive repetition, perseverance, and

[8] *Maxims and Reflections,* German Classics, *cit.,* Vol. II, p. 384.

precision are first and foremost. Clearly, these cannot well develop through a happy-go-lucky frame of mind, indifferent, or pronouncedly averse to work, meticulous and, to a degree, inevitably monotonous. Neither can they go hand in hand with the pupil's freedom of taking and leaving subject matter where and when he likes.

American students in education will recall that the dependence of our intelligence upon our will power is a *Leitmotiv* of the educational philosophy of Professor William C. Bagley and is admirably presented in his various writings. They may also be interested to know the discussion of the same point by the French philosopher and former secondary-school professor, Henri Bergson, (see p. 154) found in his paper "On Will Power and Intelligence." The principal passages of the paper are as follows:

As a rule, you call intelligent that one of your classmates who has a good memory, and a certain facility of expression, who shows flashes of wit and pleasant originality. You also often hear people mention as intelligent the man who talks well, and who can listen still better; who seizes immediately some of the broader aspects of the subject exposed to him, though frequently he is unable to penetrate the subject any deeper than the first and incomplete close-up of it, and is contented with few but clear ideas about it; a man who rapidly learns about a variety of things just as much as is necessary to know in order to be able to discuss them without blundering; in a word, a man who has the tact of talking or writing about a subject for a well-determined length of time, just long enough to bring into notice all he knows about it and short enough for dodging what he is ignorant of in the subject.

Veritable intelligence is something very different. Real intelligence is something that makes it possible for us to penetrate the inmost of the subject we are studying, to touch its very bottom, to feel the beating of its pulse and to smell its fragrance. . . . Intelligence means adjustment of the mind to the subject studied, a perfect adaptation of the attention, the ability to exercise that kind of effort which enables us each time we wish, to grasp promptly a subject, to develop it vigorously, and to remember it accurately and lastingly. . . .

All actual progress of the real intelligence is marked off with an effort by which the will brings the intellect to a superior degree of concentration. Mental concentration is the whole secret of intellectual superiority. Concentration distinguishes man from animal, which is the most absent-minded creature known to nature (*le grand distrait de la nature*). The animal is always at the mercy of impressions coming from outside, while man can concentrate his thoughts. Concentration also distinguishes a keen and sensible man from one who easily goes astray and who is given to day-dreaming. The latter abandons his mind to all sorts of fleeting ideas, while the former is constantly watchful of his thought and of realities. Finally, concentration distinguishes a superior man from an ordinary man. The latter is easily satisfied with mediocre ability, which to him is restful and inviting, while the former is moved by the aspiration to surpass himself. Concentration in all probability constitutes the essence of genius, if it is true that genius is a moment of vision which rewards years of labor, of concentration and patient expectation. . . .

Consequently, nourish in yourselves the hearth of energy and will power. Gather together your effort and concentrate your attention, give to your will power the greatest possible impetus so that your intellect may attain to the highest possible radiancy. Descend into the innermost depth of your own self in order to bring forth all there is in you, indeed, more than there is in you. Remember, your will power can perform that miracle. Demand that it be accomplished.[9]

EXAMINATIONS AS A DEVICE IN INTELLECTUAL TRAINING

Among the devices for the promotion of the habit of accurate, precise thinking there must not be overlooked the educational procedure known as examination. A good examination should be, it seems, a suitable combination of achievement test

[9] *Revue de Paris,* 1-er décembre 1928, pp. 682–684.

and intelligence test. If a man of action has to be trained through action, so a man whose job it is to do responsible thinking quickly — and no democracy can have too many such men in its service — must be trained through rapid responsible thinking. Examinations afford such occasions to train children, adolescents, and youths for speedy responsible thinking, provided that the examinations are properly organized and public significance is attached to them in the way of an alternative between promotion and non-promotion, admission and non-admission, prize winning or losing, and the like, depending on success or failure in an examination. Objections are sometimes raised against examinations on the ground that examinations breed unhealthy competition and are an inadequate test of the real value of the individual, and also on the ground that they develop ostentatiousness. Though such objections may not be entirely devoid of weight, they do not seem to invalidate the importance of examinations, either as a method of public control of the work of students and teachers, or as a method of intellectual training.

To educational policies as to human policies in any sphere of endeavor, there seems to apply the observation made by Cardinal Retz (d. 1679) with regard to international policies: " There are no good policies; but there are policies which are less bad than some others." To have examinations seems a better policy than not to have them. They may be inconclusive and leave undiscovered some fine points about the mind and character of the examined; but, on the whole, when a body of intelligent and conscientious teachers pass in review through the medium of appropriate written and oral tests the personality of the examined, they can size up his or her intellectual value, and at least certain traits of character, as well as proficiency in a given subject matter, more accurately than can otherwise be done.

Some progressives disapprove of examinations on the ground

that they are artificial situations, untrue to life. This is, obviously, an untenable objection. Concentrated, rapid, and yet exact thinking and careful, though swift, analysis and organization of data required in a properly conducted school examination are, precisely, the type of mental work which is constantly demanded in practical life.

The desirable type of examination is one that combines the new or standardized type of questions with the so-called old type. In other words, the desirable type of examination can test both the mathematically measurable exactitude of information and the rigorous reasoning on the basis of given data, on the one hand; and the meaning-getting power, that is, the power of orientation among things in accordance with their total significance, however subtle and concealed, on the other. This latter power manifests itself in actual life situations through the ability to find the right solution of complex problems and the right way out of situations laden with intangibilities. Examinations should, accordingly, be so set from the first grade on as to encourage the development of (A) the precise remembering of facts and data and a clear, rigorous reasoning about the data and facts; (B) the ability to handle the entanglements between hard facts and subtleties and intangibilities of meaning concealed in the relationships between various hard facts, in other words, the ability to find soundly " nuanced " solutions of the complex problems made of such entanglements; and — the most important of all — (C) the combination of these two orders of powers and abilities.

As an example of the C type of examination questions in letters, there may be cited the following topics characteristic of the questions set for French composition in the secondary-school graduation examinations in France.

Lessing, in order to improve the morals of the second fable of La Fontaine, wished that the cheese be poisoned and the fox die.

E. Faguet, on the other hand, seems to be in agreement with the little girl who proposed to him to correct the first fable of La Fontaine in such a manner that the ant, instead of sending away the grasshopper, chides it, but also gives it food.

Which fabulists renders the greater service to children: Those who would satisfy the child's sense of justice and sentiment of pity, or rather those who, like La Fontaine, believe that there is no more salutary lesson for children than the one that follows from an example vividly true to real life? [10]

It is said that truth is the supreme value and that, consequently, falsehood is always and necessarily bad. But it is also said that society cannot exist without falsehood. What is your attitude regarding each of the two points of view? [11]

Augustin Thierry predicted, in the Preface to his *Ten Years of Historical Studies,* that fondness for history would be the characteristic of the nineteenth century, as fondness for philosophy was that of the eighteenth century. If you think that this prediction came true give the reasons explaining the nineteenth-century taste for historical studies.[12]

In a letter to Madame Deffand of September 21, 1779, the Duchess of Choiseul speaks of Voltaire in the following terms: " Despite the defects which can be attributed to Voltaire, he will always be the writer whom I shall read and re-read with the greater pleasure because of his good taste and the universality of his interests. It does not matter that he tells nothing new. He develops and expresses so well the thoughts that I have had myself and he can say better than anyone else what others have already tried to say. I do not demand of him that he teach me something more than everybody knows, because who is that author who can tell me, as Voltaire can, something that everybody knows? "

Do you think that this opinion appraises the talent of Voltaire with sufficient exactitude? [13]

[10] Demiashkevich, M. J., " Preliminary Selection and Training of Leaders in France and Germany," *Educational Administration and Supervision,* January, 1933, p. 52.

[11] *Revue Universitaire,* juillet, 1932.

[12] *Annales du Baccalauréat,* Année 1934, Paris, Librairie Vuibert, p. 1.

[13] *Ibid.,* p. 5.

The great romantic artists love nature and sing its praise, drawing their inspiration from the humblest and most rustic forms of nature as much as from its majestic and solemn phenomena. But some of the romanticists, like A. de Vigny, dread nature and turn away from nature, as A. Dumas, the son, did. " I must confess," he wrote, " that I do not fall into ecstasy before nature. On the contrary, nature fills me with sadness, upsets me, and almost reduces me to vapour, so to speak. Solitude makes me uneasy, the infinite perplexes me."

Explain, with the help of precise examples, such contrary sentiments toward nature. Tell whether you yourself like nature and what joys you expect nature to give you.[14]

Montaigne returned at the end of 1585 to his villa from which an epidemic had kept him away for six months. He found the country devastated not only by the disease but also by marauders.

Imagine that a gentleman neighbor called on Montaigne and reproduce their conversation. They talk about the recent misfortunes visited upon the country and about the civil wars that ravage France. The visitor expressed his regret that Montaigne was not given a more important position in the government of the country. Montaigne explains why he does not think himself fit for a position of influence. He declares himself satisfied with his situation which he thinks as happy a one as can be given a man — and expresses the hope that his life will not be entirely useless to other men if they draw some profit from his *Essays* to which he will devote his forces to the end! [15]

The type A examination questions lends itself to standardization procedures, the type B and C do not. We should, of course, be grateful for the possibility, whenever it really exists, to measure, in exact quantitative formulae and yet soundly, the qualitative value of men, their abilities, and their achievements, and to express it with the help of mathematical scales independent of the differences in the opinion of individual judges and of the idiosyncrasies of the judges.

[14] *Ibid.*, p. 9.   [15] *Ibid.*, p. 17.

On the other hand, it seems right to say that mathematics ends where the human personality begins. No correct judgment, that is, as correct as is humanly possible, of the totality of a human personality appears to be possible, except when such judgment is the result of an insight into a human personality on the part of one or several persons possessing an adequate intelligence and special training.

The wondrous complexity of the human personality, even more than the complexity of the human body (in which the functioning of the physical organism and of the physiological laws to which it is subject is complicated by the play of thought, emotions, and will power or the lack of it), is prohibitive of simple, mechanical measurement of its qualities and defects, its possibilities and limitations.

Medical examination profits by the mechanical measurement of certain aspects of the organism and of some of its functions. But the correct diagnosis of the totality of the health-situation of a given human organism presupposes an auscultation, an insight into the totality of the situation, by a master physician, still better by several master physicians. A reliable and truly objective diagnosis of the patient's general vitality is not possible otherwise. An apprentice in medicine or a trained nurse may well measure, with the help of special instruments, the blood pressure of the patient, and record in exact mathematical formulae his height, weight, rate of metabolism, etc. But the final diagnosis would be a hazardous piece of medical judgment if it should be the result of a mechanical computation by an office stenographer of the data mechanically obtained. A careful auscultation by a master physician, guided by the exact measurements to which the patient was subjected, and by learning, experience, and power of insight into the value of complex and probably contradictory data, is indispensable.

Similarly, a good school examination should always include

a diagnosis of the human personality of the pupil (intelligence, character, emotional balance) in the light and in the function of his achievement or failure in the various school tasks. School examinations — except perhaps those bearing upon purely mechanical skills — seem to demand, in addition to the more or less mechanical measurements which are relative to information and which are carried out with the help of standardized achievement tests, also an " auscultation " of the student's personality by one or several experts in a given field of knowledge possessing keen intelligence, broad general culture, and adequate pedagogical training. The consensus of judgment of judges so qualified based on the observed and carefully weighed performance of the pupil in written and oral tests, which consist of complex problems in a given field of knowledge or which are relative to the general wisdom of life, is, in the final analysis, the only reliable objective estimate possible of the intellectual and moral worth and promise of the pupil. In adult life this former pupil of ours will be judged by similar methods. His prospective employer, his constituency will not put him on the scales or subject him to standardized tests, but will judge him on the basis of the total impression he makes while performing a task.

It is interesting to note the following appreciation of the value of standardized achievement tests and of the so-called old-type of examination found in one or two special studies based upon experimental evidence.

" A test composed of both old type and new type questions was preferred by the pupils to either new type or old type tests alone. . . . Each of the new tests gave poorer results as a measure of ability to think in the field of history than it gave as a measure of information." [16]

[16] Brinkley, S. G., *Values of New Type Examinations in the High School,* Bureau of Publications, Teachers College, Columbia University, Contribution to Education No. 161, pp. 59, 60.

" Their [standardized tests] * use, of course, can be easily overdone; they have, moreover, severe limitations; they are valuable in diagnosing mechanical skills, revealing factual knowledge, and in registering vocabulary achievement; they are of lesser worth in the measure of those factors which have creative values." [17]

". . . Your examinations have asked for almost no revelation of my sensitiveness to the spirit of beauty." [18]

". . . The examiners . . . would know but imperfectly, if at all, whether he were a cultivated person." [19]

Examinations, even non-competitive, contribute, of course, to the spirit of competition. But this competition is not necessarily unhealthy. Normally, it is a healthy rivalry and promotes intellectual sportsmanship among the young who are glad to see the better man win. Besides, if the competitive spirit inherent in youth is not at least partly consumed in the intellectual effort demanded by preparation for and actual performance in examinations, it may lead the young to much less healthy and worthwhile forms of competition. Furthermore, competition, which is otherwise called ambition, is one of the basic tendencies of human nature, and is base or noble depending upon the spirit in which it is carried out and the objective to which it is directed. In fact, the ambition to do away with the traditional philosophy of education, and competition with it, is the primary source of the fire with which the better, more disinterested workers of Progressive Education themselves are animated, while they inveigh against competition as a method of motivation in education.

Examinations, to be sure, may lead to an exaggerated amount of drudgery and cramming in preparatory coaching and to the

---

* Bracketed remarks are added.

[17] *Examining the Examinations in English, Harvard Studies in Education*, No. 17, pp. 209–210.

[18] *Ibid.*, p. 158.   [19] *Ibid.*, p. 159.

neglect of some other perhaps more useful forms of class work. But the vice is not an organic one. When examinations are properly organized, coaching for them means simply the training of the mind and the cultural enrichment of the students' experience conducted at the highest possible level which alone would meet the high standard of intellectual polish and of information demanded by the examiners.

Finally, the ostentatiousness of examinations is not a malignant disease inherent in examinations, either. In the first place, tactful school authorities and teachers can avoid all ostentatiousness even if the examined or their parents are inclined to stage some form of it. Second, the earnest interest on the part of the examined in their performance and the ardent desire to do their best deserve the stigma of ostentatiousness as little as does the performance of an honest artist who wishes to give the best of his art to the public. And if a certain amount of proud intellectual strutting should be an inevitable concomitant of examinations, again there is no mortal sin or anything really objectionable in being proud of a well-deserved intellectual success hard won in an examination. Whatever ostentatiousness there may be in such pride, it is a much more fruitful kind than the ostentatiousness of many of the so-called activity projects which often are accompanied by avalanches of magazine clippings and floods of picture cuttings and other similar paraphernalia covering the walls of some "new schools." Those who should benefit by such exhibits most, very often do not look at them at all.

A useful device in intellectual training for all normal children, examinations are especially important for the proper training of the more gifted, the potential leaders in the various walks of life. Plato, who seems to be one of the first to formulate the educational philosophy of examinations, has said:

. . . We must inquire who are the best guardians of their own conviction that what they think the interest of the State is to be the rule of all their actions. We must watch them from their youth upwards, and make them perform actions in which they are most likely to forget or to be deceived, and he who remembers and is not deceived is to be selected, and he who fails in the trial is to be rejected. . . . And there should also be toils and pains and conflicts prescribed for them, in which they will be made to give further proof of the same qualities.[20]

Examinations, then, can be regarded as an excellent device for training the educand in the habit of attacking problems, that is, in the habit of exercising his best thinking in an emergency. All emergencies, different though they may be in content, have one thing in common, namely, that they are emergencies. The only effective way of training the educand toward meeting emergencies is to help him to develop the habit of not being baffled or made fearful by unusual and unforeseen situations. Important unannounced examinations appear to be very useful in building up immunity from losing one's wits in the face of an emergency. Properly organized examinations will form in the educand the habit of rapidly organizing his wits in situations in which he needs them most acutely.

INDEPENDENT THINKING AND INTELLECTUAL TRAINING

Independent thinking on the part of citizens is one of the mightiest weapons of self-defense that a democracy can possess against the "Prince of Darkness," who is the worst enemy of democracies because he is the greatest ally of demagogues, dictators, and tyrants. His weapons are various kinds of blazing and dazzling show-windows, slogans, half-truths, and millennium-promising doctrines. Carlyle has made the following suggestive observation:

Truly a Thinking Man is the worst enemy the Prince of Darkness can have; every time such a one announces himself, I doubt

[20] *Republic,* III, 413.

not there runs a shudder through the Nether Empire and new Emissaries are trained with new tactics to entrap him if possible, and hoodwink him, and handcuff him.[21]

The Progressive Education literature recommends spontaneous undirected learning as the best way to attain independent thinking. Let the child work for himself at what he is interested in and let him do this in his own manner. This is the right way to make him think for himself, we are advised. Such and similar arguments are, however, more attractive than convincing. The point is that we always think for ourselves, but our thinking may be either exact or inexact, either critical or credulous. No one can get inside that intricate, almost mysterious inner chamber which is called mind. Our thinking is always our own. Yet it can be properly called independent only when it is not independent of or divorced from facts knowable by experience or from logic, but is independent of a deceptive arrangement of facts or of an incorrect interpretation of facts suggested or preached by others. An incorrect interpretation of facts is sometimes made under the influence of others who seek to " hoodwink and handcuff " our minds, and, consequently, our persons. Sometimes it is a result of our own reluctance to exercise sustained mental effort, of our own intellectual self-indulgence and self-complacency.

Such independent thinking as defined above — the only kind that really deserves the name — cannot be very well attained through the child's own undirected learning, unanalyzed by the more experienced, more critical, and more powerful intellect of a good teacher. The very opposite method, that of systematic, watchful, frank but friendly analysis and criticism of the work of the student's mind, is the road toward the treasure of enlightened independent public opinion which democracy must carefully gather and guard against the designs of the

[21] Carlyle, Thomas, *Sartor Resartus,* London, George Bell, 1898, p. 748.

"Prince of Darkness" — the machinations and propaganda of self-seeking demagogues and ruthless fanatics.

The "Prince of Darkness" must and can be defeated, if by independent thinking which the school seeks to inculcate in the young is meant thinking characterized by the fivefold independence of the mind.

(A) Independence in the face of attempts of interested persons and organizations to captivate the mind via the ear and the eye. The dangers of distortion and deception of public opinion via the ears have been great enough, but those that can come via the eyes are still greater. The historian Thucydides, a thoughtful student of the popular mind, said of the Athenian popular masses:

No men are better dupes, sooner deceived by novel notions, or slower to follow approved advice. You despise what is familiar, while you are worshippers of every new extravagance. . . . You are always hankering after an ideal state, but you do not give your minds even to what is straight before you. In a word, you are at the mercy of your own ears, and sit like spectators attending a performance of sophists, but very unlike counsellors of a State. . . .[22]

Modern propagandists and sophists have a more effective method of captivating the mind. It is to the eye that advertisers and propagandists — honest and dishonest — try to get access in the first place. The most rapid way to reach the brain is through the eye, and one of the most efficient and speedy means of transmitting varied sensations through the eye to the brain is moving pictures. The eye acts upon the mind rapidly and irresistibly. The simple spirit, the unenlightened, untrained mind, may be able to muster enough protective doubt to defend itself against suggestions pressed on it through the ear; but it can much less

[22] Thucydides, *History of the Peloponnesian War*, III, 38 (Translated by B. Jowett, Oxford, Clarendon Press, Vol. I, p. 192). Cf. Talleyrand: "It is not fools who are lacking but happily there are not enough charlatans to dupe all the fools available." Lacour-Gayet, G., *Talleyrand*, Paris, Payot, 1931, Vol. III, p. 428.

easily defend its independence of messages pressed on it through the eye. How can the school put moving pictures and printed materials to good use and forearm the maturing mind against the tendency to passive acceptance of what is planned to captivate it through this impressionable medium — the eye? No better method seems to be available than the one admired by Confucius in the *Analects:* " Seeing much with the Master and keeping it in memory." [23]

(B) Independence from intentionally deceptive slogans, that is, from the quasi-logical and quasi-scientific use of words which are left without the exact definition of their meaning. That kind of independence which is essential in the training of the citizen was aptly described by Euripides who, familiar with the ways of demagogy, referred to the latter as a parasite growing upon democracy and thriving upon the ignorance and insufficient intellectual training of the average citizen:

. . . The inflated demagogue, who, puffing the people up with words, turns them as interest prompts him. For he that is pleasant and winds himself into their hearts today offends tomorrow; then, with fresh calumnies cloaking his former errors, he escapes from justice. And then how can a people rightly guide the city who do not examine minutely the reasons that are brought forward? [24]

In political discussions the fiery terms employed are, more often than not, left undefined, or if they are defined, one unknown term is defined by another unknown term; or a term is used in more than one sense; or parallels, allegories, and comparisons are employed which are likely to produce the sentiment desired while confusing the reasoning of the listener or reader. Thus past political speeches of present-day dictators bristled with words like " progress," " liberty." Needless to say, these terms were not defined. What the future dictator meant

[23] Cf. Dawson, M. M., *The Ethics of Confucius, Cit.,* p. 63.
[24] *Suppliants,* 410 ff.

was liberty on the condition of complete submission to him, that is, as much liberty as might be left over after he had taken it away from the people; and by progress he meant anything that he might consider progress before he changed his mind and declared the opposite course of action true progress. But the gullible masses did not suspect this.

It may be observed in passing that the literature of the New Education seems to derive its power, at least in some degree, from the employment of attractive sounding undefined terms, for instance, " growth," " freedom," " initiative," " independent thinking," and the like; or slogans like "Education is not a preparation for life, but life itself." But what is life? Ask the question of a hundred different persons and you will, very likely, receive as many different answers.

In political fights one of the first things false friends of democracy do is to assume some attractive-sounding name for themselves and to give their adversaries a name which will place them in a ridiculous, contemptible, or odious light. " Words are daggers," observed Aeschylus, and Shakespeare borrowed the telling sentence.[25] They can exercise over us a power, almost mysterious. On the ninth Thermidor, Robespierre and his extremist partisans were declared outlaws by the Convention. Henriot, one of the proscribed, succeeded, however, in bringing artillerymen to train their cannon on the house of the Assembly and incited them to fire, and thus to " save liberty and revolution." When the soldiers were on the point of opening fire, the conservative deputies, naturally perturbed, turning against the extremists their own favorite weapon — the slogan — shouted to the soldiers: " Gunners, are you going to cover yourselves with dishonor? Don't listen to the rascal. He is *outlawed*." [26] When the awful word was pronounced, the soldiers

---

[25] *Libation-Bearers,* 380; *Hamlet,* Act III, Scene 3.
[26] Thiers, A., *Histoire de la Révolution Française,* Paris, Lecointe, 1834, Vol. VI, p. 463.

turned away from the man and refused to fire. The post-war revolutions present abundant examples of similar nature, with the heavy scoring of revolutionaries over conservatives.

The more combative and the less tolerant progressives have used, in the heat of war upon the essentialists, many slogans which appealed to the less mature pedagogues, some of whom came, as a result, to have a strong distrust of anything that was branded " old education." As a result, the essentialists were put, in a small way, into a position comparable to that of Socrates unjustly sentenced to die:

> How you have felt, O men of Athens, at hearing speeches of my accusers, I cannot tell; but I know that their persuasive words almost made me forget who I was: — such was the effect of them; and yet they have hardly spoken a word of truth.[27]

The employment of slogans, certainly, is not in itself a case of moral turpitude. Many honest and honorable public leaders in the various walks of life have employed slogans. A well-made slogan travels fast and wide. But the use of slogans is socially wholesome only when there is common agreement as to exactly what a given slogan means. It is, then, like dynamite which is socially beneficial when it blows passages through obstructing rocks to bring water and nourishment from regions otherwise inaccessible.

Plato would grant rulers the right to tell lies in the interest of the State: " Then the rulers of the State are the only persons who ought to have the privilege of lying, either at home or abroad; they may be allowed to lie for the good of the State." [28] It is from this passage in Plato that sprung the definition of an ambassador as a man who is sent abroad to lie there for the benefit of his country. Political experience since the time of Plato has well demonstrated that lying either abroad or — still

[27] *Apology*, 17.   [28] *Republic*, III, 389.

worse — at home on the part of even indubitably patriotic public men is more bad than good, and the maturing citizen should
be assisted toward developing the valuable capacity which is
picturesquely described by the chambermaid Françoise in a
novel by Marcel Proust: "Madame is worse than X-rays. Madame sees everything." [29] Fortunately enough, every normally
endowed mind can be sharpened to a fair degree of critical penetration into the real thought and intentions of other
people, regardless of the sonorous slogans by means of which
they may be camouflaged. And the method, again, is that of
intellectual training; or general culture, if by general culture is
meant something that remains even when all details have been
forgotten.

(C) Independence from doctrine. In our own time, and very
likely hereafter, the active citizens of good faith will constantly
have to deal with "armed doctrine." Its principal arms are the
formidable charms or witchery of words, the promise of millennium, whether a well-intentioned promise or not, direct or
implied.

That the citizen may be in a position to draw out whatever
may be good in an armed doctrine without being overpowered
and enslaved by it, he must be, in his turn, armed. The arms
the public school can and should furnish him are standards of
undisputed knowledge, of lucid, fruitful judgment, and the
habit of searching for such knowledge and of exercising such
judgment. The school should, with Marcus Aurelius, advise the
maturing educand, "If a man affronts you, do not accept his
opinion or think just as he would have you to do. No, look
upon things as reality presents them." [30] Then a vast deal of
demagogic folly will be rendered harmless and the community
will, as a result enjoy greater safety and prosperity. Then

[29] *Swann's Way*, The Modern Languages Publishers, 1928, p. 66.
[30] *Meditations*, IV, 11.

half-truths, made formidable by the grain of truth they contain side by side with untruth, will lose their sting; then sound and enlightened public opinion will function; then temptingly simple schemes of millennium, such as, to paraphrase Mark Twain, deal freely in important omissions, will be properly scrutinized by the community. The millennium-mongers will be told to go their way and their younger adepts will be given fatherly advice as was the young Lycias by Socrates: "You speak like a young man, O Lycias, who still has to learn how painfully complex is the world we live in." On the other hand, public opinion, devoid of a well-spread and solid cultural foundation in intellectual discipline, often cannot help running the risk of degenerating into "an organized ignorance elevated to the dignity of physical force." [31] The dangers of which this may be a source are obvious. Geese saved by their watchful hissing only one republic, and saved it only once. As a rule, democracies rise by their own wisdom and labor and fall when absurdities and indifference take possession of their population.

In the excellent words of a keen thinker who was also a sincere friend of democracy:

Government and civil society are the most complicated of all subjects accessible to the human mind; and he who would deal competently with them as a thinker, and not as a blind follower of a party, requires not only a general knowledge of the leading facts of life, both moral and material, but an understanding exercised and disciplined in the principles and rules of sound thinking, up to a point which neither the experience of life, nor any one science or branch of knowledge, affords.[32]

When the school education given to the average citizen has failed to accomplish a fair degree of an "understanding ex-

[31] Wilde, Oscar, *Epigrams and Aphorisms,* John W. Luce and Co., Boston, 1905.
[32] Mill, John Stuart, *Dissertations and Discussions,* Henry Holt and Co., 1874, Vol. IV, p. 344.

ercised and disciplined in the principles of sound thinking," then adult education, instead of advancing the general culture of the community, can at best unteach some of the bad mental habits acquired at school. The school should, with Euripides, advise the maturing educand:

> There is a time when it is pleasant not to build too much on our own wisdom; but then, again, there is a time when it is useful to exert our judgment.[33]

In the exercise of their vigilance over national interests, the vast majority of citizens cannot go into the detailed study of a controversial question, one, perhaps, on which experts, after years of study, have come only to sharp disagreement; but if he knows how to gather evidence and is able to judge the value of it, the citizen can arrive, with reasonable frequency, at a tolerably correct opinion about matters of national importance. If decisions rendered at the polls are often faulty, the reason is that the ballot box cannot miraculously patch up the lack of really good popular education. We hear people say that democracy as a method of government has markedly failed in recent times. Yet dictatorship, often from ignorance lauded and applauded in the midst of democratic communities, is not the only or the best remedy. There is another and better one. It is properly conducted public school instruction penetrated with the clear notion that democratic liberties cannot be preserved and the blessings of democracy cannot be fully realized without vigilance, accurate thinking, and continuous search for the necessary information on the part of all well-meaning members of a community.

In the literature of Progressive Education one comes not infrequently upon seriously presented arguments similar to the remark which Disraeli — himself a very widely read man —

---

[33] *Iphigenia at Aulis,* 924 ff.

made while in one of his moods of intellectual coquetry. This remark was to the effect that the Athenians of the age of Pericles and Socrates, the most illustrious democratic commonwealth of the ancient world, lived in the open, had very little schooling, and read no books. But we know how ingloriously Athens finished by losing national independence, together with political liberties and cultural leadership, after the Athenian state had fallen into the nets of demagogues and doctrinaires, whom Plato describes as " hookers of men, hunters after a living prey, nearly related to tyrants and thieves." [34] Small wonder that Socrates thought little of the wisdom of the Athenians of his time, who, according to him, " have no understanding, and only repeat what their rulers are pleased to tell them." [35] Less reserved in speech than the philosopher, another great Athenian, Aristophanes, says: " As often as anyone softsawdered you and called you ' sleek ' Athens, he used to obtain all his wish through the *sleekness.*" [36] To quote another passage among many of a similar nature found in the comedies of Aristophanes, he makes a personage in *The Frogs* exclaim:

> Farewell then, Aeschylus, great and wise,
> Go, save our state by the maxims rare
> Of thy noble thought; and the fools chastise;
> For many a fool dwells there.[37]

(D) Independence from our own natural tendency toward intellectual self-indulgence and self-complacency.

Ambrosio, a personage in the very instructive travel story by a young — at the time — American explorer, Henry A. Franck, served the explorer partly as a porter and partly as a guide. On more than one occasion the guide lost his way. Each

[34] *Sophist,* 221, 222.
[35] *Protagoras,* 317.
[36] *Acharnians,* 375 ff.
[37] 1498 ff. (*Aristophanes,* Translated by B. B. Rogers, G. P. Putnam's Sons, 1927, Vol. II, p. 435).

time his version of the mishap was "*se ha perdi'o el camino* — the road has lost itself."[38] The author qualifies this manner of reasoning as truly Latin-American. In reality, however, it is a weakness universal enough. The remedy against it is to be sought above all in mental discipline.

One of the serious menaces to social peace and steady social evolution is the uncritical inclination of individuals to attribute to society the failures and mishaps for which the individuals themselves are in reality responsible. We are very much inclined to camouflage the shortcomings and deliberate misdoings of the individual under lamentations against social injustice, social anarchy, social corruption, etc., as if the mysterious society which we so readily accuse and condemn did not consist of us individuals, and as if so-called social injustice and so-called social corruption did not consist in the corrupt practices of law, medicine, commerce, industry, politics, and education indulged in by corrupt individuals. Wholesale accusations against society is one of the favorite tricks of demagogues. The habit of careful reasoning can readily produce salutary self-criticism likely to prevent enough people from thinking that the existing social order is responsible for their failures even when, in fact, those failures are caused wholly by their shortcomings or vices as individuals. It would be to the common good if more men were compelled by the force of their own well-trained minds to be as critical of themselves as Confucius wanted his disciples to be: "When by what we do we do not achieve our aim, we must examine ourselves at every point. . . ."[39]

Pestalozzi, who witnessed and, in a sense, participated in the revolutionary-reformatory movement of the end of the eighteenth and the beginning of the nineteenth century, said, truthfully:

---

[38] *Working North from Patagonia*, Garden City Publishing Co., 1921, p. 624.
[39] Cf. Dawson, M. M., *Op. cit.*, p. 42.

Great ideas for improving the world, which rose out of elevated views of our subject, and which soon became exaggerated, filled our heads, confused our hearts. . . . We saw more or less all the evils under which we suffered, but no one sought for them enough and saw them where he ought — in himself.[40]

Not the least obstacle to the development of real independence of mind in the young is the natural disinclination on their part to exercise a prolonged intellectual effort and the inclination to be satisfied with a " good-enough " achievement in reasoning. Proper stimulation can overcome, to a degree, this natural aversion to a continuous mental exertion, but such stimulation cannot always be produced. A much more dependable remedy or even a preventive, would consist in the habit of intellectual craftsmanship. A properly conducted effort on the part of the school to cultivate intellectual training from the first school year on can well result in the habit of accurate clean-cut thinking. The students will like it much in the same manner as they come, under proper training, to like physical cleanliness and to dislike uncleanliness. That such an attitude is a result of training is evidenced by the fact that some of the most scrupulous housekeepers, uncompromisingly devoted to the cult of cleanliness, can remember the battles royal which they fought as children and the subterfuges and evasions of all sorts which they practiced in order to avoid washing up before going to bed or upon rising in the morning.

The ability for sustained, systematic thinking, it must be remembered, has been one of the principal though arduous roads toward civilization and away from barbarism. In fact, barbarism began to be replaced by civilization whenever and wherever a sufficient number of gifted or simply normally endowed individuals began to practice a sufficiently systematic intellectual effort. In the excellent words of Renan:

[40] *How Gertrude Teaches Her Children*, C. W. Bardeen, Syracuse, N. Y., 1898, p. 21.

Barbarism cannot have scientifically organized industries or a strong political organization, because such institutions demand and presuppose a strenuous intellectual application, and barbarism is incapable of such intellectual application. The habit of systematic intellectual application is acquired through the strong discipline of properly conducted scientific and literary training.[41]

(E) Emotional independence from the shibboleths of progressiveness and modernity.

One of the most dangerous, because the least detectable and least reparable, calamities that lie in the path to intellectual maturity is that intellectually untrained and unsophisticated boys and girls may readily fall victims to propaganda from modernity and progressiveness. This calls for a special inoculation — through intellectual training — against the emotional fever producible in untrained minds by the shibboleths of progressiveness and modernity. Many potentially good young people have become a prey to propaganda from " progress " and " up-to-dateness " and have forfeited their lives, or at least the enjoyment of morally and physically healthy and satisfying lives. It is often in this way that recruits are found to augment the sinister phalanxes of the unbalanced and uprooted, or " *détraqués,*" as the French call them.

There is a very grave, even when it is only transient and temporary, form of intellectual serfdom from which the young should be helped to remain free. It consists in servitude to quacks and demagogues of various kinds who seek to corrupt healthy youths under the disguise of initiating them into and — the highest bliss! — of admitting them to the inner circles of the really modern, advanced, up-to-the-second free thinkers and the only really bright, dyed-in-the-wool revolutionaries. It takes good mental discipline and a certain amount of coaching in psychopathology to enable adolescents and youths to distin-

[41] E. Renan, " La Jeunesse et la Vie," *Pages Choisies*, p. 219 f.

guish under the floods of red oratory and unbridled sex philosophy of some self-styled " genius " two matters which in many
such cases are the true substance of such oratory. One is some
sort of malicious self-seeking design, and the other is the tailless fox's complex, that is, absence of healthy normality, physical
or moral or both. Preaching radically new ways of life and absolute freedom from all restrictions — " decent inhibitions " —
can readily find sufficiently receptive ground in the youthful
mind which normally is a mixture of intellectual shyness, curiosity, ardent idealism, love of novelty, and thrill of noncon-
formism. Left to their own resources and unschooled in the
critical analysis of men and things the young are liable to com-
mit foolish acts under the influence of some dishonest false
" prophet of new life." These may be of any degree of gravity,
from smoking and drinking nauseating stuff, just to be well
thought of by the " bright and modern set," down to some
moral tattooing of their person with such actions as the betrayal
of the ideals and traditions of their church, their family, their
country, instigated by some " forward " individuals who thus
achieve their real goal. This goal is the ugly tailless fox's satisfaction at the destruction or mutilation of something sound and
healthy and therefore really beautiful. Not infrequently this
satisfaction is combined with the profit of recruiting new tools
for the promotion of the propagandist's personal ambition, political or financial or both.

The school is undoubtedly at fault and intellectual training
has been sadly missed or unpardonably neglected by it in each
case when the community furnishes a rich harvest to the
" Prince of Darkness " acting through agents to whose work in
this country Sinclair Lewis refers in a rather unusual passage:
" Now, since war-days, there had arisen in America a sect which
preached . . . that most people were not people at all, but sub-
human . . . , because they did not sufficiently drink, fight,

wench, denounce the church, and smoke before breakfast." [42]
And the result has been appalling crimes committed by
young descendants of perfectly honorable families, suicides and
such shipwrecks among the young who discovered too late that
they had simply been made dupes by the malicious designs of
one sort of tailless fox or another. In many cases such shipwrecks could have been prevented. For instance, a well organized analytical study of certain personages of Dostoevsky,
Zola, Balzac, Thomas Mann, and Sinclair Lewis, could have
inoculated and given sufficient immunity to the unfortunate
young people against the virus spread by the insidious degeneracy of the tailless fox's variety. Any normally endowed
adolescent can readily understand the criteria for distinguishing between really superior intelligence and mere bold intellectual blackmailing, between sincere and noble idealism and
the born tailless fox's natural sinister desire to swell the ranks
of tailless foxes by duping normal and healthy individuals into
disfiguring their persons, morally or physically or both, under
the pretext of initiation into the bliss of modernity.

FOREARMING THE EDUCAND AGAINST THE WITCHERY OF WORDS

In the course of history, philosophers have debated whether
the more powerful factors in the life of nations are sentiments or
ideas. The final solution of this problem is, naturally, still lacking because the final philosophy of history can be written only
by one who sees the last day of our world, and he will not
have time to write. In the meantime, it appears sufficiently evident that whenever a sentiment is clothed in a deceptively logical idea, a powerful historic factor, often of negative character,
can come into existence. This factor may be described as the
witchery of words. The possible injurious effects of the influence

---

[42] From *Ann Vickers*, p. 257, by Sinclair Lewis, copyright 1932, 1933. Reprinted
by permission from Doubleday, Doran and Company, Inc.

of this witchery of words, that is to say, of ideas inflated with emotions, can be checked only by a concerted effort of enlightened minds. Therefore, the witchery of words deserves the special attention of an educator in his or her work relative to intellectual training.

The prestige of extreme revolutionary leaders has always depended much upon coining slogans, or giving currency to those coined by others, which promised everything and defined nothing. The classical Jacobin triad of Liberty, Equality, and Fraternity has been paralleled with various modifications in subsequent revolutions. And many a time masses of well-intentioned but uncritical people have found — but always too late, after they have given power to a revolutionary junta — that the junta meant liberty, equality, and fraternity only for those who would obediently support it and only in proportion to the actual support given.

Some revolutionary ideas even though inflated and obscured by emotion have rendered a desirable service and have contributed powerfully toward certain desirable and lasting political and social changes. The method by which a potentially destructive influence is made constructive has always been the same. It has consisted in deflating the ideas swollen with emotion and bringing them to the right proportions by means of analysis and definition, fortified at times by the more or less costly experience of the harm done by such inflated ideas.

What can the school do with relation to forearming the educand against the witchery of words? The properly organized and conducted school can assist the maturing educand in this regard through three principal measures.

First, the school should put the student on guard against the old sophistic logic which more often than not is applied, whether consciously or not, by propagandists, especially when they are promoting their own interests by the method of the witchery of words. This sophistic logic is at the basis of wholesale assertions which would omit all gradations, distinctions, and nuances found in the realities of life. The sophistic logic consists in reasoning to the effect that A is either B or non-B. In reality things are not so simple, and A can be both B and non-B at one and the same time; in some of its aspects A can be B and in some other aspects non-B.[43] The ancient sophists (see p. 153) worked out a whole set of samples of tricky sophistic reasoning. With the help of those samples they trained their disciples toward amazing verbal trickery. Many such samples are recorded in Aristotle's work, *De Sophisticis Elenchis* (*On Sophistic Refutations*).

Among the celebrated sophisms there may be mentioned and briefly analyzed the sophism of the arrow and the sophism of the beard. A sophism is an assertion which has the appearance of a true statement but which in reality is false. It must be distinguished from aphorism, which is seemingly false, baffling, but which may be true in reality. For example, the statement " The shortest way to oneself is the way around the world " is an aphorism.

The sophism of the arrow is as follows:

An arrow cannot move. At any definite moment of time the arrow, in order to be something in existence, must be in a certain definite position in space. Everything that exists exists in a definite place and at a definite time. If this is so, then the arrow cannot move, because motion means transition from one place in space to another, it means being at a given time in no definite place in space, and this is impossible. In fact, all locomotion is impossible, because it would mean existing in no place at a definite time; and this is impossible, because it is incompatible with existence which is always at a definite moment in time and

[43] Cf. Bogoslovsky, B., *The Technique of Controversy: Principles of Dynamic Logic,* Harcourt, Brace and Co., 1928.

in a definite place in space. The trick underlying this sophism
is the logic, A is either B or non-B. As soon as this wholesale
rough logic devoid of all necessary distinctions and therefore
distortive of the complexity and subtlety of reality is rejected
and replaced by its opposite, the sophism of the arrow is exposed
and rejected. A can be both B and non-B at one and the same
time. The arrow can exist in more than one " place " in space.
While its head is in the position H, its tail is in the position
T, and other parts of the arrow are in corresponding positions.
Next, the arrow's head occupies the position H_1, the tail then
finds itself in the position T_1, etc. Therefore, the arrow's movement is not incompatible with existence.

The sophism of the beard is as follows:

The sophist asks his interlocutor whether one hair constitutes a beard or not. The answer, naturally, is in the negative.
Next, the interlocutor is asked whether or not four hundred
hairs constitute a beard. And when the reasonable answer is
given to the effect that such a number of hairs would make a
respectable-looking beard, the interlocutor is asked what he
thinks about two hairs constituting a beard, next about three
hundred and ninety-nine, then about three and three hundred
ninety-eight, and so on. Finally he is driven by apparently rigorous impeccable logic to assert — while just one hair is added
each time to the imaginary collection of hairs from one up-
ward, and just one hair is subtracted from the opposite count
— that one hundred and ninety-nine hairs do not constitute a
beard but two hundred hairs do. Next the sophist places before
his interlocutor the disconcerting conclusion that one hair constitutes a beard, because it was just one hair that constituted the
difference between the collection of hairs which the interlocutor was forced to acknowledge as non-beard and the one which
he was compelled, by the sophistic logic, to declare a full-
fledged beard. Again, as in the case of the arrow, the sophism

is solved when the wholesale logic, A is either B or non-B, is rejected as being contrary to the complex and subtle reality of things and to the general dynamic processes of life in the making, where A is at one and the same time both B and non-B. The sophism of the beard is solved as soon as we come to see that a collection, shall we say, of ten hairs is both beard and nonbeard, because it is a beard in the making. A collection of ten hairs is not a beard when the ten hairs are just an accidental collection of ten hairs. On the contrary, it is a beard — in the making — when the ten hairs are a part of the growing beard.

It is, precisely, an apparently rigorous straightforward logic, but in reality a wholesale, deceptive, sophistic logic that underlies many cases of the witchery of words with which, for instance, the present-day revolutionary propaganda in this country is bristling. We are introduced first to a vehement criticism of the traditional liberal individualistic social order. Next, to make the criticism of the existing regime (which criticism may not be devoid of a degree of justification) more drastic, the existing social order is referred to simply as capitalistic. The term " capitalistic " is employed in a clearly derogatory sense. No mention is made of the services rendered by capitalism in enlarging the volume of productive employment and in spreading comforts by reducing the cost of production through increasing its volume. Nothing is said, either, of the fact that the historic beginning of capitalism was not at all inherently bad; that in some cases it necessarily was of a noble and admirable nature. Who were among the first capitalists? The savages who were intelligent enough and had character enough to control their appetites and who saved for a rainy day something from a temporary abundance of food and of other commodities. Nothing is said by the radicals of the fact that capitalism is a social order which is characterized not only by the possibility of the accumulation of gigantic wealth by a few individuals, but also by the reasonable possibility for all individuals of the enjoyment of private homes and other forms of private property, and of the happiness which such enjoyment normally gives and which would vanish under communism or collectivism.

Next, collectivism is recommended as the only possible remedy for the abuses, actual and supposed, of capitalism. This is, obviously, a case of the sophistic logic. A is either B or non-B. In reality the true improvement of social life can come only via A being both B and non-B at one and the same time. In other words, it can come only through a reform which will strike a sound balance between economic individualism or capitalism, on the one hand, the public control, on the other; through a reform which will be cautious not to travel the irretrievable road of collectivism, common economic misery, and personal enslavement that seem to be inherent in communism or collectivism.

Similar is the logical trick underlying the theses of the *Communist Manifesto,* the supposedly perfect guide of communistic fanatics and agitators. As an example, the thesis relative to the abolition of the institution of the private family may be cited:

The abolition of bourgeois individualism, bourgeois independence, and bourgeois freedom is undoubtedly aimed at. . . .

Abolition of the family! Even the most radical flare up at this infamous proposal of the Communists.

On what foundation is the present family, the bourgeois family, based? On capital, on private gain. . . . The bourgeois family will vanish as a matter of course when its complement vanishes, and both will vanish with the vanishing of capital. . . .

The bourgeois clap-trap about the family and education, about the hallowed co-relation of parent and child becomes all the more disgusting, as, by the action of modern industry, all family ties among the proletarians are torn asunder, and their children transformed into simple articles of commerce and instruments of labor. . . . For the rest nothing is more ridiculous than the virtuous indignation of our bourgeois at the community of women which, they pretend, is to be openly and officially established by the Communists. The Communists have no need to introduce community of women; it has existed almost from time immemorial.

Our bourgeois, not content with having the wives and daughters of their proletarians at their disposal, not to speak of common prostitutes, take the greatest pleasure in seducing each other's wives.

Bourgeois marriage is in reality a system of wives in common, and thus, at the most, what the Communists might be possibly reproached with is that they desire to introduce, in substitution for a hypocritically concealed, an openly legalized community of women.[44]

Obviously, the wholesale tricky logic, A is either B or non-B, and a certain ambiguity in the employment of certain terms is at the basis of the argument for the abolition of the institution of the individual family presented by the *Communist Manifesto*. Thus " bourgeois " is a term which the communists employ in approximately the same derogatory meaning as is sometimes given by some propagandists to the expression " rugged individualism." The term " bourgeois " is not defined in the manifesto, but the manifesto insinuates that " bourgeois " is something low, self-seeking, callously cruel and greedy. Then it is insinuated, also, that for one to oppose the communistic program of " socialization " of the family means that he is one of those objectionable creatures, the " bourgeois." Next, the scattered instances of lowly or extremely unfortunate working men who, voluntarily or not, have not known family life, become the general rule of the supposedly family-less life of working men who on account of exploitation by capitalists supposedly have never had the enjoyments of family life, and therefore have nothing to lose in this regard under a fully realized communistic regime. Next, the scattered instances of infidelity and im-

[44] Marx, Karl, and Engels, Friedrich, *The Manifesto of the Communist Party,* Authorized English Translation, p. 34 ff.

morality on the part of some members of the middle and upper classes in turn become, in the logic of the *Communist Manifesto,* also a general rule, and a reason why the abolition of the institution of the private family under the communistic regime would simply mean a sort of straightforward legalization of the supposedly existing practice of universal promiscuity.

Similarly, the Marxian doctrine of historic materialism is based upon the reasoning, A is either B or non-B. It is true, of course, that the methods of production prevailing in a community exercise a profound influence upon the political and social forms of life characteristic of that community. Thus, the hand mill implied, in a sense, feudalism, while the power mill inevitably led to the concentration of industry and other features, economic, political, social, and moral, which are associated with capitalism. It is true, also, that the manner in which an individual or a group provides for material needs influences, in a measure, the general outlook upon life. Thus, the philosophy of life characteristic of the Bedouin of Ramah, on the one hand, and that of the mine owner in Pennsylvania, on the other, reveals, naturally, diverse traits resulting from the differences in the material existence of the two. Such facts do not, however, justify the wholesale assertion made by Marx that the conscience of man does not determine his mode of life, but is itself determined by man's mode of material existence; that the machine is the moving force of history. Man's mode of material existence, to be sure, has determined — in some cases to an overwhelming degree — his general outlook upon life; but in many other cases his indomitable spirit of idealism, his unquenchable thirst for the true, the good, and the beautiful have raised man to such a point of contempt for the material exigencies of life as to make him almost entirely independent of the material factors of life. Such has been the case of the great prophets and saints, of many scholars, and of some artists. And the machine, though it has been *a* maker of history, has never been *the* maker of history, because there has always been the spiritual that cannot be enslaved by the material.

Similar also is the logic underlying the question, Yes or no? when asked with relation to a proposition about which the correct answer would be, It is both yes and no.

The first important measure which it seems to be the duty of the school to practice in order to protect the maturing student against the injurious influence coming from the witchery of words, consists, then, in this: in the intellectual training of children the school must be inspired with dynamic logic — A can be both B and non-B at one and the same time — corresponding to the complexity and subtlety of reality. It is a very important residual function of the school thus to forearm the future democratic citizen against the tricky (though apparently rigorous and straightforward) wholesale static — A is either B or non-B — logic employed by radicalism in spoken and written propaganda.

The second measure toward the educand's defense against the witchery of words should consist in teaching him to investigate into the opposite of a doctrine, theory, or proposition, particularly when such a doctrine, theory, or proposition is of the extremist type. "Let us now hear the other side (*Audiatur et altera pars*)," was the rule of Rome during the best period of her history as a democratic, liberal republic.[45]

The maturing American citizen who is accustomed to practice this remedy against the witchery of words is, for example, unlikely to be readily converted to determinism (see p. 50) through such a preachment as is contained in the following and which is typical of deterministic reasoning:

---

[45] Cf. Aristophanes, *The Wasps*, 724 ff. (Translated by B. B. Rogers, G. P. Putnam's Sons, 1927, Vol. I, p. 481): 'Twas a very acute and intelligent man, Whoever it was, that happened to say, *Don't make up your mind, till you've heard both sides.*

Even the rudiments of our present scientific knowledge concerning the nature of man and his behavior serve completely to destroy the conventional view of man as a free moral agent. . . . There is nothing alarming about this conception, as it merely means that human conduct is not independent of the range of scientific causation. When we say that an individual " chooses " some action we can only mean, in scientific terminology, that the complex of conditioning which led him to the type of action " chosen " was more powerful than the conditioning which pressed him toward a different decision. That man has the power to select in an arbitrary manner the particular conditioning to which he will respond is as silly in its scientific assumptions and implications as to hold that an apple may choose whether it will rise or fall from a tree. . . .

The deterministic position carries with it very revolutionary applications to social policies. It quickly becomes apparent that no one can be held to be personally responsible for his actions, for they are the result of hereditary and social conditions over which he had little or no control. Man cannot be wilfully perverse. A man who commits a multiple murder is no more responsible for his behavior than an amiable and generous philanthropist.[46]

A student receiving proper intellectual training would in the presence of such reasoning refuse to be fascinated (without further examination into the matter) by the monopolistic authoritarian use of the term " scientific " in a statement which is merely an opinion but which pretends to be a scientific law. The educand would also investigate the opinions of other thinkers who have occupied themselves with the problem of determinism versus free will. As a result, the student would come upon some opinions issuing from distinguished men of science quite contrary to the opinion just quoted. Einstein, for instance, speaking before a communist group in New York, said: " Determinism, which lays down that everything that happens does so of necessity, as a result of cause and effect, is belief, not knowledge."

[46] Barnes, H. E., *Living in the Twentieth Century,* Bobbs-Merrill Co., 1932, p. 50 f.

He declared also that he " saw nothing to prove that the world was ' causal ' in the scientific sense of the word." As to the " first cause," he could not " even now tell which came first, the hen or the egg." According to the record of Einstein's discussion on the occasion in question found in the *New York Times* of November 15, 1930, " Dr. Einstein said that a ' physicist no longer believed in strict determinism.' He held that mankind had not really gone far in knowledge. ' The further we proceed, the more formidable are the riddles facing us.' He added, the ultimate issues were beyond our ken. ' I am not a pessimist,' he concluded. ' Let us always remember that beauty is also truth.' "

The maturing future American citizen may hear radical propagandists assert that under the social order characterized by political liberalism and economic individualism — be that social order called capitalism — the national wealth of this country is held by two or three per cent of the population, and that liberalism must be replaced with collectivism because the former has failed to achieve any progress in bringing economic benefits to the vast majority of citizens. By following the rule, *audiatur et altera pars,* the educand can readily find out that such an assertion is " grotesque," as President Butler of Columbia University rightly described it in one of his public addresses.[47] Statistical data available demonstrate that half the families in this country own the homes in which they live; 15,000,000 individuals own corporate securities; 45,000,000 had in 1932 deposits in savings banks aggregating $25,000,000,000; there were some 115,000,000 holders of insurance policies with a face value above $100,000,000,000; 10,000,000 members in building and loan associations had aggregate property of some $8,000,000,000; two out of each three families, at the time of the last Federal census, had their living quarters equipped with telephone and

[47] *New York Times,* September 3, 1934.

electric conveniences.[48] In other words, statistics demonstrate that the average inhabitant of this country possesses comforts and wealth superior to those ever possessed in any country at any time of history. To be sure, there is room for improvement even in the fundamentals of the general economic situation in this country, especially in the way of greater economic security for the average person. But the study of the " other side " of the problem would generally convince the maturing American citizen that it would be an absurd risk to try to seek for such an improvement in any way but one that would be in harmony with the American Constitution — that incomparable document dictated by reasonable idealism — under the protection of which this country has been able to accomplish within a comparatively short historic time many unprecedented grandeurs, spiritual, economic, and political.

The maturing American citizen may hear also of Soviet Russia's challenge to America through the former's supposed achievements in the way of economic security and happiness for the average man, due to the abolition of capitalism and the establishment of collectivism or communism. If any maturing American citizen would follow the rule, " hear also the other side," he or she would rapidly discover that the challenge in question is of a very dubious kind. In fact, he would see that "Soviet Russia's challenge to America " is the " challenge " of ugly poverty, amidst unlimited natural resources, and complete personal subjugation of the average person under the communistic regime — to the American regime of personal liberties, of abundant and accessible comforts of food, shelter, and recreation. The educand would further discover that the " challenge " of the communistic regime of unlucky Russia to the American democracy is the " challenge " of a regime under which free speech and thought are crimes against the " people "

[48] *Ibid.*

punishable by death or severe imprisonments equalling the agony of slow death; of a regime under which there is no trial by jury and where the Communist officials are their own law-givers, judges, and executives — to a regime characterized by freedom of speech and press and by all the fundamental liberties granted even to those who employ those liberties in order to preach and otherwise prepare the overthrow of the American Constitution and the establishment of a communistic dictatorship. The educand would also convince himself or herself that the " challenge " of Soviet Russia ruled by the Communist dictators to the American Constitution and to the social order protected by it is a case of " challenge " of a regime under which teachers, in order not only to hold their jobs but simply in order to save themselves from severe punishment, have to refrain from saying anything that would be out of harmony with Marxism or Leninism or Stalinism — to a regime under which teachers, in particular college professors, can freely teach the replacement of political liberalism and economic individualism, or capitalism, with collectivism, or communism, while receiving, as is the case of some such professors, high salaries from funds furnished by benevolent individual capitalists and while drawing high royalties from anti-capitalist writings and otherwise profiting by the system of private profits which they profess to wish to abolish, beginning this abolition with the profits of others, it seems.

This seems to be one of the cases for which Seneca intended the following observation: " And we must practice what we preach: for philosophy is not a subject for popular ostentation, nor does it rest in words, but in deeds." [49]

The maturing American citizen also hears often that the Communist party aims at the establishment of international peace, which, it is promised, will result from the abolition of

[49] L'Estrange, Sir Roger, *Seneca's Morals*, A. C. Bush, Publishers, p. 96.

all national frontiers and merging the various national groups into one united Communist World Empire. The study " of the other side " would readily show such a maturing American citizen that two important inexactitudes are contained in this communistic promise. First, the Communist party cannnot logically be called a party. The Communists or Bolshevists or Collectivists intend to rule by the method of dictatorship at least during the transition period from economic individualism and political liberalism — or capitalism — to full-fledged communism. No chronological limits are set for such " transition." In the meantime, the Communist dictators would not permit the political existence and the activities of any group or individual opposing the communistic philosophy of life and government. Consequently, the name, Communist party, is a misnomer. A party is party to something and presupposes the existence of other parties, participating as collaborators or as an opposition, in the political life of a country. The Communists or Bolshevists are not a party, but a group which is determined to be the whole and the only show. Second, the much-talked-about " peace " to be bestowed by the Communists upon the world means a peace on condition of submission to the Communist dictators and of acceptance of their de-vitalizing, de-spiritualizing regime. It is the peace of the cemetery.

To mention just one more not unimportant discovery which the maturing American citizen will make if he or she is trained to follow the rule of hearing the other side when confronted with a radical, extremist proposition. The educand so trained will discover that he or she personally does not have to be a millionaire in order to lose greatly and to gain very little, if anything, by the replacement of the American Constitution with the *Communist Manifesto* of Marx and Engels or with the decrees of Lenin, Trotzky, and Stalin. Even if the educand is just a small farmer or the son or daughter of a small farmer, the change (though it may be profitable for some communistic and pro-communistic agitators who then will become the rulers of the land) is unlikely to be a profitable one, as, for instance, an impartial and scholarly report (1934) of the School of Slavonic and Eastern European Studies of the University of London has demonstrated. This report, entitled *Collectivized Agriculture in the Soviet Union,* formulated the following conclusions:

"That the legal status of the members of collective farms is for all practical purposes equivalent to bondage.

"That the taxation and other imposts levied on the collective farms and their members are so heavy as to depress the standard of living to the lowest conceivable level.

"That social and labor conditions in both State and collective farms are extremely bad.

Lancelot Lawton, one of the contributors, writes:

"Under collectivization the U.S.S.R. has not been able to export anything like the amount of grain which was exported in pre-war times. Whatever the quantities of exports may have been, they were only rendered possible because large numbers of people were continually deprived of a sufficiency of food."

A. V. Baikalov declares that in practice the collective farms have no independence and no genuine co-operative organization, and that the laws and regulations bind the peasants for life to a collective farm.

"As a matter of fact," he adds, "the collectivized peasants have no better chance of escaping from the villages than their forefathers had before 1861." [50]

VERBAL EXPRESSION AS THE FUNDAMENTAL TOOL OF OUR MENTAL WORK

A philosopher musing over the importance of independent thinking for the stability and positive evolution of democracy said: "Every one who really thinks for himself is so far like a

[50] The *New York Times,* September 8, 1934.
Note: the year 1861, in the history of Russia, marks the abolition of serfdom.

monarch. His position is undelegated and supreme. His judg-
ments, like royal decrees, spring from his own sovereign power
and proceed directly from himself." [51] But this royal achievement and this kingly superiority depend very much upon our
skill and power in handling the supreme tool with which our
minds work in the thinking. Indeed, what is thinking? In what
does it consist? Thinking, in substance, is the process of getting
the meanings of things. Thrashing meanings out, refining them
in the mind, is done by means of the word, spoken and written,
actually or mentally. We cannot reason without the use of
words. We think about things by means of their symbols or
words and communicate with each other through the medium
of words as symbols of things and of their meanings. It is the
word that serves alike as hammer and anvil in the process of
working out meanings. It can be said: " The art of reasoning is
in the last analysis the ability for clear and exact expression." [52]

Obviously, handling words is an important part of mental
discipline. It should, naturally, hold an adequately large place in
school education, especially in a democratic commonwealth.
Therefore, the strong disapproval of " verbal learning " by
the progressives seems to be a very questionable form of progress
in educational thinking. Rather than theirs, the school teacher
should share the opinion of the ancient historian of a democracy,
Thucydides, who said: " When a man insists that words ought
not to be our guides in action, he is wanting in sense [as] he does
not see that there is no other way in which we can throw light
on the unknown future." [53]

Words symbolize meanings. Thus they enable us not only to
get other people's meanings but also to work out for ourselves
the meanings derivable from our personal and borrowed expe-

[51] Schopenhauer, A., *Parerga and Paralipomena,* II, Chapter XXII (On Thinking for Oneself), German Classics, *cit.,* Vol. XV, p. 107.

[52] Condillac, Étienne, *La Logique,* seconde partie, Ch. V.

[53] *History of the Peloponnesian, War, cit.,* III, Chapter 42.

rience into new meanings. Language is the verbal embodiment of experience. Like experience itself, language is essentially a three-dimensional matter. It records the meanings we crystallize from our present experiences, and thus transforms them into our past experiences which are available for future reference. Our direct contact with things being limited by time and space, the meanings of things preserved and transmitted through the medium of words constitute the real foundation of the kingly superiority of man over the rest of the living species. It is very probable that we are unable to recollect meanings which we have not definitely clothed in words. This perhaps accounts for the fact that we cannot recall the occurrences and impressions of our early prelingual childhood. Possibly the most important single discovery the child makes is that everything has a name. At all events, it is certain that he who cannot clearly express in words what he means does not himself know exactly what it is. Pestalozzi, an enthusiastic and gifted educational innovator, came after several " tentative and erring measures " in the direction of free, unguided, and uncontrolled expressionism, to the following conclusion regarding the training of children toward satisfying verbal expression:

In order to make children reasonable and put them in the way of a power of independent thought, we must guard as much as possible against allowing them to speak at haphazard, or to pronounce opinions about things that they know superficially. . . . Their mental freedom gains exceedingly by this; and when they have learned, and learned to use certain forms of description by many examples, they will in future reduce thousands of objects to the same formula, and impress upon their definitions the stamp of clear vision.[54]

As John Dewey (in all probability annoyed by the excessive zeal of some of his followers among the progressives) has happily put it:

[54] *How Gertrude Teaches Her Children, cit.,* pp. 72–73.

Things come and go, or we come and go, and either way things escape our notice. . . . Taken literally, the maxim, "Teach things, not words," or "Teach things before words" would be the negation of education; it would reduce mental life to mere physical and sensible adjustments. Learning, in the proper sense, is not learning things but the *meanings* of things, and this process involves the use of signs, or language in its general sense. In like fashion, the warfare of some educational reformers against symbols, if pushed to extremes, involves the destruction of the intellectual life, since this lives, moves, and has its being in those processes of definition, abstraction, generalization, and classification that are made possible by symbols alone.[55]

Democracy, which is a government by public opinion or, more precisely, a government by the vote of the majority among the adult members of a nation, is, after all, government by discussion, by talk, by persuasion. The great silent man as the last bedrock of national leadership is a myth. Great men among the true leaders of democracy were not silent. How could they be? They were men of great character and intellectual power who possessed also the adequate power of verbal expression.

As a general issue, then, it is difficult to recommend a school where they do not learn how to speak and write correctly and intelligently as a happy substitute for a school where they teach nothing but literary composition. Linguistic studies, certainly, can be abused. This sort of abuse, of course, must not have any more place in school instruction than any other. We should not endeavor to make of every student a Flaubert who would battle hour after hour against every rebellious part of speech, and when victorious would roar out his sonorous periods to the echoing walls. On the other hand, the verbal exercises done at school, both oral and written, should be so guided and controlled as to prevent the pupil from growing, under the disguise of self-

[55] Dewey, *How We Think, cit.*, p. 174, 176. Reprinted by special permission of D. C. Heath and Company.

expression, into the habit of hasty and vain productions, and from developing a crude, characterless, swaggering manner. They can and, if properly encouraged, will form a real liking for perfect verbal workmanship, or at least for honest craftsmanship.

The school must take note of the fact that the power to make a clear and well-organized statement is becoming more and more rare. Inversely, the importance of the glib propagandist is increasing in alarming proportions. The habit of correct and clear speaking and writing, like all other habits, has to be developed; very few are the fortunate persons who, like Joseph Conrad, write as the grass grows. The school should also prevent the formation of the undesirable habit in writing — a habit not at all uncommon — to which Schopenhauer objected and which consists in writing " down words, nay, even whole sentences, without attaching any meaning to them . . . but in the hope that someone else will get sense out of them." [56]

In the words of the *Leviathan,* " the most noble and profitable invention of all other, was that of SPEECH, consisting of *Names* or *Appellations,* and their Connexion; whereby men register their Thoughts; recall them when they are past; and also declare them to one another for mutuall utility and conversation; without which, there had been amongst men, neither Commonwealth nor Society, nor Contract, nor Peace, no more than amongst Lyons, Bears, and Wolves." [57] This is true.

John Locke, impressed by the defects of language, affirms, in the *Essay Concerning Human Understanding,* that if anyone " shall well consider the errors and obscurity, the mistakes and confusion, that are spread in the world by an ill use of words, he will find some reason to doubt whether language, as it has been employed, has contributed more to the improvement or hin-

---

[56] *Parerga and Paralipomena,* II, Chapter XXIII (On Style), German Classics, *cit.,* Vol. XV, p. 112.
[57] Hobbes, T. *Leviathan,* I, Chapter IV (Of Speech), Everyman's Library, p. 12.

drance of knowledge among mankind." [58] There is much truth in this also.

It can be not less truthfully said that error is very difficult to remove when it has its roots in language. Improper terms not infrequently are the chains which bind men to unreasonable practices. Every improper term contains the germ of fallacious propositions; it forms a cloud, as it were, which conceals the nature of the thing, and often presents a serious obstacle to the discovery of truth.

Let it, therefore, be repeated that no small part of education for citizenship in a democracy lies, obviously, in the critical, discriminative use of words and in intellectual training, in general. Plato, intimately familiar with the ways of democracies, thought that the power of reasoning and discourse was " truly the greatest good which gives men freedom in their own persons." [59] On the contrary, the lack of that power leaves men subject to tyranny over their minds and, by definition, over their persons. Where the majority is devoid of such an art and power, a situation can easily arise in which " equality " disunites men, " liberty " sends them to " concentration camps " and " fraternity " massacres them.

Mme. Jeanne-Marie Roland, one of the most admirable of all the innocent victims of the Terror during the French Revolution, when she arrived at the foot of the scaffold, asked for pen and paper " to write the strange thoughts that were rising in her! A remarkable request, which was refused. Looking at the Statue of Liberty which stood there, she said bitterly: ' O Liberty, what things are done in thy name! ' " [60] In saying this she spoke for innumerable innocent victims of all other revolutions, past, present, and future. And the prestige of a revolution, especially of a social revolution, as Lamartine remarked, comes from

[58] Book III, Chapter XI, Section 4 (London, Ward, Lock and Co., p. 412).
[59] *Gorgias*, 452.
[60] *The French Revolution, cit.*, Vol. II, p. 279.

defining nothing and promising everything. Consequently, Emerson gave us a valuable political and pedagogical lesson when he said, paraphrasing Plato: " He shall be as a god to me, who can rightly divide and define." [61]

THE PLACE OF INTELLECTUAL TRAINING IN THE GENERAL SCHEME OF DEMOCRATIC EDUCATION

Shall we, then, place school children in the absolute and exclusive service to Reason, in order thus to bring about the millennium? No. Ancient Rome wisely accepted in her Pantheon all gods and goddesses that sufficiently asserted themselves in the worship of the Romans themselves, and of their dependents whose friendship it was advisable to cultivate. Only the deities were granted different ranks.

The temple of pedagogy in a democracy must, by the nature of things, be also a kind of Pantheon. Reason or Intellectual Training shall not be enthroned there alone, a cold though dazzlingly magnificent goddess.

When the importance of the informational side of school learning is insisted upon in the course of this study, the purpose has not been to advocate omniscience as an educational objective. But it seems desirable that the prospective citizen should have acquired enough general information to know how and where to search for reliable information on problems he may have to face. It is still more important, perhaps, that he should possess sufficient knowledge of the fundamental truths, moral, social, and scientific, ignorance of which would make him dangerous to himself and to others. Likewise, insistence upon the significance of intellectual training in education for democracy must not be taken for a proposal to make all school students into walking philosophers at the sight of whom Plato would aban-

[61] Emerson, R. W., " Representative Men: Plato," *Works*, Bigelow, Brown and Co., Vol. II, p. 254.

don all his philosophic reserve and with loud cheers nominate them statesmen in his metaphysical republic. But, certainly, the public school in a democracy must, as best it can, imbue the mind of the pupil with the standards of lucid, profound, fruitful, and careful reasoning and inculcate in him the habit of hard and accurate thinking. In that way the school would arm him with an invaluable method of attacking problems. In the words of Socrates, the great student of the human mind:

Wisdom, viewed in this new light merely as knowledge of knowledge and of ignorance, has this advantage: — that he who possesses such knowledge will more easily learn anything which he learns; and that everything will be clearer to him, because, in addition to the knowledge of individuals, he sees the science, and this also will better enable him to test the knowledge which others have of what he knows himself.[62]

INTELLECTUAL TRAINING, INTEGRATED STUDY, AND ABSTRACT LEARNING

Partisans of the Activity Movement raise objections to what they call departmentalization of subject matter. In place of subject matter divisions into English, geography, history, physics, etc., they want a kind of panoramic culture, a synthetic or "integrated" study, a project method study. In school work, they hold, there must be no artificial chopping of the panorama of life into separate subjects, because such partitioning runs counter to the natural way in which the mind of the child works and, consequently, creates conditions unfavorable to good learning. School work, it is insisted, should not be divorced from the child's experience and from the interests of the daily life of the community, at least not in the case of children below ten years of age, or thereabouts, as these are not yet ready for dry abstract thinking. Let the child, we are advised, spend the intervening years of his school career in walking along

[62] *Charmides*, 172.

the highways of life and learning things as they present themselves all around him in his home environment. And these things can readily be seen to flow into one another, rather than be closeted in watertight compartments, we are told.

This argumentation cannot be accepted for at least three reasons which gravitate around the problem of intellectual training.

First, it can readily be seen that the school work growing around a core of interest furnished by an actual situation or a "project" implies very heavy demands on the teacher, if the learning acquired by the method of integrated instruction is to be satisfactory. One must possess a really encyclopedic education in order to be able adequately to help children in a work which would start, shall we say, from the local river, go with it into the depths of the geological story of the locality, and therefrom up to the particular chemical properties of the water yielded by the river and then further to its role in the economic past and present of the community, and still further to the pictures of the river in poetry and painting, to climax in a pictorial or verbal description of it by the students themselves. Even Tolstoy, who in his experimental school at Yasnaya Poliana tried his hand at a kind of integrated instruction, failed, as he frankly admitted himself.

Second, besides being extremely difficult in practice, integrated instruction as a general method of education is scarcely defensible in theory. Thanks to its wonderful elasticity, the human mind adapts itself excellently to the conditions of learning imposed by the complexity and variety of life. Moreover, the mind often makes pleasure as well as virtue out of necessity. The human mind generally likes variety, likes change in objects that claim its attention. This is especially true of the young mind which has not yet developed the power of discovering variety in seeming uniformity and of compensating the narrowness of a field of observation by the profundity with which it can be investigated. When the average civilized man opens his morning paper and runs through such a motley of news as " Venice by Night," " Planes Collide in Mid-Air," " Scientists and the Darwinian Theory," "Massacres at Shanghai," " Atlantic Flight News," " Bobbed Hair Ruse," etc., he is neither confused nor tired by the diversity of subjects. He can think of all these news items in any sequence, return to some of them again, and retain them in his memory for further reference. It is indeed very necessary that he should be able to do this, else he would be an ignorant man.

We must help our students to develop similar mental powers. Far from being obstructed in our educational effort by the constitution of the mind of the normal child, we shall be helped by his natural taste for variety and change in learning which diminish the fatigue. The school child does not necessarily get depressed or lost when the time schedule sends the most varied unrelated subjects to knock at the door of the child's soul and demand audience. We are told that the regime is absurdly antipedagogical under which the child has for the first period " Acids "; for the second, " The Merchant of Venice "; for the third, " The Civil War "; for the fourth, " Coffee " (Brazil); for the fifth, " Percentage " (Arithmetic). It is doubtful, however, that he would be happier or would learn better under the methodical arrangement which would treat him without any periods to one " integrated " subject, though that subject be a lovely daffodil. A teacher relates that she organized the entire instruction in one of the grades around the daffodil project. She devoted her time, first, to the anatomy and physiology of the daffodil; then, to its geography; after that, to the drawing of the daffodil; next to the poetry about it; and finally, to dancing around the flower bed. The daffodil project was still on at the time we heard about it last. We do not know how much or how little the students have learned through it in terms of information and mental habits; this depends very largely on the ability and culture of the teacher, whom we do not have the pleasure of knowing personally. But we are wondering if the majority of the daffodil project students did not finish by hating the daffodil and waiting as for deliverance for " the clang of the school bell," which some new educationists would do away with as the sinister symbol of the conventional school which " shatters valuable attitudes."

On the other hand, the reasonable correlation of subjects studied in a grade should be practiced in so far as possible. The history of South America, for example, should be studied immediately after the geographical conditions of the peninsula have been learned. Similarly, the colonial history of European countries should be supported by the corresponding geographical information relative to national industries, sources of raw materials, markets for export, commercial routes, etc.

Third, the argument relative to the panoramic or synthetical learning recommended by the advocates of integrated instruction, it appears, suffers from a misconception of synthesis. In fact, there is a synthesis which William James would have characterized as staring at a fact. Evidently, the value of such a synthesis for building experience and getting meanings is very insignificant. There is also a different kind of synthesis, a reconstructive synthesis which unites things only after their resemblances and differences have been perceived by means of dismemberment worked by analysis.

Panoramic learning can be of value only in so far as it is a synthesis alternating with an analysis, which, of course, demands some kind of division of subject matter as well as systematic study of it, that is, study proceeding in a certain definite order.

Things that the child sees while he " swims in the stream of life " or " walks along the highways of life " are too complex and too entangled for an immature mind to grasp them adequately. Pestalozzi has rightly said that the art of instruction consists in removing the confusion arising from an indefinite succession of perceptions. Rare are the minds capable — without strenuous training — of grasping things by intuition; in other words, by an immediate, direct insight into the totality of the situation. As a rule, correct knowledge has to be laboriously sought by analysis, for we generally know well only that which we can take to pieces, so to speak. No one can produce a better generalization than his knowledge of details affords.

Our uncorrected minds are apt to indulge in mere staring at facts. It is an easy occupation and can be entertaining enough. Furthermore, our minds are naturally averse to analysis, because analysis means effort. This reluctance to analyze can develop into the lack of impartiality, mental honesty, and mental courage, that is to say, into mental dispositions opposed to the spirit of true democracy.

To turn now to the problem of the educational significance of the study of the home locality, emphasized in the Activity School Movement, it is correct that the child's immediate environment offers a natural starting point for his school work. Instruction should, indeed, at the initial stage, be reasonably centered around the home environment of the children and the experience already acquired by them before entering the school. Reasonable attention should be given in the school studies to the occupations prevailing in the locality. All this should be done, of course, in an order that prevents confusion in the minds of the students, and that results in skills and informations which are reasonably accurate. The new acquisitions should be based upon the former acquisitions, the complex upon the elementary, which, evidently, can scarcely be combined with " swimming in the stream of life " pure and simple. But the home locality should hardly ever occupy the whole stage in the learning process. Other legitimate interests of the child should be given places commensurate to their relative values, even if such other things should take the child far away from his home environment and beyond the borders of his county.

Doubtless, instruction must start from where the child stands, intellectually, when he first comes to the school. But soon the curiosity of the young beckons him away into the great world. The school should certainly take this into account. Horatio, in Shakespeare's *The Taming of the Shrew,* inquired of his friend Petruchio:

> And tell me now, sweet friend, what happy gale
> Blows you to Padua here from old Verona?

Petruchio gives the following reply:

> Such wind as scatters young men through the world,
> To seek their fortunes farther than at home,
> Where small experience grows.[63]

For a while " the homely activities going on about him " are to the child " a wonderful world the depths of which he has not yet sounded, a world full of mystery and promise that attend all the doings of the grown-ups whom he admires." [64] Next, and the more intelligent he is, the sooner the child yearns to get a look, directly or indirectly, at the wide world, greatly to the enchantment of himself and sometimes to the ultimate benefit of the world. Had it not been so with the poor American farmer's boy who, " communing with himself, longed to read and know something beyond the stumps between which he planted his corn," [65] who subsequently decided that there was some great place in the world for him to fill and who eventually left upon

[63] Act. 1, Scene 2.
[64] Dewey, J., *How We Think, cit.,* p. 166.
[65] Bolton, Sarah K., *Lives of Poor Boys Who Became Famous,* Rev. ed., Thomas Crowell Co., 1925, p. 193.

the world the impress associated with the name of Abraham Lincoln? Or was not that the case of Peter Cooper? In the apt words of a biographer, Cooper, a boy living in " one of the old Dutch villages on the Hudson . . . spent many an hour up in an old apple-tree gazing across the valley to the purple peaks, beyond which lay the great world. . . ." [66]

The intellectual curiosity and imagination of the child can easily suffer under the regime of integrated instruction; and it is clearly the duty of the school to promote the wholesome curiosity and imagination of the children. It is scarcely necessary to draw up a list of the civic and scientific values of the healthy imagination. The history of civilization knows of many reveries that have resulted in great discoveries, and of many a mental flight which has revolutionized science. It is also imagination and mental experimentation that furnishes the citizen his mental watchtower from which he can see ahead instead of blindly following the propagandist. It is again imagination that enables the real leaders of humanity to climb over the walls made of the fallacies and errors of their own age. It might also be mentioned in this connection that the essence of constructive criticism is, after all, the ability to enter into modes of life and thinking different from our own.

Furthermore, it is necessary to remember that the wealth of home environment can vary all the way from that of a lonely hamlet lost in the immense expanse of a mountain to that of a large modern city. Socrates was asked by Phaedrus why he seldom, if at all, left Athens for the countryside. In reply Socrates said: " I hope that you will excuse me when you hear the reason which is, that I am a lover of knowledge, and the men who dwell in the city are my teachers, and not the trees of the country." [67] The average student also can learn more in the environment of a modern capital city than in a steppe village, coming

---

[66] *Ibid.*, p. 86.   [67] *Phaedrus*, 230.

out from which into the larger world would not fail to give him the sensation of being just hatched. Variety and novelty stimulate and feed the intellectual interest. It takes the wise to wonder at what is usual. The average youth is more likely to start wondering at what is unusual. The school, we are told, should be deeply rooted in the native soil. Yes, it should, if by native soil is meant all the cultural and moral wealth of the whole nation.

Abstract learning, to which the partisans of integrated instruction object, should begin — indeed it is actually carried on by the child of his own accord — much earlier than the age which the theory of integrated instruction sets up for it. In fact, the child begins to think abstractly when he begins to speak. Are not words, except the few onomatopœic words, merely so many abstract symbols? The moment the child becomes able to do mental arithmetic he is fairly well-equipped for successful dealing with a reasonable amount of abstract studies. Abstract studies in the true sense of the term are studies in which meanings are derived from meanings rather than from direct handling of things. The school should, without violently pushing him, lead the educand along the path of abstract learning. Through this method the child can best share in the wealth of meanings accumulated by untold generations of men during the slow process of learning things and their properties by actually handling things.

There are many things which all the members of a democratic community should learn to know as early as possible, and which can be solidly assimilated only with the help of abstract thinking and abstract learning.

For instance, without the use of abstract learning, it would be difficult to bring the young to realize the nature and the main functions of the national state. Yet, political science since the time of Aristotle knows well that the best laws will be of no avail unless the young are trained by habit and education in the spirit of the polity, unless they are habituated to think of the national state as a whole and feel attached to it. In the last few years much harm and misery has been visited upon several countries of the world because of the popular ignorance of simple verities, political and economic. The public elementary school can reasonably be held responsible for the sufficient initiation of the normal average graduate into the A B C of unadulterated social science. The school can hardly acquit itself of this obligation without considerable use of methods implying abstract learning and purely mental experimentation. How, indeed, could it otherwise teach the student the nature of money as distinct from wealth, the mechanics of the circulation of wealth, and the like? How, if not by abstract learning, can the student come to understand what is good and what is bad taxation, what are the sound, legitimate functions of trade unions and what are not; what are the duties of the producer and of the consumer, and the like?

SUGGESTIONS FOR READING

Bagley, W. C., *Educational Values* (Macmillan).

Bogoslovsky, B. B., *The Technique of Controversy* (Harcourt, Brace and Co.).

Dewey, John, *How We Think* (D. C. Heath).

Komens, G. C. and Curtis, C. P., Jr., *An Introduction to Pareto: His Sociology* (Knopf).

Martin, D. E., *Farewell to Revolution* (W. W. Norton).

CHAPTER
VI

CHARACTER BUILDING

CHAPTER VI

CHARACTER BUILDING

THE INDIVIDUAL'S GOOD CHARACTER AS THE VEHICLE OF
MORAL CIVILIZATION

Among outstanding thinkers who have occupied themselves
with the search for the best way to improve human conditions,
there can be distinguished three main schools. Of these three
schools of thought one relies entirely upon public enlightenment. According to that school of thought, social evils have their
source neither in native and incorrigible disabilities of the human being nor in the nature of the external world, but simply in
human ignorance and prejudices. The improvement of the state
of man is a matter of doing away with ignorance and removing
errors, of increasing knowledge and diffusing light. The human
reasoning power is the supreme regulator of life. According to
this — rationalistic — school of thought, the only true history of
man would be that of the five or six great ideas which have
governed civilization. The founder of this school of thought was
the celebrated French rationalist philosopher, Descartes (see
p. 70). He believed that the growth of universal reason was the
remedy for the miseries of social life.[1] What is reason? " The
power of judging aright and of distinguishing Truth from
Error which is properly what is called Good Sense or Reason." [2]
Truth to Descartes is something that is " perceived clearly and
distinctly." [3] Or, as a contemporary Cartesian has expressed it,

[1] Cf. *Les passions de l'âme*, P. III; also Descartes' letter to Queen Christine of
November 20, 1647.

[2] *Discourse on the Method of Conducting the Reason, and Seeking Truth in the
Sciences*, Open Court Publishing Co., 1903, p. 1.

[3] *Meditations Upon the First Philosophy* (Metaphysics), Third Meditation. (Tor-
rey, Henry A. P., *The Philosophy of Descartes*, Henry Holt and Co., 1892, p. 126.)

The source of life and the principal source of all harmony in life is in our mind. . . . Mind is the real origin of the just and the beautiful. Even animals and plants and inanimate bodies of nature are subject to the law of mathematics, that is to say, of reason. Nothing in nature is the result of chance. And in order to create beauty, it is necessary to imitate reason by accepting its laws of harmony. A beautiful piece of work is something marked off by the proscription of the element of hazard. It is a work in which the defects due to the lack of precision of our senses are corrected by the counsel of the intellect. . . . My friends, be faithful to reason. . . . There is no real greatness except that which issues from reason. Light surpasses in beauty both form and color.[4]

Another school of thought — the romantic — on the contrary, denies the governing role of ideas. It does not believe that ideas either rule the world or change it. The world is governed and changed by sentiments, by great longings for the ideal, and by powerful passions of all kinds.

The great modern prophet of this school of thought was Rousseau who saw the source of renovation of human society in the voice of pure emotions rising from the depth of our hearts when liberated from the obstructive influences of artificial civilization. "If reason has made man [distinct from the lower animals] * it is sentiment that guides him," declared Rousseau.[5] According to the Romanticist, great events took place when

> . . . the heart
> Stood up and answered, "I have felt."[6]

Spencer thought that the individual's sentiment or "inner conviction" was the decisive factor in building civilization. In conclusion to his *Social Statics,* Spencer says:

* Bracketed remarks are added.

4 Herriot, E., *Sous l'Olivier,* Paris, Hachette, 1930, pp. 141, 148.
Cf. Anatole France, *Credo of a Skeptic,* "Let us first of all follow reason, it is the surest guide. It warns us of its feebleness and informs us of its own limitations."

5 *Nouvelle Héloise,* P. III, Lettre VII (Paris, Barbier, 1845, Vol. I, p. 291).

6 Tennyson, *In Memoriam,* CXXIV.

The candid reader may now see his way out of the dilemma in which he feels placed, between a conviction, on the one hand, that the perfect law is the only safe guide, and a consciousness, on the other, that the perfect law cannot be fulfilled by imperfect men. Let him but duly realize the fact that opinion is the agency through which character adapts external arrangements to itself — that *his* opinion rightly forms part of this agency — is a unit of force, constituting, with other such units, the general power which works out social changes — and he will then perceive that he may properly give full utterance to his *innermost conviction;* leaving it to produce what effect it may. It was not for nothing that he has in him these sympathies with some principles, and repugnance to others. He, with all his capacities and desires, and beliefs, is not an accident, but a product of time. . . . He must remember that whilst he is a child of the past, he is a present of the future. The moral sentiment developed in him was intended to be instrumental in producing further progress; and to gag it, or to conceal the thoughts it generates, is to balk creative design. He, like every other man, may properly consider himself as an agent through whom nature works; and when nature gives birth in him to a certain belief, she thereby authorizes him to profess and to act out that belief.[7]

Still another school, the voluntaristic-rationalistic, seeks happiness like Socrates in the unity of virtue and knowledge.

Between Wisdom and Prudence he drew no distinction; but if a man knows and practices what is beautiful and good, knows and avoids what is base, that man he judged to be both wise and prudent. When asked further whether he thought that those who know what they ought to do and yet do the opposite are at once wise and vicious, he answered: " No; not so much that, as both unwise and vicious. For I think that all men have a choice between various courses, and choose and follow the one which they think conduces most to their

[7] *Social Statics; or the Conditions Essential to Human Happiness,* D. Appleton and Company, 1865, p. 516 f.

advantage. Therefore I hold that those who follow the wrong course are neither wise nor prudent."

He said that Justice and every other form of Virtue is Wisdom! [8]

It is from this third school of thought that Emile Durkheim, who may be rightly considered the founder of educational sociology, drew inspiration for his theory of moral civilization.[9] According to Durkheim's theory, civilization should be conceived dualistically, notably as the function of two forces: (a) intellect or knowledge, and (b) moral sentiment or idealistic disposition. Those two forces are not always harmonious in their relationship. Leaving out the question of priority as between virtue and knowledge — which question Durkheim justly considered idle — he insisted with great conviction and talent upon the importance of special educational effort in the promotion of moral civilization, which he defined as a code of individual action corresponding to the highest standards of moral sentiment and conduct established by what may be called moral geniuses.

Durkheim's philosophy of civilization deserves whole-hearted approval as recommended by common sense and clear lessons of history. It is well to retain from the teachings of Socrates — who inspired Durkheim — that the way toward changing a social organization for the better consists in improving the character of the individual. As did John Stuart Mill, who was a deep student of the classics and of human nature, so we also must look for permanent emancipation from the wasteful system of cruel, exaggerated individual self-interest to a moral revolution within

[8] Xenophon, *Memorabilia*, III, IX, 4 f. (Translated by E. C. Marchant, G. P. Putnam's Sons, 1923, Vol. IV, p. 225).

[9] Emile Durkheim (1859–1917), French philosopher and sociologist, Professor at the Sorbonne. Among his chief contributions are the following monographs and essays: *Les règles de la méthode sociologique, Représentations individuelles et représentations collectives, La Sociologie, De la division du travail, Jugements de valeur et de réalité, La détermination du fait moral, De la définition des phénomènes religieux, Le Suicide, Les formes élémentaires de la vie religieuse.* Cf. P. Fauconnet, "The Pedagogical Work of Emile Durkheim," *The American Journal of Sociology*, March, 1923, pp. 529–553.

the individual, rather than to economic or political revolutions, or to any particular economic system. " I regard any considerable increase in human happiness, unaccompanied by changes in the state of the desires, as hopeless." [10]

> Let us be better,
> Things will soon mend! [11]

The sense of honor, teaches Montesquieu, is the bedrock of monarchy, and virtue, the bedrock of democratic government.[12] That foundation once decayed, the whole political structure will inevitably crumble into dust. The story of the downfall of monarchical governments does, it seems, sufficiently demonstrate that divorce between privilege and honesty, between valor and social position, has been one of the principal causes of their undoing. It seems, also, that all we know about democracies gone by shows nearly as well, that without the cultivation of good character in citizens, liberty is impossible.

Socrates judged the work of Pericles as a democratic statesman in the following manner:

> The brilliant statesman had enriched and embellished the city; had erected protective walls around it; had built ports and dockyards; had launched navies; had eternalized the glory of the city by temples of undying grandeur and beauty; had multiplied in Attica the feasts of arts and reason; but he did not occupy himself with the problem of how to make the Athenians better men and women. As a result his work has remained incomplete and his creation caducous.[13]

One of the causes which in the course of history has repeatedly shattered several well-intentioned " new deals " has been the disproportion between the stress placed by prophets of drastic democratic reforms upon the rights of the citizenry, and the reluctance to emphasize the civic duties of the same citizenry.

[10] Cf. Neff, E., *Carlyle and Mill*, Columbia University Press, 1927, p. 356.
[11] Overbeck, Chr. Ad., *Gedichte*, Trost fuer Mancherlei Thraenen.
[12] *The Spirit of Laws*, Colonial Press, Revised Edition, 1900, Vol. I, pp. 20 ff.
[13] *Gorgias*, 516 ff.

WHAT CONSTITUTES CHARACTER?

Though the term " character," as it is employed by educated men and women, has a generally accepted and sufficiently clear meaning, the student in education, while discoursing upon the subject of character as an educational objective the fulfillment of which is one of the three fundamental residual services of the school to the individual, should be sure of the definition of the word. The term " character " is of Greek origin, χαρακτήρ (kharactér), *a mark engraved* or *impressed,* the *impress* or *stamp* on coins and seals. H. G. Wells ably describes character as a " gravitational centre." He says of Christina Alberta:

She had also a pitiless conscience. It was almost the only thing she could not manage in her life. It managed her. It was a large, crystalline conscience. . . . It was the gravitational centre and the rest of her could not get away from it.[14]

Among the definitions of character aptly worded by philosophers, the following may be quoted:

Kant: " To have a character means to possess this property of will power by which the acting subject remains true to the guiding principle which he has put down for himself advised by his moral sense (*praktische Vernunft*). . . . In character it is not a question of what nature makes of man, but of what he makes of himself." [15]

Schopenhauer: " Character is a permanent and an unalterable constitution and quality of an individual will." [16]

Emerson: " A character is like an acrostic or Alexandrian stanza; — read it forward, backward, or across, it still spells the same thing." [17] " Character is centrality, the impossibility of being displaced or overset." [18]

---

[14] From *Christina Alberta's Father* by H. G. Wells, p. 59. By permission of The Macmillan Company, publishers.   [15] *Anthropology,* II, p. 277.

[16] *Die Welt als Wille und Vorstellung,* Sämtliche Werke, 2 Aufl., F. A. Brockhaus, Leipzig, 1891, B. 2¹, S. 339, 346.

[17] *Essays and Poems,* " Self-Reliance," Houghton Mifflin Co., 1883, First Series, p. 53.   [18] " Character," *Ibid.,* Second Series, p. 98.

Good character, then, is the will actively to promote good and to oppose evil, and to do this with a constancy that may be described as certainty. Such certainty cannot easily be upset, in a man of good character, by his various and conflicting ideas and sentiments, or if so upset or deviated will soon reassert itself. This definition may perhaps be illustrated by the following characteristic given in *The Milner Papers* to Mr. Joseph Chamberlain:

Joe is an extraordinary man — quite on the big lines. Under a different system, he really might federate the Empire. . . . He has a most comical weakness — look at his impressionability. The most ridiculous incidents — and people — temporarily affect him, and many cause him to make great mistakes. But the effect is only temporary. In the long run he is swayed by big permanent ideas, and they are not external to him, but wherever he gets them from, they have roots inside him, which alone can insure any vitality to a policy or any greatness to its possessor. . . . I never, even to myself, criticize Joe without hastily adding, " but it is not his fault." One is so grateful for greatness anywhere. It is a sort of *lèse majesté* of the worst description to undermine it.[19]

Such deeply rooted constancy, such unalterable certainty of devotion by man to his convictions and ideals is one of the greatest assets of humanity in its search for ever higher moral civilization. As is true of all truly great human accomplishments, good character is a value not automatically produced. " He is a good man," we often say thoughtlessly. Would we not be more chary of our praise if we reflected that we could not bestow any higher praise?[20]

Even descent from good, honorable parents is not, in itself, a guarantee of good character in children. A well-planned and

---

[19] Cassell and Co., 1933, p. 629 f. Quoted by kind permission of Lady Milner.
[20] Cf. von Ebner-Eschenbach, Marie, *Aphorisms,* German Classics, cit., Vol. XIII, p. 440.

well-conducted educational effort is necessary to develop good character in the young. Pericles, we are told by Socrates, gave his sons " excellent instruction in all that could be learnt from masters, but in his own department of politics he neither taught his children himself nor gave them teachers of virtue, but allowed them to wander of their own free will in a sort of hope that they would light upon virtue of their own accord." [21] The results were of the kind to discourage a modern Pericles, great or small, from following the example of the ancient Pericles relative to the education of his children! " No man is born wise; but wisdom and virtue require a tutor, though we can easily learn to be vicious without a master." [22]

HOW IS CHARACTER BUILT?

Adherents of the New Education teach that character is built by doing, by free practice in moral actions, free personal moral experience. They appear to be convinced that character consists of moral habits and of nothing else; that the individual's character is the sum total of his or her moral habits (meaning by moral something concerning the individual's relationship with other men, that is to say, actions and disposition which affect other human beings; or, indeed, animals). There is, obviously, much truth in such a point of view, but as not all in this fashionable outlook upon the problem of character is true, and the problem is a very important one, the following analysis of it may perhaps be useful.

First, it is important to remember that the problem of how character is built is evidently the problem of building good character. If that be so, can it well be held that the badness of immoral actions has to be learned by the young through practicing them and only in this way? Such a position would be the logical counterpart of the method of building character by

[21] *Protagoras*, 320.   [22] Seneca, *Op. cit.*, p. 109.

doing. But is such a position more tenable than the idea that children should acquire all the important health habits by doing, by personal experience of the good that comes from compliance with hygienic rules and of the injury that strikes the ignorant as well as him who breaks these rules and indulges in excesses of one sort or another? Many might form bad habits in this way and some might not survive to profit by the experience.

Second, character is something more than merely a sum total of moral habits. Let us suppose, for example, that we know the moral habits of our friend. Does it follow that we can correctly predict how he will act when confronted with a moral problem? Yes and no. When the situation is similar to those under which we have seen him act before, yes. But if it is one of those occasions when a man is bound to show either the sublime nobility or the abject meanness of his heart, with no possibility of choosing a middle course, we cannot make a prediction unless we know something about our friend other than his habits, something very difficult even for the man himself to know and to describe. That something is a commanding moral attitude, fixed yet not observable in the ordinary course of events. It was there, hidden in the maze of the intimate folds of our friend's mind, before the day we saw him perform the act, divinely beautiful or demoniacally ugly, as the case may be.

How did the attitude in question come to be formed? Evidently not by actual practice. Acts of consummate sacrifice or consummate baseness are rare or even unique in the life of a man. They are not a product of habit, pure and simple. Then, how are they formed? Very probably, unless they are the results of a purely instinctive reaction to a situation, the genesis of those rare or unique attitudes and actions is as follows: The mind of our friend — who, let us suppose, shielded with his own body the person of his chief attacked by an assassin — had been impressed once, or more than once, by the sight (immediate or intermediate, obtained through what he heard or read) of similar moral action. That moral experience left behind in his mind a trace of a certain depth determined by the degree of his impressionability. He might or might not have mused over it, re-experienced it in his imagination. At any rate, the experience has taken the potential force of a directing mind-set. Until the real living situation furnished a proper stimulus, that mind-set remained slumbering in the vast chamber of past experience. Yet, it became a centrality which, however imperceptible to the casual observer, could not be displaced or upset.

It is not improbable that cases may present themselves where a diagnosis like this will not hold. Immeasurable is the variety of the mental reactions of man, and unfathomable is the brain-work where are hatched the darkest mental reactions. Equally inscrutable and impenetrable is that wonderful laboratory wherefrom spring the heavenly flames of high deeds of heroism. Nevertheless, the life story of a commanding mind-set, or super-habit if you like, as it is sketched above, appears to be the more usual course of development of that unusual and superlatively important phenomenon. Therefore, while it is proper to say that habit is will, it is inexact to say that will is habit. It is not always a habit; sometimes, and on occasions of paramount significance, it is not; it is something above and beyond habit in the common sense of the term. It is a super-habit, a key mind-set. As this is generally born — except in the case of moral geniuses, originators of the highest moral standards — of sharing in the impressive moral experiences of others, the school has evidently to do all in its power to give a desirable turn to the child's borrowed moral experience. In other words, in connection with the fundamental educational objective under consideration, we are brought by the force of the logic of things back again to directed learning, to vicarious experience, in particular to guided reading in history and literature, and especially in the drama.

Third, there is an important difference between the formation and exercise of moral habits and what might be called intellectual habits. This difference is excellently formulated by Alexander Bain:

The peculiarity of the moral habits, contradistinguishing them from the intellectual acquisitions, is the presence of two hostile powers, one to be gradually raised into the ascendant over the other. It is necessary, above all things, in such a situation never to lose a battle. Every gain on the wrong side undoes the effect of many conquests on the right. The essential precaution, therefore, is so to regulate the two opposing powers that the one may have a series of uninterrupted successes, until repetition has fortified it to such an extent as to enable it to cope with the opposition under any circumstances.[23]

It is well to remember this, as it is of capital importance to the question of the proper balancing of directed versus free development of character.

THE IMPORTANCE OF DIRECTED SECOND-HAND EXPERIENCE FOR THE FORMATION OF CHARACTER

A superman perhaps does not need the aid of the school in the matter of building his character. He may be impervious to the influence of the school. But leaving aside the question of whether there is such a thing as a superman, democracy has to

[23] Bain, Alexander, *The Emotions and the Will*, D. Appleton and Co., 1876, p. 440–441.

Cf. also Bain's *Mental and Moral Science*, Longmans, Green and Co., 1905, pp. 385–386: "In the first place, a certain repetition is necessary [for the formation of moral habits], greater or less according to the change that has to be affected, and to the absence of other favoring circumstances . . . In the second place, the mind may be more or less *concentrated* on the acquisition. Apart from the amount of repetition, moral progress depends greatly on the bent of the learner towards the special acquisition. If we are striving *con amore* to attain any important habitude, such as the Command of Attention, the currents of the brain are exclusively set in this one direction, instead of being divided with other engrossments. A less efficient, although still a powerful, stimulus, is the application of pain . . . As a large and important branch of moral acquisition consists in strengthening one power to overcome another, it is of great advantage to have an uninterrupted series of successes: which can only be secured by strongly backing at first the motive to be strengthened, and by never giving it too much to do. Defeats should be avoided, especially in the early stages."

rely on the common sense as well as on the integrity, courage, and faith of average men and women.

Not unlike the educand's intellectual experience, the building of his moral experience and his character must be accomplished largely by drawing upon borrowed experience. It is highly desirable, indeed, that children learn to avoid bad actions without having learned by actual personal experience to know their badness. Learning by doing may cause in this case irreparable injuries, or at least may lead to the formation of undesirable habits. The importance of borrowed moral experience, of sharing in the recorded moral experiences of others, does not end there. When borrowed from good sources and properly assimilated, it can be a great factor, not only in developing in the young the will to avoid bad actions but also the will to do good.

There is what may be called moral genius, or genius of morality, as there is intellectual genius. Moral genius is found in men and women who have given the noblest manifestations of the purer, higher side of human nature. For enriching and stimulating the educand's intellectual experience, an acquaintance with outstanding minds is of undisputed value. So is communion with moral geniuses valuable for building the character of the young. It is an excellent way to acquire a knowledge of the highest moral standards, as well as a desire to imitate, if not to surpass them. Living mentally through the singularly rich, dramatic trials and triumphs of a moral genius, the young pupil learns not to be elated at being somewhat better than his comrades. He will learn to strive to emulate the greatest moral achievements, never to be discouraged by difficulties or disillusioned by the existence of the base and the bad.

In answer to the question, How did moral values come into the world? Goethe said, in the *Conversations with Eckermann:*

Through God Himself, like everything else. It is no product of human reflection, but a beautiful nature inherent and inborn. It is, more or less, inherent in mankind generally, but to a high degree in a few eminently gifted minds. These have, by great deeds or doctrines, manifested their divine nature; which then, by the beauty of its appearance, won the love of men and powerfully attracted them to reverence and emulation.[24]

But, above all, the educand will, through the contact or communion with moral geniuses, store up enthusiasm for all that is noble and morally beautiful. We need not fear overheating, in this manner, the imagination of children and overstraining their emotions or sending them too high up in the air. The young mind is as elastic as the young body, if not more so. It likes stretching and breath-taking heights. Besides, the realities of life will not allow the young imagination and the youthful moral sentiment to soar too long or too high. The realities of life will remove the surplus of idealism — if there can be any surplus of that precious substance which alone can keep man from falling down into the slime. The more of that substance one takes along with him on his life travel, the greater moral satisfaction is reserved for him, and this is, in the end, the highest form of satisfaction attainable by man. " Don't drop it [idealistic enthusiasm]* when you are young," Gogol warned his readers, " because you will never be able to pick it up." [25]

If not in the immediate environment of the child, in the records of the past there can be shown to him the true patriots who served the state to their own disadvantage, the national leaders who unselfishly worked for their people. If the contemporary events of public life frequently offer to the young the spectacle of opportunism, corruption, and ineptitude, history has preserved for them brighter pictures. There they will meet public men who had and retained principles, sufficiently disdained flattery, did not court the multitude with unrealizable

* Bracketed remarks are added.
[24] *Op. cit.,* p. 184.   [25] Gogol, N., *The Dead Souls,* I, Pluyshkin.

promises, but relied, in their public careers, on the power of an incorruptible character. Surely, no attempt should be made to " arrange " the historical studies of the young. Consequently, in their wanderings through the galleries of past events and men they will come, as well, upon glib and fluent " tribunes of the people," expert in the art of darting from pole to pole of the political compass, guided solely by the lure of cash. They will see across the centuries a whole procession of public men, to quote Aristophanes, " circumstanced like those who fish for eels. When the lake is still they catch nothing, but if they stir the mud up and down, they take." [26] But the educand will also behold the unforgettable sight of high civic virtues and heroic actions. The youthful heart is hungry for the latter; they give the young hope, great hope, as well as the desire to accomplish great things.

In certain unfortunate civic conditions, those beautiful civic and moral examples will cheer the young as a voice reassures the wanderer who believes himself lost in a solitary wilderness. Furthermore, and this is perhaps a still more valuable lesson derivable from history, the young will find that humanity, as history knows it, is on the whole fundamentally moral; that " whatever their private beliefs may be, kings and statesmen must at least pretend to be on the side of right against wrong." [27] It is well said that the best reward of historical studies is the optimism which history arouses.

Shall we then recommend that all moral education or character building be carried on through the medium of the printed records of great deeds? " Must I always be a listener only? " [28] asks an ancient satirist on behalf of youths of all times. Certainly not.

Object lessons by immediate contact with living heroes and

[26] *The Knights*, 868 ff.   [27] Spender, J. A., *op. cit.*, Vol. II, p. 154.
[28] Juvenalis, *Satyrae*, I, 1.

with ordinary good men in public or private life are, naturally, very desirable for building the character of the future citizen. Unfortunately, this is a difficult method of character education fully to practice in a complex modern society where the working of civic machinery can be observed by the outsider only partially and very insufficiently. What may have been the right and natural method of education for citizenship in the case of the youth of the ancient small city-state where the young could hear national leaders speak and watch them carry out the business of the state at the *agora* (ἀγορά) or the forum, even see them in command on the battlefield, is not quite suitable for us. In fact, it is not less difficult nowadays for the young to acquire the right training in civics, both as regards information and the disposition of the mind, merely by object lessons than it is to learn the principles of modern economics through glimpses of industrial and commercial activities that can be caught by an outsider. Yet, object lessons in character building should never be neglected. Nor should the importance of the method of doing, of practicing moral actions be underestimated. This is the method appointed for the formation of moral habits. Indeed, anything else would be superfluous if character were nothing but a sum total of habits and of their functions. But it is not.

Herbert Spencer, then, grossly neglected an important educational point when he made the following statement:

Belief in the moralising effects of intellectual culture, flatly contradicted by facts, is absurd *a priori*. What imaginable connection is there between learning that certain clusters of marks on paper stand for certain words, and getting a higher sense of duty? What possible effect can acquirement of facility in making written signs of sounds, have in strengthening the desire to do right? [29]

---

[29] From *The Study of Sociology* by Herbert Spencer, p. 331. Used by permission of D. Appleton-Century Company, Publishers, New York, N. Y.

As if inspired by these words of Spencer, adherents of the New Education sometimes raise the question: Which is more important, to be honest or to be able to read and to count? Clearly, this is an instance of a false dilemma. Both are necessary, and they are not by any means mutually exclusive. On the contrary, the second may greatly help the first. In many respects honesty depends upon the ability to read and count.

Our insistence upon the intellectual aspects of character building, upon the great importance of vicarious experience in building character must not be taken as an expression of the belief that participation in activities, in first-hand experiences conducive to character building, is of secondary value. On the contrary, we believe with Emerson that " the force of character is cumulative " [30] and that every educand should take an active part in activities such as the Boy and Girl Scout movements, as well as in worthy civic projects sponsored by the school and the community. Such activities, when properly organized, contribute effectively to character building, and current educational literature justly stresses their paramount significance. On the other hand, the intellectual aspects of character building seem to be insufficiently brought into the picture, and our discussion of their importance is intended simply to call the attention of younger educators, trained under the regime of the New Education, to the significance of these factors. The intellectual factors of character building embrace insight into complex social-moral situations, critical analysis of such situations in the light of social intelligence, and the vision of a moral ideal.

SCHOOL DISCIPLINE

The motivation of an individual's attitudes and actions, through the individual's character traits, is possible, as was indicated above, from two sources: (a) the individual's moral habits

[30] " On Self-Reliance," *Essays, cit.,* p. 60.

(that is, habits concerning relationship with others); and (b) the individual's supreme moral conviction, positive or negative, described above as the key mind-set or super-habit. It is extremely difficult to determine which of the two sources of motivation has the larger share in the conduct of men. Both are, doubtless, of importance. The second may be successfully nourished through the growing child's contact with a moral genius, even though such contact should be by means of so-called second-hand experience. But how can the first-named constituent element of character, notably good moral habits, be promoted? Among other things, properly organized school discipline can contribute powerfully toward the formation of good moral habits.

A real bony physique, a body with steady nerves and tireless muscles, can be developed on the basis of normal physical endowment through exercises that form good physical habits, that is through action, by the method of doing. Similarly, a " real bony character " (to borrow this picturesque expression from J. B. Priestley's *Faraway*) [31] can be developed — to a degree — by exercise, by action, by doing. Among the school devices furnishing special occasions for character building, such devices as student government, games, and participation in the community's civic projects have been abundantly discussed and practiced in the last quarter of a century. But there is one very important device in character building which must not be neglected as has been the case in many places. It is school discipline. Because imprudently applied at times, school discipline has been unwisely attacked, on principle, by some educators, and its actual neglect has been elevated by such educators almost to the status of pedagogical virtue. This seems a very dubious sort of virtue when the meaning of school discipline is properly understood.

[31] Harper & Brothers, 1932, p. 62.

What is school discipline? It is an ensemble of rules and regulations concerning the students' conduct with relation to their work, their fellow-students, the school authorities and teachers, as well as other persons with whom they may come in contact while in the care of the school.

There are two basic kinds of discipline, the wrong or unsound, and the right or sound. The former is designed to train the student for unquestioning obedience, and to " break the spirit " of those reluctant to render such obedience. When employed in school, this sort of discipline is likely to make hypocritical serfs of the students when it does not turn them into desperate rebels, and it is to be unreservedly condemned. But then there is the right kind of discipline, designed to help the student to form good moral habits. It functions properly when sympathetic and understanding but reasonably firm educators make the student realize that the purpose of the regulations which he or she is expected to obey is to assist him or her in forming good moral habits. The educand can reasonably soon be brought to see that the acquisition of such habits, even those which he or she admires in others, is not an easy thing, as there are in us many tendencies that have to be controlled and guarded against until the right habits are formed through uncompromising adherence to certain rules of conduct. A student may sincerely admire those of his or her fellow-students or adults who possess such qualities as earnestness of purpose, perseverance in worthy undertakings, and the like, and yet be weak and unable without the watchful assistance of the school to develop those valuable traits of character; he needs an appropriate help from school discipline. In other words, the purpose and justification of sound school discipline is the development of self-discipline in the student, meaning by self-discipline the desirable moral habits which will guide his or her conduct in the right direction. " It is a paradox of the well-disciplined school," rightly observes

W. C. Bagley, " that ' discipline ' is conspicuous by its absence." [32]

If and when school discipline is organized and carried out in this spirit, then the rules and regulations will be accepted by the students as something good (or at least as an inevitable evil) because designed for their own good, and not as the hateful signs of enslavement to a stupidly heartless tyranny which it is not only a right but a sacred duty to war against, to disobey, and to cheat.

Moreover, under conditions of sound school discipline reasonable punishment is not anything objectionable in itself, though of course not anything admirable in itself. Reasonable punishment under conditions of sound school discipline is simply a more or less forceful means of attracting the attention of the student to the undesirability of some of his actions or attitudes. It is a forceful invitation (when exhortations cannot be applied or have already proved useless) to think and to see the error of his ways. *The Saturday Evening Post* some time ago carried on the cover a cartoon representing a scene in a nursery room.[33] All the new playthings which had been given the boy of three or four years of age are shown in a more or less advanced stage of destruction. A similar fate has befallen his mother's hand-mirror and a large and probably valuable vase, which objects the child had appropriated. His young mother is very angry, and is in the initial stage of administering to the youngster a certain kind of rub with a hair brush. Her hand holding the punitive hair brush is raised. But then her eye catches sight of a book. It is a *Child Psychology*. The phase to which the cartoonist carried the problem is that of the youngster stretched face down across his mother's knee, presumably yelling, while his mother, in a state of suspense, reads from the *Child Psychology*. We do not know what answer to her query she found in that particular

[32] *School Discipline*, Macmillan, 1914, p. 1.   [33] November 25, 1933.

Child Psychology — but we should not have hesitated to advise her to complete the educational action she had begun. The youngster, while sulking for some time at the experience, would reflect on his misconduct, not without some good to himself, a good which probably could not be effected by any other method.

A columnist of the *Public Ledger* tells about a woman who declared " with great pride that she and her husband were letting their children grow up perfectly untrammeled by any restraints because they wanted their youngsters to develop their own individuality. They never made them do anything they didn't desire to do. They never corrected their faults or taught them any manners. And least of all did they attempt to make them obey. ' And to what far isle do you expect them to emigrate when they are grown? ' I asked her. ' For you are entirely unfitting them for civilization.' " [34]

We must confess that we do not know of anything in the science of education that would invalidate the wisdom of the columnist's reply to the " progressive " mother.

Rousseau himself, after he pleaded with more sentiment than sense the absolute freedom of the child from all orders or prescriptions and from all obedience to any authority,[35] said:

[34] July 10, 1933.
[35] " Although we know approximately the limits of human life and our chances of attaining those limits, nothing is more uncertain than the length of life of any one of us. Very few will reach old age. The chief risks occur at the beginning of life; the shorter our past life, the less we must hope to live. Of all the children who are born scarcely one half reach adolescence, and it is very likely your pupil will not live to be a man. What is to be thought, therefore, of that cruel education which sacrifices the present to an uncertain future, that burdens a child with all sorts of restrictions and begins by making him miserable, in order to prepare him for some far-off happiness which he may never enjoy? Even if I considered that education wise in its aims, how could I view without indignation these poor wretches subjected to an intolerable slavery and condemned like galley-slaves to endless toil, with no certainty that they will gain anything by it? The age of harmless mirth is spent in tears, punishments, threats, and slavery. You torment the poor thing for his good; you fail to see that you are calling Death to snatch him from these gloomy surroundings. Who can say how many children fall victims to the excessive care of their fathers and mothers? They are happy to escape from this cruelty; this is all they gain from

Do you know the surest way of making your child miserable? Let him have everything he wants. . . . How should I suppose that such a child can ever be happy? He is the slave of anger, a prey to the fiercest passions. Happy! he is a tyrant, at once the basest of slaves and most wretched of creatures. I have known children brought up like this who expected you to knock the house down, to give them the weathercock on the steeple, to stop a regiment on the march so that they might listen to the band; when they could not get their way they screamed and cried and would pay no attention to any one. In vain everybody strove to please them; as their desires were stimulated by the ease with which they got their own way, they set their hearts on impossibilities, and found themselves face to face with opposition and difficulty, pain and grief. . . .

If their childhood is made wretched by these notions of power and tyranny, what of their manhood, when their relations with their fellow-men begin to grow and multiply? They are used to find everything give way to them; what a painful surprise to enter society and meet with opposition on every side, to be crushed beneath the weight of a universe which they expected to move at will. Their insolent manners, their childish vanity, only draw down upon them mortification, scorn, and mockery; they swallow insults like water; sharp experience soon teaches them that they have realized neither their position nor their strength. As they cannot do everything, they think they can do nothing. They are daunted by unexpected obstacles, degraded by the scorn of men; they become base, cowardly, and deceitful, and fall as far below their true level as they formerly soared above it.[36]

False parental fear of the supposed sinister effects of discipline (based on a misconception of discipline) has produced a curious case reported in the *New York Times* of July 29, 1934. It would have been merely a bizarre news item if it did not reflect, as in

the ills they are forced to endure: they die without regretting, having known nothing of life but its sorrows." *Emile*, E. P. Dutton, 1921, pp. 42–43.

[36] *Emile*, pp. 51–52.

a magnifying glass, an educational theory, false yet not unsuccessful in recruiting its adherents.

West P——, N. J., July 28, — Charles (Mickey) N——, who became addicted to tobacco when he was fourteen months old, celebrated his third birthday today by lighting a large cigar by the flame of one of the three birthday-cake candles, and then, reaching for a glass of beer, drank a hearty gulp.

Witnesses said he did well by the ice cream, candy, and cake, but seemed intent on passing through these prosaic courses with haste to reach the final course where he could "light up" and also enjoy a good glass of beer.

Ever since his father, Charles N——, a contractor of 342 J—— Avenue, permitted the child to smoke his pipe shortly after the first year was passed, Mickey has been an inveterate smoker, inclined most of the time toward cigars.

Mr. and Mrs. N—— plan a campaign to curb this habit, but Mickey will not be aware of it until after this birthday is over. While the parents were considering the most judicious method of attaining this end Mickey was sitting at the head of the party table puffing on a six-inch Havana cigar trying to blow rings.

When applying sound school discipline we must not let ourselves be frightened by spectres of the child's repressed tendencies boring subterranean channels in search of an outlet at all costs. The secret revolt against the school authorities or black hatred for the exacting schoolmaster, which adepts of the New Education seem to be inclined to suspect behind the occasionally melancholy boy's face, does not normally exist.

Facts about the emotional life of children would scarcely justify us in imagining them as easily goaded into revolt or morbidness by commands given them, and readily exasperated by interference with their freedom. The child's very nature is a declaration of fellowship and brotherhood, however unstable it may be at times. Besides, we must not forget that the difference between a repellent tyrannical command and a command accepted good-naturedly is determined by the spirit in which the command is given and received. The teacher should remember that the child's affections are the reins with which he is best guided. The teacher must also bear in mind Molière's following caution: " I must hold that we should train up youth in cheerfulness, gently reprove its faults, and never frighten it with the name of virtue. . . . Never will I follow those harsh maxims which make our children count their fathers' days." [37] It is well said that no one is fit to be an instructor of youth who does not vividly remember his own youth. The child is ready to compromise; if he loves his parents and likes his teachers, he will tolerate without resentment a reasonable amount of uninviting work and will sincerely and with reasonable wholeheartedness obey the rules of discipline. The result will be more than pleasing the child's elders. Good moral habits will be formed and the basis of self-discipline will be established.

INTEREST, EFFORT, PLAY

The growth of mechanical civilization, that is, the development of clever mechanical devices serving man's various needs, has considerably obscured in the thinking of many people the fact that, generally speaking, the real worth of machinery depends very much on the worth of the man who tends and handles the machine. Captain Alfred E. B. Carpenter, author of *The Blocking of Zeebrugge* — a gripping story of a truly remarkable exploit of the British Navy in the World War — made this thoughtful, though slightly exaggerated remark: " Those who worship *matériel* have followed a false god. The crux of all fighting lies with the personnel — a fact borne out

---

[37] *L'École des maris,* Act I, Scene ii (Ariste), Translated by Katherine P. Wormeley, Little, Brown and Co., 1919, *Molière's Works,* Vol. V, pp. 156, 157, 158.

again and again on this particular night as throughout past history." [38] Similarly, the real valor of one nation as compared at any time of its history with that of another nation is determined by moral strength. This strength seems to depend much, in our period of Western history (when the individual's rights, apparently, are emphasized by many political leaders considerably more than his duties), upon the success of the various educational agencies, and above all of public schools, in teaching the growing citizen habits of loyal recognition and fulfillment of his duties toward others. To express it in the words of one of J. B. Priestley's characters, we must educate our students to be ". . . people who see what their duty is and go and do it without a lot of fuss; people who know when they have obligations. . . . And that's what you want to see in this world in the long run. . . ." [39]

It is in the light of the foregoing considerations of self-discipline and of character building in general that the very popular doctrine of motivation of learning by interest can perhaps be properly analyzed.

One of the most attractive arguments found in the New Education literature in support of the free activity method is the affirmation that the child learns best when he works on the solution of a problem which interests him intrinsically, immediately. Learning, we are told, goes on best — both from the viewpoint of the intellectual development of the child and the development of character — when it is carried on in the " play way," when interest and effort are one. On the other hand, when the significance of a task lies in some kind of deferred satisfaction, in a distant future utility or merely in avoidance of punishment and the securing of reward, such a task is but drudgery, unproductive, and more or less harmful.

In connection with this " activist " doctrine of interest and

[38] Houghton Mifflin Co., 1922, p. 181.　　　[39] Op. cit.

effort, it may be recalled, in the first place, how much the New Education doctrine itself insists that there should be no sudden violent breaks in the methods of the child's work when he comes from one level of schooling to the next and higher level. Would not the same reasoning justify us in demanding that the student be reasonably habituated, among other things, to the relationship between interest and effort, as it usually exists in adult life? Certainly — until and unless the kind of society is established where immediate interest and effort would really coincide, where everyone could have the kind and the quantity of work he desires. But as things are now and are likely to continue, the vast majority of people have to do work that in reality interests them very indirectly. The school must reckon with this inherent part of our social heritage and must prepare the young to stand the drudgery of bread-winning work. As a social institution the school must so train children that they fit into the existing fundamental conditions of society; this, however, so far as possible without prejudice to the ability of some children to contribute in the future to the perfection of society.

To be sure, it would be the wrong kind of pedagogy not to apply in the educative process the spontaneous interests of the student to the utmost degree of reasonableness. It would be poor pedagogy not to try to create in the educand so far as possible an interest for the thing he or she is to learn. On the other hand, it is also the wrong pedagogy to include in the curriculum of a grade only the things for which the students — usually divided among themselves in such matters — seem to have an interest, and to exclude everything else.

Interest is well defined as tension toward foreseen results or aims. In distinction from the lower animals — whose learning and actions are almost invariably motivated by interest in immediate satisfactions — the grandeur of humanity lies partly in the fact that humanity has been capable of interest in and of effort toward results or aims, only distantly foreseen. Childhood, especially as represented by the more gifted, is, in a measure, capable of sharing in this grandeur of the species. It is the duty of all trustees and guardians of the child to promote that ability and to build on it in the educative process.

Herbert Spencer maintained that " the aptitude . . . to dwell on the concrete and proximate rather than on the abstract and remote " was the unfortunate peculiarity of the feminine intellect. This old Victorian compliment to the male is much too doubtful to accept. In truth, men and women alike are apt to deal " quickly and clearly with the personal, the special, and the immediate, but less rapidly grasp the general and the impersonal." In both sexes " a vivid imagination of simple and direct consequences mostly shuts out from mind the imagination of consequences that are complex and indirect." As citizens, the vast majority of people are inclined to see " what seems an immediate public good without thought of distant public evils." [40]

Preoccupation with the immediate is, indeed, one of the natural tendencies of mankind. Like nearly all other natural tendencies, it must be corrected by training; it must be pruned and guided if it is to yield all the good of which it can be the source. We must make sure that our students, in distinction from the beasts of the field, can respond to motives other than the satisfaction of momentary needs or the gratification of the love of pleasure. Consequently, deferred values must not be struck off the list of school objectives. Ability to plan for the distant future and to labor toward it is a distinct line of demarcation — in character as well as in intellect — between the civilized and the primitive man.

Furthermore, the young should know that as in the case of individuals, the people of any nation sleep in the bed they have

---

[40] From *The Study of Sociology* by Herbert Spencer, p. 346 f. By permission of D. Appleton-Century Company, Publishers, New York, N. Y.

made for themselves, except in very rare cases when blind luck or the now extinct race of kind fairies intervenes to turn rocks into down. Children must be shown that those cities whose governments planned and worked for the unborn generations have excellent sites and beautiful public parks, such as are totally absent or only to be acquired at ruinous prices by cities without intelligent and provident administrators; that nations blessed with wise, provident governments possess colonies, foreign markets, and other similar sources of employment and national income, while nations less fortunately guided have to struggle for such things in a congested world at the peril of their existence.

Nor is it difficult to make the average normal child appreciate the fact that the whole economic machinery, furnishing him the things he needs every day in order to live, is based very largely on the principle of deferred satisfaction. He can be brought to understand that, if the whole world's crop were improvidently eaten up, there would be no seed to sow and no more harvest. The average child is quite capable of seeing that " the man who spends less than he earns and who properly invests his margin keeps industry alive; that there would be no factories, railways, or other modern sources of comfort in life if there were no quiet prosaic people who have saved money for a rainy day, and put it into industry instead of indulging in immediate enjoyment that neither the brains and energy of those who have organized industry, nor the thews and sinews of those who have done the heavy work, could suffice alone; that the brains of inventors and organizers of industries and the muscles of workmen who do the heavy work would have been powerless if there had not been economical people who provided the funds indispensable for industry until the day when its product would be sold and paid for." [41]

[41] Cf. Le Mesurier, W., *Commonsense Economics,* London, John Murray, 1923, pp. 8–18, 86–87.

Doctor Kuehnel, an activist of Leipzig, takes a complacent view of the eighteen-year-old girl-student of a secondary school who under the activity regime does not know anything about the electric bell. Doctor Kuehnel argues that she can swiftly learn all that is really necessary to know about it when she has to do this in order to overcome some difficulty.[42] It is very hard, however, to accept such an argument without reservations, since it would also bind us, logically, to postpone the initiation of the child into first aid till he is wounded, and to practice other similar absurdities. There are certain things that must be thoroughly learned, disconnected as they may be from the immediate objectives or satisfactions of the student. Neglect of these things under the conditions of modern life carries its own severe punishment.

Facilitation of the struggle for life, which seems destined to be only too hard for many of us, is a worthy educational objective. This does not mean, however, that "easyism" is the right method to employ in the promotion of this objective. Far from it; as far as is the negation of self-restriction and decent inhibition from the right method of promoting liberty. Therefore, educators responsible for the organization of motivation of the child's school work seem to be justified in introducing a middle term, namely, the satisfaction or annoyance produced by competition, in cases where it is impossible to bring about the immediate coincidence of interest and effort. For competition, with its annoyances and rewards, is one of the basic phenomena of human life, and the school must take note of this. The school must not create within its walls a cloistered peace of sheltered indolence. It must think of the day when the boy and girl will have to step out into the rush and traffic of life; and it must prepare them gently but firmly for that day. Its task is so much the easier since the intelligent children who

42 *Reichsschulkonferenz*, Amtlicher Bericht, *cit.*, p. 556.

come from earnest industrious families think often enough of their own accord about the future and wish to be fitted as well as possible to get on in life.

It is superfluous to emphasize the fact that competition in life outside the school will scarcely come to an end until social conditions have come about under which the strong will gladly support the weak, the clever will work unselfishly for the common good, and individual wealth, intellect, physical strength, and craftsmanship will be placed unreservedly at the service of the community. Until and unless such a millennium be really round the corner, the school must not banish competition from its realm, even if it can do so — which is doubtful.* Competition, of course, is like everything else — capable of use and abuse; and it has two aspects. It may be a healthy rivalry in no way incompatible with the true spirit of co-operation, expressing a valuable human instinct. But when it takes the vicious form of unscrupulous over-reaching, it may be a kind of destructive onrush of the jungle upon human society. Certainly, the school should never encourage the latter variety of competition; but the former, it should put to good use. "Rivalry nourishes talent," rightly observed a philosopher, "a desire for fame, reputation, or character with others is so far from being blamable that it seems inseparable from virtue, genius, capacity, and a generous or noble disposition." Of course, students should also be taught by appropriate examples that man reaches the really superb heights of moral beauty when he

* The Communist government of Russia had tried to run its factories and collective farms on the principle, "To everybody — in accordance with his needs; from everybody — in accordance with his ability." They soon discovered that individuals were inclined, under such a regime characterized by the abolition of scaled competitive remuneration, to think more about their needs than of their possible contribution to the commonwealth; they were more ready to take than to give. In consequence, the Communist government found itself forced to encourage competition in production through capitalistic methods such as scaled wages, premiums, prizes, and even decorations, such as the Order of Lenin, the Order of the Red Banner, the Order of Labor; and the titles, Distinguished Worker, Nobles of Labor, and the like.

performs deeds of loyalty and sacrifice for the sake of others without parading his actions or seeking a reward — so that the left hand knows not what the right hand does.

Likewise, many other obligatory lessons of life await the attention of the child. The future appears to stretch endlessly before a boy; he thinks there is plenty of time and no need to worry. Therefore, it is the teacher's business to impress upon the young the well-founded observation made by a Japanese poet:

> Three things in this world never stay
> To wait man's pleasure — fading flowers,
> Rivers that seaward take their way
> And passing hours.[43]

It is essentially incorrect to say that the child lives in the present, as the activists like to stress, because the child lives very much in the future. The distinction between babyhood and childhood seems to consist precisely in the child's being a "futurist" *par excellence*. He wants to anticipate his future as soon and as fully as possible; he wants to be strong, wise, and respected like older children or adults. To use the simile of "the spirit of play" frequently employed by the activists, it appears that from the viewpoint of the general method of play there can be distinguished two fundamental play types. The first one is imaginative play, largely solitary — the game of fancy mud confections to represent dainties, cardboard or tin soldiers to impersonate intrepid warriors, a kite to become a magnificent flying machine, and paper canoes to serve as yachts, steamers, or men-of-war. This is play proper, whose difference from work has well been analyzed by Professor Bagley. The burden of the analysis is to the effect that although work

---

[43] Ki no Tsurayuki, *Permanent,* Oxford Miscellany of Prose and Poetry, 1912.
Cf. Vauvenargues, L., "He is not born to attain glory who does not consider the value of time." (*Maxims and Reflections,* 180.)

may be enjoyable and seem like play, the main difference is that one's play may be dropped whenever one feels like dropping it, but work must continue even when it becomes monotonous.[44] The second type of play is the game of skill, usually organized (like baseball). In the first type the child is entirely his own master; his activity is free, he can discontinue it when he likes and the quality of his performance is nobody's business but his own. In the second type, on the contrary, he is a member of a group and his actions are controlled, not any longer by his own pleasure but by the code of the group and the rules of the game, unceremoniously enforced.

Games of fancy are normally occupations of the kindergarten age. At the age usual for the lower grades, the child normally loses his taste for imaginative play and abandons it for the organized games of the older children. Kite-engineering, mud-pie cooking, doll-dressing, and the like, cannot serve as the pattern of general educational methods appropriate for the upper grades. The kindergarten must not be permitted to extend its dominion over the secondary school and the college, for nothing but disastrous absurdity could result from the "kindergartenization" of the levels of education beyond the kindergarten proper.

Therefore, except in pre-school education and the lower primary grades, at the latest, the teacher who would search in the play of children for suggestions relative to methods of teaching must give her attention to organized games of skill rather than to the kite and mud-pie play. The normal child early deserts his old paradise that soon appears too childish for him and good only for " small children "; he hastens to join the invigorating manliness of directed organized games of skill and strength. Now if we follow our growing students

[44] *The Educative Process*, Macmillan, 1916, pp. 101 ff. 108, 109. *Education and Emergent Man*, Thos. Nelson & Sons, 1934, p. 65.

to their field or gymnasium games in order to comply with the advice of the activists, that is in order to learn how best to organize class work, suggestions derivable from organized games of skill seem to be greatly at variance with what the activists appear to think the " spirit of play."

First, interest and effort do not immediately and directly coincide. On the contrary, there are numberless tedious exercises to undergo, hardships to suffer, humiliations to endure, all for the attainment of a rather distant end — to distinguish oneself some day by defeating the opposing team.

Second, there is also keen competition. Every child eventually takes the place that is his by the right of his ability and perseverance. Courtesy and sportsmanship are taught by stronger methods when a word does not swiftly enough produce the desired effect. The boy is told that he must learn if he wishes to get on, and that he must show that he has a firm upper lip and a stout heart before he can be admitted to sit among the victors.

Furthermore, he learns that work can conquer much, even physical disability; that perfection is realized through pain; that what is sometimes called genius is largely a great patience and perseverance; that there are no short cuts to a really high achievement, and that mere eccentricity or sophisticated shallowness cannot carry one very far.

Indeed, any school boy or school girl properly trained in games would understand and appreciate the following facts concerning the secret of the remarkable accomplishments in physical skill, endurance, and self-control, seemingly of unsurpassable perfection and therefore bordering on genius, shown respectively by the great dancer Anna Pavlova and the celebrated prestidigitator Houdini. The genius of each found its application in a different form, but the secret of the genius is probably the same.

"Pavlova knew only too well," writes her truthful and not uncritical biographer, "that the secret of perfection is in unremitting attention to detail and hard work. . . . Her life was so full of work that she never had time to do what she wanted, other than to dance. . . . She used to say: 'Art is not a flower of leisure, or a relaxation. Art means work. It is useless to dabble in beauty. One must be utterly devoted to beauty with every nerve in the body. Those who wish to achieve great things in art have no time *to cross the hands.*' " [45]

Houdini's biographer relates the following statement made by Houdini: "My chief task has been to conquer fear. My second secret has been, by equally vigorous self-training, to enable me to do remarkable things with my body, to make not one muscle or group of muscles, but every muscle a responsive worker, quick and sure for its part, to make my fingers superfingers in dexterity, and to train my toes to do the work of fingers." The biographer remarks: "This double spiritual and physical training was the foundation of his art. In his case, also, genius consisted of infinite capacity for taking pains." Next he quotes another statement of Houdini which seems also worthwhile educationally: "You know five hours is a full night's sleep for me. I can do with less. It's remarkable what a lot of work a fellow can get done during those three extra hours while the rest of the world is in bed. It's nearly eleven hundred extra hours a year. Maybe that's one of the reasons I am the Great Houdini instead of a side-show piker." [46]

Properly organized and conducted games of skill are capable of producing valuable educational results. Yet, it is important to remember that it certainly is not by watching football and baseball games, not even by playing them and, in general, not by the greatest idleness — however sportive — of the greatest

[45] Hyden, W., *Pavlova: The Genius of Dance,* London, Constable Co , 1931, p. 16. Quoted here by permission of Little, Brown and Co., American publishers.

[46] Kellock, H., *Houdini,* Harcourt, Brace & Co., 1928, pp. 3, 9.

number, that the greatest and lasting happiness of the greatest number can be achieved.

SUGGESTIONS FOR READING

Allers, R., *The Psychology of Character* (Sheed and Ward).
Bagley, W. C., *School Discipline* (Macmillan).
Hartshorne, H., *Character in Human Relations* (Scribner's).

Part Three

THE FUNCTIONING OF THE PHILOSOPHY OF EDUCATION IN THE SCHOOL'S RESIDUAL SERVICE TO SOCIETY

EDUCATION FOR SOCIAL PROGRESS IN
A CHANGING SOCIAL ORDER

EDUCATION FOR SOCIAL PROGRESS IN A CHANGING SOCIAL ORDER

DEFINITION OF SOCIAL PROGRESS

The perusal of any detailed study of the history of social progress, such, for instance, as that of Bury or Delvaille, will show the student great variety and considerable vagueness of conception by the various thinkers who have occupied themselves with this problem. There may be distinguished, however, amidst the variety of conception, five principal schools of thought.

1. Of these five schools of thought, one believes that progress is a task for humanity, a difficult but feasible task. This school of thought may be called voluntaristic-optimistic. It conditions progress upon the will and effort of humanity to achieve progress, and that condition met, it believes in the possibility of progress. All great social reformers, from the time of the writer of *Deuteronomy* and the Hebrew prophets until our time, have adhered to this school of thought on social progress. It matters little that social reformers differed in their idea as to what constitutes real happiness or that they disagreed on the question as to whether it can best be assured under the conditions of an artificial civilization, or rather under those of a simple but well-organized rural life. The important point is that they were prophets of a brighter and happier future, and believed in the attainment of better life by an ever greater proportion of humanity or even the entire human family. But, to repeat it, they also believed that better times do not come of their own ac-

cord, with men passively awaiting their coming. To achieve progress, men must choose rightly the direction for their actions and then act. Says *Deuteronomy*: ". . . I have set before thee life and death, the blessing, the curse: therefore choose life, that thou mayest live, thou and thy seed" (30:19).

2. Another school of thought is that of spontaneous progress. It may be called optimistic-fatalistic. This school is characterized by "the belief 'in a good time coming'" and regards progress "not as an ideal but as an indisputable fact, not as a task for humanity but as a law of nature, the law which we cannot escape."[1] Man's progress toward a higher state need never fear a check, we are assured; it will continue to the very last existence of history. According to Condorcet,[2] moral decadence, which may be observed in history, is a transient condition; it is a necessary phase of development. However far he has still to travel, man marches with a giant's step toward ultimate felicity. As formulated by one of its more conservative representatives, Gibbon, the historian, this line of thought can be well summed up in the following words:

The discoveries of ancient and modern navigators, and the domestic history, or tradition, of the most enlightened nations, represent the *human savage,* naked both in mind and body, and destitute of laws, of arts, of ideas, and almost of language. From this abject condition, perhaps the primitive and universal state of man, he has gradually arisen to command the animals, to fertilize the earth, to traverse the ocean, and to measure the heavens. His progress in the improvement and exercise of his mental and corporeal faculties has been irregular and various; infinitely slow in the beginning, and increasing by degrees with redoubled velocity; ages of laborious ascent have been followed by a moment of rapid downfall; and the several climates of the globe have felt the vicissitudes of light and

[1] Inge, W. R., *Outspoken Essays,* Longmans, Green and Co., 1922, p. 23 ff.
[2] *Esquisse d'un tableau historique des progrès de l'esprit humain, Oeuvres,* Paris, 1847–49.

darkness. Yet the experience of four thousand years should enlarge our hopes, and diminish our apprehensions: we cannot determine to what height the human species may aspire in their advances towards perfection; but it may safely be presumed, that no people, unless the face of nature is changed, will relapse into their original barbarism.[3]

Darwin's theory of evolution has generated in some minds an assurance that somehow good must be the final goal of ill. Progress is not an accident, but a necessity, thought Herbert Spencer. In his *Principles of Sociology,* Spencer says:

Of course deductions respecting the future must be drawn from indications furnished by the past. We must assume that hereafter social evolution still conforms to the same principles as heretofore. Causes which have everywhere produced certain effects must, if they continue at work, be expected to produce further effects of like kinds. If we see that political transformations which have arisen under certain conditions admit of being carried further in the same directions, we must conclude that they will be carried further if the conditions are maintained; and that they will go on until they reach limits beyond which there is no scope for them.[4]

3. The third school of thought on social progress conceives of the historic process as a form of repetition of cycles, each cycle being a spiral made of ascending and descending, of a rise degenerating into a decline which leads to a new rise and a new fall in the next cycle, and so on. This school of thought recognizes relative progress from the descending end of one cycle to the ascending part of another, which, however, is merely a repetition of the previous cycles. According to this school of thought, which may be called cyclic, there is no absolute progress, because there is no absolute zero from which to measure

---

[3] Gibbon, Edward, *The Decline and Fall of the Roman Empire,* The Chandos Classics, 4 vols: Vol. II, p. 581.

[4] From *The Principles of Sociology,* by Herbert Spencer. Vol. II, p. 647 f. Used by permission of D. Appleton-Century Company, Publishers, New York, N. Y.

it since the zero of progress repeats itself in each cycle of history. The only thing that is clear and unquestionable about the history of humanity is movement. Human beings are in continual movement, in action and reaction. But, as regards the opinion that they move continually forward, by unalterable laws, toward higher issues, such an opinion cannot be considered well-founded, holds the cyclic school of thought. What history best demonstrates to us is that it repeats itself. What appears to us in our limited field of vision to be progress or regression is nothing but the incoming and outgoing tides in an unchanging sea. The pulse of the universe beats in an alternate expansion and contraction. The result is a series of cycles. According to some of the Pythagoreans, each cycle repeats to the minutest particulars the course and events of the preceding one. The length of cycles was estimated differently. Plato, for example, believed that it amounted to a period of seventeen thousand solar years.[5] Oswald Spengler, the author of *The Decline of the West,* is an outstanding exponent of the cyclic theory in our own time.

4. The fourth school of thought denies any substantial change in human affairs and therefore may be called the skeptical-static school of thought on social progress. Look around you attentively, this group advises us, and compare without passion or prejudice the fundamentals in the life of our ancestors and in that of our own time, and you will see that the more things change, the more they are in reality the old things, re-appearing under a new name or under some new disguise. Adherents of this school of thought are the spiritual descendants of Marcus Aurelius, who said:

Pass in review the far-off things of the past and its succession of sovranties without number. Thou canst look forward and see the future also. For it will most surely be of the same character, and it

[5] *Republic,* VIII, 546 (Cf. *Crito,* 269).

cannot but carry on the rhythm of existing thought. Consequently it is all one, whether we witness human life for forty years or ten thousand. For what more shalt thou see? [6]

And Schopenhauer echoed:

He who lives to see two generations is like a man who sits some time in the conjurer's booth at a fair, and witnesses the performances twice or thrice in succession. The tricks were meant to be seen only once; so that, when they are no longer a novelty, and an illusion, their effect is gone. . . .[7]

5. Finally, the fifth school of thought maintains that regression is the sum total of all movements and changes that have occurred in the human world. That school of thought on social progress looks for the Golden Age in the past. It may be called the fatalistic-pessimistic or the lost-paradise school of thought. According to its views, though perhaps nature has not degenerated in her other works, there has been no physical progress in our species for many thousands of years. The splendid, vigorous, and harmoniously formed types of antiquity are no longer to be found. Moreover, whatever progress humanity may have achieved on the material side of life is more than undone by regression on the moral side. In the end, in human history every step forward has been, at the same time, though in a manner imperceptible to the immediate observer, a still longer step backward.

The historic truth known to the history of civilization and of education seems to command the educator to join with the first-named school, the voluntaristic-optimistic, which believes in the possibility of an absolute progression — in other words, in a real and not an imaginary progression of humanity in a desirable direction. This direction is toward an ever more per-

---

[6] *Meditations,* VII, 49 (Translated by C. R. Haines, Macmillan, 1924, pp. 184–185).
[7] *Parerga and Paralipomena,* II, Chapter XII, German Classics, *cit.,* Vol. XV, p. 81.

fect justice and an ever greater happiness of an ever greater number of men and women. Together with the voluntarists, the educator should bear in mind that progress is a task demanding continued effort on the part of humanity.

The educator who would attentively scrutinize, in the light of his or her responsibilities, the history of civilization and education, would hardly agree with the skeptical-static or with the cyclic or with the fatalistic-optimistic or with the pessimistic-fatalistic school of thought on social progress.

The fundamental weakness of the skeptical-static and of the cyclic theory of social progress was well summed up by a thinker in the following words:

> Nature's proceedings are held to be rhythmic in character, physical changes tending to return upon themselves and unprogressively to repeat their inherent cycles of changes, except when *psychical gains,* which wind upwards in continuous spirals, carry up the physical with them, as in all normal organization and its processes.[8]

The doctrine of spontaneous progress, ever marching or working toward higher issues of its own accord, is a very comfortable doctrine indeed. But it is difficult to hold it, in view of the facts of ugly destruction, so obvious and so frequent, and of the failure on the part of sometime great but now vanished civilizations of the world to hand on the best of what they discovered or imagined. The remains of buried empires that arose, flourished, and fell to ruins form an impressive warning for all who can read it. What we know of the rise and fall of civilizations suggests not so much a perpetual spontaneous ascent, as the possibility of disgraceful and painful relapse into barbarism. Is it not true that humanity more often than not deals in forgotten rather than in new truths? Do human groups not frequently perform, *mutatis mutandis,* the work of Penelope?

[8] Blackwell, A. B., *The Philosophy of Individuality,* G. P. Putnam's Sons, p. iii.

Indeed, they have had repeatedly to begin to weave their web afresh after having destroyed it during the night of violence, moral degradation, and mental aberration. The educator should know that the assertion of the materialistic philosophy as to the permanence and indestructibility of things applies only, if at all, to quantity, and not to quality. If it be true that matter neither perishes nor increases, but simply undergoes transformation, this would mean simply that the quantity of matter remains unchanged. The quality of things is perishable.

Though the teacher should not let himself be carried away by a fatalistic optimism, he should not, on the other hand, entertain a black and fatalistic pessimism with reference to the future of humanity. Such an attitude of mind would be as unjustified as it would be wholly unsuitable to an educator. Whatever may happen at the end of the seventeen thousandth solar year of the Platonic cycle, calm judgment decidedly pronounces itself in favor of reasonable, optimistic, joyful work toward the improvement of things human. Such an improvement is possible because it has frequently enough been achieved. Whether or not man is capable of perfection equal to that of the Olympian gods, yet he is perfectible. Though the human mind may one day come up against impassable barriers and remain there exhausted, yet the development of knowledge, of arts, of the organizing capacity of man is a tangible enough reality. Though omniscience and a perfect social state may or may not be attainable, yet the gradual triumph of reason over prejudice, of knowledge over ignorance, and of tolerance over cruelty and oppression are possible, as history shows.

Our own time, despite its hypocrisies, is certainly an improvement, even in its very hyprocrisies, upon the times when cruelty, tyrannical abuses of political power, and various other forms of injustice were practiced without restraint or apology. In our time, man, however high and safe in his power over other men, no longer robs, plunders, or murders openly without the frank disapproval of at least some group or groups of men. He may rob or murder, to be sure, in a " kid-gloved " manner, but even then, not without society's making at least some show of bringing him to justice, or at least to censure. Nor can he violate openly the welfare of others, even within the law, without receiving the condemnation of at least a part of society. The ideals of liberty, justice, and human dignity have progressed beyond the power of tyrants and demagogues to destroy them or even temporarily to bury them deeply enough not to be disturbed by the unquenchable voice of the ideal of social justice and individual liberty.

The educator, then, is advised by the historic truth to lend to the voluntaristic-optimistic idea of social progress at least as much confidence as does the philosopher, Hans Driesch:

It is certain that the world is a vale of tears. But we are its inhabitants, whose task it is as it is our privilege to alleviate the ill even if we cannot dry the tears. That doctrine is nefarious which denies man even the capacity of alleviation. It is true that man is bad, but he is not so bad nor so weak that he cannot alleviate if he has the will, though its manifestations may be hindered or even turned in a wrong direction by error or by lack of rational understanding. True rational instruction can set it free. We can never fashion a realm of pure spirit on earth. But we have the power to strive after it and to realize it if only fragmentarily. . . . Let us believe in freedom and in our power to alleviate. . . .[9]

SOCIAL PROGRESS CONCEIVED AS MOVING EQUILIBRIUM

The teacher or the educational administrator who has understood the historic objectivity of the voluntaristic-optimistic theory of social progress is not at the end of his inquiry into the problem of social progress and its educational implications. In

[9] Excerpt from *Man and the Universe,* Allen and Unwin, 1929, p. 170. Quoted by permission of Long & Smith, the American publishers.

order that in the performance of his daily work he may best serve universal social progress and, at the same time, properly discharge his responsibilities toward certain more or less limited groups of humanity, such as the family and the nation, he must, it appears, still further particularize his conception of social progress. Considering the residual nature of the responsibilities of the school, would it not be appropriate for an educator to think of progress in terms of moving equilibrium? He must accept the movement side of social progress as a fact. History unfolds before his eyes the scene of the endless drama of human action and reaction, of struggle and triumph and defeat. But history seems to justify the hope that the movement observable in history is fundamentally directed toward the better state of things, however frequent and disconcerting may be the deviations from true progress.

How is it possible to prevent such disastrous deviations and to avoid collapses? Again, history suggests the answer: the human groups which achieved a more solidly rooted and more rapid progress were precisely the groups that had a well-developed sense of economy in the expenditure of their collective force. The sense of economy of collective force lends equilibrium to the movement of the group (which is sufficiently possessed of such a sense) toward further progress.

For instance, consider the English nation and its rapid, and to all appearances, solid political progress in building up the British Empire and the civilization for which it stands.

The English occupy a more prominent position in the world than do their closest rivals, some of whom, like the Germans, are more numerous than the English; or, like the French, were more numerous than the English until the middle of the nineteenth century — because, in the course of history, the English, much less than any other nation, have engaged in the work of Penelope — *mutatis mutandis*. The other nations only too frequently, in the night of unrest and blindness, be it called revolution, or dictatorship, or unlucky war, destroyed the tissue laboriously produced during the day of constructive effort and healthy inspiration. To paraphrase the poet, the English are "strong in will," not only "to strive, to seek, to find"; but above all, "not to yield." [10]

The English have understood better than any other nation that continuity is a virtue, and that each generation of men is much stronger against the various adversities of life when the young people preserve the results of the effort expended by their elders. Throughout their history the English seem to have realized that the desire for the durability of one's own creation is a supremely human quality which has contributed very largely to man's superiority over the lower animals. In the animal kingdom each family begins, in its effort of self-assertion against the external world, exactly where its most distant ancestors began. The lower animals thus practice the most wasteful and disastrous kind of originality.

The more one studies England, the more one appreciates the truth of Emerson's statement, "The English power resides in their dislike of change." [11] They may preserve some unnecessary and even not altogether desirable customs, institutions, and laws; but this drawback does not appear too high a price for maintaining their power of preserving customs. "It was England he had wanted," says John Galsworthy of a personage in *Swan Song*, "something in the way the people walked and talked; in the smell and the look of everything; some good humored, slow, ironic essence in the air, after the tension of America, the shrillness of Italy, the clarity of Paris. For the first time in five years, his nerves felt coated. Even those features of his native land which offended the aesthetic soul, were com-

---

[10] Tennyson, *Ulysses* (closing stanza).
[11] Emerson, *English Traits*, Houghton Mifflin Co., 1883, p. 109.

forting . . . all seemed comforting . . . all seemed comfortable, a guarantee that England would always be England." [12]

Such mental traits as these — to the fostering of which the
school in England has powerfully contributed — have been the
source of the equilibrium which has been characteristic of social
progress among the English and which explains, to a large degree, the magnitude of the historic achievements of the English
nation.

The residual function of the school in any country seems to
make it one of the principal tasks of the school, in the promotion of social progress, to contribute to the equilibrium-aspect
of social progress. Normally the mobility-aspect of social progress can be left by the school to look after itself; not so the
equilibrium-aspect. There are always numerous individuals and
groups who, disinterestedly or not, clamor for change and work
toward it. It is safe to predict that the day will never come when
people will open their morning newspaper to find on the front
page the joyful announcement that everything is either perfect or good enough, and that good citizenship from now on
should consist in not changing anything in the organization
or functioning of government, industry, commerce, and education.

On the other hand, human nature carries in itself something
that constantly threatens to upset, and often actually and ca-
lamitously does upset, the equilibrium so as to make the preservation of it a worthy residual function of the school. Many
contradictions torment and unbalance mankind. These become
ever more numerous as civilization grows more complex. Philosophers call our attention to various sets of dualisms residing
in man, such as flesh and spirit, mind and body, necessity and
freedom, etc. Gerhart Hauptmann, in *The Sunken Bell,* makes
Heinrich try to explain this to the little Rautendelein:

[12] Charles Scribner's Sons, 1928, p. 42.

I am a man. Can'st understand me, child?
Yonder I am at home . . . and yet a stranger,
Here I am stranger . . . and yet I seem at home.
Can'st understand? [13]

The tangible truth of the matter is that man contains within himself those two homes of which Hauptmann speaks. The basic dualism of human nature seems to be man's tendency to oscillate between the egotistical and the non-egotistical or altruistic, between the material and the spiritual. That is what makes him what Emerson calls "this old Two-Face creator-creature, mind-matter, right-wrong, of which any proposition may be affirmed or denied." [14] Undisciplined, untrained, unenlightened men are capable of most disconcerting and costly inconsistencies. They are capable of being not only lovers of law and order but also of anarchy, of stability, and of wanton change.

Our insistence upon the school's residual duty to contribute to the conservation-aspect or the equilibrium-aspect of the movement toward social progress (as over and against the change-aspect of this movement) is not intended to mean that the school should be made an agency of die-hard conservatism and the instrument of a sort of Byzantine immobility. Not at all. Free discussion and questioning of moral values, even of the most fundamental moral values, must not be banished from the school. It should be given a place in the student life of the school, only the time and the form should be properly chosen. It may be reasonably doubted whether an unexamined life is worth living.

It is justly said that the people to be feared are not those who dispute, but those who concede. The believer who has never

---

[13] Act IV., German Classics, cit., Vol. XVIII, p. 189.
[14] "Nominalist and Realist," Essays, Houghton Mifflin Co., 1883, Second Series, p. 233.

doubted will hardly convert a doubter. The skeptical spirit has done much to liberate humanity from its own initial errors. When confronted by a startling doctrine, we should be most concerned in knowing, not how far it is degrading, but how far it is true. Tennyson has well said that "there lives more faith in honest doubt . . . than in half the creeds."[15] Our pupils should not leave school furnished with moral precepts of a sort similar to paper money which is not backed by an adequate reserve of precious metal. Paper money may pass and be accepted, doing its part in the economic life of a community without mischief to anyone, and may even be very useful, so long as no question arises as to its value. On the other hand, our students should be brought up in the habit of carefully distinguishing between a really great reformatory message of lasting value and that which Tennyson so well describes:

> Our little systems have their day,
> They have their day and cease to be. . . .[16]

Youth desires the epoch of youth. It is a natural and beautiful and, on the whole, a useful peculiarity of youth, to strive toward and to dream about new, better forms of life, individual and social. To achieve a desirable lasting improvement, however small, in human affairs, it is necessary to dream about and to strive toward the grandiose. Goethe's predictions still hold good:

So it was fifty years ago, and so it will probably be fifty years hence. Let us not imagine that the world will so much advance in culture and good taste that young people will pass over the ruder epoch. What a young man has written is always best enjoyed by young people. Even if the world progresses generally, youth will always begin at the beginning, and the epochs of the world's cultivation will

[15] *In Memoriam,* XCVI.
[16] *Ibid.,* (Fifth stanza of the Introductory Canto).

be repeated in the individual. This has ceased to irritate me, and long ago I made a verse in this fashion:

> Still let the bonfire blaze away,
> Let pleasure never know decay;
> Old brooms to stumps are always worn
> And youngsters every day are born.[17]

But it was also Goethe who wished to impress upon the young that "the most foolish of all errors for clever young men to believe is that they forfeit their originality in recognizing a truth which has already been recognized by others."[18]

Education for social progress has, then, a twofold task. One part of this task should be inspired by the historic truth embodied in the voluntaristic-optimistic view of social progress. The other part of the school's task in education for social progress should be guided by the residual function of the school resulting from the importance of the equilibrium-aspect of social progress. These two parts of the school's task may readily conflict with each other. How shall we reconcile them and bring them to a fruitful co-operation? The way to such co-operation seems to lie through a proper balance in the educative process between the changing and the unchanging aspects of civilization, and through harmony between the physical and spiritual elements in school work. The first of these two tasks of the school relative to education for social progress can be obstructed by what may be called the Neo-Heraclitean philosophy of education.

THE NEO-HERACLITEAN PEDAGOGY

The philosopher Heraclitus was born at Ephesus toward the middle of the sixth century B.C. He taught a doctrine of change. He believed that nothing remained stable in the world or identi-

---

[17] *Conversations with Eckermann, cit.,* p. 152.
[18] *Maxims and Reflections,* German Classics, *cit.,* Vol. II, p. 371.

cal with itself even a single instant; that everything changed incessantly and that, consequently, change was the only constant characteristic of the universe. Textbooks in history of philosophy usually quote a passage from the Heraclitean fragments illustrating his doctrine of change: " Everything flows; it is impossible to step twice into the same river." For that statement Heraclitus, according to Aristotle, was criticized by his disciple Cratylus, who appears to have been a more consistent Heraclitean than Heraclitus himself, when he said that it was impossible to step even once into the same river.

And again, because they saw that all this world of nature is in movement, and that about that which changes no true statement can be made, they said that of course, regarding that which everywhere in every respect is changing, nothing could truly be affirmed. It was this belief that blossomed into the most extreme of the views above mentioned, such as was held by Cratylus, who finally did not think it right to say anything but only to move his finger, and he criticized Heraclitus for saying that it is impossible to step twice into the same river; for he thought one could not do it even once.[19]

Several conditions, in various combinations in different countries of Western civilization, united early in the present century to create a fertile soil for the development of a Neo-Heraclitean philosophy of education. Those conditions were re-enforced by the need of relaxation from the exhaustive effort and privations (or merely from the excitement) produced by the World War and its aftermath, primarily in the belligerent but to some extent in the so-called neutral countries also. The wave of despondent skepticism, paralleled by the desire for short cuts, had surged over the cultural Atlantic and washed, through the field of education, as well as that of politics, art, and economics, in the entire Western world, flooding some parts of the field in every country, not excepting large educational areas in America.

[19] *Metaphysics, cit.*, 1010^a7 ff.

These two waves would in all probability already have rolled back, as they ultimately will, to the resting place of all receding tides, if many minds, prompted by various urges, had not applied themselves to dam up the flood in order to bring it on their own mill or to send it to destroy the mills of others. Not unlike some other structures, the pedagogical dam in question is made of both solid, honest gravel and evasive, deceptive dust, receiving its significance from the gravel with which it associates itself.

Whatever are the underlying motives, the preaching, and still more of course, the practice, of the pedagogical doctrine inspired by an exaggerated impression that everything changes in civilization, can readily result in the neglect of certain fundamentals which protect the very roots of civilization.

The doctrine of the constant mutability of all things can logically lead just to one practical conclusion, the one drawn by Heraclitus himself. He returned to the mountains, having renounced all activity, including research work in physics. What is the use of scientific research, if things incessantly change? All knowledge except the knowledge that change is ceaseless is bound to be invalid, since things are never identical even with themselves. It is interesting to note that Heraclitus seems to have been guilty of an inconsistency with relation to his own doctrine of the invalidity of all human knowledge, when, afflicted by a disease of the stomach, he descended from his mountainous retreat near Ephesus to consult the physicians of that city.

The present-day Neo-Heraclitean educators do not go quite so far as Heraclitus. But, being hypnotized by the element of change in life, they insist that the general educational method be wholly guided by the immediate actual interests of the students and by the purpose of catching up with the changing present. Translated into the actualities of school life the Neo-

Heraclitean method of education easily results in an exaggerated degree of pedagogical chaos. This chaos is characterized by the absence of emphasis upon sustained, sequential, and robust programs of study, as well as by the anathema put on direct teaching and directed learning, especially with regard to teaching the appreciation of fundamental moral values, which is usually stigmatized as indoctrination. Under the Neo-Heraclitean regime, the ignorance even of what, in the old-fashioned pedagogical terminology, were regarded as fundamental facts and notions essential to every cultured person, is excused not only in the student but also in the teacher, in the name of freedom from indoctrination, of education for initiative, for attacking problems, and the like. Fortunately enough, the excellent teacher's end of it does not have to be taken very tragically. Her culture and fine personality will attract her pupils to her, like so many plants instinctively bending toward the sun, even though the educational philosophy of her employer should have intended her to stay in the farthest corner of the room so that she might not interfere with the self-activity of the little lads and lassies who are preparing themselves for life in a changing civilization.

One's outlook can scarcely be joyous when one considers the effects of the Neo-Heraclitean pedagogical regime upon the average student, and, indirectly, upon his parents and community.

The Minister of Public Instruction in one of the Western European states, himself an adept of the " new method," was visiting a Gymnasium type of school, run on the principle of " curriculumless curriculum." The visitor attended a " civic discussion hour," which term is supposed to be an improvement on the conventional " history lesson." The form visited was the senior form of the school. The Minister, himself a student of the history of the Near East, had what proved to be an embarrassing inspiration. " Suppose that you hear the word ' Mo-hammedanism,' " he addressed the class. " What historic as-sociations does the word evoke in your mind? " And then ensued a painful silence in the entire form. Indeed, they all shook their heads, because, it was reported, not a single gradu-ating boy had ever studied anything relative to the history of Mohammedanism. The history of Mohammedanism had not happened to come up before the boys who lived under the regime of " curriculumless curriculum."

Doubtless, the members of university entrance examining committees in every country could relate many similar or even more appalling instances of ignorance furnished by pupils of " curriculumless " schools. It is to be feared that this is typical of the average student's end under the regime of the " new pedagogy." As to the unfortunate father's side of it, if he only realized what was happening to his children and were not entirely dazzled by the sonorous slogans and elaborate, almost mystically technical vocabulary of the " new education," he would probably deliver before the forum of Neo-Heraclitean educators a rebuke similar in spirit to that addressed by a humble Roman citizen to his vaguely grandiloquent lawyer, Postumus, and reported in an epigram by Martial (VI, 19). " My law-suit," he remonstrates, " is about three goats, which I complain, have been stolen by my neighbor. This the judge desires to have proved to him; but you, with swelling words and ex-travagant gestures, dilate on the Battle of Cumae, the Mith-ridatic War, and the perjuries of the insensate Carthaginians, the Syllae, the Marii, the Mucii. Now, pray, say something about my three goats." It appears that an increasing number of parents of boys and girls attending schools governed by the Neo-Heraclitean doctrine demand that teachers instruct the children in the three R's, or better, threefold excellence — in reading, writing, and reckoning, taken in a broad sense.

THE FUNDAMENTAL ERROR OF THE NEO-HERACLITEAN PEDAGOGY

It seems that Heraclitus himself and our Neo-Heracliteans of Progressive Education are guilty of an old error against logic. They have this error in common with certain modern schools of artists. The error consists in taking a part for a whole in space or in time or in both. When a cubist painter draws the hatted head of a young lady, using exclusively straight lines — in fact, using cubes — he is partially right, because normally there is a certain amount of geometrical squareness and angularity even in a very round-looking face or hat. But the cubist is more wrong than right because there is more roundness than angularity in a normal human face and also in a normal hat. The cubist, then, has taken a part for the whole — in space. When an impressionistic painter makes the oak in his picture entirely violet, he, again, is partially right, because it is very likely that the foliage of an oak, if watched long enough, may, on some day and at some hour in certain conditions of light, " present a violet appearance," as the futurist phraseology puts it. But the impressionistic painter is also more wrong than right, because, ordinarily, for the major part of its life, the oak presents an appearance that is anything but violet. Consequently, he also, like his cubist *confrère,* has committed the error of fixing in his picture as a whole something that was merely a part — in time. When Heraclitus himself, standing on the bank of a river and watching its waters flow past, thought that this was a perfect symbol for his doctrine of change, his error was twofold. He took a part in space and in time for a whole in space and time. Indeed, it was thanks to the sufficient immobility of the river bank, or, to be exact, of the spot where Heraclitus stood, that he could perceive the mobility of the water in the river.

The error of the Neo-Heraclitean pedagogy, inspired by the fact that civilization changes, is also of the nature of taking a part for the whole, in space and time. The school of pedagogical thought which insists that education be for a changing civilization, neglects the fact that there are certain unchanging elements in civilization which have necessarily been operative wherever and whenever civilization has existed. To be sure, the school has to reckon with changes in civilization that are produced by numerous unceasing influences of varying respectability and purity of intention. The school has also the duty of training students to profit by desirable changes in civilization and in turn be able to make such improvements. But when all is told, it remains true that a significant residual function of the school in our time of tacit and open revolutions, is to educate children for the respect and preservation of fundamental social values. Not that those values need our protection; the higher social or moral values, such as justice, filial piety, gratitude, loyalty, the love of the true and the beautiful, the thirst for knowledge of the ultimate reality, and dissatisfaction with mere material animal satisfactions, will reassert themselves even when they are neglected or directly attacked in the school, publishing houses, and other public places. " Sans-culottism will burn much; but what is incombustible, will not burn," [20] Carlyle has pointedly observed.

Yet it may be permissible to repeat that, though the fundamental moral values are indestructible, they can be temporarily submerged, in the life of a society as in the life of an individual, by an unrestricted onrush of the lower tendencies of human nature. Then they are as good as lost to many contemporaries of such a moral, or rather immoral, deluge, and the happiness of all concerned will, accordingly, be greatly diminished, if not entirely ruined. When the Athenians banished Anaxagoras, the philosopher, because he was telling them unpleasant truths, the philosopher said that it was not he who was banished from

[20] *The French Revolution, cit.,* Vol. I, p. 184.

Athens, but that the Athenians had banished themselves from intercourse with him. The same may be said with relation to the neglect of or opposition to the fundamental moral values, in the name of the doctrine of change or of any other doctrine.

Education for a changing civilization has a very real and important objective which consists of implanting in students appreciation of the eternal social values. Fortunately, there are such values, whatever the chronic revolutionary may say to the contrary. To paraphrase Pascal, there are truths on this side of the Pyrenees which are not at all errors on the other side of the mountains,[21] truths not only in space but also in time, persistent truths. Whenever and wherever those truths have been obstructed by Neo-Heraclitean propaganda, real progress has been arrested and set back.

INDOCTRINATION VS. INDOCTRINATION

"In other words," somebody may object, "you recommend that the school should try to make up the minds of the young with regard to moral issues. In plain language, you recommend the indoctrination of the young with conventional morals." The answer to such an objection would be that it is necessary first of all to agree on the meaning of the term "indoctrination." This term is in reality vague, though unmistakably condemnatory. It lacks a very necessary clarity and needs a careful definition. Indeed, when a mother teaches her child to practice gratitude, loyalty to friends and country, tolerance or respect for other people's religious beliefs, and the like, is it a condemnable indoctrination in which she is engaged? Would it not be more exact to use an expression such as "sharing with the child the tested moral values of humanity"? The term "indoctrination" may better be reserved for two kinds of pedagogical activity, one more respectable than the other: (a) teaching

[21] *Pensées*, Sec. V, 294.

things which have not really been verified scientifically but which it is clearly for the good of the learner to believe, for example, the infinite perfectibility of human nature and human science; and (b) teaching things which likewise have not been scientifically verified, but which it is primarily, if not exclusively, to the benefit of the supreme educational authorities that the learner practice, for instance, the teaching, in one form or another, of respect for the despotic head or oligarchic heads of a state.

Besides, it is necessary to bear in mind the fact that every immature and, in general, every easily influenced person is not a *res nullius,* no one's property. On the contrary, almost invariably there is somebody, an individual or a group, wishing to enlist the obedience of that immature person for their own interest or profit of whatever description. The talk about the child's finding out for himself moral truths in complete independence of all indoctrination is at variance with reality. The denunciation of indoctrination leveled by nihilists, dressed up as free-thinkers, against those teachers who perceive permanent moral values and teach them, is the old line of tactics well described in the French saying, " *Ote-toi de là que je m'y mette* (Get out in order that I may take your seat)." Certain fundamental truths should be repeatedly brought to the attention of the educand, because various irresponsible or deliberately sinister agencies never cease repeating or insinuating to the young certain fundamental untruths.

As educational administrators and teachers, we are among the trustees of the young and of the civilization for which the majority of our thinking fellow-citizens stand. This civilization cannot endure, free from disastrous unnecessary upheavals, unless we strive to impart to the young a devotion to the permanent ideals on which all civilization rests. If we fail to perform this duty, from a false fear of practicing indoctrination, or for any other reason, or without any other reason than indolence, we are guilty of desertion from duty. The progress of civilization is conditional upon the association and co-operation of persons of good will and sufficient intelligence. To be an association we may differ in some things but those things may not be important things. With regard to important, fundamental things we must be in agreement.

It may be useful also for educational administrators and teachers, as well as for parents, to remember that some of the more attractive, because playfully discoursive and apparently non-partisan, promoters of unprincipledness rouged up as "broadmindedness," are prompted by a psychology implied in a statement of the French symbolist poet, M. Régnier, who said: "As soon as any one of my books is printed and published, I forget it; it does not interest me." To this M. de Mun, of the *Académie française,* very pointedly retorted: "You are out of it. That is fine, but what about us, your readers?" [22]

THE TWO FUNDAMENTAL CONSTANTS OF CIVILIZATION

Impressive — at least on the surface — are the "variables" of civilization, the changes actually taking place or proposed by would-be reformers and clamored for by journalists. Unostentatious are the constants of civilization which uphold social mobility and prevent its lapsing into chaos, and which help restore equilibrium to the movements of social progress, when the equilibrium is violated by a powerful attack of blind fanatics or deliberately self-seeking individuals disguised as tribunes of social justice and friends of the oppressed. There are at least two such constants of civilization. The school should impart to the young a deep-seated appreciation of those constants; such appears to be the primary task of the school in education for

---

[22] *Le matérialisme actuel* par MM. Bergson, Poincaré, Ch. Gide, Paris, Flammarion, 1913, p. 110.

social progress under the conditions of a changing civilization
and of a changing social order.

The first of these two constants is the permanent moral truth.
It is important, in education, not to treat together the truths of
a day and those that are properly called " eternal truths." It is
vital to distinguish between *a* moral, or a moral code, and *the*
morals. The first is an ensemble of rules and criteria of good conduct professed by just a group of men during an epoch. The second is the ensemble of rules and criteria of conduct considered
valid always by all men, or at least by their better selves, the rules
and criteria of which John Locke has said: " This gives me the
confidence to advance that conjecture which I suggest, that
morality is capable of demonstration as well as mathematics." [23]
True morals may laugh at morals; but true morals never laugh
at true morals. Jesting Pilate asked the question, " What is
truth ? " As is the habit of a jesting Pilate, he did not wait for an
answer or try to answer his own question. Yet there is an answer.
It was given by Antigone, whom Sophocles makes speak of

> The immutable unwritten laws of Heaven,
> They were not born today nor yesterday;
> They die not; and none knoweth whence they sprang. . . .[24]

Classical antiquity was acquainted with a story told by an
anonymous Attic philosopher:

" I observed Jove one day," Silenus related, " talking of destroying
the earth; he said it had failed; they all were rogues and vixens, who
went from bad to worse as fast as the days succeeded one another.
Minerva said, she hoped not; they were only ridiculous little crea-

---

[23] *An Essay Concerning Human Understanding,* Book IV, Chapter XII, Sec. 8,
Ward, Lock & Co., London, p. 547. Cf. Book IV, Chapter III, Section 18: ". . . I
doubt not, but from self-evident propositions, by necessary consequences, as incon-
testable as those in mathematics, the measures of right and wrong might be made
out to any one that will apply himself with the same indifferency and attention to
the one as he does to the other of these sciences." *Ibid.,* pp. 447–448.

[24] *Antigone,* 456 ff. Translated by Storr. In the Loeb Classical Library, Harvard
University Press.

tures, with this odd circumstance that they had a blur, or indeterminate aspect, seen far or seen near; if you called them bad, they would appear so; and if you called them good, they would appear so; and there was no one person or action among them which would not puzzle her owl, much more all Olympus, to know whether it was fundamentally bad or good." [25]

The implication of this witty Attic story was answered by another Athenian, Sophocles, in the above reference to " The unwritten laws of God which know not change."

Among those divine laws are found the fundamental moral values accepted by the consensus of humanity — moral values such as filial piety, loyalty, dissatisfaction with material satisfactions, the love of justice and beauty, and the like. No normal person anywhere ever rejoiced at the sight of a son maltreating or insulting his parents, or of a friend betraying a friend; nor has anyone ever really respected a traitor to his country. Around the fundamental and permanent moral values of humanity — or moral categories — there can be built a reasonably convincing code of morals, which will not be in conflict with really praiseworthy broadmindedness. The latter is an empty term unless it means simply the willingness to give hearing to the other side; it must not be confused with ignorance, with cowardly lack of courage and convictions, or with licentiousness camouflaged under the cloak of sophisticated " superior " independence from all permanent moral criteria of conduct and of conventionalities in general.

A skeptic may object: Study the universal history of ideas and of morals, and then ask yourself the question, What ideals has man not cherished? He has adored ferocious gods; he has professed atheism.

Very true; man has lived under various moral codes. But is it not also true that, as soon as a primitive human community was

[25] Emerson, R. W., "Manners," *Essays,* cit. p. 245.

introduced to certain moral ideals, such as are fully expressed in
the unadulterated Christian moral code, that community abandoned its pristine standards of conduct, in so far as they were less
beautiful than the Christian ideal of brotherhood, service, and
pardon. Consequently, these ideals may well be regarded as potentially existing in all places and at all times. The admiration
for these moral ideals is inherent in the better part of men; indeed it is contemporary with humanity. The conclusion of a
monumental ethnographical study on the unity of moral conscience of humanity is given in these words:

This much can be stated: though primitive peoples, not unlike
civilized ones, do not always act in accordance with the principles
which they profess, the recognition of the good seeks constantly to
translate itself into practice and to struggle against the evil. The conception of guilt and innocence of crime and retribution, is found
everywhere. . . . The sense of right, that is to say, of rightfulness
proper, with related virtues of truthfulness, loyalty, generosity, hospi-
tality, politeness, gratitude, is known everywhere and is practiced
to a certain degree, even though it finds among primitive peoples
not always the same expression as among civilized peoples.[26]

The eternal moral ideals of man must be put on the list of unchanging objectives in education. They are very largely responsible for the existence and growth of all civilization. The skeptic
should again and more carefully study universal history; then
he will not fail to notice that a civilization was doomed to vanish when moral corruption, egoism, and violence came to be
prevalent in the home of that civilization. One of history's clear-
est lessons appears to be that the real strength of a nation and of
the civilization it represents is equal to the surplus of its good
qualities over its defects. On this point contemporary international history offers enlightening illustrations.

[26] Cathrein, Victor von, *Die Einheit der sittlichen Bewusstsein der Menschheit.
Eine ethnographische Untersuchung,* 1914, 3 Bde, B. III, S. 563 f.

" Alarmists are cowards," a thinker correctly remarks. " That piety is infantile which apprehends that knowledge is fatal to reverence, devotion, righteousness and faith." [27] This is true on condition, however, that the variety of knowledge presented to the growing generation includes also the kind of knowledge which Plato has Socrates define in a dialogue with Adeimantus:

> You have often been told that the idea of good is the highest knowledge, and that all other things become useful and advantageous only by their use of this. . . . Do you think that possession of all other things is of any value if we do not possess the good? Or the knowledge of all other things if we have no knowledge of beauty and goodness? — Assuredly not.[28]

The search for the Good — to repeat it — should be not by way of submissive unquestioning acceptance of criteria handed down to the young by adults. Among the dangers to true social progress is the inability or unwillingness to protest. In the words of a poet,

> To sit in silence when we should protest,
> Makes cowards out of men. The human race
> Has climbed on protest. Had no voice been raised
> Against injustice, ignorance and lust,
> The Inquisition yet would serve the law,
> And guillotine decide our least disputes.
> The few who dare must speak, and speak again,
> To right the wrongs of many. . . .[29]

On the other hand, in order that criticism and protest against existing political and social abuses may not degenerate into mere tactics for replacing the abuses, actual or imaginary, denounced by revolutionary critics, with the new, and usually worse, tyr-

---

[27] Gilman, D. C., " Academic Freedom," Modern Eloquence, cit., p. 219.
[28] Republic, VI, 505.
[29] Wilcox, E. W., " The Bravery of Protest," The Franklin News (the private periodical of the Franklin Society), November, 1932.

anny of the false "tribunes of the people," who, in reality, seek to obtain for themselves supreme dictatorial power, the maturing citizen must have "his intellectual vision" so ordered by the school "as to have the most exact conception of the essence of that which he considers." [30]

Thus, under the conditions of a changing civilization, the educator should heed the philosopher's advice, that one ought not always to be changing his mind on the most important subjects.[31] Is it not true that, in our own time of extreme mobility and multiple, almost chaotic change, the school can contribute much to real social progress by devoting sufficient educational effort to building in the young minds a kind of centrality, made of moral convictions which cannot be easily upset? That centrality should be based, in the first place, on the appreciation of permanent moral values. Education for such appreciation will safeguard considerably the equilibrium aspect of social mobility.

There is still another great constant of civilization and another important educational objective, whose unchanging significance is enhanced, if anything, by changes of civilization. The effort and the ability of man to perceive relationships among the various phenomena of the universe has undoubtedly been among the principal sources of civilization. The power to crystallize and state those observed relationships, be they called scientific laws or lessons of history, is one of the most valuable among human capacities. The urge to search incessantly after unity in multiplicity, after the unchanging in the changing, and the ability to capitalize the findings of those who lived before us, is one of the greatest advantages man possesses over the lower animals. Science as well as statesmanship consists in the discovery of relationships among phenomena; therefore, what Montaigne called "the well-formed head" [32]

---

[30] *Phaedo*, 65.   [31] *Gorgias*, 527.
[32] "De l'institution des enfants," *Essais*, I, 25.

has been, from the beginning of civilization, an educational objective pursued by the best teachers and the best pupils the world over. Indeed, if the word "education" has not lost all its meaning, then one of the permanent objectives of school education is to introduce students to the highest standards of accurate and fertile thinking, through direct or indirect contacts with the best minds of humanity, and in that way to put them on solid ground for the critical judgment of their own thinking and that of others.

In the fitting words of Walter Lippmann: " If the schools attempt to teach children how to solve the problems of the day, they are bound always to be in arrears. The most they can conceivably attempt is the teaching of a pattern of thought and feeling which will enable the citizen to approach a new problem in some useful fashion." [33] Intellectual training, then, is another unchanging educational objective, which, in proportion as it is realized in conjunction with the moral improvement of humanity, helps civilization to change for the better.

The task of the school to contribute to social progress by achieving a proper balance between the changing and the permanent in civilization has been viewed in the light of historic truth embodied in the voluntaristic-optimistic theory. It may be here stressed, also, that man is man not only because he remembers, but because, in general, he makes himself to be what he is. His civilization and its strength result from his effort as individual and as species, to promote, in his dualistic nature, the inclination to physical conservation as over against the inclination to physical dissipation; his rational soul, to use the Kantian term (that is, the love of the just, the beautiful, and the true) [34] as against the less beautiful tendencies born of

[33] From *The Phantom Public* by Walter Lippmann, p. 27. By permission of The Macmillan Company, publishers.
[34] *Critique of Judgment* (Division I, Sec. 16 ff.) Macmillan, 1931, p. 83. Cf. *Prolegomena,* Open Court Publishing Co., 1933, p. 136.

his mere physical cravings; his social altruistic tendencies against his narrow egoism, in the end self-defeating. The assistance to be given by the school to the maturing member of society toward growth in the better direction is an unchanging aim of education. The conditions created by rapidly changing aspects of civilization only enhance the importance of that unchanging educational objective, and the duty to promote it on the part of the school as a trustee of the young and of the civilization cherished by the nation into which they are born.

Civilizations do not grow spontaneously, through no organized effort on the part of anyone. In many respects they are a fragile outcome of the long and arduous effort of an untold number of men and women, many of whom did not live to see better times. Neo-fatalism, suggesting that things, in their change, will somehow get better, is a cheerful optimistic version of fatalism, but it is scarcely less harmful than the pessimistic fatalism of the Oriental who does not try to improve his condition because he thinks it is written that he be poor and destitute. The major part of the best way to the best education for a changing civilization lies, therefore, through education for the appreciation and capitalization of the unchanging elements in civilization. This goal can be properly achieved only by the method of education which makes a sufficiently large place for a well-organized and adequately controlled study of sequential curricula taught by competent teachers who can really " deliver the goods."

SOCIAL EFFICIENCY THROUGH SOCIAL HARMONY

It now remains to consider the other of the two ways in which the school can fulfill its double task (see p. 351) relative to education for social progress. One of these ways has just been discussed; namely, the proper balance, in the educative process, between the changing and the unchanging aspects of civilization. The other way lies through harmony between the physical and the spiritual elements in school life and work.

Thinking people in every country of the world are asking themselves the anxious questions: What ails society? What is wrong with it? Is it possible to arrange things so that the individual can have more economic security for himself and his family? How can society be made really efficient in guaranteeing, at least to all reasonable individuals, a reasonable amount of happiness? Some educators demand that the school build a new social order to remedy the present and possible future social inefficiency, under which an individual may readily be deprived of his right to the pursuit of reasonable happiness. Generally, such proposals that the school should build a new social order seem to imply: (a) that this new social order must be what is known as socialism, and even its extreme or complete form, collectivism or communism; and (b) that this new social order can issue only from a social revolution toward which the school should work.

It is difficult, for several reasons, to agree with such an interpretation of the duties and responsibilities of the school.

First, on account of its very nature, the school cannot change, by revolutionary methods, the society amidst which it functions. The governing powers of the society, so doomed by its school to be roasted on the revolutionary frying pan, are unlikely to furnish fuel long enough to energize the work of the men and women handling that revolutionary frying pan.

Second, the ethics of the situation would be of a very questionable sort. Indeed, the plan would amount to sending young impressionable pupils to a head-on collision with the existing political and social powers, with certain stern elemental laws of life which " never apologize." Don Quixotes fighting against skyscrapers would not have the novelty of Don Quixotes fighting against the windmills, and would have still less success.

Third, the study of social revolutions, past and present, appears to justify a skeptical attitude toward social revolution (but not toward political democratic revolution) as a method of making the world safe for social justice and social efficiency. The principal reason why social revolutions seem to be doomed to failure in accomplishing social justice and social efficiency, despite the great enthusiasm and energy of the better, more unselfish persons among revolutionaries, is, in all probability, the fact that social revolutions direct their primary effort toward the equalization of material enjoyments. This is likely to remain forever a utopia.

Men's appreciation of their material needs is relative in character; at least it becomes relative in character as soon as the hunger for basic satisfactions, such as food and shelter, is stilled. If a communistic state succeeded in furnishing every inhabitant with sufficiently abundant and sufficiently varied food and with comfortable shelter (the possibility of which accomplishment it is legitimate to doubt seriously, in the light of the material misery obtaining in Soviet Russia after many years of communistic administration, despite the vast natural resources of the country), the problem of social justice and efficiency would still be far from solution. The naked realities of the life of Russia under the Bolshevist regime are far from refuting the celebrated jibe made by the late Lord Balfour in a note to the Soviet government: " Communism, while an excellent means of making rich men poor, is a dubious means of making poor men rich." Those inhabitants of the communistic state whose standard of living under the capitalistic social order was lower than under the new order would, however — at least for some time — be satisfied with the new regime, supposing for the sake of argument, such an achievement of the communistic regime. But their progeny born under the new regime would take those elementary satisfactions for granted and would feel unhappy at not having the luxuries of life, which, by definition, are exclusive and can be accessible only to a few. Even if the communists succeeded in putting, on the day of the week which is the communist equivalent of Sunday, a chicken in the pot of every collective cafeteria — so far the egg from which this communistic chicken is to issue does not seem to have been hatched, and perhaps has not even been laid — there would not be enough caviar for all, not enough silk for all, not enough Rolls-Royces (or equivalent) for all, and the like. In the course of time there would be accumulated much class hatred in the communistic state, although the communists overthrew the capitalistic order on the plea and for the purpose of equalization of material satisfactions and abolition of all class-distinctions.

Material wealth, in a capitalistic state as well as in a communistic state, is but a zero that can multiply a quantity. That quantity can be furnished only by spiritual wealth. The spiritually rich hut has always been and always will be richer than the sumptuous but spiritually indigent palace. Socrates, in a dialogue with Critobulus, has well said that man is rich, not by what he has but by what he can do without.[35] An individual or a group, once the primary material needs are satisfied, can " do without," and yet be happy and contented, in proportion as they are capable of finding spiritual satisfactions, intellectual, aesthetic, or religious. Therefore, the school, in order to fulfill its task in promoting social progress, must educate the young, not for social efficiency to be achieved through social revolution, in the accepted meaning of the term, but for social efficiency to be realized through social harmony, the basis of which seems to be harmony between the physical and the spiritual in the life of the individuals of whom a given society consists. In a World-War novel, a young man while in the trenches writes to his father: " My dear, dear Father, I am grieving and grieving — and

[35] Xenophon, *Oeconomicus*, II, 2 ff.

it's altogether nonsense. And all mixed up in my mind. . . ." [36]
When in the present-day war which the young — even more
than the adults — have to lead against the problem of finding
work, they feel very much like that young man at the front;
and when they address similar confidences to us, directly or
indirectly, our answer, it seems, should be to advise the
young to work not toward social revolution, but toward social
harmony.

By harmony we mean not a prescribed, unquestioning harmony of stagnation, but a voluntary, conscious, and purposive
harmony resulting from the individual's social intelligence;
that is, from the individual's capacity for purposive freedom and
for self-control.

THE SCHOOL'S ROLE IN THE HISTORIC QUEST FOR HARMONY

When reduced to simple terms and stripped of the mystery of
big words, the substance of all social problems is simply the lack
of harmony between the desires, aspirations, and interests of the
individuals composing society. For instance, social problems
relative to labor are frequently created by the employer's desire
to get out of his workers as much as possible for as little as possible, and the workers' desire to the contrary. Similarly, social
problems concerning banking sometimes result from some
bankers' wish to get rich quick at the expense of their depositors,
and the latter's natural dislike of such banking. Then the remedy
to be applied at the very source of social evil is the increase of
harmony. Indeed, the meaning of the term *social,* as Aristotle
and Hegel have clearly shown in their theory of the state, is only
then employed in its true sense when it designates something
relative to the common good, that is, to the good of all at the expense of all as over and against the individual egotistical good of
one at the expense of all. For example, it is social to have law and

[36] Wells, H. G., *Mr. Britling Sees It Through,* Macmillan, 1917, pp. 365–366.

justice under which the reasonable rights of everybody are reasonably protected, and it is made impossible, at least in theory, for anyone to enslave another human being or to arrogate to himself the property and the products of the labor of others, and thus to have some good for himself at the expense of others.

What is, then, the true role of social institutions? It is to harmonize by means of laws and regulations the conflicting interests and desires of the individuals who constitute society. How? By forcing, and still better by educating (with the help of the radio, the theater, the cinema, the school, the pulpit, the press, and courts of justice) the individuals to restrict their individual egoism. The amount of social harmony and of true socialness, as over against social disruption and discord, seems to be proportionate in any society to the number of hours in which every individual living in the society is his better self. To help to increase these hours, when — to paraphrase Hobbes — man is not a wolf but a man to another man is the supreme contribution to social efficiency of which the school is really capable.

But how can we work toward this goal? Humanity has already tried several methods of bringing about social harmony. Those several schemes have, not unnaturally, gravitated toward the problem of attainment of harmony between the physical and the spiritual.

The earliest philosophers in Western civilization — that is to say, the men who were interested in detecting the general behind the particular, the unchanging behind the changing, and who sought thus to establish their scale of values — have rapidly discovered the fact that, after all, man is the greatest source of happiness as well as of misery to another man. They could not help noticing that while man was evermore increasing his physical comforts by harnessing the various forces of nature, and while he was evermore successfully defending himself from the various pestilential insects and animals, he was not successful in securing peace from other men, particularly from civil and international strifes; this despite all the wise laws and eloquent exhortations against such evils. As a result, the earliest thinkers already understood that — as Socrates later taught — in order to improve society, the individual had to be improved and made more capable of living in harmony with other individuals. And he can be improved and made more capable of living in harmony with others only in proportion as harmony will have been worked out within the individual himself. That harmony, according to the best thought of Greco-Roman antiquity, must be threefold: (a) harmony between the physical in him and the spiritual in him; (b) harmony within the physical, for instance, between his physical force and physical grace; and (c) harmony within the spiritual, for example, harmony between his cold, calculating, dissecting reason and his sentiment for the beautiful, the just, and the good.

Greco-Roman civilization went into bankruptcy, in all probability because of the disproportionate growth of hedonistic egoism; in other words, because, instead of harmony between the physical and the spiritual, the physical came to dominate the spiritual. As a result, instead of reasonable real harmony among the individuals, there grew within the Greco-Roman world a kind of sham harmony which we can often hear preached and see practiced nowadays within nations, and especially between nations. It was not only a sham harmony, but also a forced harmony, similar to that between an unkind horseman and his horse. In the end the horse, that is to say, the destitute popular masses, unsaddled the horseman — the ruling class — and then went wild.

The medieval ideal of life, which grew on the ruins of the bankrupt antique civilization, was characterized by a new scheme of social harmony. It consisted in the belief that men can establish the kingdom of God on earth, *i.e.,* true Christian brotherhood, only when they will have restricted and in fact suppressed their earthly wishes, have given undisputed domination to the spiritual over the physical, and have come to regard one another as so many children of the same God. Hence, the medieval philosophy of life — within the one and united Christian church, by the church and for the church. It so happened that it was soon enough vitiated and compromised, partly by exaggerated neglect of and contempt for the physical and the worldly, but probably still more by the fact that evermore numerous individuals, whose task it was to preach the medieval ideal of life, did not themselves by any means live up to their own preaching, and callously exploited others in order to give carnal enjoyments to themselves.

At all events humanity began to long for another ideal of life, more human and more pagan. And so came the Renaissance with its motto borrowed from the Latin poet Terence, " I am a man and nothing human is alien to me." [37] When considered as a philosophy of life, the Renaissance is nothing but the renewed Greco-Roman doctrine of harmony between the physical and the spiritual. But again, as in ancient times, mankind has not been able to work out a real balance between the physical and the spiritual. The physical has been predominant under, or without, various disguises. Hence arose the social discord and strife, open or covert, which, alas, has never been absent from our history since the Renaissance.

In so far as the philosophy of life is concerned, distinctive or inarticulate, of the majority of men and women, we are still in the period of the later Renaissance with its tense disillusionment. Who knows that we are not on the eve of the return of medievalism? However this may be, the fact remains that many people are today in the state of mind which may be called pre-Bolshevist, the state of mind so admirably sensed by Dostoevsky

[37] *Heautontimeroumenos* (The Self-Tormentor), Act I, Scene 1, 25.

when he made Ivan Karamazov, a pre-Bolshevist character in *The Brothers Karamazov,* speak as follows: "Freedom, free thought, and science will lead them into such straits and will bring them face to face with such marvels and insoluble mysteries, that some of them, the fierce and rebellious, will destroy themselves; others, rebellious but weak and unhappy, will crawl fawning to our feet and whine to us: 'Yes, you were right; you alone possess this mystery and we come to you; save us from ourselves.'" [38]

Great and depressing as is the disillusionment of many of us, there seem to be other and better ways out of the anxieties and disappointments of political and economic crises than the propagation of the pre-Bolshevist state of mind. If not remedied, it would inevitably lead to Bolshevism, because, as a historian has pointedly observed, people when they fall always do so on the side toward which they were already leaning.[39] The school can worthily and powerfully participate in the preparation and spread of a valuable remedy against this ever-recurring disease of social unrest, economic depression, and moral despondency. What can the school do toward this end? Three things, at least.

First, the school can make students reasonably immune to the extreme and wholesale pessimism and cynicism which are steps that lead toward Bolshevism. How can the school do this? By following the advice of a great Romantic writer to younger fellow writers, warning them against the much over-praised and much-abused realism. For realism in literature and in art has, unfortunately, often degenerated into the sinister occupation of picturing the ugly side of life, with almost total indifference to the more attractive, sound, and fresh aspects. To offset the disastrous effect of such one-sided realism on the reader, a thoughtful Romantic writer advised as follows:

[38] *Modern Library,* 1929, p. 317.
[39] Guizot, F., *Discours prononcé à la Chambre des Députés,* le 5 mai 1837.

In times when great evils are manifest, born of the fact that men misunderstand and hate one another, it is the duty of the artist to emphasize sweetness, confidence, friendship, and in this way to remind the embittered and the disillusioned that high characters capable of real attachment, of loyalty and of straight, unsophisticated justice still can be found in this world of ours.[40]

One of the duties of the school in its work toward real social efficiency is of a similar nature. Plato in his *Republic* holds this opinion as follows:

We would not have our guardians grow up amid images of moral deformity, as in some noxious pasture, and there browse and feed upon many a baneful herb and flower day by day, little by little, until they silently gather a festering mass of corruption in their own soul. Let our artists rather be those who are gifted to discern the true nature of the beautiful and graceful; then with our youth dwell in a land of health, amid fair sights and sounds, and receive the good in everything; and beauty, the effluence of fair works, shall flow into the eye and ear, like a health-giving breeze from a purer region, and insensibly draw the soul from earliest years into likeness and sympathy with the beauty of reason.[41]

Second, the school can and should contribute to the humanization of the mechanistic progress of our times. How? By presenting to the young well-balanced curricula in and through which the students would be led, not only to measure natural forces and interrogate nature about its secrets, but also to penetrate as deeply as they can into the intricacies of the world of men, a world at one and the same time so near and yet so distant, so open to our observation and yet so nearly impenetrable. The key to these mysteries of intimate human reactions and sentiments is what the Greek philosophers have happily baptized " sym-

[40] Sand, Georges, *La petite Fadette,* Henry Holt and Co. 1930, Preface, p. iv.
[41] *Republic,* III, 401.

pathy." It is important that our students develop unshakable human sympathy and become humanized through the study of humanities. No better method is available (see p. 23).

Third and last, the school, in addition to inculcating in the student reasonable optimism and reasonable humanism, can and should contribute toward moral harmony, and consequently toward the real socialization of society, by philosophizing the student, if one may say so. In other words, the school should assist the student in working out the right scale of values. It should lead the student forward in the comprehension of the fact that in social relations and the moral order everything holds together as well as in physical matters; that, for instance, in the moral order no less than in the physical order, man cannot cut down his fruit tree and yet have the tree and the fruits; and that it is impossible to have real social and political democracy without real moral democracy. More especially should the school impress upon the young by appropriate lessons from the past and present that the keystone to the vaulted edifice of society is justice. There can be no social peace or social efficiency without social justice; as there can be no international peace and international co-operation without international justice.

Hence, we, as educators, should be inspired in our work toward social peace and social efficiency by the following admonition which Socrates addressed to his friend and disciple Glaucon:

The time has arrived, Glaucon, when like huntsmen, we should surround the covert and look sharp that justice does not steal away, pass out of sight, and escape us; for beyond doubt justice is somewhere in this country: watch therefore and strive to catch sight of her, and if you see her first, let me know. . . . Offer up a prayer with me and follow. . . . Here is no path . . . and the wood is dark and perplexing; still we must push on. . . .[42]

[42] *Republic*, IV, 432.

Educational writers opposed to the general method of directed education use, among the various arguments in support of their position, an argument which may be called the argument from nature. Full freedom of activity and self-expression is demanded for the child in the name of nature and for the sake of harmony between education and nature, from which harmony social progress is declared to draw, indirectly, much of its subsistence.

This argument from nature has a strong appeal to the general public. Small wonder that it has, since it contains a good deal of truth, but it is not wholly true. This is the old trouble about arguments from nature which repeats itself each time when nature is summoned to testify for or against a proposition relating to a social or educational problem. The source of the trouble is invariably the same; disputants do not define what they mean by nature, the word unfortunately having more than one meaning. Cicero, who in his capacity of an ingenious lawyer knew well how to win an argument by the skillful marshalling of words, found that the term " nature " had at least four different meanings: (a) nature as the ensemble of facts and phenomena of the universe; (b) nature as the particular constitution of each living being; (c) the laws to which all beings are subject; (d) a certain mystic power.[43] This is not at all, however, a complete list of the meanings of the word " nature." In fact, it is one of those vague and equivocal terms which do not correspond to any clearly defined reality and which lend themselves admirably to the construction of purely verbal proof.

In discussions concerning political and economic subjects Nature (usually capitalized to increase the effect) has often been employed in a similar role. In substance, the scheme of reasoning has all the appearance of logic and regularity. A is X, X is B,

[43] *Academicorum Posteriorum*, I, 15. *Academicorum Priorum*, II, 44.

consequently A is B. X stands, however, for an ambiguous idea, or more exactly, for a sentiment which is complex and undetermined and of which one meaning dominates in the premise, A is X, another in the premise, X is B. As a result, X is in reality of double meaning, but many accept the conclusion, A is B. Needless to say, X is left undefined. For instance, in the early socialist literature there is found the following argument: " To live in accordance with Nature is good; Nature does not admit property; consequently, good life is incompatible with the institution of property." [44] Evidently, in the first premise " Nature " stands for something which agrees with one's tendencies or dispositions in distinction from something which one does but under pressure. Accordingly, the premise is approved. The second premise causes one to separate the artificial creations of man, among which many are certainly far from being perfect, from the complex body of things and phenomena which exist independent of the action of man, of which many are beautiful and pure, and among which the detection of the institution of property is not easy for one who is guided by sentiment alone. Once it has been granted that the institution of property is not the work of nature (as if nature did not have its " institution of property," like the dog's bone or the bird's nest, etc.), very logically the conclusion is accepted that the good life excludes property.

In the second half of the eighteenth century, there was established among the intellectuals in Europe (as a reaction against the exaggerated rationalism of the previous hundred years) a sort of new, or supposedly new, religion the divinity of which was Nature. The high priest of this new deity and the prophet of this new creed of naturalism was Rousseau. It is interesting to recall in this connection that the " Nature " with which Rousseau was intimately familiar was that of Switzer-

[44] Cf. Pareto, V., *Les systemes socialistes,* Girard et Brière, 1902.

land, Savoy, and France; in other words, a nature already corrected by civilization. Even in Savoy, in the beautiful hills of Chambery, Rousseau could not come in contact with anything more wild than a rabbit or a wild rose. One is involuntarily wondering what would have become of Rousseau's naturalism if he had known as much about nature as David Livingstone and other experienced tropical explorers knew.

Rousseau's imaginary picture of the perfect "natural man" has become the powerful *Leitmotiv* of romantic literature and philosophy. Fichte eulogized the natural sense of truth in man and regretted his initiation into the self-conscious intellectual life:

I will choose voluntarily the destination which the impulse imputes to me. And I will grasp, together with this determination, the thought of its reality and truth, and of the reality of all that it presupposes. I will hold to the viewpoint of natural thinking, which this impulse assigns to me, and renounce all those morbid speculations and refinements of the understanding which alone could make me doubt its truth.[45]

Carlyle declared nature the sure guide in all cases. Wordsworth believed that

> Nature never did betray
> The heart that loved her.[46]

and that

> One impulse from a vernal wood
> May teach you more of man,
> Of moral evil and of good,
> Than all the sages can.[47]

The influence of the naturalism of the romanticists in literature, philosophy, and education, though somewhat offset by the

[45] *The Destiny of Man*, German Classics, Vol. V, p. 31.
[46] *Lines Composed a Few Miles Above Tintern Abbey*, I, 123.
[47] *The Tables Turned*, 21 ff.

revival of the materialistic philosophy in the latter part of the nineteenth century, has never ceased. At present, a kind of neo-romantic naturalism seems to have many adherents among the followers of the New Education movement, though again it has a serious enough rival, within the New Education group as well as elsewhere, in the Bolshevist or Marxist materialistic " realism," which has influenced some of the influential progressives. As has frequently occurred in the history of thought, the exaggerated doctrine of the infallibility of crude nature produced a reaction. Many thinkers fell into the opposite extreme and, like some people at present, denied nature or the natural man anything good. Horrified at the sight of " Nature, red in tooth and claw with ravine," Tennyson asked:

> Are God and Nature then at strife,
> That Nature breeds such evil dreams? [48]

John Stuart Mill had little difficulty in showing that this glorification of undisciplined human nature was based on false anthropology and false psychology.

Mill told his readers that, according to anthropological investigations, savages as a rule are liars, unclean, and cowardly. " In the times when men were nearer to their natural state," he says, " cultivated observers regarded the natural man as a sort of wild animal, distinguished chiefly by being craftier than the other beasts of the fields; and everything that makes character was deemed the result of a sort of taming; a phrase often applied by the ancient philosophers to the appropriate discipline of human excellence belonging to human character which is not decidedly repugnant to the untutored feelings of human nature." Mill concedes that undoubtedly most instincts of the race were

---

[48] *In Memoriam,* LV, LVI. Cf. also *Maud,* I, IV, 4:
For nature is one with rapine, a harm no preacher can heal;
The mayfly is torn by the swallow, the sparrow spear'd by the shrike,
And the whole little wood where I sit is a world of plunder and prey.

" directed to things needful or useful for its preservation." On the other hand, he points out that " destructiveness, domination and other selfish instincts, which had helped man to supremacy among animals, were handicaps in his civilized state." These instincts, if they are not to make human life an exaggerated likeness of the odious rest of the animal kingdom, and so fill human life with misery, must be eliminated or controlled. Consequently the reference to " Nature" as an ethical standard tends to confuse and pervert moral judgment.

Mill is convinced that the non-human world is entirely unfit for human imitation:

In sober truth, nearly all the things which men are hanged or imprisoned for doing to one another, are nature's everyday performances. . . . If, by an arbitrary reservation, we refuse to account anything murder, but what abridges a certain term supposed to be allotted to human life, nature also does this to all but a small percentage of lives, and does it in all the modes, violent or insidious, in which the worst human beings take the lives of one another. Nature impales men, breaks them as if on the wheel, casts them to be devoured by wild beasts, burns them to death, crushes them with stones like the first Christian martyrs, starves them with hunger, freezes them with cold, poisons them by the quick or slow venom of her exhalations, and has hundreds of other hideous deaths in reserve, such as the ingenious cruelty of a Nabis or a Domitian never surpassed.[49]

Thomas Huxley, who, in his Romanes Lecture on Evolution and Ethics, attempted " to find out whether there is, or is not, a sanction for morality in the ways of the cosmos," decided that " cosmic nature is no school for virtue, but the headquarters of the enemy of ethical culture."

And Maupassant says, in a similar anti-naturalist strain:

[49] " Nature," *Three Essays on Religion,* Henry Holt, 1874, pp. 28-29.

We have had to invent civilization, which includes so many things, so very many things of all kinds, from socks to telephones. To soften our brutish fate, we have discovered and manufactured everything, beginning with houses, and going on to delicate foods, sweets, cakes, drinks, tapestries, clothing, ornaments, beds, hair mattresses, carriages, railways, innumerable machines: more, we have discovered science and art, writing and poetry, music, painting. Everything that belongs to the imagination comes from us, and all the gay conceits of life, feminine dress and masculine talent, which have managed to make the merely reproductive existence . . . a little more beautiful in our eyes, a little less naked, less monotonous and less harsh. . . . Think what we have done, in spite of nature, in opposition to nature, to establish ourselves in barely tolerable conditions, hardly decent, hardly comfortable, hardly elegant, unworthy of us.[50]

Again, as almost always is the case with passionate controversies, the truth lies somewhere between the two extremes. Obviously, if not all is good in the non-human world nor in the " natural man," not all about them is bad. It is certainly an exaggeration to say that " nature never foresaw gentleness nor peaceful way." On the other hand, an uncorrected " natural world " hardly assures the survival of the morally fittest, because tiger-rights and brutal powers hold in it precedence over gentle methods. Social morals develop to a higher degree only in the artificial, or better, artful moral world. They come and increase with the rise of general culture in the masses and with the growth of the sense of responsibility and emulation among the actual or potential leaders of the group.

Our civilization, though certainly no unmixed good, appears to have achieved the best there is in it, not so much by imitating as by perpetually striving to amend the course of nature and by bringing phenomena over which we can exercise control more

[50] Reprinted from *Useless Beauty*, by Guy de Maupassant by permission of and special arrangement with Alfred A. Knopf, Inc., authorized publishers.

nearly into conformity with the higher standards of justice and goodness than those found in uncorrected, "natural" nature. To repeat, our morals are artful, and consequently "unnatural," both as social philosophy and as governmental machinery.

Equality of opportunity and all the liberties and rights implied in democracy would strike a savage, or even a civilized man of certain political preferences, as a perfectly absurd and unnatural arrangement. Similarly, certain tribesmen would be astonished at our social provisions for the support of the old or disabled members of the community. Aristotle himself would be not a little surprised at the "unnatural" condition of modern society where there is no legal institution of slavery. In fact, concentrated, prolonged thinking, the greatest instrument of all progress and of all civilization, is not quite a "natural" occupation. It interferes with one's indisputably "natural" pleasure — that of enjoying food — and can, normally, be set into motion not without resistance. William James, in his twenty-fourth year, writing a friend about his studies at Harvard, said in the refreshingly frank, pointed, vivid manner which was habitual with him:

I have been studying now for about two weeks, and think I shall be much more interested in it than before. It was some time before I could get settled down to reading. But now I do it quite naturally, and even *thinking* is beginning not to feel like a wholly abnormal process; all which, as you may imagine, is very agreeable — altho' I confess that as yet the philosophical *rouages* * of my mind have not attained even to the degree of lubrication they had before I left.[51]

Now, by what methods are certain reprehensible and injurious natural ways of the non-human natural world amended and made subservient to physical and moral good, in other words, to progress? In fairy tales, the malicious schemes of evil

* wheels   [51] *Letters, cit.,* Vol. I, p. 74.

fays are checked by the intervention of good ones. Similarly, we can and actually do tame and harness evil or indifferent natural forces by the help of those that are favorable or simply accessible to us. As Francis Bacon advised, we must command nature by obeying it.[52]

Among the natural tendencies of the child, that is, of the "natural," not yet civilized, human being, there are good as well as undesirable tendencies. Clearly, a pedagogical system based on the belief that the child is naturally good, is as ill-founded as the one based on the conviction that every child is born naturally evil. Froebel believed the child a "channel through which heaven floweth." This is partly true and partly false. The experienced teacher, however, knows his

> Race of real children, not too wise,
> Too learned or too good, but wanton, fresh,
> And bandied up and down by love and hate,
> Not unresentful where self-justified,
> Fiery, moody, patient, venturous, modest, shy.[53]

He knows also that children can

> Run lightly after bright butterflies
> And often, laughing, kill what most they love.[54]

To become a civilized man is, indeed, an art. Society has the right to demand a certain measure of that art from everyone who comes to live within it. Otherwise the dearly acquired social values would be exposed to the danger of destruction by home-bred Vandals. Intelligent parents and the school have the duty of helping the child to acquire certain habits, the possession of which is necessary if he is to be spared perilous conflicts with the established and on the whole desirable ways of the world,

[52] "On Nature in Men," *Works,* London, Longman & Co., 1858, Vol. VI, p. 469 f.
[53] Wordsworth, *Prelude,* V, 410 ff.
[54] Hauptmann, *Op. cit.,* Act. IV, p. 184.

and is to attain, more or less safely, mature age. If he has to rely on his own devices, the average adolescent is likely to prove woefully unfit. The school should not turn out, if it can help it, young people accustomed to listen to nothing but their unchecked impulses. In our congested modern society such members would be as unbearable as mastodons or dinosaurs in a city park, or porcupines in a crowded train. To paraphrase the little Jude in Thomas Hardy's *Jude the Obscure:* "We are too menny," [55] to afford complete freedom of self-expression as the general method of education in the name of dubious "naturalism."

The belief of Plato and Aristotle, that the young, by steady discipline, should be habituated in exact knowledge and right conduct, is unlikely ever to become a grotesque anachronism, good for nothing but pedagogical archives.

If we cannot let the child give free expression to all his tendencies and desires, what shall we do with those that must not be encouraged? Shall we try simply to repress them? No, we must avoid doing that unless forced by solid reasons of moral health; for instance, a vicious disposition must be stopped before it contaminates others, or when it threatens to take on the strength of habit in the child affected by it. Then it must be forcibly stopped and its repetition eliminated. We can best accomplish this by setting up against the undesirable natural tendency one or several desirable natural tendencies; in other words, we can best control nature by obeying it.

SUGGESTIONS FOR READING

Bagley, W. C., *Education, Crime, and Social Progress* (Macmillan).

Bury, J. B., *The Idea of Progress: An Inquiry Into Its Origin and Growth* (Macmillan).

Todd, A. J., *Theories of Social Progress* (Macmillan).

[55] Harper & Brothers, 1923, p. 405.

EDUCATION FOR NATIONALISM, PATRIOTISM,
AND INTERNATIONALISM

CHAPTER VIII

EDUCATION FOR NATIONALISM, PATRIOTISM, AND INTERNATIONALISM *

THE FUNCTION OF THE INDIVIDUAL IN WORLD AFFAIRS

In the novel *The Magic Mountain,* at the moment when the principal character is marching into battle at the beginning of the World War, the author takes leave of the lad thus:

Farewell, honest Hans Castorp! Farewell, Life's delicate child. Your tale is told. Farewell — and if thou livest or diest! Thy prospects are poor. The desperate dance in which thy fortunes are caught up will last yet many a sinful year; we should not care to set a high stake on thy life by the time it ends. We even confess that it is without great concern. We leave the question open. Adventures of the flesh and in the spirit, while enhancing thy simplicity, granted thee to know in the spirit what in the flesh thou scarcely couldst have done. Moments there were when out of death and the rebellion of the flesh there came to thee as thou tookest stock of thyself a dream of love. Out of this universal feast of death, out of this extremity of fever, kindling the rain-washed evening sky to a fiery glow, may it be that Love one day shall mount.[1]

Millions of men and women all over the world, full of anxiety, have lately been asking a similar question, and many proposals as to how to find international justice and security for

* Adapted from Demiashkevich, Michael, *Shackled Diplomacy: The Permanent Factors of Foreign Policies of Nations.* (Chapter VI Conclusion: Educational Implications of the Permanent Factors of Foreign Policies of Nations). Courtesy Barnes & Noble, Inc., Publishers.

[1] Reprinted from *The Magic Mountain,* II, 899, by Thomas Mann by permission of and special arrangement with Alfred A. Knopf, Inc., authorized publishers.

all nations have been advanced. As a rule, such projects suffer from a very common defect of our thinking on social problems that has been characteristic of Western humanity since the great revolutionary movements of the end of the eighteenth century and the beginning of the nineteenth. We have been trained in a school of political thought which has been forgetful of the defects and shortcomings of the individual himself, and has placed the whole responsibility for our evils on a rather vague and mystic society, as if society were not the sum total of its individuals. This fashionable verdict on the imperfections of our life was very favorably received because of the natural tendency of the individual to blame somebody else for his misadventures rather than himself. It would immeasurably promote the common good if more men were as critical of themselves as is the archer in the *Analects* of Confucius, who says: " In archery we have an illustration of the procedure of the superior man. When the archer misses the target, he turns round and seeks for the cause of his failure in himself."

Existing social institutions, to be sure, leave ample room for improvement. But in seeking that improvement in domestic or international affairs it is useful to remember Descartes' advice to proceed from the simple to the composite. A penetrating student of human affairs has well said:

The government does not exist in statehouses or halls of Congress. It is a relation of personal wills, as all society is likewise a relation of personal wills with their background of conscious affection, ideas, purposes. It is in this hidden realm that we live, love or hate, obey or disobey, and live in peace or strife. Wars have not existed in space, and real battlefields are in the unseen. They are conflicts of ideas, of aspirations, of mental tendencies; and all the fighting that ever took place in space was but a symbol and expression of the inner unpicturable strife.[2]

[2] Bowne, B. P., *Personalism*. By permission of and special arrangement with Houghton Mifflin Company, 1908, p. 273.

It is only from the moral and mental improvement of the individual that a better society can come. Would not, for instance, the spiritualization of human pleasures contribute to the softening of international commercial and industrial rivalries? When the individual members of a nation with useless extravagance consume its natural resources, such as iron or oil, there is less of these necessities left for the coming generations of that nation and for the rest of the world. But when Beethoven, Verdi, Rossini, or Rimsky-Korsakov is enjoyed in the various countries, that source of pleasure is not diminished through everybody's partaking of it. No amount of international law can give real and lasting security to a small nation that possesses natural resources badly needed by a large nation, nor can it remove the resulting jealousy and suspicion which inevitably develop into active hatred and animosity. " But the fruit of the Spirit is love, joy, peace, long-suffering, gentleness, goodness, faith, meekness, temperance; against such there is no law " (Gal. 5:22–23).

We must, then, concentrate upon the individual and seek to give him the right education for world co-operation. In determining the method of such an education, should we not follow the counsel of the ancient philosopher who taught that the right education consisted in the right attitude and in the right knowledge (see p. 293)?

With regard to the former, it is demanded by many sincere champions of international peace and justice that education for internationalism should replace education for nationalism. The persistent frequency and the strong popular appeal of this educational program seem to justify a special, however brief, analysis.

DEFINITION OF SOUND NATIONALISM, PATRIOTISM, AND INTERNATIONALISM

The concepts of nationalism and internationalism belong to the class of ideas which may be designated as deceptively clear

ideas. To begin with, there are, in truth, two kinds of nationalism and two kinds of internationalism.

Of the two kinds of nationalism, one is unhealthy, narrow
nationalism, commonly called jingoism, or chauvinism. This
kind of nationalism is characterized by an exaggerated national
pride and a contempt or suspicion or both of other nations,
which sentiments make the narrow nationalist blind to shortcomings of his own nation and to the good qualities and accomplishments of other nations. The narrow nationalist is, as a
result, not only incapacitated for international co-operation,
but is unable to make a calm, detached, scientific study of other
nations. Thus narrow nationalism, being morally unhealthy, becomes unsound politically and economically. As the French
say: "*Bienveillance est la moitié de la clairvoyance*" (Good
will is half the solution of a problem).

Fortunately, there is another kind of nationalism, which may
be called sound, reasonable nationalism. In order to understand
its nature, and to give a satisfactory definition of it, it is necessary to analyze the concept "nation." What is a nation? As
the Latin root of the word, *nasci,* shows, nation originally meant
a human group bound together by birth relationship. But
modern nations have outgrown that stage of development.
Modern nations appear to be human groups characterized by
six fundamental features which are the factors of national
cohesion:

1. Statistical or demographic. A nation is a human group that
has in common the consciousness of its numerical size. How
large a human group should be to be a nation sociologists cannot tell us. Albania, for instance, has, according to the latest
census, a population of 1,003,124; Luxemburg, 299,782; Monaco,
22,153; Lichtenstein, 11,000; Andorra, 5,231.

2. Geographical. A nation is a human group that owns certain
territory.

3. Political. A nation is a human group bound together by obedience to one central authority, whose purpose is to watch over the most important common interests and to reconcile and co-ordinate conflicting interests of individuals or groups within the nation.

4. Economic. Nations as well as individuals have to earn their living. A nation is a human group bound together, among other things, by common economic interests, such as safeguarding basic national industries, and the like.

5. Social. Besides the constituted authority, members of a nation obey certain unwritten laws, national mores — that is to say, customs and habits which regulate certain aspects of our domestic life and social intercourse; for instance, our manners, types of habitation, dress, cooking, and the like, fall under this caption. When one travels abroad, among the first things which make one feel foreign are precisely the strange mores, because sometimes linguistic differences do not present more novelty or difficulty than dialects of the native country.

As examples of those different national mores, the following may be mentioned:

In English-speaking countries, when two persons are introduced courtesy demands that they at once pronounce each other's names: " I am glad to meet you, Mr. So-and-So." As the names are often indistinctly pronounced by the person making the introduction, embarrassments result. In France, on the other hand, to address the new acquaintance at once by name is a shocking familiarity. The correct form, according to the French code, is: " I am delighted to make your acquaintance, *Monsieur* or *Madame* or *Mademoiselle* " — period, or one or several points of exclamation in one's voice, depending entirely upon one's conception of the occasion.

The Japanese stir their tea or coffee in the direction opposite to the one in which the hand of a clock moves and which is the right direction for stirring one's tea or coffee in Western lands. Six helpings from a course must be taken by the polite guest in Japan. If those were of the size and consistency of helpings in pre-Bolshevist Russia, the guest, unless he were a giant, would be subjected to a very grave danger. Fish, which is eaten in countries of English civilization like meat, with the help of both fork and knife, must be eaten in polite society on the Continent with the help of the fork alone; and should one wish to lift from the plate a morsel escaping the fork, this must be done with the assistance of a piece of bread. The most insecure form of social eating in civilized countries seems to be that of partaking of refreshments at an American or English afternoon tea, where one's canapes, tea, ice cream, etc., are piled up on a tray, itself perched at a dangerous angle on one's knee. The European continent provides itself with tables on such occasions.

When, at a social function, one is accosted by somebody who is inclined to buttonhole one, an extremely complicated maneuvering is necessary, under the European code of good manners, to extricate oneself from the unwanted interview. Civility demands that some more or less convenient and convincing urgent necessity be invented to justify the breaking away. This country furnishes one, for just such an occasion, with the cheerfully polite formula, " I'll see you later! "

A German father prudently advised his boy, who was sailing for England on board an English vessel, as follows: "When she gets rocky and the man from the upper berth shouts to you, ' Look out! ' be sure that you don't look out."

6. Moral, or *communio sacrorum,* as the Romans had it. A nation is a human group bound together also and probably above all by common memories, traditions, aspirations, and ideals sacred to the group. As Sully Prudhomme said: " Our fatherland is not a syndicate of interests, but a bundle of noble

ideas, and of noble follies toward which the fatherland has struggled."

The total cumulative effect of such common memories, traditions, and ideals of the group seems to be stronger than the community of race, language, and religion. History shows that peoples of the same race, language, and religion have not only formed themselves (of their free will, in some instances) into separate and distinct national states, but can even go to war against one another, if necessary, almost as whole-heartedly as against a nation or nations of distinctly alien race, language, and religion. On the other hand, human groups sufficiently different in race, language, and religion have formed themselves into stable and well-knit national states. Such is, for instance, the case of Switzerland, where the memory of the common struggle of the mountain people for independence from the political ambition of neighboring national states, formed in the surrounding plains, and the political ideal grown out of that struggle have been the factor of national cohesion between Protestants and Catholics, between Italians, Frenchmen, and Germans. In the fitting words of Ernest Renan:

To have in common the remembrance of glories achieved in common in the past, to have a common will in the present time, to wish to do in the future great things like those accomplished through common effort — such is the essential condition for being a nation. The national existence of a people is a kind of plebiscite renewed every day, exactly as the individual existence of a man is a perpetual affirmation of the will to live.[3]

It follows, then, that a human group is a nation in proportion as all these six features are present in it and in the degree in which members of the group, the popular masses, have a sense of ownership and participation in all those features which constitute a nation.

[3] *Discours et conférences*, IV, Calmann-Lévy, 1925.

That feeling of ownership and participation in the numerical strength, in the territorial possessions, in the government, in the mores or social customs, in the vital economic interests, and in the moral values of a nation seems to be what should be called sound nationalism, a nationalism not to be ashamed of, a worthy educational objective.

But what is patriotism if sound nationalism means the feeling of ownership and of participation in the fundamental elements that make the concept of nation?

Patriotism is doing for the sake of our nation something that may be contrary to our personal egotistical interests. Nationalism is more abstract. Patriotism is concrete. Nationalism is of more cognitive and affective nature, it has more of thinking, feeling. Patriotism is of more volitional nature; it is carrying some action to a successful or abortive issue for the sake of one's country. Nationalism is the attitude of taking, getting, and keeping; patriotism is the attitude of giving. Nationalism is appreciation; patriotism is service and sacrifice. Such is sound patriotism, a patriotism worthy of pursuit. Education for patriotism clearly merges with the training of character. As Renan, again, has aptly put it

Defend jealously your freedom but respect that of others. Preserve the independence of your judgment; but do not abandon your country either physically or spiritually. Find your satisfactions in life by means of holding to something permanent. Many things will change around you. You will probably witness changes more considerable than all the preceding changes that the history of humanity remembers. But among such changes and the uncertainties which they produce, there is one thing that remains certain — in all social conditions that you may have to pass through, there will always be some good to accomplish, truth to search for, and the fatherland to love and to serve.[4]

[4] Renan, E., " La Jeunesse et la Vie," *Pages Choisies,* cit.

But again, as in the case of nationalism, true patriotism must be clearly and surely distinguished from another kind which Lamartine, in his *Discourse on the Abolition of Slavery,* describes as follows:

"I can hate others thoroughly; I can despise others profoundly; and this capacity I love to exercise on the nations rival to mine." This kind of patriotism does not cost the "patriot" much. All that he has to do is to be ignorant, profusely abusive, and full of hatred.

A distinction between the concept "nation," on the one hand, and the concepts, "nationality" and the "state," on the other, is probably also useful to the clarity of each and not without value from the educational point of view.

It appears that a nationality considered as a human group [5] differs from a nation chiefly in the fact that it does not possess a territory or, to use the terminology of political science, does not possess sovereignty.

Yugoslavians were for centuries merely a nationality within the Turkish Empire and the Austro-Hungarian Empire. Now, after the abolition of the Turkish and Austro-Hungarian sovereignty over the territories populated by the Yugoslavians, they are a nation and not merely a nationality.

The concept of the state has in common with the concept of nation four of the elements of the latter as listed above: 1, 2, 3, and 4. Number 5 (mores) and 6 (*communio sacrorum*) are lacking in the state as such. Take for example Poland or Rumania or any one of the so-called buffer countries that came into existence as the result of the Bolshevist revolution in Russia. They all are sovereign states now. Are they so many nations? Yes and no. They are nations or national states only in propor-

---

[5] Nationality has another meaning, a legal capacity of the individual before international law as in the question, What is your nationality? asked by consuls, pass control officers, etc.

tion as their population possesses the cohesion of common customs, habits, ideals, memories, and aspirations. Post-war Rumania, for example, whose population counts some thirty per cent of non-Rumanian elements, is a sovereign state, but it is a nation only to the extent of sixty-five per cent, because the Russians of Bessarabia annexed by Rumania, or the Hungarians given to her by the treaty of Versailles, do not have much in common with their new masters in the point of mores or *communio sacrorum*. Evidently, other conditions being equal, the country in which the state and nation coincide is a real national state and is a stronger, more stable and more harmonious human group than the state which is not entirely, or very little, a nation. To be sure, even a state which is entirely free from unassimilated and unassimilable racial elements is not necessarily and of itself a nation once and forever. A nation does not grow as the grass does. It is a perpetual creation in which the role of the public school and other national educational agencies instrumental in the " nationalization " of oncoming generations is as great as it is obvious.

But is education for nationalism, even for sound nationalism, justifiable from the higher human point of view of world co-operation, and is it not both adverse and inferior to internationalism as an educational objective?

To answer this question, it is necessary to remember that there are two kinds of internationalism. One is moderate and feasible and should certainly be promoted through educational activities. An excellent definition of it is given by President Nicholas Murray Butler of Columbia University in his well-known analysis of what he calls the international mind:

The international mind is nothing else than the habit of thinking of foreign relations and business and that habit of dealing with them which regard the several nations of the civilized world as friendly and co-operative equals in aiding the progress of civilization, in developing commerce and industry, and in spreading enlightenment and culture throughout the world.[6]

With this kind of internationalism sound nationalism is entirely compatible; for as Petrarch has observed, it is possible for a man properly educated to be " one of those whom love for their country does not make hate all other nations."

Another version of internationalism is the complete or extreme kind which preaches the abolition of all national states and the uniting of all men in one world community. To this form of internationalism sound nationalism is clearly averse. But does it follow that sound nationalism is morally inferior to extreme or complete internationalism? Hardly so, unless one believes that buying castles in Spain is an occupation superior to honest and modest home-building at home.

THE ROOTS OF NATIONALISM

Sound nationalism is a noble human attitude of mind, for it seems to be the broadest form of altruism to which men can normally attain. At the bottom of sound nationalism lies the proud human instinct of beating the physical death and escaping the humiliation of complete extinction with which the cessation of his individual egotistical existence menaces man. Hence the honorable disposition of all honorable men to seek survival after death by serving the group through labor, and if necessary through the supreme sacrifice of the very life of the individual, in order that the group may live, and through it the individual who has identified himself with the group as a permanent part and particle of it and has acted accordingly.[7] The

---

[6] *Message to the American University Union in Europe.*

[7] A very interesting instance of the working of this human instinct is furnished by the will of Epicurus. He did not believe in the immortality of the soul, which was logical because he did not believe in the existence of the soul. Adhering to the atomistic philosophy of Democritus, Epicurus, again logically enough, declared: " Death is nothing to us: for that which is dissolved is without sensation; and that which lacks sensation is nothing to us." Less logically but very humanly, Epicurus

group in question was originally just the family, and next it was the tribe. These groups the individual could readily embrace with his physical vision, and touch, so to speak. He could naturally feel himself as belonging to them and vice versa. For their sakes he could with comparative ease limit his egotistical tendencies. It demanded a far greater effort of moral imagination, if one may say so, to raise oneself to the next phase of "altruization" of the ego, which is service to the nation at the expense not only of oneself but also of one's family. Some people have never reached this superior stage of moral development. Such is, for instance, the case with the Chinese, who are not yet a nation in the true sense of the term because their method of survival after death is still very largely by merely serving the interests of the family, or at best of the clan.

To be sure, the ideal situation would be to internationalize nationalism; in other words, to place at the service of humanity as a whole the noble passions that make nationalism, even sound nationalism, at once admirable and formidable. The problem is, figuratively speaking, to take the sting out of the bee and yet preserve its honey-bearing power. But is this possible?

So far it has not been possible. One of the shortcomings of human nature has been that the nation is the highest point which the average man has been capable of reaching in the

wrote in his will: ". . . The income of the property left by me to Amynomachus and Timocrates shall be divided by them as far as possible, with the advice of Hermarchus, for the offerings in honour of my father and my mother, and for the customary celebration of my birthday every year on the tenth of Gamelion, and likewise for the assembly of my disciples which takes place on the twentieth of each month, having been established in recollection of myself and Metrodorus." Thus Epicurus, the materialist and atheist, who negated the existence of the soul and wrote many long discourses in support of this negation, was anxious to perpetuate the memory of his name through the establishment of a philosophic school, or, as it would be called today, of a foundation bearing his name. He sought a kind of immortality for himself through posthumous association with a group. Epicurus wished, as do his successors in our own time, and hoped to survive his own physical death by means of a continuous symbolic membership in the group which he had founded and which he expected, or at least wanted, to exist perpetually. (*Cf.* Bailey, Cyril, *Epicurus*, Oxford University Press, 1926, p. 151.)

noble effort to transcend the limitations of his purely animal egoistical existence. Group life has not yet been able to attain real universality or real cosmopolitanism. Why? Voltaire has answered the question probably as well as it can be answered when he makes Palmire, a slave of Mahomet, give this definition: " Fatherland is the place to which one's soul is chained." [8] Man seems capable of just one great passion, even though men are expansive beings. A man can belong at the same time to various groups, such as the family, nation, religious denomination, political party, industrial or recreational organization, etc. But the strength of his attachment to each of the various groups to which he belongs is not the same. We cannot embrace what cannot be embraced, as the South-Russian popular philosopher Kuzma Prutkov remarked. Humanity, conceived as one big family having everything in common, free from all national distinctions and frictions, is to man — save in rare exceptions — something that cannot really be embraced as a basis upon which to build his daily life, though it may be a good topic for postprandial eloquence at various international gatherings.

A sincere, fruitful, and complete internationalism presupposes many conditions which appear to be incompatible with human imperfections and infirmities. It seems that nothing short of a common high and ardent religious experience can make men over into beings really capable, day in and day out, of embracing in their hearts and minds all other mortals as so many brothers and sisters. Marcus Aurelius, who is sometimes mentioned as the earliest internationalist of note, said: ". . . mankind are under one common law; and if so, they must be fellow-citizens, and belong to some body politic. From whence it will follow, that the whole world is but one commonwealth; for certainly there is no other society in which mankind can be incorporated. . . ." [9] Now reason and social principles are

---

[8] *Mahomet ou le Fanatisme,* Acte I, scène 2.   [9] *Meditations, cit.,* III, 4.

suited to my nature; and my city and country, so far as I am
Antoninus, is Rome, but so far as I am a man, it is the world.
The things then which are useful to both these societies, are
alone useful to me." [10] But it is not certain that the philosopher
in the attire of the Roman Caesars would not have been opposed
to having any town other than *Roma aeterna* for the center of
that fatherland of his, large as the world itself. On the contrary,
it is rather certain that he was opposed to a different interpretation of his internationalism by the Roman subjects of Egypt
and Greece and Asia Minor, who wanted to secede from Rome
and against whom Marcus Aurelius sent military expeditions.

So much is suggested regarding the education of the individual for the right attitude toward world co-operation.

In closing, a few observations concerning the right knowledge, the popularization of which through the medium of
public educational institutions seems to be the necessary pre-
condition of an effective world co-operation.

KULTURKUNDE AS A METHOD OF EDUCATION FOR INTERNATIONAL CO-OPERATION

The modern Delphic oracle would, it seems, be well advised
to prevail on peoples that they should never rest from learning
to know themselves and finding out the truth about their own
nation, but should strive with equal zeal to learn the truth, not
only the bad truth but also the good, concerning other countries,
their national character, their strength and weaknesses, vital interests and grievances. Even leading nations have neglected in
the past this aspect of education. The outbreak of the World
War found mutual ignorance — in fact was to a large extent
due to it — instead of solid mutual knowledge of one another
on the part of the belligerent nations, as represented not only
by the much-abused man-in-the-street, but also by responsible

[10] *Ibid.,* VI, 44.

leaders. The appalling mutual error of judgment, be it over-estimation or underestimation, by statesmen, and by the General Staff officers, is too well known to insist on it here. The case of Germany (that as a result of such error of judgment — of which her opponents were, to be sure, not at all innocent — experienced the most stupendous downfall) is probably the most instructive one and, therefore, may be briefly referred to. She deserves special attention because hers is also the case of a nation that seems to have applied itself — at least until the advent of the Nazi — to profit most by the lesson of the World War relative to the education of the young for the right knowledge of the world situation and of its principal agents.

From her experience of the World War Germany has undoubtedly drawn the lesson of patience and careful calculation of her own and others' strength. It is significant that she has since the war been the leading country in the promotion of a comparative study of the mentality of the various nations — to which she has given the label *Kulturkunde*. In distinction from the conventional or old manner of studying foreign nations, characterized by the inclination to slander or at least to minimize other countries in order to bring into sharp relief the actual or imaginary virtues of the home people, *Kulturkunde* strives to be an objective study. It places before the student the materials relative to a foreign land which the native children of that land study; in other words, the materials of ethical, aesthetic, historical, economic, political, and cultural character selected from scholars and authors representative of the nation in question. Such materials, properly selected, can naturally reveal the face of the nation as it is and can adequately reflect the national character with both its strong and weak points.

Surely, the study of the vital interests and cultural forces of foreign nations in schools should serve as an effective means of diminishing the danger to international peace. Ignorance of what a certain nation can suffer without going into a fight for its life and of what is the real power of mutual resistance and expansion of the various nations has been responsible for several wars even before the World War.

The diffusion of a better comprehension of the history of nations through the study of history and political science is also invaluable to accelerate and correct the process of improving society through the improvement of the individual. There is much truth in the saying that there would have been no history if people always understood. That is to say, history contains appalling records of ruinous unnecessary conflicts within and among nations. Very pertinent is a discussion by Hippolyte Taine in the prospectus written by him for the since famous School of Political Sciences in Paris [11] established in 1871 by far-seeing statesmen and distinguished scholars who were convinced that one of the causes of the unfortunate Franco-Prussian War was the insufficient comprehension of international affairs by the French public. In that prospectus Taine raises the question, " Is there a political science? " and replies to it as follows: " At all events there is a body of positive lessons which, in matters political, lend precision to discussion, guide judgment, and diminish the element of speculation, extravagance, and error."

The treatment of history and political science in schools and for the general public should be as far as possible a philosophic treatment — in two regards.

First, it should seek to clarify and connect the multiple facts relative to international relations by showing students the permanent factors underlying the changing and apparently chaotic facts. Even very young students should be trained in such a treatment of the history of international relations, for it is er-

---

[11] *L'Ecole Libre des Sciences Politiques,* of which the eminent scholar, M. Emile Boutmy, was founder and director until his death in 1906.

roneous to think that young persons are averse to or incapable of abstract thinking, by which is meant thinking in the form of generalizations. The child begins his abstract thinking when he begins to use words as symbols of objects. Normal children, and especially the more gifted ones, like generalizations which serve as so many towers from which the mind can look with more efficiency and amplitude into the sea of indiscriminate facts.

Second, the study of history and political science in schools should be inspired by the Ciceronian definition of philosophy as " Knowledge and practice of all that is best." The successive purposes of human science and thought were once enumerated as contributing, first, to the maintenance of life; second, to the explanation of life; and third, to the elevation of life, national and international. It seems that we have to change the order of succession today, for in order to survive, a modern nation must begin with the elevation and explanation of life. History is said to be a father who teaches his children. And one of the salutary lessons of history seems to be patience and hope.

This patience and this hope will certainly be better rewarded if and when, instead of proceeding by the method of trial and error — which not infrequently degenerates into trial of old errors — society will have in its midst many men who have received in the schools the right knowledge of the history of international relations. Is not history a prophet looking backward?

Students should be taught, however, to keep their feet on the ground while philosophizing about world affairs. In fact a philosophic scanning of the history of international relations would show the educand that foreign policies of nations are determined by three fundamental factors, or motives, which function sometimes singly but more often in conjunction. These three permanent factors of international relations are: (a) the sentiment of *revanche*, or revenge and retaliation for grievances, actual or imaginary, sustained at the hands of a foreign nation or nations; (b) political mysticism, or belief in a special mission with which nations think themselves entrusted by Providence or " humanity" and the fulfillment of which justifies in their eyes expansion at the expense of other nations believed less worthy than the conquering nation; (c) vital interests, rightly or wrongly conceived.[12]

SUGGESTIONS FOR READING

Gooch, G. P., *Nationality* (Swarthmore Press).

Hayes, C. J. H., *The Historical Evolution of Modern Nationalism* (R. R. Smith).

Kandel, I. L., *Comparative Education,* Ch. I. Education and Nationalism (Macmillan).

---

[12] For further discussion of the permanent factors of foreign policies of nations see *Shackled Diplomacy, cit.*

CHAPTER
IX

EDUCATION FOR LEADERSHIP IN A DEMOCRACY

EDUCATION FOR LEADERSHIP IN A DEMOCRACY

WHO SHAPES HISTORY, THE MASSES OR INDIVIDUAL LEADERS?

Approximately a hundred years ago the intellectuals in almost every country of Western civilization were debating the problem as to which is the more influential in shaping history, the individual or the masses. Tolstoy, in *War and Peace,* echoed the controversy.

In the majority of European countries, it fell to the task of bureaucracies to "canalize" — as the expression went — the chaos following in the wake of the Napoleonic Wars. Happily, in every chaos there are germs of a cosmos; but it takes the penetrating and properly trained eyes of really gifted leaders to perceive them. The autocratic hereditary regimes, served by practically hereditary bureaucracies, then prevalent in the majority of Western countries, did not produce the soil in which really constructive leadership could grow, and, as the saying is, it is not the cowl that makes the monk. As a result, the chaos was painfully long. Political philosophers of the time were divided in distributing the blame. Some thought that the popular masses were responsible in the last analysis. Such philosophers believed, as Walter Lippmann seems to believe, that history is made by movements of the popular masses; that " the real law in the modern state is the multitude of little decisions made daily by millions of men." [1] The opposite school of thought maintained that history is made by leaders, by inspired individuals.

[1] *Preface to Morals,* The Macmillan Company, 1929, p. 275.

It appears that the controversial problem in question has been settled with satisfactory clarity by the history of the last hundred years. This was the century of liberalism during which the masses, or the so-called lower classes, exercised greater political activity and influence than ever before. Yet that century of liberalism seems to have vindicated the theory that it is individual leaders who shape history. The historic lessons on leadership derivable from the World War and its continuing aftermath are particularly illuminating in this respect. England, France, and the United States are the nations in which "circulation of the elite" had been practiced on a larger scale before the war began, and more sincerely during the war, than was the case in such countries as Russia, Germany, Austria-Hungary, or Rumania. Circulation of the elite is the social process which consists in the recruitment and training, on the competitive basis, of future leaders in the various walks of life selected from among the children best endowed or "chosen" intellectually and morally; further, it consists in bringing the right man, the gifted and properly trained man, to the right place by displacing the wrong man from the wrong place. It is scarcely a mere accident that the three first-named countries made in the war a far better showing, on the whole, regarding the supreme national leadership, political, social, and economic, which contributed to the outcome of the war. In this group of belligerent states the circulation of the elite made possible a more effective employment of the potential services of the more capable individuals.

Pre-war Germany had some very capable civil servants, but they were debarred by social barriers from posts of higher authority and remained in subordinate positions, while titled mediocrities possessing "pull" were the masters of Germany. Germany had in the World War many excellent generals; but these were not in the supreme command, at least not during the initial phase of the war — August-September, 1914 — which predetermined the final issue. In the closing chapter of the remarkable study of the World War, *Der Weltkrieg,* by General Hermann von Kuhl, there are found almost literally repeated such aphorisms as the one attributed to Philip of Macedon: " An army of stags with a lion at their head is better than an army of lions with a stag at their head "; or that found in Aristophanes: " It often happens that less depends upon the valor of an army than upon the skill of the leader." [2] What was true of the higher Imperial German civil and military administration was certainly not less true of the Russian. The new evidence furnished by public and private documents seems to have elevated to the quality of historic truth the opinion professed by many military experts that Germany lost and France won the decisive battle of the Marne of September 6–11, 1914, for the reason that the German armies were commanded at the time by the sickly, nervous, and confused von Moltke, but the French, by the robust and self-possessed Joffre.

Even much more appropriately it might be said that if at the time of the World War Russia had had a more capable ruler than Emperor Nicholas II and Germany a more fit one than Emperor William II, the condition of these two countries and of the world at large would have been in all probability immeasurably better than it is now. Or how differently the February revolution of 1917 in Russia would have turned out if Kerensky had had determination and vision more nearly commensurate with his good intentions, and if the Bolshevist group had been led during the initial phase of its rule by a man of less intrepidity, ruthlessness, and clarity of judgment than Lenin.

But these and similar illustrations of the predominance of

[2] Kuhl, Hermann von, *Der Weltkrieg 1914–1918,* Berlin, Verlag Tradition, 1929, B. I, S. 45, 46, 47, 61 ff.; B. II, S. 553 ff.

the specific gravity of leaders over that of the masses in shaping the historic process may fail to impress some people in a democratic country. The illustrations are taken from the history of autocratically governed countries. Though, in truth, in this case the point relative to the origin of the evidence is beside the point, still it is interesting to recall that the clearly tangible turning-points in the political history of a democratic country such as the United States are connected with the names of individual leaders like George Washington, Abraham Lincoln, Theodore Roosevelt, Woodrow Wilson, Franklin D. Roosevelt. And are not the important stages in the economic history of the United States connected with the names of Vanderbilt, Astor, Rockefeller, Carnegie, Morgan, Ford? Or the significant phases of the cultural history of the United States with the names of Henry Barnard, Horace Mann, Thomas Alva Edison, Charles W. Eliot?

THE HISTORIC NOSTALGIA FOR LEADERSHIP

Even free democratic masses, whenever some uncontrollable or poorly controlled circumstances bring them into an impasse, instinctively look for a leader to guide them out of their political, economic, or religious wilderness. Thus the American masses, moved by the depression, flocked in the election of November 1932 to the reassuring and optimistic personality of Franklin D. Roosevelt, and forced Democratic congressmen and senators, not at all uniformly willing, to grant to the new President unprecedentedly vast powers.

Is it not rooted in a social instinct — this nostalgia for leadership, and this willingness of even politically free masses to submit themselves in situations of grave complexity to the authoritative leadership of individuals whom they trust? That instinct consists in a subconscious feeling on the part of the masses (even when their judgment runs a fair danger of being beguiled by the flattery of demagogues) that it is the individual who " has the spirit." History demonstrates that inventions and discoveries — intellectual, artistic, moral, economic — in other words, the most lasting and creative among the influences which shape the historic process, are essentially the creations of outstanding individuals. Millions of men for thousands of years — *vox populi!* — had believed and repeated that the sun went round the earth until a gifted, studious individual discovered that the contrary was true. Are not men of genius, " whom keener sensibilities, stronger intellects, and more resolute wills had equipped for fruitful discoveries," the greatest benefactors of the race, as John Stuart Mill believed? [3]

It will not be denied by anybody, that originality is a valuable element in human affairs. There is always need of persons not only to discover new truths, and point out when what were once truths are true no longer, but also to commence new practices and set examples of more enlightened conduct, and better taste and sense in human life. . . . There are but few persons, in comparison with the whole of mankind, whose experiments, if adopted by others, would be likely to be any improvement on established practice. But these few are the salt of the earth; without them, human life would become a stagnant pool. Not only is it they who introduce good things which did not before exist; it is they who keep the life in those which already existed. . . . Persons of genius, it is true, are, and are always likely to be, a small minority; but in order to have them, it is necessary to preserve the soil in which they grow. . . . [4]

Similarly, history shows that popular masses have always experienced nostalgia for self-confident and confidence-inspiring leadership with relation to problems intellectual, political, economic, surpassing the resources of the average individual in intellectual power or learning or experience or leisure or all

[3] Neff, E., *Carlyle and Mill*, Columbia University Press, 1926, p. 288.
[4] Mill, J. S., *On Liberty*, The Harvard Classics, Vol. 25, pp. 269–270.

of these. It is in the light of such nostalgia that the Fascist and the Hitlerite revolution can be properly understood. In these cases the nostalgia has taken a hysterical form owing to certain specific political and historic conditions of Italy and Germany.

John Stuart Mill, in the essays on *Representative Government* and on *Parliamentary Reform,* vainly regretted that Democracy meant counting votes, while for the sake of the common good votes should be weighed. Some votes are being weighed, indeed. The votes of some people — to be exact, the leaders' — exercise a weighty influence upon the votes of their followers. The real problem is that the right votes should receive the right weight. And this is very largely an educational problem. It cannot be satisfactorily solved by a national commonwealth except through the systematic work of an educational system that possesses satisfactory arrangements for developing among the future adult citizens a reasonably sufficient number of guiding lights; or, to continue Mill's figure of speech, by insuring sufficient number of votes worthy of great weight, while not neglecting any possible measures for educating the popular masses in order to enable them properly to select and intelligently to follow the guiding lights.

EQUALITY OF EDUCATIONAL OPPORTUNITY AND OPPORTUNITY FOR THE ELITE

The history of education, like any other branch of the history of human endeavor, has known its revolutions with their witchery of words or inflated ideas (see p. 259). Rousseau's theory of natural education furnishes a pedagogical equivalent to Jacobinism and its influence upon the political history of the Western world. In more recent times many an oppressive feudal or neo-feudal wall that obstructed the career of the less fortunate children born into the economically lower strata of society has crumbled before the banners proclaiming equality of educational opportunity. Unfortunately, though not unlike many other constructive revolutionary slogans and doctrines, this wholesome doctrine of equality of educational opportunity readily lends itself to inflation and the witchery of words, from which all persons concerned inevitably suffer, sooner or later, unless a careful and critical watch is exercised regarding the application of this doctrine.

Indeed, has not the doctrine of equality of educational opportunity shown a tendency to degenerate into a kind of democratic counterpart of the autocratic doctrine of divine right of kings? Every royal prince born, irrespective of mental ability or character, is entitled, in the countries which have royal houses as a part of their systems of government, to all the privileges that go with royal birth. Inflation of the idea of educational opportunity in the popular mind in a democratic country inevitably results in an educational philosophy and practice to which the reproach in Act V of Beaumarchais' comedy, *The Marriage of Figaro,* closely applies. Then practically all that we have to do to the following passage to make it fit criticism of those false democratic educational theories is to substitute John Doe for Count Almaviva and " citizen " for " nobleman ":

What! Because you are a nobleman you fancy yourself a great genius? — Which way? — How came you to be the rich and mighty Count Almaviva? Why, truly, you gave yourself the trouble to be born! . . . And what, most noble Count, are your claims to distinction, to pompous titles, and immense wealth, of which you are proud, and which, by accident, you possess? For what one of your virtues? . . .[5]

Equality of educational opportunity can reasonably mean only an educational arrangement characterized by the accessibility of each type and level of public education beyond the

[5] Act V, Scene 3.

elementary grades, obligatory for all, only to those adolescents and youths who can prove through their intellectual endowment, scholastic achievement, and character that they are fit for the continuation of their education at public expense in a particular type of school. John Quincy Adams, taking exception to the doctrine that all men are created equal, declared this doctrine " as gross a fraud as ever was practiced by Druids, by Brahmins, by Priests of the immortal Lama, or by the self-styled philosophers of the French Revolution. . . . Nature has ordained that no two objects shall be perfectly like and no two objects perfectly equal. . . . No two men are perfectly equal in person, property, or understanding, activity, and virtue. . . . Every being has a right to his own, as clear, as moral, as sacred as any other being has." [6] The elite, then — the intelligently and morally " chosen " children, adolescents and youths — has the right to an appropriate educational opportunity, which it is the duty of the commonwealth to observe and to promote as fully as possible, at the same time offering the largest possible educational facilities for unselected masses of students.

The masses of well-intentioned citizenry, and more especially the younger and less experienced educators themselves, should be warned of the dangers concealed in an inflated — non-selective — conception of equality of educational opportunity, a conception that inevitably leads to the violation of the first and foremost rule of sound educational administration, which demands that the right student should be brought to work with the right teacher in the right subject matter.

GREAT WASTE INSTEAD OF GREAT INVESTMENT

The devastating result of the false, inflated version of the democratization of education, according to which post-elemen-

6 Merriam, C. Edward, *A History of American Political Theories,* pp. 130, 131. By permission of The Macmillan Company, publishers.

tary education should be given freely to all in non-selective public schools in non-classified groups, hazardously formed on the basis of the pupils' chronological age, is that it irresistibly degenerates into wasteful lowering of standards of education. The inevitable consequence of this would be the substantial, if not the statutory, abrogation of democracy itself and the establishment of the rule of demagogues and racketeers exploiting the actual, if not advertised, backwardness of the popular masses, fostered through the weakened public schools. Moreover, the masses are then left unprotected by true democratic leadership. Under the regime of an inflated conception of equality of educational opportunity, the elite — that is to say, the gifted and keen children, adolescents, and youths attending public schools — are thrown in with poorly endowed, incurious, and unwilling pupils whom the teachers must try to occupy in some worth-while manner.

Thus the public secondary school in which the capable adolescents should, normally, receive an enriching and stimulating liberal education (in other words, a general cultural education preparing toward no definite vocation but necessary for practicing competent leadership in any vocation), is often forced down to the role of an entertaining establishment for any adolescent of secondary school age. It becomes then impossible to follow in public secondary education the only reasonable policy, which, in the fitting words of Professor F. T. Spaulding, is one of " discriminating selection of those pupils for whom continued schoolwork may mean reasonable profit to the state, rather than an effort to hold all pupils in school indefinitely, regardless of their ability to learn or their willingness to learn." [7] Thus, also, virtual " grade schools and high schools are made out of colleges because a great many young people fail to do

[7] " A Brief for the Selection of Secondary School Pupils," *The Harvard Teachers Record*, November, 1931, p. 106.

their grade and high school work before they go to college." [8]
The eager, inquisitive boys and girls ambitious for learning and
culture, are then held back, if not entirely submerged, by the
crowds professing what a heroine of Sinclair Lewis called the
" cheerful antipathy to scholarship." [9]

Next, the public is disappointed in its colleges. In the words
of Professor J. W. Shepherd,[10] " The public sees too little studying, too light an attitude towards life's problems, too much
professional incompetence. . . . The final product of the college — its graduates — is being criticized for lack of scholarly
knowledge, for lack of cultural attitudes, for lack of leadership, and for lack of ability to do successfully the things demanded by a cold and unsympathetic world." Then, the disappointed public reduces its support to higher educational
institutions, and the vicious circle is formed in consequence of
which the circulation of the elite is blocked, the commonwealth
does not obtain a sufficient supply of gifted and carefully trained
potential leaders from among whom it could choose, on the
basis of electoral competition and civil service examinations, its
actual leaders in the various walks of life. As a result, such a
commonwealth, as surely as water flows downward, is weakened in comparison with those commonwealths which have in
their educational system an adequate arrangement for preliminary selection and training of their future leaders in public
educational institutions.

In order that the elite of a democratic nation may have an
appropriate educational opportunity, and the nation an appropriate circulation of the elite, which alone can promise that
the right man will be brought to the right place in the service
of democracy, it is necessary, then, that equality of educational

---

[8] J. W. Shepherd, " Our Educational Goose-Step," *The American Scholar*, May,
1933, p. 293 ff.
[9] *Ann Vickers, cit.*, pp. 55–56.
[10] *Op. cit.*

opportunity should be reduced to its right proportions, and educational opportunity for the elite should be adequately provided.

TWO HISTORIC TYPES OF LEADERSHIP: THE AGAMEMNONIAN AND THE PERICLEAN

The question may be asked if this is really so necessary, for is it not a legitimate belief that leaders are "born" and cannot be either produced or reduced by an educational system? Have not gifted men entirely unschooled, or with very little schooling, left a profound imprint in the history of empire-building? Such questions can probably be best answered in the light of the history of national leadership.

It appears that history has known two fundamental types of national leadership. One is the heroic, impetuous, knot-cutting kind. The other is the reflective, urbanized, or diplomatic type, the knot-disentangling kind. The first type may conveniently be called Agamemnonian, and the other the Periclean. Agamemnon is portrayed by Homer as a man with whom willingly

> . . . a world of men
> Most strong and full of valor went, and he in triumph then
> Put on his resplendent armor, since he did overshine
> The whole heroic host of Greece.[11]

This is a type of leader more evidently "by the grace of God," a man who leads while actually going himself through the same thick and thin as his followers, above whom he towers by sheer physical and mental strength and daring. It is a type of "born" leader, born for a "pure act." On the other hand, a leader of the Periclean kind is formed on the basis of a sufficiently high intellectual endowment through a careful, sys-

[11] *Iliad*, II.

tematic culture and training. His is " the delegated intellect," to use the expression found in Emerson's essay, " The American Scholar." [12]

The Agamemnonian leadership is indispensable in hard though often obscure conquests accomplished by every great people in the frontier period of its history; while the Periclean leadership is imperative in the congested political, economic, and cultural conditions concomitant with the more advanced phases of civilization. Leadership is more fertile when, as rarely occurs, the two types are blended in one personality. Memorable examples are Peter the Great, George Washington, Frederick the Great, Napoleon Bonaparte.

Now that the Western world has definitely passed the frontier period with its Agamemnonian romance of open-field generalship and horseback statesmanship, the less colorful but not less difficult Periclean leadership is the great necessity for nations living in this changeful and evermore complex civilization. Such leadership can reasonably be found only in well-informed, broadly cultured men and women, trained through sustained, precise thinking and capable of perceiving with the magnifying glass of a well-formed and adequately informed intellect the almost intangible indications marking off the right course through the maze of complex modern conditions.

One of the vital residual functions of the public school is to foster and develop the reflective, learned leaders, capable of far-sightedness through the perspective of the accumulated experience of centuries. Unless the school lives up to its mission of furnishing potential Periclean leaders to the nation which has matured into the Periclean conditions of life, two equally great evils will fall upon its national leadership. First, when Periclean leaders have to adapt themselves to the out-of-date but still glorified Agamemnonian standards, more often than not many

[12] *Nature, Addresses and Lectures,* A. L. Burt Publishers, p. 79.

such leaders, for fear of being accused of assuming a superior attitude, will become a sort of Greek slave in Rome, a writer of the master's opinions, quite often to the greater detriment of the master — the popular masses — than of the slave. Second, when uninformed, untrained Agamemnonian leaders have to act in a Periclean situation, they usually either fall into the disastrous policy, " I am their leader, therefore I must follow them "; or they become the proverbial blind bull in a china shop, with this important modification of the hilarious old simile — instead of china it is our lives that are broken by raw, clumsy, incompetent leadership, however spectacular or brave.

The school as a social institution is a great, though not always a properly used, human device in the economy and development of physical, intellectual, and moral forces. Therefore it seems that now, when Western empires have been built and the Agamemnonian period of Western civilization is closed, it is a task of the school in the Western world to contribute toward maintaining and perfecting the empires by increasing in the Periclean commonwealths social justice, prosperity, and happiness and diminishing the elements of disorder, discord, insecurity, and misery. This task cannot be fulfilled if the schools fail in preliminary selection and training of Periclean leaders, for whom there is great nostalgia, however inarticulate it may be at times. To borrow from Henry W. Holmes:

The hand of fate is moving us forward to another stage wherein we shall have to place greater reliance on learning, trained capacity, and co-operation.

Greatness no longer lies for us along the road of *laissez-faire*. Our conquests must be spiritual as well as material, our vision broadened and refined, or we shall court the fate which Spengler predicts for Western civilization.[13]

[13] " The Training of Teachers and the Making of the Nation," *N. E. A. Proceedings,* 1928, p. 899.

"DIALECTICS" OF THE HISTORY OF EDUCATION FOR LEADERSHIP

The philosopher Hegel teaches that the development of the universe proceeds by the "triad of dialectics" or certain creative contradictions. The triad consists of position (thesis), negation (anti-thesis), and higher unity (synthesis). Thus, for instance, in the moral development of the individual or humanity at large, innocence (position) gives place to doubt (negation) out of which grows conviction or rationally established faith (higher unity). In the physical world, a seed (position) undergoes disintegration through germination (negation) to give life to a plant (higher unity).[14] Some historians, observing how humanity has been in the habit of finding more or less balanced solutions of its problems only after a jump from an extreme into its opposite, have spoken of the Hegelian "dialectical process" in history.

The history of education certainly affords many examples of such a "dialectical process" of contradictions out of which only very slowly and painfully emerge reasonably balanced practices relative to the organization, administration, and method of the educative process. Confining ourselves to the history of education for leadership, it is interesting to remember how in this regard also (as in many other educational matters, for instance in those relative to educational method), *praejudicium antiquitatis,* or the bigotry of tradition, would be replaced by a sort of *praejudicium novitatis,* the bigotry of novelty. Out of the resulting conflicts, there begins only now to emerge in some countries a more or less balanced solution of the problem of education for leadership.

At the beginning of all organized educational effort in each Western country, as well as elsewhere, the primary purpose was

---

[14] *Enzyklopädie der philosophischen Wissenschaften im Grundrisse,* Hegels Werke, Bd. VI–VII.

almost exclusively the training of leaders. At first the leading members of the community rose to their position through their personal ability and effort, or because they were — in the terminology of Jefferson — " natural aristocrats," the best endowed members of the group. They wished, however, that their children, whom they naturally wanted to succeed them, be trained for leadership through theoretical learning — that is to say, through the assimilation of past experience sufficiently crystallized into theory.[15] In doing so, fathers did not simply try to smooth out for their progeny the rough path of life. They understood also that the tasks of their sons as public authorities were necessarily going to be more difficult than their own, because those tasks of the sons would be complicated by the various improvements and developments made under the fathers, since the imperfection of human kind willed that progress should mean the greater complexity of life. The fathers understood also that it was only through a sequential assimilation of the accumulated experience of the group that the sons could become prepared to exercise safely the inherited authority. Hence, the organization or institutionalization of education. At the dawn of the history of education, then, training for leadership was the only formal intellectual education given. Only much later did it begin to dawn upon the authorities of the tribe, clan, or absolutist national state that it was necessary to do something for the masses in order to make of them more intelligent and more efficient followers. They were intended, however, to receive just a modicum of practical training and much indoctrination.

Thus at the beginning of the history of organized education the opportunity of education toward leadership existed primarily, if not exclusively, for the descendants of " natural

15 The term " theory " is taken here to mean a set of guiding principles of action and conduct in specific situations demanding a well-analyzed, clearly understood specific experience; for instance, theory of bridge construction, fortress building, warfare, navigation, government, etc.

aristocrats " who, though already hereditary aristocrats, were still willing and capable of undertaking the hard work necessary at all times in good training for leadership. But it is rightly said that history is the cemetery of aristocracies. They rapidly enough degenerate into mere " vested interests " which would not relinquish, however, of their own accord the dominant positions inherited from their truly aristocratic forefathers — that is, forefathers who were the members of the group best endowed, intellectually and morally — unless and until such vested interests are forced out by the new " natural aristocracy " rising from the so-called lower strata and supported by the masses. Before this happens, however, education for leadership is monopolized by vested interests. The educative process, serving then the deteriorated progeny of the pristine " natural aristocracy " of intellect and will power, is deliberately facilitated by the allotment of a large place to social adornments, sports, and other occupations not demanding much intellectual ability and effort.

Sooner or later the dissatisfied real elite that happened to be born into the plebeian strata of society, usually assisted indirectly by the blunders, ineptitude, ostentatious satiety, and inefficiency of the self-perpetuating vested interests, succeeds in revolutionizing the chronically dissatisfied lower masses and marching them, literally or figuratively, into the revolt intended to destroy the weakened, degenerated ruling class.

In consequence, another extreme sets in with relation to the accessibility of higher levels of education preparing toward the Periclean leadership, unless the aristocratic tradition is sufficiently shared and endorsed by the masses — as it has been in England, for example — and thus protects the new democracy against harmful equalitarian illusions. Unless a joint check, combining common sense and a reasonable aristocratic tradition, is kept, an inflated doctrine of equality of educational opportunity is produced. Then for a long time this doctrine virtually obstructs the development of the elite through the medium of the public school, until a national crisis demonstrates to the well-intentioned but unimaginative citizenry the wasteful absurdity of the situation. Meanwhile the public school, despite the generous increase of funds given to it by the community, would fail to turn out a reasonably sufficient number of enlightened and patriotic potential leaders, whose presence and competitive public activity would make it impossible for racketeers and demagogues virtually to enslave whole communities and to undermine the very foundations of democracy to the point of creating in many minds the desire for a sort of Fascist, authoritarian, and supposedly paternalistic, unpartisan government.

Such, briefly, seems to have been the thesis (or position) and the anti-thesis (or negation) of the dialectics of the history of education for leadership. But, though this is a historic fact, it is important to insist that there is no fatality about this fact in the sense that it must produce itself everywhere. It did not produce itself in some communities; and where it did, it did so with greatly varying degrees of wastefulness and harm. Whatever may be the fatality of the development of matter in accordance with the Hegelian dialectics, human society (that is, human minds in their interrelationship) can be free from that fatality, if it is enlightened enough and tries hard enough. The principal difference between matter and mind is that matter is uncritical of itself and its actions. The realm of matter is where facts, such as they are, have the last word; while in society, *i.e.,* in the realm of the interrelationship of human minds, it is a mind that may have the last word over facts when it is clear enough, creative enough, and determined enough to produce new and better facts. Thus the human mind has successfully replaced, in many societies, the facts of cruelty, fanaticism, and injustice with a reasonable measure of tolerance, co-operation, and justice.

DEMOCRATIC SELECTION AND " ARISTOCRATIC " TRAINING OF THE ELITE

To be able to assist toward placing the problem of democratic leadership on the sound basis of circulation of the elite,
the school in a democracy must first free itself from the inflated
notion of equality of educational opportunity, for this notion
results in depriving the nation's " natural aristocracy " of the
opportunity adequately to prepare themselves in public educational institutions for proper service to the nation.

It is suggested, therefore, that in order to eliminate the
dilemma of the dialectics of the history of education concerning
education for leadership, " higher unity " should be substituted for the distortions of education for leadership via the
dialectics of the thesis and anti-thesis. Such distortions come
either from above and are made by vested interests or they come
from below and then they are made by intentionally or unin-
tentionally false friends of democracy. To achieve the higher
unity in question, there must be offered a special educational
opportunity to " natural aristocrats " from wheresoever they
may come. In other words, the elite, or potential future leaders,
should be democratically recruited, but should be trained
" aristocratically," that is, in the manner which " natural aristocrats " naturally desire — through systematic and exacting
intellectual work properly interspersed with physical, aesthetic,
and religious activities.

Under such conditions, the future leaders who have received
their valuable training, both general and specialized, free in
public educational institutions will contract, in a sufficient number of instances, a debt of gratitude toward the nation. Then
there will be only a very small place for the quite intelligible
suspicion and fear that the popular masses used to have of superior persons as leaders, aloof and contemptuous. The majority of
leaders will then be directly and literally flesh from the flesh

and bone from the bone of the people. Why is it not a reasonable belief that such leaders, many of whom would have borne the real brunt of life, would understand, at least merely egotistically, that it is not possible to be happy save in a happy world? Why not believe that among such " natural aristocrats," elevated to leadership through the training given them under special provision made by the nation, there would be enough great souls, of whom the Indian philosopher Kalidasa has well said that they are like the skies; they accumulate only in order to spread and distribute? They will be close enough to the people and will understand the people and be understood because they are, in the words of a thinker, " the condensed people." [16]

AMERICAN DEMOCRATIC ARISTOCRACY

A unique experience of leadership exercised by a democratically selected aristocracy of the mind and character is furnished by eighteenth-century America. Was not, indeed, the eighteenth-century leadership in this country distinguished by a blending — unprecedented in modern times — of superior intellect and character, disinterested love of letters and science, and democratic sentiment? The leading members of the Continental Congress were precisely men who embodied in themselves this happy blending. Was not such a great democrat as Benjamin Franklin, for instance, not only a member of the committee to draw up the Declaration of Independence and later the first ambassador of the American republic to France, but also the founder of the American Philosophical Society? Small wonder that Benjamin Franklin, skillful not only in practical affairs, both public and private, but at the same time very sensitive to literary and artistic elegancies, was heartily welcome to associate with the intellectual aristocracy of France. Alexander Hamilton advised the people of New York that " the

[16] Brunner, Constantin, *Die Lehre von dem Geistigen und dem Volk, cit.*, S. 57.

aim of every political constitution is, or ought to be, first to obtain for rulers men who possess the most wisdom to discern, the most virtue to pursue the common good of society," [17] in other words, aristocrats of mind and character.

Jefferson, who, it will be remembered, was the founder of the University of Virginia, distinguished between a natural aristocracy based upon virtue and talent and an artificial aristocracy based upon wealth and birth. He believed that " natural aristocracy " was " the most precious gift of nature," and eminently valuable for the instruction and government of society. He maintained, " That form of government is the best which provides the most effectively for a pure selection of these natural *aristoi* into the offices of government." [18]

The American Commission headed by John Quincy Adams and including Commissioners Bayard, Gallatin, Clay, and Russell, who negotiated with the English the treaty of peace in 1814, undoubtedly was also composed of such " natural aristocrats " of excellent culture. To them the Marquis of Wellesley paid a tribute by declaring in the House of Lords that the Americans " had shown a most astonishing superiority over the British during the whole of the negotiations." And James Truslow Adams justly remarks in a comment upon this statement made before the Lords, " It must be recalled that the Americans had been dealing not with the British negotiators but through them with the British Government itself." [19]

Truly, their own intellectual and moral power in achievement, even more than their theory of government and of leadership in a democracy, is an undying monument and an impressive lesson in the unadulterated democratic philosophy of education bequeathed to the American people by their great

[17] *The Federalist*, p. 377.
[18] Merriam, C. Edward, *op. cit.*, p. 156.
[19] Adams, James Truslow, *The Adams Family*, Little, Brown and Co., 1930, p. 156.

leaders of the eighteenth and the early nineteenth centuries. Unfortunately, this philosophy of education was subsequently distorted by the inflation of the idea of equality.

SELECTIVE ADVANCED COURSES IN THE HIGH SCHOOL AS AN OPPORTUNITY FOR THE ELITE

The establishment of advanced courses in the high school for the selected, brighter, more ambitious, and more scholastically-minded adolescents should probably be the first step in the direction of selective public education for the elite under the condition of local support and control of public education. With the good will and tact of really competent school superintendents and principals who are converted to the idea, much can be accomplished even without special funds, and without setting up a war between the parents of the more intelligent and those of the less capable students. Why, for example, in large, even non-selective high schools, should not a certain fair percentage of funds and personnel be assigned to the service of the select students? Adolescents found in high schools are often lacking in interest, or in ambition, or in intelligence, or in all of these together, and therefore are not qualified to pursue more difficult systematic studies. To be sure, it is in the end a better policy to occupy such adolescents in public high schools and continuation schools as worthily as possible, rather than leave them at the mercy of the street, only later to spend in the increased budgets of the police force, prisons, criminal courts, and the like, whatever savings might be effected by refusing admission to or turning from post-elementary education the incapable or non-studious pupils. But it seems to be also imperative that a certain just percentage of funds and personnel should be set aside for the special care of the elite. Teachers more suitable for handling the less gifted students should fill about seventy-five per cent of the faculty appointments of non-selective secondary schools and should conduct with the mass of students some suitable work of more elementary nature in the humanities, and of utilitarian, practical nature in mathematics, natural science, and crafts. The other twenty-five per cent of the faculty should be selected and developed in service to appeal to the brighter and keener pupils by the broadness and richness of their general culture as well as by expertness in some definite field or fields of knowledge.

LIBERAL EDUCATION AS THE BASIS FOR PRELIMINARY TRAINING OF THE ELITE

Now, supposing that the problem as to whom to give preliminary training toward the Periclean leadership is solved with a reasonable degree of satisfaction by the educational authorities through the establishment of selective advanced courses in the high school, the next problem would be, what to teach. It would not be necessary, it seems, to set up expensive curriculum research committees in order to determine the curriculum for a preliminary general training of the elite. The research has been made, checked and rechecked over long periods of time in the course of history of education.

Briefly, the selection should take place after some four years of study in a non-selective common elementary school. Next, for six years the elite should be given in selective advanced courses of the secondary school, or better, the adolescent school, a general or liberal education. (Continuous selection and transfer elsewhere of the failing students should be practiced at the end of each school year.) Next, the worthy students should be admitted to a three-year college where the preliminary training should be finished, again under a curriculum of liberal studies but with some appropriate individual admixture of pre-specialization training. Specialization should be the purpose of graduate schools.

Leaving out the problem of specialization and confining our-selves to the general preliminary training of the adolescent elite, it is suggested that a crossing between the curriculum of the French seven-year *lycée* and of the German nine-year *Real-gymnasium* could yield a satisfactorily wide and rich sequential curriculum for the six-year adolescent school and the three-year college for the elite.[20]

To repeat, investigations concerning the curriculum for the preliminary training of the elite have been abundantly made in practice in the course of history of education. Cicero some two thousand years ago formulated an outline of preliminary gen-eral education for what is, in our terminology, the Periclean leadership when he said:

Then [in the Greek time] * as now, the greatest rewards were annexed to this profession [public leadership] * — popularity, in-terest, and honor: and besides, the capacities of Romans, as we may judge from many other instances, were far superior to those of the rest of mankind. All this being considered, have we not reason to be surprised that in so long a span of time, and despite so many oppor-tunities, and such a variety of states, the number of *good* orators [leaders] * should be so inconsiderable? But the truth is, that in this art there is something more, and it must be attained by an acquain-tance with more arts and sciences than mankind generally imag-ines. . . .[21] In my opinion, no man can deserve the praise of an ac-complished leader [orator] * without a knowledge of everything that is great and of all liberal arts.[22]

In saying this, Cicero did not merely theorize. Rather he suc-cinctly described the procedure of education for leadership exist-ing during the advanced or Periclean period of Greco-Roman civilization.

---

* Bracketed remarks are added.
[20] For details see Kandel, I. L., *Comparative Education*, Houghton Mifflin, 1933, and Demiashkevich, M. J., "Preliminary Selection and Training of Leaders in France and Germany," *Educational Administration and Supervision*, January, 1933.
[21] *De Oratore*, I, 4.   [22] *Ibid.*, I, 6.

After the wilderness of the Dark Ages, which were one long frontier or Agamemnonian period in Western Europe, Western humanity entered upon the Renaissance period. As civilization grew evermore Periclean, *i.e.,* more complex and rich, it was a modernized, enlarged curriculum of liberal arts (*liberalia studia*) that was offered to the elite — or supposed elite — very largely the progeny of vested interests. When recently the English, the French, and the Germans began to grapple with the problem of democratic reorganization of education for leadership, they wisely adhered, with some minor retouches, to the traditional conception of the curriculum appropriate for the education of the elite prevailing on the continent of Europe since the time of the Renaissance.

With regard to the problem as to what pupils should be selected, recent years have witnessed in Western Europe a fundamental change in the tradition that, since the revival of liberal education during the Renaissance, reserved primarily for scions of the ruling classes both secondary and higher education and the positions of leadership to which they led. This traditional privilege of vested interests has been practically abrogated in recent years under the pressure of the need for the circulation of the elite. But, on the other hand, recent educational reforms in this direction in England, France, and Germany have prudently left intact the fundamentals of the Renaissance tradition relative to the objectives and curriculum of the secondary school which have persisted in Western Europe throughout all the external changes because they have stood the test of time. The purpose of the secondary school — which is aimed to be the school for the adolescent elite — is, as of old, a preliminary general preparation toward the Periclean leadership in any walk of life, while higher education is intended for the acquisition of expert knowledge in a specific field of research or practical work.

Such a general disinterested education, when based upon a

sequential curriculum composed of both the humanities and the sciences and studied with properly trained and selected teachers, can reasonably be expected to result in strong saturation of the student with the highest standards of achievement, intellectual, moral, and aesthetic, known to humanity. An analytical familiarity with the great accomplishments and the instructive failures of outstanding individuals and of human groups in the realm of practical life, as well as in disinterested arts and sciences, will contribute powerfully to the formation of mature judgment in the future Periclean leader.

In substance, this is the old classical educational philosophy relative to the study of liberal arts, with this difference: In the ancient Greco-Roman civilization, liberal education was traditionally conceived as something to which only the free-born were entitled and something which was naturally appropriate for them. Nowadays every man is supposed to be born free — except in the countries governed by dictators. But man is in reality free only when he is liberated from the multiple impressions on his mind that are managed (offered or imposed) by numerous agencies of varying respectability and purity of intention. The agent of this liberation is the proper general cultural education, and intellectual training built upon sufficient native endowment; or it may be the guidance offered by enlightened and loyal leaders, true guardians of the state. Indeed, it is only then that — to paraphrase John Stuart Mill — the individual is adequately forearmed against any agency seeking to establish " despotism over the mind, leading by natural tendency to one over the body." [23]

Our general position relative to the curriculum appropriate for the preliminary training of the elite is, then, to the effect that the curriculum of preliminary instruction of the future Periclean leaders should be a systematic curriculum of liberal education

[23] *On Liberty, cit.*, Ch. V, p. 315.

graduated, to be sure, in accordance with the maturity of the student and somewhat varied in accordance with the peculiarly desirable gifts and peculiarly worth-while inclinations of the student.

Through the study of, and saturation with, the method of the mathematical and natural sciences, our future Periclean leaders, in addition to acquiring indispensable information of high practical value, will acquire certain valuable habits of mind by submitting to scientifically established facts (see p. 22).

The humanities — literature, philosophy, social science, art — on the other hand, when properly studied, will teach the maturing citizens to revolt against certain ugly facts and to apply themselves to create new facts, more just and more beautiful. The humanities will also show the student that there are reasons which the analytical scientific faculty of reason cannot understand; they will train him in the art of discovery and proper evaluation of experimentally non-measurable intangibilities, which art distinguishes in our Periclean civilization more than ever, a statesman from a mere, though eminent, statistician. This is a rare and difficult art, long to acquire. John Dewey well said in the *Quest for Certainty*: "Man has never had such a varied body of knowledge in his possession before, and probably never before has he been so uncertain and so perplexed as to what his knowledge means, what it points to in action and in consequences." [24]

TRAINING THE ELITE FOR THE KNOWLEDGE OF MEN

The difficult and rare art of statesmanlike insight into the complexities of both the changing and the unchanging conditions of life, like any other art, is teachable, to a degree, when it is taught by the right teachers to the right students in the right way. How, then, can our future Periclean leaders acquire some

[24] *Op. cit.,* pp. 312–313.

of this invaluable art in the course of their general preliminary training?

Best of all, probably, this art can be acquired through the study of men with the help of the analysis of subtle, intricate facts of the human heart and mind. Instruction in those fields, however, must be sought in many more places than in psychological laboratories. To many other ways than the quantitative methods of the natural sciences our future leaders must turn for help and enlightenment. It appears that those other ways must be sought in the study of the humanities.

Even the finest and most ingenious among laboratory methods are still — and are likely to remain — too crude to be capable of a reliable analysis of the complex and recondite psychological situations such as are, however, clearly perceived and clearly described by the greatest psychologists humanity has known — the so-called fiction writers possessed of the genius of a Sophocles, a Goethe, a Dostoevsky, a Tolstoy. William James, for instance, summarized his impressions, as a psychologist, from reading Tolstoy's *War and Peace* and *Anna Karenina,* in the following lines found in a letter to Theodore Flournoy of August 30, 1896:

Of course you have read Tolstoy's *War and Peace* and *Anna Karenina.* I never had the exquisite felicity before this summer, and now I feel as if I knew *perfection* in the representation of human life. Life indeed seems less real than his tale of it. Such infallible veracity! The impression haunts me as nothing literary ever haunted me before.[25]

Great historians, men of the philosophic turn of mind, for example, Polybius, Tacitus, Mommsen, Sorel and the like, who are interested in the detection of historic laws, will also teach our future Periclean leaders many a valuable lesson about men and their ways.

Not less than this knowledge of man in general, another ele-

[25] *Letters, cit.,* Vol. II, p. 48.

ment is valuable in giving the future leader statesman-like insight; this is communion between him and his predecessors, the past leaders of humanity, to be obtained through the study of their biographies, memoirs, diaries, and letters, as well as through the study of historical investigations into the life and work of these men. It is a wholesome humility for the future leader to suppose that there were capable and honest leaders before his time and to try to learn from their experience. We need not fear that the originality and initiative of the future Periclean leader will be impaired in this way. Much room will be left for him to exercise his real originality and initiative in the course of his historical studies, by analyzing the lessons of history and distinguishing the more valuable from the less valuable ones. Even the Scipionism of Scipio — as a typical ancient Periclean leader — consisted in a large measure of selecting from and improving upon the experience of the Scipios of preceding times.

THE RIGHT ATTITUDE TOWARD TRADITION

In addition to the general suggestions relative to the education for good character presented in the chapter on " Character Building," a special emphasis, it seems, should be placed, in the case of the elite upon the right attitude toward tradition. The future Periclean leader should be properly impressed with the social value of tradition as an instinctive and noble human device that helps to preserve some equilibrium amidst the desirable or simply inevitable changes in civilization, making the phenomenon of change less dangerous and less degradingly chaotic. Therefore, the future leader should be brought up in a careful and cautious, though constructively critical, attitude toward traditional values. The nihilism of the palace — be that even a subtle nihilism of an unadvertised collective democratic palace made of the pulpit, the floor of parliament, the college chair, and the city hall — such will inevitably sooner or later (and rather sooner than later) implant itself in the market place where parishioners always grow to resemble their parsons. Nihilism will then produce the same fundamental political and social consequences as it has always produced. The exaggerated nihilism of the Renaissance in the fifteenth and sixteenth centuries produced, among the sounder element of the free classes of society, a yearning for authority, and brought about the absolutism of the seventeenth century, which was *par excellence* the century of authority with all its inevitable abuses. After a long and painful struggle, led by freedom-loving leaders, the absolutism of the seventeenth century gave place first to the enlightened absolutism of the eighteenth century and then to the liberalism of the nineteenth century.

It is probably owing in a large degree to the moral and intellectual nihilism of leaders that liberalism in Italy and the incipient liberalism in Germany and Russia went down before the new forms of autocracy, such as Bolshevism, Fascism, and Hitlerism. Mussolini proclaims the twentieth century the century of authority. It is a warning that is to be properly heeded in the training of future democratic Periclean leaders, not because it comes from an apparently successful dictator, but because it comes from stern facts. The support of Hitlerism by the wider masses of the middle and lower middle classes in Germany cannot be fully explained in abstraction from the nihilism, moral and metaphysical, shown by many outstanding political and cultural leaders of post-war Germany, and the resulting yearning for authority on the part of the middle and the lower middle classes.

"PHILOSOPHIZING" THE FUTURE LEADERS

A thoughtful student of antiquities observed, wisely: "The facts of life are like the . . . Sphinx: if its riddles are not rightly answered it devours men and nations." [26] The curriculum for the general preliminary training of the future Periclean leaders should, therefore, give also an adequate place to philosophizing on the part of the more mature elite students about the general ultimate meaning of the facts of life in their entirety, about the " general hang of things," and, in particular, about the problem of the ultimate reality. Such students should be assisted by properly qualified instructors toward the acquisition of as much certainty as is humanly possible relative to the ultimate goal of human existence. Similar provision should, of course, be made also for the rank and file adolescent pupils, but the elite need it all the more because it is in the nature of the elite to be more acutely stimulated by, or suffer more from, anxiety relative to the final value and ultimate meaning of things.

This important curricular detail must be specifically insisted upon in view of the exaggerated influence of pragmatism upon contemporary educational theory. Pragmatism, as has been shown above, would not only excuse the school, but would actually prevent it from treating metaphysical issues — as well as the permanent moral values — in a planned manner, as a worthy educational objective. Seneca, in a letter to Lucilius, pities mortals because they " spend a great part of their life in doing evil, the larger part in doing nothing, and the entire life in doing other things than what they ought to do." The future leaders should be educated to guard against the development of similar incapacity in themselves.

One qualification — if not the primary qualification — of a good Periclean leader is the ability to take with conviction correct long views and to abide by great ultimate goals, while making only absolutely inevitable concessions to the immediate, narrowly pragmatic clamors of the day. " Why could they, centuries

[26] Nelson, L., *Politics and Education,* Translated from the German, London. Allen & Unwin, 1928, P. II, p. 71.

ago, create cathedrals like this, and why cannot we now?" asked a tourist visiting a medieval Italian cathedral. "Because they then held convictions and now we entertain only opinions," was another tourist's answer. The majestic social cathedrals — the beneficent civic, industrial, cultural, and aesthetic institutions — cannot be built in any other way.

Good character, it will be probably also conceded, valuable in every man, is pre-eminently valuable in a leader. A good character has been likened to an acrostic, for whether it is read forward, backward, or across, it still spells the same thing. A high character presupposes, indeed, a degree of certainty and conviction that must go even beyond the consensus of humanity on the fundamental moral values. In fact, a certainty as to the final metaphysical issues seems indispensable for the make-up of leaders of high character. It is such a certainty that can enable them well to fill positions demanding a high degree of responsibility.

It would be poor pragmatism to neglect, or still worse to try to prevent — as some extreme pragmatists are apt to do — an adequate acquaintance of the future Periclean leaders with the fact, for instance, that there is such a thing as the soul, at least in the sense of something in us that makes it impossible for a normal man or woman to be content with mere material satisfactions. The future guardians of the state — to use the celebrated Platonic term — should be duly prepared to meet situations arising from the fact that precisely as soon as men find themselves in a perfectly satisfactory environment, materially, they begin to be perplexed and pained with those more fundamental maladjustments which exist, not between man and society, nor between man and nature, but primarily between man's rational reason operating on the basis of the senses and his anxiety for the ultimate, super-sensible certainty and purpose.[27]

Likewise, it would not be good pragmatism to omit from the

[27] Edman, Irwin, *The Contemporary and His Soul,* Viking Press, 1931.

curriculum for the general preliminary training of the future Periclean leaders the provision under which they would be amply informed of the role of faith in human life and undertakings. They should know that it is not only the more or less naïve and vague pragmatic faith — the belief in the salutary effect of optimism, in other words, the belief that things will go better if we believe them capable of so doing — that is the great factor in life. Still greater is the stern and definite belief in an ultimate metaphysical reality linked with moral faith in a transcendent ideal.

Knowledge possessing a satisfactory degree of final certainty has been found possible by many human beings — not at all the duller element of humanity — in a morally founded faith. Faith is here taken in the sense of the residue of thought remaining after the subtraction of thought belonging to the realm of science. In other words, this residue consists of scientifically unanalyzed and undemonstratable, but also irrefutable, convictions regarding the ultimate purpose of life. The residue in question — by which in reality men are primarily guided in life — is accompanied, however, by a greater or smaller degree of certainty as to its ultimate truth and reality. That certainty is founded (a) in an immediate or direct and clear feeling of the moral beauty of such believed ultimate reality; (b) in the beauty of the ideal of life implied in such believed reality; (c) in an immediate, direct, and perfectly clear feeling of the utter ugliness of the idea of the unreality of such believed reality; and (d) in the instinctive horror of moral — or rather unmoral — life in logical conformity with such disbelief.

To look at the problem of curricular provisions for the metaphysical education of the future Periclean leaders from a different angle, it is very largely some kind of final metaphysical certainty that has sustained the greatest heroes of humanity, however unadvertised and obscure, in the production of a kind of moral surplus value — to paraphrase economists — in the form of altruism and self-sacrifice which has contributed much to social progress. The secret of a good social organization is not wholly deciphered by the formulae, give-and-take and live-and-let-live. These, in substance, are a modernization of the primitive motto, *do ut des* (" I give you in order to receive from you "). The greater portion of the real advance of civilization seems to be due to the fact that there were and still are enough people who, though not at all beguiled and intellectually inferior persons, give through their talent and their toil or even with their very blood much more than they take. Such persons are usually moved toward altruism by their scale of values, formed in the light of their metaphysical certainty and their transcendent moral ideal, which elevates them above and beyond their selfish material inclinations and interests.

If and when the highest principle determining the relationship of men does not rise higher than the take-and-give, it will, as always in the past, inevitably result in the rather general attempt to take more than to give, and will create a serious danger of the dissolution of society in a war of all against all. Are not international relations, which have practically never surpassed the principle of *do ut des,* or the take-and-give, a sufficiently convincing proof and a warning?

The elite should be " philosophized " also in another sense of the term. The future leaders should be trained especially through the study of the thought and work of great leaders of the past toward the ability to seize the principles underlying a variety of conflicting facts, and to grasp the grand lines of the course of events in whatever may be the sphere of action and of leadership. The real leader and the real statesman is the person capable of serene judgment amidst the turmoil of uncontrollable or seemingly uncontrollable events. Such serenity of judgment can come only from the art of perceiving the simple reality beneath a motley of contradictory appearances. This art alone can give man a certain degree of dominion over the future; this power over the future comes from the prevision of the future and is one of the sublime secrets of true leadership.

TEACHING THE ELITE

The problem of method of the general preliminary training of the elite does not seem to demand any long elaboration. It is almost automatically solved whenever the elite of students is brought to study with the elite of teachers.

The question of method of teaching has recently acquired a large — in fact disproportionately large — place in educational theory for two reasons. First, under the regime of the inflated conception of equality of educational opportunity, the teachers of adolescents and youths have been confronted with the really difficult problem of handling unselected masses of pupils often unwilling and almost as often incapable. The problem seems insoluble via method, but not unnaturally the real issue was camouflaged under the problem of method and curriculum, of how to teach, and what to teach, while the real basic issue is whom to teach and where.

Second, contemporary pedagogy is suffering from lack of discrimination between educational tactics, or method of the educative process, and educational strategy, or the guiding principles or the philosophy of education (see p. 29).

It appears sound strategy in education that elite students be taught by elite teachers because only men and women themselves of the calibre of Periclean leaders, intellectually and culturally, can give the right general preliminary training to the future Periclean leaders. Bring together, then, an elite of students and an elite of teachers and you may practically turn them loose. The result will be a systematic, solid growth of the elite satisfying to themselves, their teachers, their parents, and their nation. An interesting and promising attempt at promoting " higher unity " in this country through the special undergraduate training of elite teachers of the elite has been made by Professor Thomas Alexander in the establishment in 1931 of New College at Teachers College, Columbia University. A noteworthy project of organization of superior graduate work for the elite teachers and educational administrators was announced by Dean William F. Russell of Teachers College, Columbia University, in his annual report for the academic year 1933–34. An impressive statesman-like program for the recruitment of a superior body of teachers and educational administrators has been proposed by Dean Henry W. Holmes, of the Harvard Graduate School of Education, in several of his recent papers, for example, in " Pedagogical Racketeering," published by Scribner's (XCVII: 157–161).

Teachers of the elite should in the first place be themselves an elite in the sense of possessing intellectual acumen, character, and general culture. They should, of course, possess knowledge of their special fields and of the fundamentals of the science of education. They should be well-grounded also in the fundamentals of the history of philosophy, irrespective of their specialities.

Again, why philosophy? First, because a teacher of the elite in order to be a competent guide in the matter of character building must himself have a scale of values — moral, scientific, political, aesthetic — as firm and clear as possible. In other words, the teacher of the elite must have a critically worked out general outlook upon life and its fundamental problems. Above all, the teacher has to know how humanity stood in the past and appears to stand in his own time with regard to the fundamental problem of certainty — epistemological, metaphysical, and ethical. Then he will be better prepared to answer their questions and guide the youths in their inherent urge for the ideal.

Educational administrators and teachers must be able to measure experimentally measurable facts of life, but they must also be capable of leading the students, even while following them, in their speculations and in their flights of imagination toward the ideal.

Second, the importance of the philosophic studies to the teacher of the elite seems to be enhanced by the increasing specialization of the different subjects of secondary and college education. That specialization, though valuable and desirable in many regards, has created a considerable degree of isolation among the various fields of knowledge. But it is precisely one of the tasks of philosophy, properly taught, to co-ordinate the findings of the different sciences, to serve as a sort of clearing house for them, to work out a synthesis showing how these fundamental findings are related to one another and to the final goal of knowledge, which is to find truth and certainty. Therefore, it is with the help of the philosophic studies that the future teachers of the elite can better comprehend and appreciate the place which their respective special fields occupy in the general scheme of things, cultural, moral, political, and economic.

WORKING TOWARD " HIGHER UNITY "

When a democratically recruited and " aristocratically " trained elite of teachers will have been placed in charge of the " aristocratic " training of a democratically recruited elite of students, then the educational precondition for the circulation of the elite will be fulfilled and the future of democracy will be much better assured than it is now. The preceding hundred years have seen ushered into the history of education the new age in which free compulsory elementary education has been achieved and facilities for public secondary education have been enlarged. Now is the time and the next logical step, as well as a vital social need greatly increased under our complex social and economic situation, to open a new epoch in the history of education. This should be the epoch of "higher unity" — to use again the Hegelian simile of the "dialectical triad" — to be brought about by placing, through the medium of the school, at the service of a Periclean democratic civilization a real democratic Periclean leadership for which there is a real demand and nostalgia in the democratic world. Some hundred years ago, Pestalozzi described, truthfully and poignantly, the existing educational "opportunities" for the masses as follows:

I could not hide from myself that school-instruction, at least as I saw it actually practiced, was for the great majority and for the lowest classes of no use at all.

As far as I knew it, it seemed to me like a great house of which the upper story was bright with the highest and best art, but inhabited by few men. In the middle many more dwelt, but there were no steps by which in a *human way* they could mount to the upper story; and if a few showed a desire to clamber up to the higher story, animal-fashion, whenever they were seen, sometimes a finger, here and there an arm or a leg, by which they were trying to climb, was cut off. Lastly, below lived a countless herd of men who had an equal right with the highest to sunshine and healthy air; but they were not only left in nauseous darkness, in starless dens, but by binding and blinding the eyes they were made unable to look up even to the upper stories.[28]

The preceding hundred years have accomplished a great advance in democratic civilization by establishing the free public elementary, higher elementary, and, in some countries, free secondary schools. The unpardonably selfish and obdurate neglect — self-defeating, in the end — of popular education by the ruling classes, or vested interests, has been in a large degree corrected in the countries of Western civilization. Now a new injustice and a new neglect, also inevitably self-defeating, in the

[28] *How Gertrude Teaches Her Children, cit.,* p. 125 f.

end — the neglect of the democratic elite by democratic educational authorities, must be carefully guarded against and avoided as much as possible. An educational franchise has been created permitting the more ambitious children of the so-called lower classes to rise to a more satisfactory economic, cultural, and political condition from the economic misery and demoralizing subjection into which their forefathers had been cast and in which — to paraphrase again the *Marriage of Figaro* — more ability was necessary to gain a mere subsistence than was ever requisite to govern empires.[29] Next, it is to the vital interest of true democracy that the capital of brain and character deposited in the children of a nation should not be wasted, either on account of the inaccessibility of secondary and higher education to the gifted but impecunious persons, or because an inflated and deceptive conception of equality of educational opportunity prevented the public school from giving those persons proper training toward the preservation and embellishment of democratic empires through the true Periclean leadership of which gifted youths are potentially capable.

Public education in a democracy does not exist, to be sure, for the purpose of helping a genius to be a genius. But, on the other hand, its mission is not limited to helping the average to be a good average, though this is, doubtless, a very vital task of public education. To fulfill its mission, democratic public education, in addition to devoting a great effort to the worth-while development of the average child, should also have adequate provisions for the formation and mobilization of talents for the service of the nation. In the words of the late President Gilman of Johns Hopkins University:

Genius takes care of itself. Nobody can tell how it comes to pass that men of extraordinary minds are born of commonplace parents and bred in the school of adversity away from books and masters.

[29] Act V, Scene 3.

Institutions are not essential to their education. But everyone who has observed in a series of years the advancement of men of talent, as distinguished from men of genius, must believe that scholars, investigators, reasoners, orators, statesmen of enduring reputation, poets, discoverers are rarely produced in the freedom of the wilderness. . . . The history of civilization declares that promising youth should have the most favorable opportunity for intercourse with other minds, living as well as dead, comrades as well as teachers, governors as well as friends. It declares that in most cases talents will seize opportunity, and opportunity will help talents. . . .[30]

May it be repeated, in conclusion, that special educational opportunities for the gifted children of the nation should be provided only in so far as such opportunities would not materially detract, financially or otherwise, from the educational opportunities provided for the mass of average children and youths. History seems to have vindicated the idea of Aristotle to the effect that without good followers good leaders are of little avail to the commonwealth. " The few best," when deprived of the supporting strength to be found only in " the many " — intelligent and willing followers — are as plants possessing superficial roots. They are destined to wither rather than to fructify. Besides, Aristotle seems to be also right when he says: " Again, the many are more incorruptible than the few; they are like the great quantity of water which is less easily corrupted than a little." [31]

Even Hegel, though by no means a great admirer of democracy, conceded that " public opinion deserves . . . to be esteemed for its essential fundamental principle, which only shines, more or less dimly, through its concrete expression. . . . Anything great and rational is eventually sure to please public opinion, to be espoused by it, and to be made one of its posses-

---

[30] *The Characteristics of the University.* Quoted by courtesy of Johns Hopkins University.

[31] *The Works of Aristotle, cit., Politica,* Vol. X (1921), 1286a.

sions. . . . Public opinion is the unorganized way in which what a people wants and thinks is promulgated. . . . Public opinion contains, therefore, the eternal substantial principles of justice, the true content, and the result of the whole constitution, legislation, and the universal condition in general. The form underlying public opinion is sound common sense, which is a fundamental ethical principle winding its way through everything, in spite of prepossessions." [32] It is the fundamental duty of educational authorities in every community to work, through the medium of public education, toward such an organization of public opinion as would enable the average citizen to exercise, firmly and promptly, those beneficial powers which even Hegel, the absolutist and the prophet of the absolutist autocratic state, concedes to the popular masses.

SUGGESTIONS FOR READING

Babbitt, J., *Democracy and Leadership* (Houghton Mifflin).

Brent, C. H., *Leadership* (Longmans, Green).

Briggs, T. H., *Secondary Education* (Macmillan).

Kandel, I. L., *History of Secondary Education* (Houghton Mifflin).

Maurois, A., *Captains and Kings* (John Lane).

National Council of Education. Theses on Freedom, in Relationship to Culture, Social Planning, and Leadership.

Nelson, L., *Politics and Education* (Allen and Unwin).

St. Andrews University, *Walker Lectures on Leadership.*

[32] *Philosophy of Law,* German Classics, *cit.,* Vol. VII, pp. 87, 88, 89.

SELECTED INDEX *

Absolute, 37f., 55
Abstract learning
  child's early aptitude for, 287
  and democracy, 287f.
Activity method, *see* New Education
Activity movement, *see* New Education
Adams, J. Q., 408, 420
Adams, J. T., 420
Aeschylus, 249
Agnosticism, definition, 59
Alembert, J. d', 131
Alexander, Thomas, 435
" Algebra " of civics, 197ff., 205
  definition, 199
Anaxagoras, 348
A posteriori knowledge, 77, 79
  contrasted with *a priori* knowledge, 50
A priori knowledge, 56, 77, 79
  contrasted with *a posteriori* knowledge, 50
Aristophanes, 254
  on communism, 202f.
Aristotle, 60, 362, 375, 377
  definition of experience, 167
  on politics, 174
  on the spirit of the polity, 287f.
" Arithmetic " of civics, 203ff.
Auscultation
  definition, 11f.
  use in educational administration, 17
  use in examinations, 241ff.

Bacon, Francis, 68, 376
  forerunner of Comte and Dewey, 69
  on reading, 172
  reviver of the experimental method, 69
Bagley, Wm. C.
  as an essentialist, 147
  on intelligence tests, 127
  on play, 320f.
  on relationship between will power and intelligence, 235
Bain, Alexander, on moral habits, 301
Behaviorism
  as evolutionistic psychology, 88ff.

influences upon the New Education, 125ff.
  insufficiencies of, 98ff.
  materialistic ethics, 131
  in the role of epistemology, 129f.
Bergson, Henri
  dualistic vitalism, 149ff.
  as an essentialist in education, 154f.
  on evolution, 85f.
  on intuition, 56f.
  pedagogy, 153ff.
  on relationship between will power and intelligence, 235f.
Berkeley, 73
Book learning
  as an activity, 173f.
  contributions to democracy, 171ff.
  and creative originality, 192ff.
  as a method of intellectual training, 231ff.
  role in the history of civilization, 189ff.
Boring, Edwin, on the weaknesses of behaviorism, 100
Briggs, T. H., as an essentialist, 147
Butler, N. M., definition of international mind, 390f.

Cabanis, 76
Carlyle, 169f., 245f., 348, 371
Carr, H. W., on theory of relativity, 12
Cartesianism, *see* Descartes
Categorical imperative, 80
Categories of pure reason, 78
Category of universality, as the basis of language, 78
Character
  definition, 296f.
  intellectual factors of character building, 306
  methods of building character, 298ff.
  and moral habits, 300f.
  and vicarious experience, 301ff.
Cicero, on literary studies, 190
Circulation of the elite, definition, 402

* Compiled by Madeline Pond

441